COLLECTED POEMS

JM

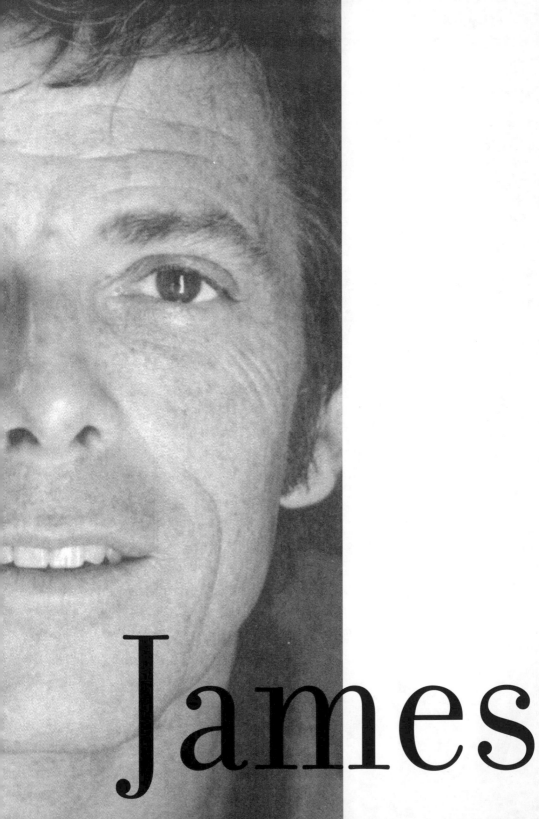

James

COLLECTED POEMS

edited by

J. D. McClatchy and Stephen Yenser

Merrill

Alfred A. Knopf • New York • 2002

This Is a Borzoi Book
Published by Alfred A. Knopf

Copyright © 2001 by The Literary Estate of James Merrill
at Washington University

www.randomhouse.com/knopf/poetry

Knopf, Borzoi Books, and the colophon are registered trademarks
of Random House, Inc.

Library of Congress Cataloging-in-Publication Data
Merrill, James Ingram, 1926–1995.
[Poems]
Collected poems / edited by J. D. McClatchy and Stephen Yenser.
p. cm.
Includes index.
ISBN 0-375-70941-X
I. McClatchy, J. D., 1945–   II. Yenser, Stephen, 1941–   III. Title.

PS3525.E6645 A17   2001
811'.54—dc21   00-040542

Manufactured in the United States of America

Published March 3, 2001

First Paperback Edition, November 2002

EDITORS' NOTE

The *Collected Poems* of James Merrill includes all the poems in ten trade volumes that the poet saw through the press (omitting "The Book of Ephraim" from *Divine Comedies*). It also contains the poems in his first book, *The Black Swan*, published in a limited edition, that were not reprinted in *First Poems*; *The Yellow Pages*, which gathers poems Merrill had excluded from earlier volumes; his translations of twenty-one poems from several languages; and forty-four previously uncollected poems. Of the latter, some were published in magazines or special editions, and some are published here for the first time. In choosing these previously uncollected poems from among a much larger number, we have tried to imagine the selection their always discriminating author would have made. The time will come for a complete poems and then a variorum edition. Unless we have indicated otherwise in the textual notes, the poems printed here appear in the order in which they appeared in the original volumes and in the forms that they took there—or, if not published in books, that they took in magazines or typescript—except for misprints and inconsistencies in usage or spelling, which we have corrected.

This *Collected Poems* excludes Merrill's epic work, *The Changing Light at Sandover* (which comprises "The Book of Ephraim," "Mirabell's Books of Number," "Scripts for the Pageant," and "Coda: The Higher Keys"), available in a separate volume, as well as juvenilia, many occasional poems, and other minor verse.

We are indebted to Jack W. C. Hagstrom for his bibliographical efforts and to Daniel Hall and Patrick Merla for their editorial work. Their labors have facilitated this book.

JDMcC and SY

CONTENTS

CONTENTS

CONTENTS

CONTENTS

CONTENTS

THE FIRE SCREEN (1969)

BRAVING THE ELEMENTS (1972)

CONTENTS

xii

CONTENTS

THE INNER ROOM (1988)

CONTENTS

CONTENTS

CONTENTS

CONTENTS

CONTENTS

CONTENTS

FIRST POEMS

(1951)

For Frederick Buechner

Black on flat water past the jonquil lawns
    Riding, the black swan draws
A private chaos warbling in its wake,
Assuming, like a fourth dimension, splendor
That calls the child with white ideas of swans
    Nearer to that green lake
  Where every paradox means wonder.

Though the black swan's arched neck is like
    A question-mark on the lake,
The swan outlaws all possible questioning:
A thing in itself, like love, like submarine
Disaster, or the first sound when we wake;
    And the swan-song it sings
  Is the huge silence of the swan.

Illusion: the black swan knows how to break
    Through expectation, beak
Aimed now at its own breast, now at its image,
And move across our lives, if the lake is life,
And by the gentlest turning of its neck
    Transform, in time, time's damage;
  To less than a black plume, time's grief.

Enchanter: the black swan has learned to enter
    Sorrow's lost secret center
Where like a maypole separate tragedies
Are wound about a tower of ribbons, and where
The central hollowness is that pure winter
    That does not change but is
  Always brilliant ice and air.

Always the black swan moves on the lake; always
    The blond child stands to gaze
As the tall emblem pivots and rides out
To the opposite side, always. The child upon
The bank, hands full of difficult marvels, stays
    Forever to cry aloud
  In anguish: I love the black swan.

THE BROKEN BOWL

To say it once held daisies and bluebells
     Ignores, if nothing else,
Its diehard brilliance where, crashed on the floor,
The wide bowl lies that seemed to cup the sun,
Its green leaves curled, its constant blaze undone,
Spilled all its glass integrity everywhere;
     Spectrums, released, will speak
Of colder flowerings where cold crystal broke.

Glass fragments dropped from wholeness to hodgepodge
     Yet fasten to each edge
The opal signature of imperfection
Whose rays, though disarrayed, will postulate
More than a network of cross-angled light
When through the dusk they point unbruised directions
     And chart upon the room
Capacities of fire it must assume.

The splendid curvings of glass artifice
     Informed its flawlessness
With lucid unities. Freed from these now,
Like love it triumphs through inconsequence
And builds its harmony from dissonance
And lies somehow within us, broken, as though
     Time were a broken bowl
And our last joy knowing it shall not heal.

The splinters rainbowing ruin on the floor
     Cut structures in the air,
Mark off, like eyes or compasses, a face
Of mathematic fixity, spotlight
Within whose circumscription we may set
All solitudes of love, room for love's face,
     Love's projects green with leaves,
Love's monuments like tombstones on our lives.

THE GREEN EYE

Come, child, and with your sunbeam gaze assign
Green to the orchard as a metaphor
For contemplation, seeking to declare
Whether by green you specify the green
Of orchard sunlight, blossom, bark, or leaf,
Or green of an imaginary life.

A mosaic of all possible greens becomes
A premise in your eye, whereby the limes
Are green as limes faintly by midnight known,
As foliage in a thunderstorm, as dreams
Of fruit in barren countries; claims
The orchard as a metaphor of green.

Aware of change as no barometer
You may determine climates at your will;
Spectrums of feeling are accessible
If orchards in the mind will persevere
On their hillsides original with joy.
Enter the orchard differently today:

When here you bring your earliest tragedy,
Your goldfish, upside-down and rigidly
Floating on weeds in the aquarium,
Green is no panorama for your grief
Whose raindrop smile, dissolving and aloof,
Ordains an unusual brightness as you come:

The brightness of a change outside the eye,
A question on the brim of what may be,
Attended by a new, impersonal green.
The goldfish dead where limes hang yellowing
Is metaphor for more incredible things,
Things you shall live among, things seen, things known.

The matriarch with eyes like arrowheads
Sat in a shawl of sunlight, amber beads
Hung from her tribal ears. Orange the noon.
Ah, Dr. Johnson kept the peels, she said,
In his coat-pocket till they withered quite.
The rinds of noon like orange-rinds had blown

Out of her lap across the bright, dazed grass,
Lay shriveling flat upon a scorched perspective,
As though her gaze imperial had expressed
No wish to fix them or, since all flesh is grass,
Fix poets, gross eccentrics who exist
High in the shallowest stratum of the past.

These learned gentlemen are frivolous soil,
She said, that one plows up for relics—skulls
And pottery. There is a base of stone:
Pure rock that bears no pinchbeck marigolds,
Intelligent with age which is the skill
To endure accumulations of deep time.

She rose; her head built in a blossoming
That recognized no facile season swung
Beyond the orange hour. So it passed.
And on the lawn the gardener gathered up
The scattered orange-peels, whether to keep
Them or destroy them, one could only guess.

She watched as though her eyes of artifact
In a profound age had from darkness cut
Clean diagrams in vaults of perfect rock
That no air dampens. Luminous in these schools
Language is glittering of flint rituals
And a race of sober children learns long smiles.

MEDUSA

The head, of course, had fallen to disrepair
If not to disrepute. The bounteous days
When the blank marble gaze
Was blind in its own right, did not need moss
To mar its sightlessness,
Brilliantly blind, the fabulous days are rare
And spiraling in the ear
Of time; the fountain-mouth
Whitens with bird-droppings. The birds are south
That whistled on the basin's rim and circled
Delightfully where the white water sparkled.

The snake-haired head with overturned eyeballs,
Being all our summer's pleasure, has become
Our mouldering autumn;
We are still fixed as by a stone-eyed spell
Where only brown ferns tell
How summerlong the makeshift waterfalls,
Birds and their songs were false
As all imperishables,
As the stone mask itself, its parables
Of wingèd-heeled assassins, mirror-armed:
For, to believe this face, it must be dreamed.

As birds assault a blind eye it must be dreamed;
It must like godhead in a world of sense
Be that slight crystal lens
Whose scope allows perfection to be conceived.
Yet when chill air first sieved
Twigs to the fountain's peeling floor, it seemed
This mask was not the same,
For we were studying
The blemishes of stone no longer young,

And turning each to the other we declared
Our lives were failing like a bleeding bird.

It was our lives somehow without our living,
Our poppied summer with no sunlight in hand
Or hand's shade on the ground.
O noons and surfaces, brute hours drain
Us like the moulting fountain
Whose walls are parched, where since the water's leaving
No sunlight has been diving,
No splashings to arrest
The formal face whose change is meaningless,
Since all is change; for still in the still heart
Of time the snakes will writhe, the stone lips part,

The blank eyes gaze past suns of no return
On vast irrelevancies that form deforms,
The maladies of dream
Where the stone face revolves like a sick eye
Beneath its lid: so we
Watch through the crumbling surfaces and noons
The single mask of stone
And the dry serpent horror
Of days reflected in a doubtful mirror
With all their guileful melody, until
We raise our quivering swords and think to kill.

ACCUMULATIONS OF THE SEA

I

The hand with a seagull purpose falls upon
Sand where the beach is barren: through clean light
From eye's blue zenith, past seascapes of blue,
Falls on gray sand; yet stenciled in its fall

Against a band of ocean flaked with sunlight:
Touches at last the sand, as one descending
The spiral staircase of association
Around the well of substance. The dry sand crumbles.

A leanness in the atmosphere prevails,
Euclidean monotony of bone,
Music and chill perspective of the shore
Where nothing blurs unless it is the eye.

The beach extends, peopled with solitudes:
Dune-grass, dead starfish brownish with red navels,
Glass changed from ornament to element
In oval lumps, weed, wood and skeletons

Of beach umbrellas. And with the nimble wrist
Buried in sand, palm and its curling fingers
Protrude remote as breathers of the sea,
As sea's accumulations shored and salted.

2

At noon the swimmers pink and shining sprint
Across the beach in the green shallows sporting,
Explore the miniature monsters of the reef
And plunge beyond cold fathoms in the sea.

A while they float, eyes lidded in the sun;
Then play at drowning, smilingly submerge,
Describe in strings of light impossible curves,
Wrist, throat and ankle clothed in a green cold;

9

The sunlight, submarine, entangles them,
Fearlessly sunken from the lilting ceiling,
As in a trail of bubbles they withdraw
Deeper to where upon invisible floors

The coldest darkness sprouts. They touch clam-shells
Perhaps, or tangled plants or a blind stone,
Then plummet upward, leap half out of the sea
To greet with waterfall eyes the gentle air;

And swim to shore, trampling on wind and waves,
And gaze upon the surface of the sea,
And turning, wring the water from their hair
And rub the cold from their cold eyes and bodies.

3

We watch the skeletons of childhood sunken
In sockets of the beach, oyster-white stone,
Bone, shell, sophistications of nostalgia,
A music as of time on the victrola.

Composed among misfortunes of smooth bone
A pearled illusion in the ear creates
Familiar madrigals like those of sleep,
Builds these organic trophies. So coral builds

Its chamber music in the skull; the ear
More labyrinthine than the coiling shell
Will echo it. The pebbled eye propelled
By the elastic rhythms of the tide,

The hand that falls to quiet each swelling wave
Are ambered in a cone of time. But children
Barefoot with baskets holding starfish come
To skim the flat stones, stare at cloudlessness;

And a gull carousing in angelic weather
Prints with its image white cascading octaves
Mounting beyond perception; and the sky
Is vibrant and the sea again unsounded.

CLOUD COUNTRY

How like a marriage is the season of clouds.
The winds at night are festive and constellations
Like stars in a kaleidoscope dissolve
And meet in astounding images of order.
How like a wedding and how like travelers
Through alchemies of a healing atmosphere
We whirl with hounds on leashes and lean birds.

As though the air, being magician, pulled
Birds from a sleeve of cloud, birds drop
To warm grass dented by a smile asleep.
Long odysseys of sunlight at this hour
Salute the gaze that of all weariness
Remains unwearied, and the air turns young
Like reddening light in a corridor of pines.

The landscape where we lie is creased with light
As a painting one might have folded and put away
And never wished to study until now.
How like a marriage, how like voyagers
We come upon this season of right clouds,
Valors of altitude, white harbors, hills
Supple and green, these actions of the sun.

THE DROWNING POET

The drowning poet hours before he drowned
Had whirlpool eyes, salt at his wrists, and wore
A watery emphasis. The sea was aware
As flowers at the bedside of a wound
Of an imminent responsibility
And lay like a magnet beside him the blue day long
Ambiguous as a lung.

He watched the divers learn an element
Familiar as, to the musician, scales,
Where to swim is a progression of long vowels,
A communication never to be sought
Being itself all searching: certain as pearls,
Simple as rocks in sun, a happiness
Bound up with happenings.

To drown was the perfection of technique,
The word containing its own sense, like Time;
And turning to the sea he entered it
As one might speak of poems in a poem
Or at the crisis in the sonata quote
Five-finger exercises: a compliment
To all accomplishment.

ENTRANCE FROM SLEEP

To wake into the afternoon for you
Is a familiar gesture. Upon the eye,
As dawn to the shade-embroidered fountain brings
The young fern's wisdom, the first world takes shape
Where shadow and light on a white ceiling meet;
And the late garden builds its trellises
And the machinery of light begins.

To wake is to become what one first sees.
So, waking upon beaches, one is a shell,
A tide; or, afternoons in an apartment
Above a garden, levels of shade and sun
Through which you wade like eyes in tapestries
That wake only when struck by light and take
Advantage of this grace to change our sleep

Or plant an image of our wakening.
So you, with a Medici smile, becoming not
A twilight personage but the danceable gloom
And music of all shade, wake trailing song
As in an hour of hot brilliance what
Happens is a wrung memory of light
And all shade is what music we have rung.

And all throughout a Breughel matinée
Those buxom waltzes rang. Good people, cried
The fiddler, dance! Fiddler, the dancers cried,
Addressing perhaps the sun, teach us this joy
That is no more than dancing it in shade
Or on bright streets, teach us this simple trade.

The fiddler was a man of consequence,
Responsive to a morning's imperfections;
He found too many elbows in the dance
And too much pity in the cobblestones;
And flowers shriveling in the pride of hands
Dropped to the ground as dancers in a dance.

And daring to be gracious the fiddler grew
Unmoved by all but his most private music,
Drew then cold pulses with his fiddlestick,
So cold the dancers halted in their whirlings,
So long the dancers lost their worlds and knew
The different musics and steps of solitude.

And in each one there was a kind of dance
Such as breath makes upon a frosted air
And in this stillness there was a kind of joy.

And for three days such was the dancing there.

POEM IN SPRING

Being born of earth, we've come to sit
On fecund ground and fondle it—
A filial diversion this.
Then brother-sisterly we kiss
Who cannot tell one branch for buds
Nor see, for trees, the April woods
Cloudy with green nor, amorous,
Think autumn looks askance at us.

Our father by his hourglass
Drowsing, approves the pretty pass;
Our mother dresses even now
In young girls' finery, as though
To tempt her sons to a Greek deed
In the green shade of her great need.
Come, with their prime example, love
Only those things we're parcel of.

For innocence is useful, too,
In springtime. Sister, let us woo
Complications of limb and leaf
And our own limbs and their one life,
As all is wooed by earth and season.
The single beauty in such treason
—Apart from penance done too late—
Is that it is immediate.

In good time enough there'll be
No more, dear orphaned love, to see
The trees for the sapped forest, or
Dropped leaves for the brown forest floor:
Gold they will fall, incestuous gold
The personal, and soon be mould,
Indictment of our days that in
Such curious vividness begin.

HOURGLASS

Alone, one can but toy with imagery.
I watch this hourglass that has been taught
    Calm flowing such as you teach me,
        For inasmuch as we
Are drop-clear crystal and fine red sand brought
From where sun makes a stab at majesty,
With which each crystal feeds its counterpart,
    This form most holds you to my heart.

For this perhaps a baffled century,
Given to grand personifications, feeling
Women had secrets they were not revealing,
        Made it a norm of beauty,
    Called sumptuous figures by its name,
Placed it in rooms where, bland and beautiful
And more genteel than the memorial skull,
    It took their glances, kept them tame,

Kept tame their beauty, but their utterance urged
To a fine indulgence, to a finer trust
That the soul's crystal and the body's dust
    Should never finally be merged.
        What portliness of wit
Held them from seeing what we smile at now
In the expensive crystal, knowing how,
    Teller of time, time tells on it:

How at last the sand so gently grinds the glass
That, years before it shows, the minutes fil-
    ter swifterly through the waste all will,
        While still the waist holds, pass
    As toward his overturn each moves.
Alone I cannot bear this image. You
Are the kind gathering I most falter to.
Love only is replenishment of halves.

CONSERVATORY

Nothing is not so wasted, my dear wastrel,
That of our shelters you should fear to say
They totter, all that damask, one last day
Like roses tattered, waiting for the mistral,
Or red cape rippled by a mad bull's nostril.

And say it in a blowzy idiom.
The anger of this wind is a strange anger,
Blows light, blows dark, blows vicious, blows humdrum:
Wryness is all, say, hearing the wind come,
And none of us is getting any younger.

Say
Bull in a rosebed, bull in the arena,
Wind in the red room where the flowers are kept,
Rose behind the jalousies, bull in Barcelona,
At the whine of blood, olé! the rowdy ladies clapped.

But, back to roses, if anything will save them,
Pleading rosefever, keep them in a wide bowl
Where wind through the wide window may unleaf them.
For risk is finer than bargain. And when the bull
Stomps out in France, thick ropes of roses wreathe him.

To kill the bull would be to spoil the game.
The French pluck roses back from the bull's black shoulder.
And this, I mean, is delicacy, a name
For the fighter less than for the skilled beholder.

Flowers inside the thirteen-year high walls
Rehearse the profane virtues: Golden Coins
For constancy; and Sweet Indulgence twines
Above the small pale bells
That natives call White Lies. Here children run
Among the blossoms, pointing, calling,
Each with his toy behind him trailing,
A deformity worshipped, an introduction to pain.

I have loitered by the wall, being somewhat taller,
Wanting to die, but that life was a flattery,
And seen the children pose in their vanity
Of pearls round a throat of color
Beside the peepholes they have made in the brick,
Rolling their eyes at these, although
No one but God knows what they know
Playing I-Spy, Red Light, the Marriage Trick.

In such games one shuts his eyes, unclosing them
Only to find all playmates hidden, never
Completely sure of how he will recover
Those vanished in the sun-stream;
A deportment formal as his cries at birth,
The roulades of relinquishment,
Shows him how change is never sent
Like a valentine, but waits, a plot of earth,

A green conspiracy against the heart who is It,
Counting his pulse, face in the slick leaves pressed,
Feeling at first just the thrill of being lost
In leaves; then the flavor bit-
By-bit of learning how utterly they have gone,
How only he is prisoner, must
Love and forswear them and, at last
Outplayed, play out his Patience quite alone.

VARIATIONS:
THE AIR IS SWEETEST
THAT A THISTLE GUARDS

I

The air is sweetest that a thistle guards
And purple thistles in our blue air burn
And spiny leaves hold close the light we share.
The loose tides sprawl and turn and overturn
(Distant pearl-eaters gorging) on the shore,
While taut between those waters and these words,
Our air, our morning, the poignant thistles weave
Nets that bind back, garland the hungering wave.

2

Midsummer spreads the ticklish mullein leaf,
Rambler and brambles, and his ankles bleed
Who wanders less than gingerly among them;
In winter, holly; later, the bittersweet rose;
Leaves harsh and somber, nettles in November.

Burr, cactus, yucca, the moral thorn that only
A snail can master; plants that bring to mind
Porcupines (bad for dogs), sea-urchins, scorpions:
Near by what silkiest blows a sharp thing grows
And this is good for lovers to remember.

3

Flowers are people
Enchanted by witches—
This we were able
To learn in the nursery,
But thought, being mercenary,
How witches brought candy,

Were easy to hide from
Or frighten with matches.

Listening to Nanny
We laughed till we died
At her warnings, her funny
Despairs, her enticements:
"Be good!"—while in basements
We broke eggs on grindstones,
Pulled apart flowers
And tracked snow inside.

Ah, people are flowers.
They fall helter-skelter
In their first witching weather
Or turn wry like thistles
Who, bristling together,
Brag of their shelters,
Insist that each latest
Is safest, is sweetest.

4

When at midnight Jane took off her mask, the red-
Checkered-lavender and bordered with seed pearls,
She kissed her lover as though she had never had
Nor wanted another. Some girls
Snorted, for this was beautiful. One could
But wander alone then through the tropical dark
And ask what comforts lurk
In such disordered gleams from under the tide.

Now not the answer, for of course there were
No helpful answers, but the air of questioning
Is what one needs to remember, to let ring clear
As a sea-cave widening
The little noise of loss. What barrier
Holds up, what is not vulnerable? Down, down,

Sand on a sunken crown
Settles; but that shape is always there.

Just as beneath her mask there was always Jane:
She let it drop, we saw her jubilant smile,
Thought, "Beauty is not so temperate, nor is pain,
But that they burst the seal
We stamp upon them." Remembering love, but fearing
The memory of the beloved, I once cut
Three thistles which I put
In a glass of water, then sat beside them, staring,

Asking the flowers, silver under water,
To tell me about time and love and doom,
Those great blue grottos of feeling where the rank intruder
Is moved to think in rhyme;
But the thistles could indicate only that face which came
Abruptly to mock with its usual witty anger
My nakedness, my hunger,
And the thistles jabbed my wrist when I reached for them.

5

Three days I wept in the snow, feet bare,
Then to Canossa waved goodbye.
Absolution was a luxury
Only the innocent could snare.
I went where the pearl-eaters were.

The air was dazzling in my eye
Accustomed to the mountainous shade
So lately left behind: this showed
I was still far from purity
But it would come assuredly.

Pearl-eaters met me on the road,
Glimpsing me first as down foothills
I stumbled, rising from their meals,

And every courtesy bestowed
To make me at their tables glad.

In a chair of pearl I sat while gulls
Croaked Cheer! and ate the priceless food—
There was always more, my hostess said.
I knew those pearls were pure, or else
Purity was the pace that kills.

So with the pearl-eaters I stayed
Till memory drove me back inland
Where, to my wonderment, I found
Whatever I tasted wherever I strayed
Became at once of pure pearl made.

6

Friday. Clear. Cool. This is your day. Stendhal
At breakfast-time. The metaphors of love.
Lucky perhaps, big Beyle, for whom love was
So frankly the highest good, to be garlanded
Accordingly, without oblivion, without cure.
His heedful botany: not love, great pearl
That swells around a small unlovely need;
Nor love whose fingers tie the bows of birth
Upon the sorry present. Love merely as the best
There is, and one would make the best of that
By saying how it grows and in what climates,
By trying to tell the crystals from the branch,
Stretching that wand then toward the sparkling wave.
To say at the end, however we find it, good,
Bad, or indifferent, it helps us, and the air
Is sweetest there. The air is very sweet.

RIVER POEM

This old man had lavender skin, a handkerchief
Toppling from his breastpocket like an iris.
We on the riverbank watched the gracing rowers
Leaving the shore and watched him watch them leave,
And Charles said: I wonder if they mean to him
As much as I can imagine they mean to him.

Charles was like that. But as evening became
A purple element we stayed there wondering
About the old man—talking of other things,
For although the old man, by the time we all went home,
Had moved away he stayed there wandering
Like a river-flower, thinking of rivery things

(We supposed) well into the twilight. We would never
Know, this we knew, how much it had meant to him—
Oars, violet water, laughter on the stream.
Though we knew, Charles said, just how much *he* meant to the river.
For he moved away, leaving us there on the grass,
But the river did not vanish, or not then at least.

KITE POEM

"One is reminded of a certain person,"
Continued the parson, settling back in his chair
With a glass of port, "who sought to emulate
The sport of birds (it was something of a chore)
By climbing up on a kite. They found his coat
Two counties away; the man himself was missing."

His daughters tittered: it was meant to be a lesson
To them—they had been caught kissing, or some such nonsense,
The night before, under the crescent moon.
So, finishing his pheasant, their father began
This thirty-minute discourse, ending with
A story improbable from the start. He paused for breath,

Having shown but a few of the dangers. However, the wind
Blew out the candles and the moon wrought changes
Which the daughters felt along their stockings. Then,
Thus persuaded, they fled to their young men
Waiting in the sweet night by the raspberry bed,
And kissed and kissed, as though to escape on a kite.

FOUR LITTLE POEMS

1 / PROCESSION

Virgins and kings: the very fields aquiver
Moving through which the long procession moved.
But others mused beside that ardent river.
Each white field-flower they had gathered shed
Its petals, wanting to tell them they were loved.
If a girl looked, she looked as in still water
At maidens, village suitors—where instead
He rode, her least familiar most real lover.

Gazing the flowers gave up all to gaze
After the great procession, longer, greater
For having passed unfathomed. Nowadays
Not many comprehend the language of flowers.
It will soon be dusk on the reflective water.
As girls love daisies, love dismembers hours.

2 / PORTRAIT

A youth last seen by an undecipherable
Artist. Or not a painting at all. A young man
With his comic hat on, waiting in the middle
Of many things for his painter to come and make
Most of them plausible.

One arm perhaps on the sideboard where would be shown
A lute, cold meats, a snifter somewhat full
Like a crystal ball predicting what's unknown;
Ingots of nougat, thumb-sized kumquats sodden
With juice not quite their own.

The other arm akimbo; eyes askance
Follow the crook of his elbow pointing out
The window, where might be a bird, for instance,
A blue tree, or a woman picking her way
Through what he sees as distance.

3 / PARABLE

After the child laughed, and the Emperor
Had been hurried back to the palace, he stood before
His mirror long enough to see that, yes,
He was indeed quite naked. What a mess.

The children, more impressionable for all
Their accuracy, could not but recall
The solemn music before the Embarrassment,
And naked down the avenues they went.

4 / PROVERB

And so at winter's end her perennial bounty
Put forth leaves, having become a small tree
By then, and was set near the window in its urn;
Really a marvel—six years to have gone, and still
That astounding florescence, white and sinewy green,
While ours would flag long before summer did.
Not that we had inferior seed or mould,
Or were stingy with water, or that none of us had
Green fingers. But hers throve. It was like a child
Who waits for Something Awful to happen, tense
Beyond distraction and shining and all the while
Fixed in indifference, tree in the tight urn.

FOLIAGE OF VISION

As landscapes richen after rain, the eye
Atones, turns fresh after a fit of tears.
When all the foliage of vision stirs
I glimpse the plump fruit hanging, falling, fallen
Where wasps are sputtering. In the full sky
Time, a lean wasp, sucks at the afternoon.

The tiny black and yellow agent of rot
Assaults the plum, stinging and singing. What
A marvel is the machinery of decay!
How rare the day's wrack! What fine violence
Went to inject its gall in the glad eye!
The plum lies all brocaded with corruption.

There is no wit in weeping, yet I wept
To hear the insect wrath and rhythm of time
Surround the plum that fell like a leper's thumb.
The hours, my friend, are felicitous imagery,
Yet I became their image to watch the sun
Dragging with it a scarlet palace down.

The eye attunes, pastoral warbler, always.
Joy in the cradle of calamity
Wakes though dim voices work at lullaby.
Triumph of vision: the act by which we see
Is both the landscape-gardening of our dream
And the root's long revel under the clipped lawn.

I think of saints with hands pierced and wrenched eyes
Sensational beyond the art of sense,
As though whatever they saw was about to be
While feeling alters in its imminence
To palpable joy; of Dante's ascent in hell
To greet with a cleansed gaze the petaled spheres;

Of Darwin's articulate ecstasy as he stood
Before a tangled bank and watched the creatures
Of air and earth noble among much leafage
Dancing an order rooted not only in him
But in themselves, bird, fruit, wasp, limber vine,
Time and disaster and the limping blood.

THE GRAPE CURE

For two days feed on water. The third morning
Drink water and eat, some twenty minutes after,
The first of your grapes. In as many weeks as you need
You shall be cured. What happens, in plain words,
Is a purging, a starving not of yourself but of what
Feeds on you, hangs down like a crab from your heart.

The first days have a tang: in a bone cup
Wild honey, locusts, the gracile hermit's lunch,
And goglets cooling among walls; the verb
Of Handel in a starlit attic sounding
The question of how much one ever needs
—Which is high naughtiness in a grave man.

And the ruddy colossus who had guarded you
Moves to a pillar above those crawling sands
In which his absence plants the splendor plucked
By late visitors to that place. And only then,
With the last illusion that anything matters lost
Like a bad penny, do such languors come

That, pulled two ways at once by the distant star
Called Plenitude and the bald planet Ebb,
Your body learns how it is chained to fear.
You learn you need one thing alone which, pressed
Against your palate, is not yet joy, nor even
The hope of it. Your body is like a coast

At sunset, whose morbid flats, the blacks and beggars
Straggling with their hideouts on their backs,
Burn like the cities of antiquity caught
For once without the patina of time;
And at full tide, though winsome, still suspect,
Laid on too thick, but (though suspect) held dear

Lest everything fail: lest after Handel stopped
The listening beasts had not lain down appeased:
Or lest, tomorrow morning, when the sun
Bestrides the vineyards, a sick man should pretend
Somehow that of this chryselephantine air
The gold cannot be pity, nor ivory charity.

When the picnic-basket lovers who had been dangling
Grapes between every kiss (thus interfusing
Leavings with their loving) left the bruised glade,
Then for three hours each weed and tendril sprang
With a tingling back to its proper bend in the sun,
Small reconciliations not to be counted.

Or not perhaps to be counted dear, being
So plural and of such a delicate vim.
Where the grapes' wet skeleton fell, swift points of light
Clustered like maggots or the remembrance of green fruit
Darklier ribbed now where no sun may ripen.
It became at last possible to watch the entire clearing,

The thick light ruminant, lit branches gently
Heaving, muscles of a beast asleep, watch it
Assimilate the lovers, what they meant
With their refreshments and their temporal soundings,
Till the flesh of the beast is burning history
Of what they endured in the glade, persisting there.

For they went, mouths plundered by the dark beast
Who with his gold twin broods on happenings:
The black beast sluggish from a thousand graces
Swallowed each day, crisper of grasses, whose
Mere odor salts the sensitive tongue with autumn.
—Greedy themselves, they had deserved no less.

Yet where they lay, light in a Maltese cross
Through branches halts them amberly from this,
Like the good gold beast for whom even now at dusk
The villagers leave meat by the black woods' edge;
Then hurry back, already too long afield,
To friends and firelit rooms and the late retelling

Of how, from the time when the world was a tall young tree,
He comes to graze, transmutes with a father's pride
The frail or bitten and, by the least of his cares,
Reddens the ashen trunk where fungus clings
Like the incidence of pleasure to his children
Committed to doom, denial, airier things.

TRANSFIGURED BIRD

I

That day the eggshell of appearance split
And weak of its own translucence lay in the dew.
A child fond of natural things discovered it.

Though it was broken it was very blue,
Pearly within, and lit by sun enough
For it to glow, though broken clean in two.

He ran home with it wrapped in a handkerchief
To where he kept his findings. Here, in a nest,
Robins' eggs hollowed with a pin and a puff;

Moths spread like ferns, then ferns and flowers pressed
Like moths on cotton; a bullfrog, once green;
Minerals, and a few smutched feathers—lest

The world be part forgotten if part unseen.
No longer glowing, but blue as the sky that day,
The shell went on the top shelf. What had been

Inside was nimble and hungry and far away,
And had left behind only this envelope
For a child to find and fancy it was gay.

2

As one who watches two days in some hope
A fertile yolk, until there throbs at last
The point of blood beneath his microscope,

Then rises rinsed with the thought of what has passed,
I watched the big yolk of remembrance swallowed
By the throbbing legend there, that broke its fast,

Grew into shape, now to be hatched and hallowed,
Whether a bugling bird or cockatrice;
And when the wild wings rose, on foot I followed.

And much was legend long days after this.
I mean that much was read and read aright.
Where the bird went gold plumes fell, which were his.

3

Philippa raised her elbows to the light
As though to lean there watching the red deer
Leap through it, blonde as her hair unpinned at night

When by her bed she took a comb to her hair
And gave it lessons in simplicity
Till each long strand was docile and severe;

Then turned as if to smile, smiled then at me,
And in the sudden dark stretched with no fear,
For whom the night was a warm nubility.

Reynard, Cock Robin, Bruin and Chanticleer,
Dreaming she ruled these clever animals
She had laughed aloud in her sleep when they came near.

And had herself shown other valuables:
Fabergé's royal Easter eggs she kept
To look at in her moods. The enameled shells

Sprang wide at her touch, and out each marvel stepped:
In one, some great-grandchildren's miniatures
That a Russian prince smiled at before he slept;

Then from a gold yolk with sharp ruby spurs
A little rooster flaps gold wings and crows
—Inside of it a thumbnail engine whirs;

"And this I think has a fox, but one never knows."
Nor did she know, nor would I tell her ever
How close she was to the flood of time that flows,

Or rather flies, a yellow bird, forever
Beyond, stops only if we stop, to trill
In the thicket yonder, loudest to a lover.

34

Close in the thicket under her windowsill
The bird of prophecy no song decoys
Sang, while she dreamed and I was somewhat still;

Sang, while the darkness would not mute its noise,
First of its past, the teeming yolk; sang then
Of fables, findings, shelves of fabulous toys,

Its various images in the minds of men;
Of love. At which she woke. The bird in me
Sang on, a panic in my blood, a pain.

Strange how that music made a woman's beauty,
Most notable for being frail, of such
A power one could have wept for frailty;

Her hair too much like sun, her love too much
Like ignorance, perhaps. I must begin
To tell her of this music in my touch:

Of God who like a little boy with a pin
Shall prick a hole in either end of the sky
And blow it clean away, the thing within,

Away, before it waste, or hatching fly
Out of his reach in noisy solitude,
Or kill him with the oracle in its eye;

Blow all away, the yolk with its X of blood,
The shelves of jewels away, this drowsing girl
At whose hand, away, the shapely animals fed;

Till the egg is void of all but pearl-on-pearl
Reflections and their gay meanderings;
Shall, tiring, burst the shell, let the fragments whirl.

4

That day the year, eager to hatch new springs,
Nested in russet feathers by the bare lake.
That day a child who was fond of natural things

Went where light dangled like a bait to take
And found a blue egg which had airily dropped,
A freak of season, down to the hooked brake,

Lifted it out, as children will, but stopped:
He had thought to blow it clean, but there had broken
From the cold shell his chilly fingers cupped

The claw of the dead bird, clutching air, a token
Of how there should be nothing cleanly for years to come,
Nor godly, nor reasons found, nor prayers spoken.

And though it was still early morning he went home
And slept and would not till nearly dusk be woken.

THE PARROT

I am impatient of the myth that numbs
    A spinster as she hums
Sweet nothings to her parrot in its cage.
The haggard eye set in white crinkled paint
Meeting her eye over the cracker crumbs
    Tells much about old age
  Beyond what is serene or quaint.

Our revels now are ended, pretty Poll,
    For midnight bells extol
The individual face behind the mask.
Each dancer seeks his partner to embrace
As if he had seen deep into her soul
    And gave what it dared ask,
  While knowing but a woman's face.

As she grew older, old, it was to sense
    A sad irrelevance
About the Moment she had so long wanted,
When mask *did* matter least, and face *did* tell
More than it knew of private riches, whence
    Came surely the enchanted
  Eye, the enchanting syllable.

Think how the parrot masked always not young,
    Selecting as from dung
The oaths and greetings she let fall when most
She suffered or felt joy was possible,
Destroys the personal with its gray tongue,
    That frail and talkative ghost
  A bird of utterance can dispel;

Speaks with no human voice, which is pretense
    Of gentleness and sense.
Against such masks, its ancient cry awoke
Jungles within her, sunsets of its flight,
Being the music that informed her dance
    Until all music shook
  To stillness in the bestial night.

THE PELICAN

Squatter on water, ingenuous fisherman,
    Behold the pelican
Slapped by a wave, all grinning or aghast
At the enormity of his habitat,
The famous pouch, half stomach and half chin,
    Quick to show off unguessed
  Capacities: few things do that.

Always the postures foolish yet severe
    Of Empire furniture
Assist him in a courtesy nowadays
Only among artists fashionable, who like
Being in public each a caricature
    The world may recognize
  And still be free to overlook.

Like great men he already is in part
    A myth or work of art
Sparing the watcher as it spares itself
By an apt gaiety, gay ineptitude,
Who floats, no evident concern at heart,
    Above the bluest gulf
  Upon the wind as on a tide.

But when the human fishermen cast their bait
    At times they see too late
The ponderous bird avail of it in midair,
And are made to witness by their stratagem
Hurt and embarrassed over the pleasure-boat
    A creature of desire
  As crude as theirs, involved with them.

Yet, lacking food, this bird must be, to feed
    His offspring flesh and blood,
Himself his own last supper, and die then
Fattened upon the sense of how they thrive.
Almost one fancies charity is not greed,
    Seeing the pelican
  From air to emptier water dive.

THE PEACOCK

I speak to the unbeautiful of this bird
    That, celestially bored,
On feet too little under willows trails
Too much of itself, like Proust, a long brocade
Along, not seen but felt; that's never spared,
    Most mortal of its trials,
  Lifting this burden up in pride.

The spreading tail is pallid seen from the back
    But it's worthwhile to look
At what strenuous midribs make the plumage stretch:
Then, while it teeters in the light wind, ah
It turns, black, green and gold, that zodiac
    Of eyes—not these so much
  As idiot mouths repeating: I.

Consider other birds: the murderous swan
    And dodo now undone,
The appalling dove, hens' petulant sisterhood;
And then the peacock that no cry alarms,
Tense with idlesse, as though already on
    A terrace in boxwood
  Or graven in a coat of arms.

In all these there's the common wound of nature
    No natural hand can suture,
A lessening—whether by want of shape they fail,
Of song, or will to live, or something else.
How comforting to think blest any creature
    This short of beautiful!
  But some have known such comfort false.

A beatitude of trees which shall inherit
    Whoever's poor in spirit
Receives the peacock in their cumbersome shade.
Some who have perfect beauty shall not grieve,
As I, for diminution: they know merit
    In body, word and deed,
  Lone angels round each human grave.

PRIMER

A final lassitude, of snapdragons
Puckering in their plot, the air like bronze,
Ringing of bronze, even the fieriest ones

Too weary in their exile to deny
Taste of the forbidden fruit of the bare sky.
"Blessed is what is born, for it shall die,"

Our prophet uttered from his porch. We stood
Cowed by the benison of his platitude,
Then filed in silence out of the mystic wood

Into an orchard, perishable, lit
With novelty, as before: our altered wit
Found each thing altered by our sense of it.

And as before by orchard springs, where all
Was clear, day-clear, we saw the apples fall
That hung above a babbling prodigal

Of autumnal water, sweet to overflowing
With dissolution; taste of which was knowing
Much about age, old age, the going-going-

Gone of the senses, how they putrefy
In the black sun, weeping-ripe, or infancy
From drunken water sip. And the bare sky

Shed on us, children swaddled all in earth,
A vernal dawn, a more than personal mirth:
Blessed is what shall perish into birth.

—The words were next to nothing, but we shook
Enhancement from them, like the childhood book
Wherein, since then, we had not thought to look:

How much we had forgotten. The first page
Bespeaks a pang no worldliness can gauge:
Once more its glimmering scripture to assuage

Calls from within us cypress and flowering thorn,
Carpets, the woman and the god each morn
Naming the creatures to their latest-born.

VARIATIONS AND ELEGY:
WHITE STAG, BLACK BEAR

for my father

1

      . . . and chiefly shone,
Set in red gold upon his forefinger,
A cameo, black bear and milk-white stag
In mortal conflict.

2

The lion's resounding profile and the pride
That called it proud walk side by side.

And Envy, seeing the magpie envious,
Flies with it everywhere.

Violent, the thief and glutton, all of us
Find grateful creatures to ensnare.

While the lecher, spry at the zoo's center,
Spies no cage he may not enter,

To a tired man, winter
Recommends the bear.

3

Could we have wondered at the mere
Animal, then the honey in his maw,
All brute, wet tongue, all body, shaggy claw,
Would have been sensual and clear.

But spirit loomed where most we saw
Body: wonderful shapes in the white air
Transfigured Bruin; by the time our ear
Froze to his growl, the growl had ceased.

We called the autumn night his lair,
Yet knew it ours, who long ago released
Movements of such persuasiveness in the beast
That seven stars became a bear.

4

Hunters choke the golden clearing
With apertures: eye, nostril, ear: for there
The white stag prances, unicorn-rare,
Whose hooves since dawn were steering

His captors toward beatitude:
Yet, when to pouring horns the hunters, nearing
The mound where he should stand subdued,

Find once more the shining puzzle
They stalk is constantly disappearing
Beyond the hounds and musket-muzzles,

How shall they think that, fearing
He might too blissfully amaze,
The white stag leaps unseen into their gaze,
Into their empty horns, past hearing?

5

Naked we lie in the black night
As on the lepers' island, where
Against a white and crumbling shore
Two lovers lie in full delight
Watching, while the sun climbs, upon
The corpulence of passion spread
Those pale restrictive flowers that shed
Glistering petals from the bone.

All you who lie in the black night,
Blacker than flesh in darkness, never
Inspired to tell love from lover,

How far the flesh past touch and sight
Moves in its felicity
You shall never understand,
Until the leper says (your hand
Resting in his white hand) Kiss me.

6

They married, but kept journals. *First*, he wrote,
Coffee with Psyche by the river. Later
Three hours upon the water.
I think she liked the blue and yellow boat.
Too tired to write further. She
Made other reckonings: *When I said Yes,*
Did the frail ear that grows within me guess
What my next word would be?

So, where he slept in the dark bed, she took
A candle, wooed his profile with the kiss
Of all things bodiless,
Until his hand, fighting this new light, struck
Quick tears and knowledge from her gaze
And it was him she pardoned, not his hand
That, holding hot advantage like a wand,
Conjured its own disguise.

In this way, through the first woods before dawn
Seeking only themselves, white stag, black bear,
Engaged at sunrise where
Trees with a timely red stood overgrown,
—The bear's teeth sunk in light's lean shoulder,
White horns calling blood from the dark flank—
Fought on the brink of loving, reared or sank
Together, as foretold.

Thank God it happened at the root of sense,
Their earliest battle, near the cave's mouth. O
Then did we undergo
Subliming dreams, or wake incarnate? since
All surfaces we live by flash

With whiteness of the white stag who demands
Of veined black stone on which he stands
Reflection into flesh.

ELEGY

Sickness, at least, becomes us. Like red leaves pulled
By autumn, the fingertips throb with fever—
As though their place were elsewhere, at temples
Other than their own—and a panic scores
The trunk like the antlers of remembered bucks.
Lichen and Indian pipes, fretwork of twig and knuckle
Under a sheet of sky: from which, as vantage,
All might have happened among encompassing dun or green;
But from within
Three hundred tints approximate
The single color of decline. Or seen
From a further point in time, all might
Have given away, as life to the afterlife,
To a brilliant prospect of
Black lines in snow. But from within,
Chilled to such red, scarlet on red, the branches
Facet the sunset, cyclops Rose,
Or, if the eye is shut,
The small veins of the eyelid, red on rose,
Emblaze the blinding petals
As with a sigil of the passing year.

So that, like anything
About to die, everlasting,
Eye-deep in malady, the grove
Preserves from horn, tongue, crown, their melody,
Its own delirium, steep in a hollow tree,
Honey-cells rich and orderly as graves:
Heavy the woods with Self,
With selves, *our*selves, sniffing as children at dusk
The century plant at the top of a red stair:
Tiptoe on amber spires, all shall sleep

But that the bear,
Matted with bittersweet and the wakeful burr,
The future dancing in his nostrils, ambles
Panting, black, to the base of the honey-tree.
Unmindful of the nodding court,
Like a cannibal come upon Sleeping Beauty
He hugs the tree, then clambers
Through shaking color and minor breakage
Up to the sweet weight there.
                            And for an hour
The grove does wake! stirs as to a suddenly
Localized pain. Beneath his paw, a branch
Snaps. Twelve prongs of fern
Relinquish the moist air
They held entranced. Blink
Of mute sap. A stem,
Being still green, relents.
At last they know themselves, these two:

A grove of autumn trees, no more; a creature
Greedy against the smell of snow.
Two human lovers in their place
Might have left the altar and the rose-window
Happy forever after, so. But honey
Undoes a bear that yawning
Crashes from their embrace, the lick and lop,
One revel nearer sleep:
Abandoned, a grove once more extends itself
Hopelessly into meaning.

It appears we seek whatever we do seek only
That we may cry Enough! For the bear,
Under the glittering horns, the snowy pelt,
The whiteness reared from which the whiteness falls,
Must sleep, pores closing, eyes,
That huge body growing
Weaker than the spell it broke, or nearly broke,
Slinking, while the spell holds,
Into its ashen dream, the scar of claws . . .

There, where a tree is scarred, they pause,
Hunters, burning in the vast autumn:
Which beast they chased they were hard put to say.
When at last it hesitated among red leaves,
White as the underside of summer leaves,
Its eyes like split pods and two rising
Branches of ice from these,
They knew, and to this day
Speak of its capture as a man who has never been ill
Tells everywhere of disease.

PERIWINKLES

You have seen at low tide on the rocky shore
How everything around you sparkles, or
Is made to when you think what went before.

Much of this blaze, that's mental, seems to come
From a pool among the creviced rocks, a slum
For the archaic periwinkle. Some

Are twisting, some are sleeping there, and all
(For sun is pulse, and shade historical)
Cling in blotched spirals to the shadiest wall

—Whose cousins, shingled by the finding tide,
Purpled the cloths of kings. Place one upside-
Down in your hand. If at all satisfied,

The little creature stretches from its shell
One lucent, speckled horn by which to tell,
Touching your skin, if that is safe as well;

Then turns with much interior shifting over
Into your palm, so that its spirals cover
Whatever suddenly takes hold. You shiver,

Touched by the fecund past, a creature curled
In a flaky cone which inside is all pearled
With nourishment sucked out from the pulsing world:

Knowing that ancient liveliness undone,
For having crept within, where there was none
To feel it but yourself, squinting in sun,

Caught by the crazy trustfulness of the past:
Its gentle sucking, our old nurse at last
Demented, crooned to revery at our breast.

It is ourselves shall tell her fairy tales
Of fountains we scooped dry with bottomless pails.
Then we grow old; her lunacy prevails.

WILLOW

If not, why should the willow bend? It bends
High in the air, but to the stream descends
Dipping its as-we-call-them finger-ends

In weedy water: hence, a weeping tree,
We say, invoking in our imagery
Not much of willows: for to such as we

It was that branches lent, though covertly,
Movements more suave, guiding what pangs there be
Into a bearable choreography:

Our hands rehearsed the eloquent charade
Of willows: from the simple noises made
By creatures come to drink in the trees' shade

Came sobs of women weeping into their hands,
Performing easily all their pain demands,
Gesture and sound no child misunderstands:

Because of this we never could recall
What we *did* bear, as under water all
Becomes a silvery weightless miracle

In which, presuming on the certitude
Of bodily grace, movements that in us wooed
Profounder levels rose to air renewed:

Thus, rocked by sorrows, never could we tell
How grave they were, our bodies knowing well
The signs to charm them, alter or dispel:

At times we thought, Gesture is all that grieves:
The hand has slanted (like the willow's leaves)
From touching faces it alone conceives

Downward to drop its pennies on shut eyes
Before the habit fades of their surprise
Past blood and tissue where remembrance lies.

THE HOUSE

Whose west walls take the sunset like a blow
Will have turned the other cheek by morning, though
The long night falls between, as wise men know:

Wherein the wind, that daily we forgot,
Comes mixed with rain and, while we seek it not,
Appears against our faces to have sought

The contours of a listener in night air,
His profile bent as from pale windows where
Soberly once he learned what houses were.

Those darkening reaches, crimsoned with a dust
No longer earth's, but of the vanishing West,
Can stir a planet nearly dispossessed,

And quicken interest in the avid vein
That dyes a man's heart ruddier far than stain
Of day does finial, cornice and windowpane:

So that whoever strolls on his launched lawn
At dusk, the hour of recompense, alone,
May stumbling on a sunken boundary stone

The loss of deed and structure apprehend.
And we who homeless toward such houses wend
May find we have dwelt elsewhere. Scholar and friend,

After the twelve bright houses that each day
Presume to flatter what we most display,
Night is a cold house, a narrow doorway.

This door to no key opens, those to brass.
Behind it, warning of a deep excess,
The winds are. I have entered, nevertheless,

And seen the wet-faced sleepers the winds take
To heart; have felt their dreadful profits break
Beyond my seeing: at a glance they wake.

THE COUNTRY OF A THOUSAND
YEARS OF PEACE

(1959; revised edition, 1970)

I

THE COUNTRY OF A THOUSAND YEARS
OF PEACE

to Hans Lodeizen (1924–1950)

Here they all come to die,
Fluent therein as in a fourth tongue.
But for a young man not yet of their race
It was a madness you should lie

Blind in one eye, and fed
By the blood of a scrubbed face;
It was a madness to look down
On the toy city where

The glittering neutrality
Of clock and chocolate and lake and cloud
Made every morning somewhat
Less than you could bear;

And makes me cry aloud
At the old masters of disease
Who dangling high above you on a hair
The sword that, never falling, kills

Would coax you still back from that starry land
Under the world, which no one sees
Without a death, its finish and sharp weight
Flashing in his own hand.

THE OCTOPUS

There are many monsters that a glassen surface
Restrains. And none more sinister
Than vision asleep in the eye's tight translucence.
Rarely it seeks now to unloose
Its diamonds. Having divined how drab a prison
The purest mortal tissue is,
Rarely it wakes. Unless, coaxed out by lusters
Extraordinary, like the octopus
From the gloom of its tank half-swimming half-drifting
Toward anything fair, a handkerchief
Or child's face dreaming near the glass, the writher
Advances in a godlike wreath
Of its own wrath. Chilled by such fragile reeling
A hundred blows of a boot-heel
Shall not quell, the dreamer wakes and hungers.
Percussive pulses, drum or gong,
Build in his skull their loud entrancement,
Volutions of a Hindu dance.
His hands move clumsily in the first conventional
Gestures of assent.
He is willing to undergo the volition and fervor
Of many fleshlike arms, observe
These in their holiness of indirection
Destroy, adore, evolve, reject—
Till on glass rigid with his own seizure
At length the sucking jewels freeze.

FIRE POEM

How unforgettably the fire that night
Danced in its place, on air and timber fed,
Built brightness in the eye already bright.
Upon our knees, held by a leash of light
Each straining shadow quietly laid its head
As if such giving and such taking might
Make ripe its void for substance. The fire said,

If as I am you know me bright and warm,
It is while matter bears, which I live by,
For very heart the furnace of its form:
By likeness and from likeness in my storm
Sheltered, can all things change and changing be
The rare bird bedded at the heart of harm.
We listened, now at odds, now reconciled.

I was impatient when the laughing child
Reached for the fire and screamed. Pointless to blame
That splendor for the poor pain of an hour.
Yet fire thereafter was the burnt child's name
For fear, and many ardent things became
Such that their fire would have, could fire take fear,
Forgot the blissful nester in its flame.

OLIVE GROVE

The blue wave's slumber and the rocky brow
Almost submerged where while her father slept
Sleep of the blue wave from his forehead leapt
The goddess, dropped her gift, this silvery bough

On him who among olives drowses now
Among these drowsing boughs their trunks express,
Pale paint from tubes so twisted, emptiness
Might sooner have put forth the slumbering green

Than these whose gnarled millennium bestows
(Upon his slumber tentatively marine
For whom endurance, lacking theirs, had been
Too bare an ikon of the mind's repose)

A dream, not of his dreaming, or to wean
Roots from deep earth, rather of how each delves
To taste infusions by whose craft ourselves,
Once dreams in the mind of earth, like olive trees,

Houses, the sleeper and his smile, the quais
And tall sail bent on the blue wave, have grown
Out of that molten center now alone
Uneasy for its melting images.

THISTLEDOWN

First clan of autumn, thistleball on a stem
Between forefinger and thumb,
Known for the seeds
That make a wish come true when the light last of them
Into air blown subsides,

Feathery sphere of seeds, frail brain
On prickly spine,
I feared their dissipation, deeds of this crown aspin,
Words from a high-flown talker, pale brown
Thistledown.

Yet when, bewildered what to want
Past the extravagant
Notion of wanting, I puffed
And the soft cluster broke and spinning went
More channels than I knew, aloft

In the wide air to lift its lineage
Ha! how the Scotch flower's spendthrift
Stars drifted down
Many to tarn or turf, but ever a canny one
On the stem left

To remind me of what I had wished:
That none should have clung, lest summer, thistle-bewitched,
Dry up, be done
—And the whole of desire not yet into watched
Air at a breath blown!

A TIMEPIECE

Of a pendulum's mildness, with her feet up
My sister lay expecting her third child.
Over the hammock's crescent spilled
Her flushed face, grazing clover and buttercup.

Her legs were troubling her, a vein had burst.
Even so, among partial fullnesses she lay
Of pecked damson, of daughters at play
Who in the shadow of the house rehearsed

Her gait, her gesture, unnatural to them,
But they would master it soon enough, grown tall
Trusting that out of themselves came all
That full grace, while she out of whom these came

Shall have thrust fullness from her, like a death.
Already, seeing the little girls listless
She righted herself in a new awkwardness.
It was not *her* life she was heavy with.

Let us each have some milk, my sister smiled
Meaning to muffle with the taste
Of unbuilt bone a striking in her breast,
For soon by what it tells the clock is stilled.

THE GREENHOUSE

So many girls vague in the yielding orchard,
None at my pausing but had seemed therefore
To grow a little, to have put forth a tentative
Frond, touch my arm and, as we went,
Trailingly inquire, but smilingly, of the greenhouse
—One had heard so much, was it never to be seen?
So that it would always have appeared possible
To be distinguished under glass
Down ferned-faint-steaming alleys of lady-slipper,
Camellia, browning at the fingertip,
Yet always to find oneself, with a trace of humor,
In perhaps the least impressive room.
It was hotter here than elsewhere, being shadowed
Only by bare panes overhead,
And here the seedlings had been set to breeding
Their small green tedium of need:
Each plant alike, each plaintively devouring
One form, meek sprout atremble in the glare
Of the ideal condition. So many women
Oval under overburdened limbs,
And such vague needs, each witlessly becoming
Desire, individual blossom
Inhaled but to enhance the fiercer fading
Of as yet nobody's beauty—Tell me (I said)
Among these thousands which you are!
And I will lead you backwards where the wrench
Of rifling fingers snaps the branch,
And all loves less than the proud love fastened on
Suffer themselves to be rotted clean out of conscience
By human neglect, by the naked sun,
So none shall tempt, when she is gone.

THE LOVERS

They met in loving like the hands of one
Who having worked six days with creature and plant
Washes his hands before the evening meal.
Reflected in a basin out-of-doors
The golden sky receives his hands beneath
Its coldly wishing surface, washing them

Of all perhaps but what of one another
Each with its five felt perceptions holds:
A limber warmth, fitness of palm and nail
So long articulate in his mind before
Plunged into happening, that all the while
Water laps and loves the stirring hands

His eye has leisure for the young fruit-trees
And lowing beasts secure, since night is near,
Pasture, lights of a distant town, and sky
Molten, atilt, strewn on new water, sky
In which for a last fact he dips his face
And lifts it glistening: what dark distinct

Reflections of his features upon gold!
—Except for when each slow slight water-drop
He sensed on chin and nose accumulate,
Each tiny world of sky reversed and branches,
Fell with its pure wealth to mar the image:
World after world fallen into the sky

And still so much world left when, by the fire
With fingers clasped, he set in revolution
Certitude and chance like strong slow thumbs;
Or read from an illuminated page
Of harvest, flood, motherhood, mystery:
These waited, and would issue from his hands.

SOME NEGATIVES:
X AT THE CHÂTEAU

Where skies are thunderous, by a cypress walk
Copied in snow, I have you: or
Sitting beside the water-jet that here
Is jet. You could be an Ethiop with hair
Powdered white as chalk

Instead of simple diffidence on her tour
Of monuments. Yet these first
Images of images I shall keep.
Once they have testified, immersed
In a mild Lethe, to what you really are,

These insights of the mind in sleep,
May they recall you as you never were!—
Your charming face not lit
But charred, as by dark beams instructing it
In all to which you were the latest heir,

In lake, lawn, urn and maze
Plotted by your dead rivals with no care
That I should love you next, find milky ways
To leave the grotto where I grieved for them.
Slowly you might have learned to bear

Estates no deed can alter. Only whim
Holds sway like gossamer
Till never breath dispels the water-wraith.
Here where no image sinks to truth
And the black sun kindles planets in noon air

The lover leads a form eclipsed, opaque,
Past a smoked-glass parterre
Towards the first ghostliness he guessed in her.
He bends her to a dazzling lake . . .
If the lens winks, it winds them who knows where.

A RENEWAL

Having used every subterfuge
To shake you, lies, fatigue, or even that of passion,
Now I see no way but a clean break.
I add that I am willing to bear the guilt.

You nod assent. Autumn turns windy, huge,
A clear vase of dry leaves vibrating on and on.
We sit, watching. When I next speak
Love buries itself in me, up to the hilt.

KYOTO: AT THE DETACHED PALACE

Struck by the soft look
Of stone in rain, wet lake,
By the single evergreen
Wavering deep therein,
Reluctantly I sense
All that the garden wants
To have occur.
Part of me smiles, aware
That the stone is smiling
Through its tears, while
Touched by early frost
Another part turns rust-
Red, brittle, soon
To be ferried down
Past where paths end
And the unraked sand
Long after fall of night
Retains a twilight.

HÔTEL DE L'UNIVERS ET PORTUGAL

The strange bed, whose recurrent dream we are,
Basin, and shutters guarding with their latch
The hour of arrivals, the reputed untouched Square.
Bleakly with ever fewer belongings we watch
And have never, it each time seems, so coldly before

Steeped the infant membrane of our clinging
In a strange city's clear grave acids;
Or thought how like a pledge the iron key-ring
Slid overboard, one weighty calm at Rhodes,
Down to the vats of its eventual rusting.

And letters moulting out of memory, lost
Seasons of the breast of a snowbird . . .
One morning on the pillow shall at last
Lie strands of age, and many a crease converge
Where the ambitious dreaming head has tossed

The world away and turned, and taken dwelling
Within the pillow's dense white dark, has heard
The lovers' speech from cool walls peeling
To the white bed, whose dream they were.
Bare room, forever feeling and annulling,

Bare room, bleak problem set for space,
Fold us ever and over in less identity
Than six walls hold, the oval mirror face
Showing us vacantly how to become only
Bare room, mere air, no hour and no place,

Lodging of chance, and bleak as all beginning.
We had begun perhaps to lack a starlit Square.
But now our very poverties are dissolving,
Are swallowed up, strong powders to ensure
Sleep, by a strange bed in the dark of dreaming.

II

At last through a deprived dusk we felt
Snow fall, white seed that would outpeople us
Were we not sown with many darknesses,
Were we not ourselves grown on the glimmering road
Soldiers of shade, with footholds dark in snow.
But as the snow ermined our passage, so
Of the miles beneath us, undermined and dim:
A wince of mole-blind noses in dense air
Met that cold dazzle floating down on them
—Of whom the slow upheavals, pain or fear,
Having so riddled and debased our ground,
Seemed now but slender hungers of a stem
For its right blossom. Spiraling down came
Billions hexagonal, unique, to kiss and crown
Melting, then clinging white, while, sense withdrawn,
Like springtime lawns under a blossomfall
We slept. We slept. But not by this we grew.
The gray snow shrank, turned hard
As the rich woman weary of a young man
Who bites his lip till it is numb with shame
Less for his soiling suit than her deceit
Nor by her grace the blood rose to a cheek
More pinked, more rife, a tuft of wry persistence
In the stunned road waking beneath his feet.

UPON A SECOND MARRIAGE

for H. I. P.

Orchards, we linger here because
Women we love stand propped in your green prisons,
Obedient to such justly bending laws
      Each one longs to take root,
    Lives to confess whatever season's
Pride of blossom or endeavor's fruit
    May to her rustling boughs have risen.

    Then autumn reddens the whole mind.
No more, she vows, the dazzle of a year
Shall woo her from your bare cage of loud wind,
      Promise the ring and run
    To burn the altar, reappear
With apple blossoms for the credulous one.
    Orchards, we wonder that we linger here!

    Orchards we planted, trees we shook
To learn what you were bearing, say we stayed
Because one winter dusk we half-mistook
      Frost on a bleakened bough
    For blossoms, and were half-afraid
To miss the old persuasion, should we go.
    And spring did come, and discourse made

    Enough of weddings to us all
That, loving her for whom the whole world grows
Fragrant and white, we linger to recall
      As down aisles of cut trees
    How a tall trunk's cross-section shows
Concentric rings, those many marriages
    That life on each live thing bestows.

SAINT

Wanting foreknowledge of eternity
It may be you must learn
From an illumination, from an ivory triptych,
How the young martyr, stripped
And fastened to the trunk of a fruit-bearing
Tree, could in a fanfare
Of tenderness for their reluctance summon
Those hooded archers: *Come!*
The arrows! Come! He loves me best who nearest
To my heart hits! In love and fear
They let fly. Wanting endurance of that moment's
Music, you are afraid. Below
Your hotel window, the piazza blackens
And hisses. You do not draw back,
You hold it all in your eye's mind. The women
Limp toward the chapel named for him.
Their gums water. They mumble hocus-pocus
Before the painted wood baroque
Sebastian. Already his left foot is missing.
The strong white ankle, kiss by kiss
Borne past the dyed breaths and the human acids,
Celebrates elsewhere its mass—
While the saint, trammeled not at all by worm-drilled drapery
In his ambition to escape
No least caress, studies the whole procedure
Exuberantly. He appears, indeed,
To dip himself into their unfathomable craving
As into a pure, upholding wave:
He kisses me who kills, who kills me kisses!
And what is learned? Just this:
He is the flaw through which you can glimpse meadows,
Herds, the lover piping with bent head.
Full of the scene, you turn back in
To serve your time. The damask bed
Creaks under you. The board groans, the stone wrinkles—
Eternity refusing to begin.

THE CHARIOTEER OF DELPHI

Where are the horses of the sun?

Their master's green bronze hand, empty of all
But a tangle of reins, seems less to call
His horses back than to wait out their run.

To cool that havoc and restore
The temperance we had loved them for
I have implored him, child, at your behest.

Watch now, the flutings of his dress hang down
From the brave patina of breast.
His gentle eyes glass brown

Neither attend us nor the latest one
Blistered and stammering who comes to cry
Village in flames and river dry,

None to control the chariot
And to call back the killing horses none
Now that their master, eyes ashine, will not.

For watch, his eyes in the still air alone
Look shining and nowhere
Unless indeed into our own

Who are reflected there
Littler than dolls wound up by a child's fear
How tight, their postures only know.

And loosely, watch now, the reins overflow
His fist, as if once more the unsubdued
Beasts shivering and docile stood

Like us before him. Do you remember how
A small brown pony would
Nuzzle the cube of sugar from your hand?

Broken from his mild reprimand
In fire and fury hard upon the taste
Of a sweet license, even these have raced

Uncurbed in us, where fires are fanned.

WHO GUESSED AMISS THE RIDDLE OF THE SPHINX

In the night my great swamp-willow fell.
I had run home early, dark by five,
To find the young sphinx and the hearth swept bare
By the lazy thrashing of her tail.

A scraping on my window woke me late.
Circling those roots aghast in air
I asked of wind, of rottenness, the cause,
As yet unaware of having forgotten

Her yellow gaze unwinking, vertical pupil,
Stiff wing, dark nipple, firelit paws
—All that the odor of my hand brings back
Hiding my face, beside the boughs

Whose tall believed exuberance fallen,
Bug goes witless, liquors lack,
Profusion riddled to its core of dream
Dies, whispering names.

She only from the dead flames rose,
Sniffed once my open palm, but disdained cream,
Civilities of the aftermath.
Now even the young tree branching in that palm

Is gone, as if for having blocked a path.

A NARROW ESCAPE

During a lull at dinner the vampire frankly
Confessed herself a symbol of the inner
Adventure. An old anxiousness took hold
Like a mesmerist hissing for each of us
To call up flitterings from within,
Crags and grottos, an olive dark that lured
Casements to loosen gleamings onto the Rhine.
More fluently than water she controlled
The vista. Later, von Blon said he had known
Her expressionless face before, her raven braids
—But where? A tale . . . a mezzotint? The tone
Was that of an 1830 pianoforte.
There followed for each a real danger of falling
Into the oubliette of that bland face,
Perfectly warned of how beneath it lay
The bat's penchant for sleeping all day long
Then flying off upon the wildest tangents
With little self-preserving shrieks, also
For ghastly scenes over letters and at meals,
Not to speak of positive evil, those nightly
Drainings of one's life, the blood, the laugh,
The cries for pardon, the indifferences—
And all performed with such a virtuoso's
Detachment from say their grandmothers' experience
That men in clubs would snort incredulously
Provided one escaped to tell the story.
It was then Charles thought to wonder, peering over
The rests of venison, what on earth a vampire
Means by the inner adventure. Her retort
Is now a classic in our particular circle.

MIDAS AMONG GOLDENROD

Divine uncultivation, and look, invariably
He shows up, at once lighter and darker, also
More intermittent because more independent
Than golden masses nodding in a noon breeze.
Next, barely hushing the trebled voices, he
Comes jerkily closer, see, and carries a net.
Damp, flushed, his eyes are streaming, his mouth
Shuts and opens like a ventriloquist's dummy
Eloquent with opinions it does not really believe.
Does he suffer? Yes. But you who believe that only
The mind suffers, that tears flow from its chasms,
Ought, enviously perhaps, to admit the sly
Irritant in the gold of an environment.
You might even make out some flighty flattering thing
A bit too languid and a bit too quick,
For sake of which the sufferer persists.
Remember, now that he is close enough to call,
The tears flow from his eyes, from nowhere else.
It is helpful to think of him fast in a golden fist.
Is he protected? Yes. But mischievously.

SALOME

1

No wonder, shaggy saint, breast-deep in Jordan's
    Reflected gliding gardens,
That you assumed their swift compulsions sacred;
Nor that, dreaming you drank, so cool the water,
Regeneration, of which the first taste maddens,
    You let spill on the naked
  Stranger a pure and tripled mitre;

Nor that later, brooding on the sacrament
    Of flowing streams, you went
Back where none flow, and went in a new dread
Of water's claspings, whose rapt robe, whose crown
Make beggar and prince alike magnificent.
    A dry voice inside said,
  "Life is a pool in which we drown."

Finally then, small wonder the small king,
    Your captor, slavering
In a gold litter, bitten to the bone
By what shall be, pretended not to hear
His veiled wild daughter sinuous on a string
    Of motives all her own
  Summon the executioner.

2

Our neighbors' little boy ran out to greet
    The chow, his runaway pet,
And was fearfully mauled. Breaking its mouth on fences

Down the struck street the orange mad dog tore
Until my father's pistol made of it
    Pinks, reds, a thrash of senses
  Outside the stationery store.

I was crying, but stayed on to watch. I saw
    The swelled tongue, the black maw,
And had seen earlier this meek dog trot off
Into the brambles of a vacant lot,
Suspecting then what I now know as law:
    That you can have enough
  Of human love. The chow forgot

The dim back porch, whistle and water-bowl;
    Confessing with a growl
How sweetly they subdued, forgot caresses;
Began to suffer the exactitude
Of its first nature, which was animal.
    Back in the child's oasis
  It told what it had understood.

3

The camel's vast thirst is the needle's eye.
    Whosoever faithfully
Desires desire more than its object shall
Find his right heaven, be he saint or brute.
But in a child's delirium never he
    Who next appears, the hale
  Young doctor from the Institute,

Atwirl like any exalted princess, or
    The ego of Pasteur,
Imperious for prophetic heads to probe
Upon a platter. "Ha!" cries he, "this brow

Swaddles a tangleworld I must explore!
    Stout vein and swaying lobe
  Redden beneath my knives. And now

"Let chattering apes, let the last proud birds screech
    Abuse, well out of reach—"
Or later, quiet, drinks in the hiss and hurl
Of burning issues down to a pronged pool
Soon parched, mere clay, whose littlest crown ableach
    Suns lighten and winds whirl
  Back into earth, the easier school.

THE DUNES

To have a self, even of salt and sand!
The loud, the marble-maned—at last a way
Out of its insane frothing, those white jaws
In which they were nothing, do you understand!

Now that they are no longer prey to that thing,
But for chill flushes which would come anyway
To anyone, in moonlight or a storm,
It is like a dream, it is past their remembering.

Before long they have ceased to be makeshift.
Wiry grasses keep them from blowing away,
As does a certain creeper yearning seaward
Over a dry admonitory drift.

Seen from the crest, two cities catch the light
At opposite ends of a black and white highway.
People come out here to lose things. The dunes
Permit themselves the first airs of a Site.

A flowered compact, lying too deep for tears,
Remains unsought. Yet, "We do not give away
Our secrets to all comers," say the dunes
Bridling like sphinxes at the hush of gears.

Once I think I caught them looking back.
The tide had gone far out that bright calm day
And small fish danced in death ecstatically
Upon the flashing mirror of its track.

In heaven there must be just such afternoons.
Up rose a burning couple far away.
Absolute innocence, fiery, mild. And yet
Soon even they were lost behind the dunes.

I grow old under an intensity
Of questioning looks. *Nonsense,*
I try to say, *I cannot teach you children*
How to live.—*If not you, who will?*
Cries one of them aloud, grasping my gilded
Frame till the world sways. *If not you, who will?*
Between their visits the table, its arrangement
Of Bible, fern and Paisley, all past change,
Does very nicely. If ever I feel curious
As to what others endure,
Across the parlor *you* provide examples,
Wide open, sunny, of everything I am
Not. You embrace a whole world without once caring
To set it in order. That takes thought. Out there
Something is being picked. The red-and-white bandannas
Go to my heart. A fine young man
Rides by on horseback. Now the door shuts. Hester
Confides in me her first unhappiness.
This much, you see, would never have been fitted
Together, but for me. Why then is it
They more and more neglect me? Late one sleepless
Midsummer night I strained to keep
Five tapers from your breathing. *No,* the widowed
Cousin said, *let them go out.* I did.
The room brimmed with gray sound, all the instreaming
Muslin of your dream . . .
Years later now, two of the grown grandchildren
Sit with novels face-down on the sill,
Content to muse upon your tall transparence,
Your clouds, brown fields, persimmon far
And cypress near. One speaks. *How superficial*
Appearances are! Since then, as if a fish
Had broken the perfect silver of my reflectiveness,
I have lapses. I suspect
Looks from behind, where nothing is, cool gazes
Through the blind flaws of my mind. As days,
As decades lengthen, this vision
Spreads and blackens. I do not know whose it is,

But I think it watches for my last silver
To blister, flake, float leaf by life, each milling-
Downward dumb conceit, to a standstill
From which not even you strike any brilliant
Chord in me, and to a faceless will,
Echo of mine, I am amenable.

III

AMSTERDAM

"Au pays qui te ressemble"

There is a city whose fair houses wizen
In a strict web of streets, of waterways
In which the clock tower gurgles and sways,
And there desire is freed from the body's prison.

Into a black impasse deep in the maze
A mirror thrusts her brilliant severed head,
Mouth red and moist, and pale curls diamonded.
A youth advances towards the wraith, delays,

Squints through the window at a rumpled bed,
Cat, the familiar, lolling on batik,
The leman's person now no more unique
Than any hovel uninhabited,

Then turns, leaving her wrappered in a reek
Of realism, back the way he came.
Her jewels rekindle in their sooty frame
Lights for a future sleuth of the oblique.

(Once, once only to have laid absolute claim
Upon that love long held in readiness,
Not by the flesh in any stale undress,
Nor by the faithful ghost whose lips inflame

Lips curling dry, licked once to evanesce;
One night one autumn, so to have taken hold
Of certain volumes violent yet controlled
As to leave nothing for regret, unless

A strand of hair, pale auburn not quite gold
On the creased cushion, being what you must bear,
Guided the passion to its hush, like prayer,
And paler, cooler, tapered, as foretold,

Into the sheer gold of nobody's hair,
The fragrance of whatever we suppose
Wafted, as music over water flows
Into the darkened sleeper, now elsewhere . . .)

Next day, is it myself whose image those
Sunning their own on the canal's far side
Are smiling to see reel at the downglide
Of one leaf, wallow, painfully recompose?

My head has fallen forward open-eyed.
Word of somebody's Schumann—"like a swan
That breasts a torrent of obsidian"—
Idles below me in formaldehyde.

Have I become my senses, all else gone?
A warm gust from the luxurious act
Interrupts reflection, leaves it tracked
With dust, like water sunlight moves upon.

By dark the world is once again intact,
Or so the mirrors, wiped clean, try to reason . . .
O little moons, misshapen but arisen
To blind with the emotions they refract!

LABORATORY POEM

Charles used to watch Naomi, taking heart
And a steel saw, open up turtles, live.
While she swore they felt nothing, he would gag
At blood, at the blind twitching, even after
The murky dawn of entrails cleared, revealing
Contours he knew, egg-yellows like lamps paling.

Well then. She carried off the beating heart
To the kymograph and rigged it there, a rag
In fitful wind, now made to strain, now stopped
By her solutions tonic or malign
Alternately in which it would be steeped.
What the heart bore, she noted on a chart,

For work did not stop only with the heart.
He thought of certain human hearts, their climb
Through violence into exquisite disciplines
Of which, as it now appeared, they all expired.
Soon she would fetch another and start over,
Easy in the presence of her lover.

THREE CHORES

1 / WATER BOILING

When Polly's reddening hand
Let fall into the kettle
The greenest few of all
Her backyard's victuals

Which early underground
Imbibed from the hot metals
A cooking lacking little
To set them on her table

How while each knowing bubble
Jolted ebulliently
Good it felt to be going
At last where the ideal

Erupting of an eyeball
That dwelt more than its fill
On summer's flame shall scour
The kitchen from the hill!

2 / NIGHT LAUNDRY

Of daily soilure laving
Fabric of all and sundry
With no time for believing
Loving might work the wonder

Who among clouded linen
Has scattered blueing then
Well over wrist in grieving
Dismissed all but the doing

May see to clotheslines later
A week of swans depending

From wooden beaks take flight
Flapping at dawn from water's

Jewel of the first water
And every dismal matter's
Absorption in its cleansing
Bring the new day to light.

3 / ITALIAN LESSON

It will not do Luigi
You in this fireless room
Tirelessly expounding
The sense of so much sound

As if to speak were rather
Those promenades in Rome
Where each cool eye plays moth
To flames largely its own

Than the resounding Latin
Catacomb or labyrinth
Corinthian overgrown
With French sphinx or the heated tones

Of all these quenched at nightfall
Yet sparkling on a lip
At whose mute call I turn
To certain other lessons hard to learn.

THE CRUISE

Poor little Agnes cried when she saw the iceberg.
We smiled and went on with our talk, careless
Of its brilliant fraction and, watchful beneath,
That law of which nine-tenths is a possession
By powers we do not ourselves possess.
Some cold tide nudged us into sunny gales
With our money and our medications. No,
Later in shops I thought again of the iceberg.
Mild faces turned aside to let us fondle
Monsters in crystal, tame and small, fawning
On lengths of ocean-green brocade.
"These once were nightmares," the Professor said,
"That set aswirl the mind of China. Now
They are belittled, to whom craftsmen fed
The drug of Form, their fingers cold with dread,
Famine and Pestilence, into souvenirs."
"Well I'm *still* famished," said a woman in red
From Philadelphia. I wondered then:
Are we less monstrous when our motive slumbers
Drugged by a perfection of our form?
The bargain struck, a thin child parted curtains.
We took to lunch our monsters wrapped in silk.
They have become our own. Beneath them stretch
Dim shelves adrowse, our hungers and the dread
That, civilizing into cunning shapes,
Briefly appeased what it could not oppose.

THREE SKETCHES FOR EUROPA

I / THE TOURIST

Now Henry (said his Aunt) take care.
She may not realize who you are.
And if her speech is less than lucid
Try to remember always that in
Her day she spoke, not counting Latin,
Nine languages. Think what she did,
Or meant to do, before the war.
Was there anyone like her?

Palermo lay at her feet. Madrid
Trembled, a moonstone from her ear.
Avoid all mention of your Grandfather.
Poor soul, she's peevish now, an invalid,
Has lost her beauty, gets things wrong.
Go now. But do not stay too long.

2 / GEOGRAPHY

The white bull chased her. Others said
All interest vanished. Anyhow, she fled,

Her mantle's flowing border torn
To islands by the Golden Horn,

Knee bared, head high, but soon to set
One salty cheek on water, let

Flesh become grass and high heart stone,
And all her radiant passage known

Lamely as Time by some she dreamt not of.
Who come to pray remain to scoff

93

At tattered bulls on shut church doors
In black towns numberless as pores,

The god at last indifferent
And she no longer chaste but continent.

3 / AT THE BULLFIGHT

Deep in the gaunt mask arenas blaze.
To creaking music now appear
Champions of her honor, with fixed gaze
And slow parading through a maze
Where the thing waits. Just once in fear
She stiffens, wonders that her people cheer
Pelting down roses and berets.
Then on the mask a smile plays, absent, queer.

In a fringed shawl of blood the bull
Moans and kneels down. His huge eye glazes
On the confusing candor of her gauzes
Who called, who of her own young will
Hung him with garlands, tickled his nostril
And urged him into the foam with gentle phrases.

A VIEW OF THE BURNING

Righteous or not, here comes an angry man
Done up in crimson, his face blackened
If only by the smoke of a self-purifying flame.
Now he is thrusting his hand into the flame
To sear away not, as he said, a moment's folly
So much as his hand, the useful part of it.
I must confess this fails, after a bit,
To produce the intended effect on us.
We had loved each other freely, humanly
With our own angers and our own forgiveness
—Who now, made light of by his seriousness,
Gases on which flame feeds, are wafted up
With lyre and dart, public, hilarious,
Two cupids cuddling in a cupola.
Useless to say he is acting for our sakes.
One does not care for those who care for one
More than one cares for oneself. Divine or not,
At the end he calls upon justice. But, my dear,
Little shall startle from the embers, merely
A grinning head incensed, a succulence
On which to feast, grinning ourselves, I fear.

MARSYAS

I used to write in the café sometimes:
Poems on menus, read all over town
Or talked out before ever written down.
One day a girl brought in his latest book.
I opened it—stiff rhythms, gorgeous rhymes—
And made a face. Then crash! my cup upset.
Of twenty upward looks mine only met
His, that gold archaic lion's look

Wherein I saw my wiry person skinned
Of every skill it labored to acquire
And heard the plucked nerve's elemental twang.
They found me dangling where his golden wind
Inflicted so much music on the lyre
That no one could have told you what he sang.

ORFEO

Ah downward through the dark coulisse,
Impelled to walk the stage of hell,
Unwind as in a theater gilt and puce
His opulence of pain until

Each damned soul dropped its trembling fan
(Which in the gusts of wooing trembled still)
And wept to hear him: it was then
Sickeningly he divined, but with an odd thrill,

Among the shadows of a box
That brow, that hand outspread upon
The plush worn bare, a white peacock's
Genius at dusk on a dissolving lawn,

Her loss within his music's rise and fall
Having become perpetual.

THE DOODLER

Most recent in the long race that descends
From me, welcome! and least askew of ikons
That grow on a new page like rapid lichens
Among the telephone numbers of new friends.

These I commune with every day. Hellos,
Goodbyes. Often by dusk a pair of eyes
Is all I draw; the pencil stupefies
Their lids with kohl until they almost close

But then do not, as if, more animate
Than any new friend's voice flattened by news,
Guessing some brilliant function I refuse,
And why, and wanting to accept their fate.

Noses as yet, alas, revert to profile.
Lips, too, are pursed in this or that direction,
Or raised to other lips from sheer distraction;
To mine, not once. While still, just as at Deauville

Off-season, tiny hands are better hidden
By great muffs of albino porcupine.
Indeed, nothing I do is at all fine
Save certain abstract forms. These come unbidden:

Stars, oblongs linked, or a baroque motif
Expressed so forcibly that it indents
A blank horizon generations hence
With signs and pressures, massing to relief

Like thunderheads one day in sultry foretaste
Of flashes first envisioned as your own
When, squat and breathless, you inscribe on stone
Your names for me, my inkling of an artist—

He-Who-endures-the-disembodied-Voice
Or *Who-in-wrath-puts-down-the-Black-Receiver*—
And, more than image then, a rain, a river
Of prescience, you reflect and I rejoice!

Far, far behind already is that aeon
Of pinheads, bodies each a ragged weevil,
Slit-mouthed and spider-leggèd, with eyes like gravel,
Wavering under trees of purple crayon.

Shapes never realized, were you dogs or chairs?
That page is brittle now, if not long burned.
This morning's little boy stands (I have learned
To do feet) gazing down a flight of stairs.

And when A. calls to tell me he enjoyed
The evening, I begin again. Again
Emerge, O sunbursts, garlands, creatures, men,
Ever more lifelike out of the white void!

IV

THE PERFUME

Ticklish no longer
With tangibility
Nor rooted, crimson, over
The worm's inching stupor

Little but a spirit
Costly and volatile
Am I, want of my touch unstoppers
Now that you suffer it.

THE DAY OF THE ECLIPSE

Summer, until today, burned thought
Away like dross, refined or stunned
Into a life mask golden blind
The face fixed upward with eyes shut;
On either lid a rose-red coin was put;

And upon water rapt and sheer
A single eye of fire held sway;
A single rower just off shore
Could sit becalmed day after day,
A world from oar to dripping oar;

While anyone who walked at noon
Upon the mirror of the tide's
Retreat, turned every drunken sun
His bare feet tarnished, to a stepping-stone,
Or, sped by glares from the banked pride

Of light at heel, put dunes between
Himself and town (the wharves, the saltbox inn,
One lamp above its door lit even
In sunshine, like a freethinker in heaven)
And came back with red skies beneath his skin.

Today is different. The sky pale,
The rower absent, is it warm or cool?
Up from the sound one thin pole
Totters beneath a sudden gull.
Its wing, folded, is hard to tell

From sky. The walker drops onto the beach
In a turmoil he still cannot define.
There is a lone, burned child to watch
Digging so furiously for fun
As to stir up a chaos into which

They both might slip, their muscle yield
To something blinder and less skilled
Than maggots, and their boniness
Flex, fracture, effervesce,
Before the lacy vortex can be healed.

Turning to heaven for relief
He sees it happening. The world's dark half
Clears like a spring, a galaxy
Flows from its severed veins. And he,
He tries to give himself.

He rises, peers up through smoked glass.
A black pupil rimmed with fire
Peers back. Some thin clouds pass.
Afterwards, in the atmosphere
Of any dusk, he sits, depressed, unsure.

Here she is, pacing the dim pier,
The girl of whom he has been aware all summer
With her white face and short red hair.
He knows that she belongs to a far more
Exciting world, which soon will claim her.

Look! as the gull fades from its pole
She stiffens, unique caryatid
Of the unthinkable. A coal
Inhaled glows where her eyes bid
Grayness to overrun the whole

Dunescape she must undergo.
Then other far, blurred lights go on,
Causing an unseen buoy to moan.
He waits for the strange girl to follow
The gull into oblivion.

Some evenings he can watch her dine
Across a cellar's flames and murk.

Relaxed, convivial over wine
And looking beyond the fallen dark
To her next morning's work

Companionless in a skylit shack,
She has told the nodding waitress how to take
Gobbets of gray-blue clay, refine
Them to an eyelid, a jawline,
Circling the figure, stepping back

To judge it. She arrived in May
With someone dark and handsome to a fault
Who promptly left. Last night he heard her say
She would be fetched back soon. He felt
The need for many another day

Of radiance before the end.
He felt he had begun to understand
Those mounds of matter cold and blind
She loves, how even they respond
To the least pressure of a shaping hand.

WALKING ALL NIGHT

Now each has climbed to the uninhabitable
My song rings oddly. Soot floats down the street.
Behind plate glass rot sweets no one shall eat,
While overhead on its iron grill
Somebody's shape a sheet
Unwinds from slowly tosses in our moonless heat.

Those others, who knows where they are?
The lonely man. He steals through doors ajar
Up to some breathing pen
Of brothers, pours a phial of his own pain
Into each sleeper's ear, then slips unseen
Down towards day, the happy din.

The sleeper knows. Rivers inside of him
Rise. His palms glide upon his own dark skin.
His eyes sleep-blind but gleaming wide
Fill with the same warm tide
That laps our piers come morning. In his dream
The highest watermark stands for wisdom.

I, I know only that when the dawn mist
Discourages one bare gold dome like rust,
When stones fume I shall rest,
Loving my neighbor as I love myself,
No more, no less, for I do not love myself . . .
But something stirs, stirs now. At love's name? No,

No apparition, neither any abrupt gust
Of roses' fragrance, here where none grow:
The hair rises almost,
The throat just tries to close, so quietly do
You find me, topple at my feet, poor ghost,
Sung to sleep by a first and faraway cockcrow.

You I forget, you whom the immemorial
Wraps round with many a foolish vow,
Hush! all at once our graying prospects billow
Like cloths, a canvas town.
My eyes fill with a seeing not their own.
Those cloths aside, your sleep is what I know.

A SURVIVAL

I have forgotten how. I try to wake,
I want to. But an eye, when morning comes,
Weeps grains of sand, an ear a bitter wax,
The linen winds and wrinkles like shed skin.

Outside, the angel fumbles with a rake.
He has forgotten, too. And by fall, albums
Are full of studies done in browns and blacks
For one stilled figure, rarely a face drawn in.

Father, your blind hound fleetest when he lies
In the familiar dream of weapon and flight
Stirring, will puzzle at my outstretched palm,

Then let me merge into those images
Whose odors guide, that can no more excite,
His silvering muzzle towards your perfect calm.

ABOUT THE PHOENIX

But in the end one tires of the high-flown.
If it were simply a matter of life or death
We should by now welcome the darkening room,
Wrinkling of linen, window at last violet,
The rosy body lax in a chair of words,
And then the appearance of unsuspected lights.
We should walk wonderingly into that other world
With its red signs pulsing and long lit lanes.
But often at nightfall, ambiguous
As the city itself, a giant jeweled bird
Comes cawing to the sill, dispersing thought
Like a birdbath, and with such final barbarity
As to wear thin at once terror and novelty.
So that a sumptuous monotony
Sets in, a pendulum of amethysts
In the shape of a bird, keyed up for ever fiercer
Flights between ardor and ashes, back and forth;
Caught in whose talons any proof of grace,
Even your face, particularly your face
Fades, featureless in flame, or wan, a fading
Tintype of some cooling love, according
To the creature's whim. And in the end, despite
Its pyrotechnic curiosity, the process
Palls. One night
Your body winces grayly from its chair,
Embarks, a tearful child, to rest
On the dark breast of the fulfilled past.
The first sleep here is the sleep fraught
As never before with densities, plume, oak,
Black water, a blind flapping. And you wake
Unburdened, look about for friends—but O
Could not even the underworld forego
The publishing of omens, naively?
Nothing requires you to make sense of them
And yet you shiver from the dim clay shore,

Gazing. There in the lake, four rows of stilts
Rise, a first trace of culture, shy at dawn
Though blackened as if forces long confined
Had smouldered and blazed forth. In the museum
You draw back lest the relics of those days
—A battered egg cup and a boat with feet—
Have lost their glamour. They have not. The guide
Fairly exudes his tale of godless hordes
Sweeping like clockwork over Switzerland,
Till what had been your very blood ticks out
Voluptuous homilies. Ah, how well one might,
If it were less than a matter of life or death,
Traffic in strong prescriptions, "live" and "die"!
But couldn't the point about the phoenix
Be not agony or resurrection, rather
A mortal lull that followed either,
During which flames expired as they should,
And dawn, discovering ashes not yet stirred,
Buildings in rain, but set on rock,
Beggar and sparrow entertaining one another,
Showed me your face, for that moment neither
Alive nor dead, but turned in sleep
Away from whatever waited to be endured?

Presently at our touch the teacup stirred,
Then circled lazily about
From A to Z. The first voice heard
(If they are voices, these mute spellers-out)
Was that of an engineer

Originally from Cologne.
Dead in his 22nd year
Of cholera in Cairo, he had KNOWN
NO HAPPINESS. He once met Goethe, though.
Goethe had told him: PERSEVERE.

Our blind hound whined. With that, a horde
Of voices gathered above the Ouija board,
Some childish and, you might say, blurred
By sleep; one little boy
Named Will, reluctant possibly in a ruff

Like a large-lidded page out of El Greco, pulled
Back the arras for that next voice,
Cold and portentous: ALL IS LOST.
FLEE THIS HOUSE. OTTO VON THURN UND TAXIS.
OBEY. YOU HAVE NO CHOICE.

Frightened, we stopped; but tossed
Till sunrise striped the rumpled sheets with gold.
Each night since then, the moon waxes,
Small insects flit round a cold torch
We light, that sends them pattering to the porch . . .

But no real Sign. New voices come,
Dictate addresses, begging us to write;
Some warn of lives misspent, and all of doom
In ways that so exhilarate
We are sleeping sound of late.

Last night the teacup shattered in a rage.
Indeed, we have grown nonchalant
Towards the other world. In the gloom here,
Our elbows on the cleared
Table, we talk and smoke, pleased to be stirred

Rather by buzzings in the jasmine, by the drone
Of our own voices and poor blind Rover's wheeze,
Than by those clamoring overhead,
Obsessed or piteous, for a commitment
We still have wit to postpone

Because, once looked at lit
By the cold reflections of the dead
Risen extinct but irresistible,
Our lives have never seemed more full, more real,
Nor the full moon more quick to chill.

THE POWER STATION

Think back now to that cleft
In the live rock. A deep voice filled the cave,
Raving up out of cells each time in some way left
Huger and vaguer. There was a kind of nave

Strewn with potsherd and bone.
The tribe's offspring, converted now, rejoice
In our sane god. But two or three hours south, not known
To them, the charges of the other's voice

Break into light and churn
Through evening fields. Soon a first town is lit,
Is lived in. Grounded. Green. A truth fit to unlearn
The blind delirium that still utters it.

DREAM (ESCAPE FROM THE SCULPTURE MUSEUM) AND WAKING

Softening the marbles, day
Is dawning, which two elms vein.
Presently, slow as crochet,
White veils grow across the scene.
Now that my life has lost its way
I watch for it, through a cold pane

Out past all this eloquence
Inside: look, gesture, flowing raiment
Done in porphyry or jasper whence
One white arm, for a long moment
Raised to strike, relents
(Not to spoil one's enjoyment)

Back into stone, back into being
Hard, handsome to the fingertips,
With eyes that bulge unseeing
To call down an immaculate eclipse
Upon the world. It began snowing
Because of the statues, perhaps.

Or because for a long time now
I have wanted to be more natural
Than they, to issue forth anew
In a profusion inimitable
As it is chaste and quickly through.
White void, my heart grows full

With all you have undone!
Starwise, from coldest heights, a gong
Of silence strikes *end of an eon*,
Reverberates keen and strong
Until a far veil lifts. Someone
Is stumbling this way. Neither young

Nor old, man nor woman, so
Propelled by cold, a human figure
Barely begun, a beggar, no,
Two by now, and ever nearer, bigger,
Cause me to stiffen in a show
Of being human also, eager

For what never, never occurs.
In the tradition of their kind
Exhaustingly the wayfarers
Breathe out white and pass by blind.
After them trot two ermine-yellow curs.
These look up, almost lag behind,

Then follow with two unheard shakes
Of bells. As my eyes close, nearby
Something unwinds and breaks.
Perhaps the Discus Thrower has let fly
Or Laocoön stepped from his snakes
Like old clothes. The scene changes. I

Am mounted in a village common.
A child calls. Early lamps and sunset
Stream together down the snowman's
Face and dazzle in his jet
Eyes. He lives, but melts. I summon
All my strength. I wake in a cold sweat.

You are beside me. It is dawn
In a friend's house in late
Summer. I softly rise, put on
A robe, and by the misty light
Watch you sleep. You moan
Once in your own dream, and are quiet.

I turn to look outdoors
At the formal garden our friend made.
A figure kneels among the flowers,
A limestone river-god,

Arm raised so that a clear stream pours
From the urn level with his head.

But a white, eyeless shape
Is gesturing deep in my dream.
I turn back to you for companionship.
At once there rises like perfume
To numb me, from your too heavy sleep,
What we said last night in this room—

All of it muffled to protect
Our sleeping friend—when for a wild
Half-hour the light burned, the clock ticked.
You called me cold, I said you were a child.
I said we must respect
Each other's solitude. You smiled.

Well, I shall wake you now,
Smiling myself to hide my fear.
Sun turns the stone urn's overflow
To fire. If I had missed before
The relevance of the road in snow,
The little dogs, the blinded pair,

I judge it now in your slow eyes
Which meet mine, fill with things
We do not name, then fill with the sunrise
And close, because too much light stings,
All the more when shed on these
Our sleeps of stone, our wakenings.

STONES

1

To a head at daybreak
Abolishing its dreams
No use naming the forms
Numbed in one small rock

Which, for it understands
That blind necessity
Neither to suffer, grow nor die,
Hangs heavy on my hands.

2

Now just the least part of you
Can be reached by love, as when
The world coming between
Causes a crescent moon.

3

O to have traveled
Far in the oblong emerald,
Learned how to endure
Thresholds diminishing
To a green vanishing . . .
How small and pure
We should have turned
Before our journey's end.

THE LOCUSTS

The plain dries outward from its heart.
The wise flat-bottomed clouds depart
With all their secrets. Green and gold
The land still tries to look controlled
But one leaf panics. It will start

Now. A chirring numbs the air.
Live shrouds abruptly from nowhere
Fill up the failing streams like dirt.
Each tree puts on a dull brown shirt
And slumps, bowed down with care.

You think first: This is no rain
Of locusts, rather my own brain
At work, whose preconceptions dye
The whole world drab. Or bluntly: I
Am dreaming, or insane.

The next day dawns upon no dream.
There is wide evidence of Them,
Such as the myriad dead or maimed
In furrows, in that yet unnamed
Trickle of corpses, once a stream.

Step gingerly; for they were real,
The locusts, after all.
Wearing opaque goggles (proof
Of a vestigial inner life?)
They have the dead hue of the useful,

The weak husk of no great event.
You feel nothing. It is time you went
Back to where everything was clear,
Where trouble was a limpid source to peer
Deep into, heaven-sent

Mirrorscope, green, wet,
All echo, orchid, and egret
In pure transports recalling you.
Go. A young man before you do
Is apt to roll a cigarette

And talk. Come spring (he says)
The grubs will hatch from crevices
To eat up anything that may have bloomed.
How strange, with all of it foredoomed,
His caring for that scant green is!

What can be said to him? The glue
Of dead wings thickens on your shoe.
Indeed, only when far behind
Does the experience make a kind
Of weird sense. One night over the bayou

Certain great clouds you have seen before
Move in, give way to a downpour.
They have been told at last, it seems,
About the flayed trees and the choked streams.
Rain wakes you, pounding on the door.

IN THE HALL OF MIRRORS

The parquet barely gleams, a lake.
The windows weaken the dark trees.
The mirrors to their bosoms take
Far glints of water, which they freeze
And wear like necklaces.

Some pause in front of others with
Glimmers of mutual admiration.
Even to draw breath is uncouth.
Steps make the silver marrow spin
Up and down every spine.

You feel that something must begin.
To clickings from the chandeliers
A woman and a man come in
And creak about. She sighs, he peers.
A guide hisses in their ears,

"Your seeresses of sheer Space
In argent colloquy despise
Anything personal or commonplace."
Looked at, the mirrors close their eyes.
Through the guide's good offices

In one glass brow a tree is lit
That multiplies itself in tiers,
Tempting the pair to populate
Those vistas from which visitors
Ricochet in fours,

Eights, sixteens, till the first two gaze
At one another through a glazed crush
Of their own kind, and the man says,
"Complex but unmysterious,
This is no life for us."

He shuts the camera whose cold eye
Far outshone his own or hers.
The woman, making no reply,
Scans the remotest mirrors within mirrors
For grander figures,

Not just those of herself and him
Repeated soothingly, as though
Somebody's wits were growing dim—
Those! those beyond! The guide says, "Time to go."
They turn to do so,

And of a million likenesses
The two had thought to leave behind
Not one but nimble as you please
Turns with them, masterfully aligned.
Then all slip out of mind

And in the solitary hall
The lobes of crystal gather dust.
From glass to glass an interval
Widens like moonrise over frost
No tracks have ever crossed.

A DEDICATION

Hans, there are moments when the whole mind
Resolves into a pair of brimming eyes, or lips
Parting to drink from the deep spring of a death
That freshness they do not yet need to understand.
These are the moments, if ever, an angel steps
Into the mind, as kings into the dress
Of a poor goatherd, for their acts of charity.
There are moments when speech is but a mouth pressed
Lightly and humbly against the angel's hand.

WATER STREET

(1962)

For Robert and Isabel, Eleanor and Grace

Out for a walk, after a week in bed,
I find them tearing up part of my block
And, chilled through, dazed and lonely, join the dozen
In meek attitudes, watching a huge crane
Fumble luxuriously in the filth of years.
Her jaws dribble rubble. An old man
Laughs and curses in her brain,
Bringing to mind the close of *The White Goddess*.

As usual in New York, everything is torn down
Before you have had time to care for it.
Head bowed, at the shrine of noise, let me try to recall
What building stood here. Was there a building at all?
I have lived on this same street for a decade.

Wait. Yes. Vaguely a presence rises
Some five floors high, of shabby stone
—Or am I confusing it with another one
In another part of town, or of the world?—
And over its lintel into focus vaguely
Misted with blood (my eyes are shut)
A single garland sways, stone fruit, stone leaves,
Which years of grit had etched until it thrust
Roots down, even into the poor soil of my seeing.
When did the garland become part of me?
I ask myself, amused almost,
Then shiver once from head to toe,

Transfixed by a particular cheap engraving of garlands
Bought for a few francs long ago,
All calligraphic tendril and cross-hatched rondure,
Ten years ago, and crumpled up to stanch
Boughs dripping, whose white gestures filled a cab,
And thought of neither then nor since.
Also, to clasp them, the small, red-nailed hand
Of no one I can place. Wait. No. Her name, her features

Lie toppled underneath that year's fashions.
The words she must have spoken, setting her face
To fluttering like a veil, I cannot hear now,
Let alone understand.

So that I am already on the stair,
As it were, of where I lived,
When the whole structure shudders at my tread
And soundlessly collapses, filling
The air with motes of stone.
Onto the still erect building next door
Are pressed levels and hues—
Pocked rose, streaked greens, brown whites.
Who drained the pousse-café?
Wires and pipes, snapped off at the roots, quiver.

Well, that is what life does. I stare
A moment longer, so. And presently
The massive volume of the world
Closes again.

Upon that book I swear
To abide by what it teaches:
Gospels of ugliness and waste,
Of towering voids, of soiled gusts,
Of a shrieking to be faced
Full into, eyes astream with cold—

With cold?
All right then. With self-knowledge.

Indoors at last, the pages of *Time* are apt
To open, and the illustrated mayor of New York,
Given a glimpse of how and where I work,
To note yet one more house that can be scrapped.

Unwillingly I picture
My walls weathering in the general view.
It is not even as though the new
Buildings did very much for architecture.

Suppose they did. The sickness of our time requires
That these as well be blasted in their prime.
You would think the simple fact of having lasted
Threatened our cities like mysterious fires.

There are certain phrases which to use in a poem
Is like rubbing silver with quicksilver. Bright
But facile, the glamour deadens overnight.
For instance, how "the sickness of our time"

Enhances, then debases, what I feel.
At my desk I swallow in a glass of water
No longer cordial, scarcely wet, a pill
They had told me not to take until much later.

With the result that back into my imagination
The city glides, like cities seen from the air,
Mere smoke and sparkle to the passenger
Having in mind another destination

Which now is not that honey-slow descent
Of the Champs-Elysées, her hand in his,
But the dull need to make some kind of house
Out of the life lived, out of the love spent.

FROM A NOTEBOOK

The whiteness near and far.
The cold, the hush . . .
A first word stops
The blizzard, steps
Out into fresh
Candor. You ask no more.

Each never taken stride
Leads onward, though
In circles ever
Smaller, smaller.
The vertigo
Upholds you. And now to glide

Across the frozen pond,
Steelshod, to chase
Its dreamless oval
With loop and spiral
Until (your face
Downshining, lidded, drained

Of any need to know
What hid, what called,
Wisdom or error,
Beneath that mirror)
The page you scrawled
Turns. A new day. Fresh snow.

A VISION OF THE GARDEN

One winter morning as a child
Upon the windowpane's thin frost I drew
Forehead and eyes and mouth the clear and mild
Features of nobody I knew

And then abstracted looking through
This or that wet transparent line
Beyond beheld a winter garden so
Heavy with snow its hedge of pine

And sun so brilliant on the snow
I breathed my pleasure out onto the chill pane
Only to see its angel fade in mist.
I was a child, I did not know

That what I longed for would resist
Neither what cold lines should my finger trace
On colder grounds before I found anew
In yours the features of that face

Whose words whose looks alone undo
Such frosts I lay me down in love in fear
At how they melt become a blossoming pear
Joy outstretched in our bodies' place.

POEM OF SUMMER'S END

The morning of the equinox
Begins with brassy clouds and cocks.
All the inn's shutters clatter wide
Upon Fair Umbria. Twitching at my side
You burrow in sleep like a red fox.

Mostly, these weeks, we toss all night, we touch
By accident. The heat! The food!
Groggily aware of spots that itch
I curse the tiny creatures which
Have flecked our mended sheets with blood.

At noon in a high wind, to bell and song,
Upon the shoulders of the throng,
The gilt bronze image of St. So-and-So
Heaves precipitously along.
Worship has worn away his toe,

Nevertheless the foot, thrust forward, dips
Again, again, into its doom of lips
And tears, a vortex of black shawls,
Garlic, frankincense, Popery, festivals
Held at the moon's eclipse,

As in their trance the faithful pass
On to piazza and café.
We go deliberately the other way
Through the town gates, lie down in grass.
But the wind howls, the sky turns color-of-clay.

The time for making love is done.
A far off, sulphur-pale façade
Gleams and goes out. It is as though by one
Flash of lightning all things made
Had glimpsed their maker's heart, read and obeyed.

Back on our bed of iron and lace
We listen to the loud rain fracture space,
And let at first each other's hair
Be lost in gloom, then lips, then the whole face.
If either speaks the other does not hear.

For a decade love has rained down
On our two hearts, instructing them
In a strange bareness, that of weathered stone.
Thinking how bare our hearts have grown
I do not know if I feel pride or shame.

The time has passed to go and eat.
Has it? I do not know. A beam of light
Reveals you calm but strangely white.
A final drop of rain clicks in the street.
Somewhere a clock strikes. It is not too late

To set out dazed, sit side by side
In the one decent restaurant.
The handsome boy who has already tried
To interest you (and been half gratified)
Helps us to think of what we want.

I do not know—have I ever known?—
Unless concealed in the next town,
In the next image blind with use, a clue,
A worn path, points the long way round back to
The springs we started out from. Sun

Weaker each sunrise reddens that slow maze
So freely entered. Now come days
When lover and beloved know
That love is what they are and where they go.

Each learns to read at length the other's gaze.

Light into the olive entered
And was oil. Rain made the huge pale stones
Shine from within. The moon turned his hair white
Who next stepped from between the columns,
Shielding his eyes. All through
The countryside were old ideas
Found lying open to the elements.
Of the gods' houses only
A minor premise here and there
Would be balancing the heaven of fixed stars
Upon a Doric capital. The rest
Lay spilled, their fluted drums half sunk in cyclamen
Or deep in water's biting clarity
Which just barely upheld me
The next week, when I sailed for home.
But where is home—these walls?
These limbs? The very spaniel underfoot
Races in sleep, toward what?
It is autumn. I did not invite
Those guests, windy and brittle, who drink my liquor.
Returning from a walk I find
The bottles filled with spleen, my room itself
Smeared by reflection onto the far hemlocks.
I some days flee in dream
Back to the exposed porch of the maidens
Only to find my great-great-grandmothers
Erect there, peering
Into a globe of red Bohemian glass.
As it swells and sinks, I call up
Graces, Furies, Fates, removed
To my country's warm, lit halls, with rivets forced
Through drapery, and nothing left to bear.
They seem anxious to know
What holds up heaven nowadays.
I start explaining how in that vast fire
Were other irons—well, Art, Public Spirit,
Ignorance, Economics, Love of Self,

Hatred of Self, a hundred more,
Each burning to be felt, each dedicated
To sparing us the worst; how I distrust them
As I should have done those ladies; how I want
Essentials: salt, wine, olive, the light, the scream—
No! I have scarcely named you,
And look, in a flash you stand full-grown before me,
Row upon row, Essentials,
Dressed like your sister caryatids
Or tombstone angels jealous of their dead,
With undulant coiffures, lips weathered, cracked by grime,
And faultless eyes gone blank beneath the immense
Zinc and gunmetal northern sky . . .
Stay then. Perhaps the system
Calls for spirits. This first glass I down
To the last time
I ate and drank in that old world. May I
Also survive its meanings, and my own.

THE GRAND CANYON

It is still early, yet
Clear waves of heat,
Eye-watering, dilute
What powers drive
The warped pine to the brink.
You, too, must conquer
Involuntary nausea
Before you look. Far under-
foot are your wept-over
Sunsets, your every year
Deepened perspectives, layer
On monstrous layer of mouse,
Marigold, madder—
All petrifying, not
To be approached without
Propitiatory oohs.
By all means undertake
A descent on gargoyle-faced ass-back
To the degrading yellow
River. This first mistake
Made by your country is also
The most sublime.
Now let its convulsions
Mimic your heart's
And you will guess the source.
Be strong then. Find no fault
With the white-wigged, the quartz-
Pated up there, wrapped
In whipping vestments, neither
Man can corrupt
Nor heaven wholly melt.
They have sat a long time
In one of our highest courts.

PRISM

a paperweight

Having lately taken up residence
In a suite of chambers
Windless, compact and sunny, ideal
Lodging for the pituitary gland of Euclid
If not for a "single gentleman (references),"
You have grown used to the playful inconveniences,
The floors that slide from under you helter-skelter,
Invisible walls put up in mid-
Stride, leaving you warped for the rest of the day,
A spoon in water; also that pounce
Of wild color from corner to page,
Straightway consuming the latter
Down to your very signature,
After which there is nothing to do but retire,
Licking the burn, into—into—
Look: (Heretofore
One could have said where one was looking,
In or out. But now it almost—) Look:
You dreamed of this:
To fuse in borrowed fires, to drown
In depths that were not there. You meant
To rest your bones in a maroon plush box,
Doze the old vaudeville out, of mind and object,
Little foreseeing their effect on you,
Those dagger-eyed insatiate performers
Who from the first false insight
To the most recent betrayal of outlook,
Crystal, hypnotic atom,
Have held you rapt, the proof, the child
Wanted by neither. Now and then
It is given to see clearly. There
Is what remains of you, a body
Unshaven, flung on the sofa. Stains of egg
Harden about the mouth, smoke still
Rises between fingers or from nostrils.

The eyes deflect the stars through years of vacancy.
Your agitation at such moments
Is all too human. You and the stars
Seem both endangered, each
At the other's utter mercy. Yet the gem
Revolves in space, the vision shuttles off.
A toneless waltz glints through the pea-sized funhouse.
The day is breaking someone else's heart.

FOR PROUST

Over and over something would remain
Unbalanced in the painful sum of things.
Past midnight you arose, rang for your things.
You had to go into the world again.

You stop for breath outside the lit hotel,
A thin spoon bitter stimulants will stir.
Jean takes your elbow, Jacques your coat. The stir
Spreads—you are known to all the personnel—

As through packed public rooms you press (impending
Palms, chandeliers, orchestras, more palms,
The fracas and the fragrance) until your palms
Are moist with fear that you will miss the friend

Conjured—but she is waiting: a child still
At first glance, hung with fringes, on the low
Ottoman. In a voice reproachful and low
She says she understands you have been ill.

And you, because your time is running out,
Laugh in denial and begin to phrase
Your questions. There had been a little phrase
She hummed, you could not sleep tonight without

Hearing again. Then, of that day she had sworn
To come, and did not, was evasive later,
Would she not speak the truth two decades later,
From loving-kindness learned if not inborn?

She treats you to a look you cherished, light,
Bold: "Mon ami, how did we get along
At all, those years?" But in her hair a long
White lock has made its truce with appetite.

And presently she rises. Though in pain
You let her leave—the loved one always leaves.
What of the little phrase? Its notes, like leaves
In the strong tea you have contrived to drain,

Strangely intensify what you must do.
Back where you came from, up the strait stair, past
All understanding, bearing the whole past,
Your eyes grown wide and dark, eyes of a Jew,

You make for one dim room without contour
And station yourself there, beyond the pale
Of cough or of gardenia, erect, pale.
What happened is becoming literature.

Feverish in time, if you suspend the task,
An old, old woman shuffling in to draw
Curtains, will read a line or two, withdraw.
The world will have put on a thin gold mask.

SCENES OF CHILDHOOD

for Claude Fredericks

My mother's lamp once out,
I press a different switch:
A field within the dim
White screen ignites,
Vibrating to the rapt
Mechanical racket
Of a real noon field's
Crickets and gnats.

And to its candid heart
I move with heart ajar,
With eyes that smart less
From pollen or heat
Than from the buried day
Now rising like a moon,
Shining, unwinding
Its taut white sheet.

Two or three bugs that lit
Earlier upon the blank
Sheen, all peaceable
Insensibility, drowse
As she and I cannot
Under the risen flood
Of thirty years ago—
A tree, a house

We had then, a late sun,
A door from which the primal
Figures jerky and blurred
As lightning bugs
From lanterns issue, next
To be taken for stars,
For fates. With knowing smiles
And beaded shrugs

My mother and two aunts
Loom on the screen. Their plucked
Brows pucker, their arms encircle
One another.
Their ashen lips move.
From the love seat's gloom
A quiet chuckle escapes
My white-haired mother

To see in that final light
A man's shadow mount
Her dress. And now she is
Advancing, sister-
less, but followed by
A fair child, or fury—
Myself at four, in tears.
I raise my fist,

Strike, she kneels down. The man's
Shadow afflicts us both.
Her voice behind me says
It might go slower.
I work dials, the film jams.
Our headstrong old projector
Glares at the scene which promptly
Catches fire.

Puzzled, we watch ourselves
Turn red and black, gone up
In a puff of smoke now coiling
Down fierce beams.
I switch them off. A silence.
Your father, she remarks,
Took those pictures; later
Says pleasant dreams,

Rises and goes. Alone
I gradually fade and cool.
Night scatters me with green

Rustlings, thin cries.
Out there between the pines
Have begun shining deeds,
Some low, inconstant (these
Would be fireflies),

Others as in high wind
Aflicker, staying lit.
There are nights we seem to ride
With cross and crown
Forth under them, through fumes,
Coils, the whole rattling epic—
Only to leap clear-eyed
From eiderdown,

Asleep to what we'd seen.
Father already fading—
Who focused your life long
Through little frames,
Whose microscope, now deep
In purple velvet, first
Showed me the skulls of flies,
The fur, the flames

Etching the jaws—father:
Shrunken to our true size.
Each morning, back of us,
Fields wail and shimmer.
To go out is to fall
Under fresh spells, cool web
And stinging song new-hatched
Each day, all summer.

A minute galaxy
About my head will easily
Needle me back. The day's
Inaugural *Damn*
Spoken, I start to run,
Inane, like them, but breathing

In and out the sun
And air I am.

The son and heir! In the dark
It makes me catch my breath
And hear, from upstairs, hers—
That faintest hiss
And slither, as of life
Escaping into space,
Having led its characters
To the abyss

Of night. Immensely still
The heavens glisten. One broad
Path of vague stars is floating
Off, a shed skin
Of all whose fine cold eyes
First told us, locked in ours:
You are the heroes without name
Or origin.

THE LAWN FÊTE OF HOMUNCULUS ARTIFEX

for Fred and Sandra Segal

Moisten me, press me,
Mold me to tumbler, to tin,
The shallow, the tall, confuse me
With straw and leave me
Where sun is hottest, patted into hills.
Do not forget this bit of mirror:
Half buried in my breast, it will store up
The white blues and the yellow blues of skies
Under which one dreams of living.
There, it is done! Meanwhile
The dishes shall be ceremoniously dotted
With petal of geranium, berries or pebbles,
That there may arise from them
An illusion of food and drink,
A hunger then, a zest for life
Peculiar to those not quite alive,
Who only dream of living, who are not born
In childbed, rather in some hour tense with charms
Glancing off the alembic's giant scrotum
Till sun and moon conjoin, and all is dark
As the wizard's robe, as his drenched brow.
When he could do no more
He fell back spent. Our little party
Got under way as best it could. The twigs
Unclenched, the greedy rosebuds caked with smut.
The ill-knit creatures, now in hues
Of sunstroke, mulberry, white of clown,
Yellow of bile, bruise-blacks-and-blues,
Stumped outward, waving matchstick arms,
Colliding, poking, hurt, in tears
(For the wound became an eye)
Toward the exciting, hostile greens
And the spread cloths of Art.
Already openly in love

With what he saw, one of us disregarded
Common background or future union
Through dissolution in the first real rain
Enough to cry, addressing who
Or what he could not say, "Invest me
With nuance, place on me
Your conical hat of stars,
Hand me the hazel wand
That was my hand—
It stirs! It bends!
When I am base again, and my name mud,
You'll have this likeness of me with a dozen
Of my three billion closest friends."

THE WORLD AND THE CHILD

Letting his wisdom be the whole of love,
The father tiptoes out, backwards. A gleam
Falls on the child awake and wearied of,

Then, as the door clicks shut, is snuffed. The glove-
Gray afterglow appalls him. It would seem
That letting wisdom be the whole of love

Were pastime even for the bitter grove
Outside, whose owl's white hoot of disesteem
Falls on the child awake and wearied of.

He lies awake in pain, he does not move,
He will not scream. Any who heard him scream
Would let their wisdom be the whole of love.

People have filled the room he lies above.
Their talk, mild variation, chilling theme,
Falls on the child. Awake and wearied of

Mere pain, mere wisdom also, he would have
All the world waking from its winter dream,
Letting its wisdom be. The whole of love
Falls on the child awake and wearied of.

CHILDLESSNESS

The weather of this winter night, my dream-wife
Ranting and raining, wakes me. Her cloak blown back
To show the lining's dull lead foil
Sweeps along asphalt. Houses
Look blindly on; one glimmers through a blind.
Outside, I hear her tricklings
Arraign my little plot:
Had it or not agreed
To transplantation for the common good
Of certain rare growths yielding guaranteed
Gold pollen, gender of suns, large, hardy,
Enviable blooms? But in my garden
Nothing is planted. Neither
Is that glimmering window mine.
I lie and think about the rain,
How it has been drawn up from the impure ocean,
From gardens lightly, deliberately tainted;
How it falls back, time after time,
Through poisons visible at sunset
When the enchantress, masked as friend, unfurls
Entire bolts of voluminous pistachio,
Saffron, and rose.
These, as I fall back to sleep,
And other slow colors clothe me, glide
To rest, then burst along my limbs like buds,
Like bombs from the navigator's vantage,
Waking me, lulling me. Later I am shown
The erased metropolis reassembled
On sampans, freighted each
With toddlers, holy dolls, dead ancestors.
One tiny monkey puzzles over fruit.
The vision rises and falls, the garland
Gently takes root
In the sea's coma. Hours go by
Before I can stand to own

A sky stained red, a world
Clad only in rags, threadbare,
Dabbling the highway's ice with blood.
A world. The cloak thrown down for it to wear
In token of past servitude
Has fallen onto the shoulders of my parents
Whom it is eating to the bone.

GETTING THROUGH

I wrote the postcard to you and went out
Through melting snow to mail it. Old Miss Tree
Buttonholed me at the corner with something about
Today being our last chance. Indeed! Well, well,
Not hers and mine, I trusted gallantly,
Disengaging her knuckle from my lapel.

First thing on entering the Post Office,
I made out through my pigeonhole's dim pane
An envelope from you. Cheered up by this,
Card between teeth, I twirled the dials; they whirred
But the lock held. One, two, three times. In vain,
At the stamp window I called for Mr. Bird,

Our friendly Postmaster. Not a soul replied.
Bags of mail lay in heaps, lashed shut, the late
Snowlight upon them. When at last I tried
To avail myself of the emergency stamp machine,
A cancelled 20 franc imperforate
From Madagascar slid out, mocking, green.

Nerves, I thought, wishing more than ever now
You had not gone away, considering mailing
My card unstamped, presuming that somehow . . .
What's this! Your envelope lies at my feet,
Ripped open, empty, my name running, paling
From snow tracked in by me. Outside, Main Street

Is empty—no: a Telephone Company truck.
Why, I can phone! The mere sound of my voice
Will melt you, help decide you to come back.
But as I hurry home a water drop
Stops me, then little rainbow husks of ice—
From the telephone pole. There at the shivering top

Two men in rubber boots are cutting wires
Which heavily dangle from a further pole.
(Oh, May Day ribbons! Child our town attires
As Queen in tablecloth and paper crown,
Lurching down Main Street blindly as a mole!)
When the last wire is severed I lurch down

The street myself, my blankness exquisite.
Beyond juniper hedge sits Mrs. Stone,
Mute on her dazzling lawn. Bracing to sit
In such fresh snow, I brightly call. Her hard
Gaze holds me like amber. I drop my own,
And find I cannot now read the postcard

Still in my grasp, unspotted and uncrushed.
My black inkstrokes hover intensely still
Against the light—starlings gunshot has flushed
That hover one split second, so, then veer
Away for good. The trees weep, as trees will.
Everything is cryptic, crystal-queer.

The stationery store's brow drips, ablaze
Where the pink sun has struck it with the hand
Of one remembering after days and days—
Remembering what? I am a fool, a fool!
I hear with joy, helpless to understand
Cries of snow-crimson children leaving school.

FIVE OLD FAVORITES

1 / A DREAM OF OLD VIENNA

The mother sits, the whites of her eyes tinted
By a gas lamp of red Bohemian glass.
Her one gray lock could be a rosy fireworks.
She hums the galop from Lehár's Requiem Mass.

Deepening a blood-red handkerchief the father
Has drawn over his face, the warm beams wreathe
Its foldings into otherworldly features
Now and then stirred lightly from beneath.

The child, because of his extreme pallor,
Acquires a normal look as the lamp glows,
For which the mother is and is not grateful,
Torn between conflicting libidos.

To wed the son when he has slain the father,
Or thrust the brat *at once* into the damp . . . ?
Such are the throbbing issues that enliven
Many a cozy evening round the lamp.

2 / THE MIDNIGHT SNACK

When I was little and he was riled
It never entered my father's head
Not to flare up, roar and turn red.
Mother kept cool and smiled.

Now every night I tiptoe straight
Through my darkened kitchen for
The refrigerator door—
It opens, the inviolate!

Illumined as in dreams I take
A glass of milk, a piece of cake,
Then stealthily retire,

Mindful of how the gas stove's black-
Browed pilot eye's blue fire
Burns into my turned back.

3 / SUNDOWN AND STARLIGHT

He licks the tallest tree, and takes a bite.
His day's excess has left him flushed and limp. Then, too,
It is time she changed for the evening. Hadn't she better
Be thinking what to wear? Nothing seems quite

To match her mood. Women! She must consider
One dress after another of pale or fiery hue.
At the hour's end, as foreseen, her favorite dark blue
Comes fold by fold out of its chest of cedar.

His jaws have closed on the tree's base.
Moments like this, he turns into a compulsive eater.
Men! Let him burn all night. She has other things to do
Than care for him. She opens her jewel case.

4 / EVENT WITHOUT PARTICULARS

Something will be hanging from the ceiling—
A dagger fern in chains? Shroud of a chandelier?
One feebly blinking bulb? Be that as it may,
Something you notice right away.

Something will decorate the wall—a calendar?
A looking glass? A scorched place? One never can say.

And something lie on the table—a teacup or book
You may care to read if you dare to look.

Then comes the opening of the door.
Somebody enters—young, face deep in a nosegay,
Or with a drink, or a crutch and milk-blind eyes.
In any case *you will rise*

And go to her over whatever is underfoot
To make you feel at home, since you have come to stay—
Black and white marble might be used for some;
For others, roses of linoleum.

5 / THE DANDELION SERMON

In the heat of a sentence I stopped. You waited
Complacently, but the mind
Had been breathed upon at last.
Innumerable feathery particles rose in less than wind

Out over the nude waters where both suns
Fierily, the reflected and the seen,
Strove to be one, then perhaps were, within
A white haze not at once or ever with ease construed.

ROGER CLAY'S PROPOSAL

I may be oversusceptible to news
But what I see in the papers leaves me numb.
The bomb. The ultimatum. Wires hum—
Adult impersonators giving interviews,

As if that helped. What would? I've thought of it.
With all due ceremony—flags unfurled,
Choirs, priests—the leaders of a sobered world
Should meet, kneel down, and, joining hands, submit

To execution: say in Rome or Nice—
Towns whose economy depends on crowds.
Ah, but those boys, their heads aren't in the clouds.
They would find reasons not to die for peace.

Damn them. I'd give *my* life. Each day I meet
Men like me, young, indignant. We're not cranks.
Will some of them step up? That's plenty. Thanks.
Now let's move before we get cold feet.

Music we'll need, and short, clear speeches given
Days of maximum coverage in the press.
We'll emphasize disinterestedness,
Drive the point home that someone could be driven

To do this. Where to go? Why not Japan,
Land of the honorable suicide.
And will the world change heart? Until we've tried,
No one can say it will not. No one can.

THE RECONNAISSANCE

Up from the ranks a body volunteers
For the difficult assignment, hears
That it may not come back, smartly replies
Far better I than you, Sir. Tears
Spring to the General's eyes.

The body now dons a disguise
That turns it thin and sallow. It is gowned
In white, and given to memorize
Things to be heard by none but a renowned
Leader of the Underground.

Fevers. Vigils. Not till the sixth moon's
Dead shimmer gloats upon the last
River struggled across, is the pigeon released
Whose return to Headquarters invariably means
Mission Accomplished.

The General stiffens. He began
As a young officer learning strategy,
Also the languages of flower and fan.
In those days would he have made so free
With the life of any man?

Dully he lifts a gloved fist to his face.
The tears however do not fall.
Too few are left and he will need them all
Now word has come of an unassailable place
Far from the sirens' call.

THE WATER HYACINTH

When I was four or so
I used to read aloud
To you—I mean, recite
Stories both of us knew
By heart, the book held close
To even then nearsighted
Eyes. It was morning. You,
Still in your nightgown
Over cold tea, would nod
Approval. Once I caught
A gay note in your quiet:
The book was upside down.

Now all is upside down.
I sit while you babble.
I watch your sightless face
Jerked swiftly here and there,
Set in a puzzled frown.
Your face! It is no more yours
Than its reflected double
Bobbing on scummed water.
Other days, the long pure
Sobs break from a choked source
Nobody here would dare
Fathom, even if able.

With you no longer able,
I tried to keep apart,
At first, or to set right
The stories you would tell.
The European trip,
The fire of 1908—
I could reel them off in sleep,
Given a phrase to start;

Chimneys of kerosene
Lamps only you could clean
Because your hands were small . . .
I have them all by heart

But cannot now find heart
To hinder them from growing
Together, wrong, absurd.
Do as you must, poor stranger.
There is no surer craft
To take you where you are going
—A story I have heard
And shall over and over
Till you are indeed gone.
Last night the mockingbird
Wept and laughed, wept and laughed,
Telling it to the moon.

Your entire honeymoon,
A ride in a rowboat
On the St. Johns River,
Took up an afternoon.
And by that time, of course,
The water hyacinth
Had come here from Japan,
A mauve and rootless guest
Thirsty for life, afloat
With you on the broad span
It would in sixty years
So vividly congest.

ANNIE HILL'S GRAVE

Amen. The casket like a spaceship bears her
In streamlined, airtight comfort underground.
Necropolis is a nice place to visit;
One would not want to live there all year round.

So think the children of its dead, emerging
From shadow by the small deep gates of clay,
Exclaiming softly, joyful if bewildered,
To see each other rouged, heads bald or gray.

Some have not met, though constant to the City,
For decades. Now their slowly sunnier
Counterclockwise movement, linked and loving,
Slackens the whirlpool that has swallowed her.

Alone, she grips, against confusion, pictures
Of us the living, and of the tall youth
She wed but has not seen for thirty summers.
Used to the dark, he lies in the next booth,

Part of that whole, poor, overpopulated
Land of our dreams, that "instant" space
—To have again, just add stars, wind, and water—
Shrinkingly broached. And, as the brief snail-trace

Of her withdrawal dries upon our faces
The silence drums into her upturned face.

ANGEL

Above my desk, whirring and self-important
(Though not much larger than a hummingbird)
In finely woven robes, school of Van Eyck,
Hovers an evidently angelic visitor.
He points one index finger out the window
At winter snatching to its heart,
To crystal vacancy, the misty
Exhalations of houses and of people running home
From the cold sun pounding on the sea;
While with the other hand
He indicates the piano
Where the Sarabande No. 1 lies open
At a passage I shall never master
But which has already, and effortlessly, mastered me.
He drops his jaw as if to say, or sing,
"Between the world God made
And this music of Satie,
Each glimpsed through veils, but whole,
Radiant and willed,
Demanding praise, demanding surrender,
How can you sit there with your notebook?
What do you think you are doing?"
However he says nothing—wisely: I could mention
Flaws in God's world, or Satie's; and for that matter
How did he come by *his* taste for Satie?
Half to tease him, I turn back to my page,
Its phrases thus far clotted, unconnected.
The tiny angel shakes his head.
There is no smile on his round, hairless face.
He does not want even these few lines written.

TO A BUTTERFLY

Already in midsummer
I miss your feet and fur.
Poor simple creature that you were,
What have you become!

Your slender person curled
About an apple twig
Rebounding to the winds' clear jig
Gave up the world

In favor of obscene
Gray matter, rode that ark
Until (as at the chance remark
Of Father Sheen)

Shining awake to slough
Your old life. And soon four
Dapper stained glass windows bore
You up—*Enough*.

Goodness, how tired one grows
Just looking through a prism:
Allegory, symbolism.
I've tried, Lord knows,

To keep from seeing double,
Blushed for whenever I did,
Prayed like a boy my cheek be hid
By manly stubble.

I caught you in a net
And first pierced your disguise
How many years ago? Time flies,
I am not yet

Proof against rigmarole.
Those frail wings, those antennae!
The day you hover without any
Tincture of soul,

Red monarch, swallowtail,
Will be the day my own
Wiles gather dust. Each will have flown
The other's jail.

THE PARROT FISH

The shadow of the little fishing launch
Discreetly, inch by inch,
Crept after us on its belly over
The reef's uneven floor.

The motor gasped out drowsy vapor.
Seconds went by before
Anyone thought to interpret
The jingling of Inez's bracelet.

Chalk-violet, olive, all veils and sequins, a
Priestess out of the next Old Testament extravaganza,
With round gold eyes and minuscule buckteeth,
Up flaunted into death

The parrot fish. And for a full hour beat
Irregular, passionate
Tattoos from its casket lined with zinc.
Finally we understood, I think.

Ashore, the warm waves licked our feet.
One or two heavy chords the heat
Struck, set the white beach vibrating.
And throwing back its head the sea began to sing.

When our son died
We cured his little frame,
Scoured, pickled, overlaid head to toe
The ultimate forged antique
With augmentingly non-literal translations
Into gold, of the boy, into alabaster,
His face's full moon setting
Beneath an earth chewed bare by beetles,
And all at length, with tutors and possessions
Packed into a gold—into *four* gold
Garages at the heart
Of four three-sided glassy slopes
Upheaved through layers of blue and yellow gas.
The gods our cousins were reduced
To looking on, bird-eyed or jackal-eyed,
His guests who had been theirs.
My sister and I stood
As we stand now, in red
Granite, chins high, fists drugged
Upon symbols of rank. We must
Apparently have felt
Shock of a sort. We are shown taking
A rigid backward step
Into this world of giant papyrus-sheaves,
Sunwashed, pitted with inventory.
It was "the dawn of history."
Do not judge us unkindly, friend
Whose heart still beats and bleeds.
States noway known till we induced them
Propel one bride and groom, your autumn night,
Into the living area
Of a first apartment. Open-armed,
Goat-footed chairs the worm has drilled,
A quarter year been traded to possess,

In the bronze glow of missiles become lamps
Receive the pair. His cup
Poured, sweetened, her small voice goes on:
Each day should be *composed*,
Should have "shape" and "texture"—living was an art! . . .
He nods, on fire. Back of her fair young face
Is hung her other, her unchanging face
Launched free of earth between sun-whitened waves.
Her slaves, his senses, rend their clothing.
Eyes she will never look through look through him
To chill themselves in a transparence
On whose far side, all night
Enthralled, press wings, press tiny wings.
Illumined therefore unbudging, we rule here.
Exerting no pressure. Only
When stones he gave her, that will cost one year,
Glitter, glittering back.
Too late the ritual of blinds.
Both now, as all before them, have seen us—grown
Taller than buildings, masked in magnets,
Traffic of stars, the myriad needles plunged
Green into that arterial heaven
Our loss, which is your gain.

THE SMILE

It was going to rain.
Beneath his scalp
The silver ached. He got
With no one's help
To his feet. A cane
Steadied him up the stair.

It was warm there
On the sleeping porch.
His jacket hung
Over a chair would not
Let go his form.
He placed his round gold watch,

Unwound, among
Dimes, quarters, lunatic change . . .
He woke in bed,
Missing his spectacles.
He felt the strange
Palms laid on his forehead.

Then he heard other palms
Rattling in wind.
More time passed. He had dreams.
In one, rain fell
And fell, and when
The sun rose near at hand

Stood his life gleaming full.
The bubble-beaded
Tumbler magnified
A false and grinning friend
No longer needed.
He turned his face and died.

SWIMMING BY NIGHT

A light going out in the forehead
Of the house by the ocean,
Into warm black its feints of diamond fade.
Without clothes, without caution

Plunging past gravity—
Wait! Where before
Had been floating nothing, is a gradual body
Half remembered, astral with phosphor,

Yours, risen from its tomb
In your own mind,
Haunting nimbleness, glimmerings a random
Spell had kindled. So that, new-limned

By this weak lamp
The evening's alcohol will feed
Until the genie chilling bids you limp
Heavily over stones to bed,

You wear your master's robe
One last time, the far break
Of waves, their length and sparkle, the spinning globe
You wear, and the star running down his cheek.

A TENANCY

for David Jackson

Something in the light of this March afternoon
Recalls that first and dazzling one
Of 1946. I sat elated
In my old clothes, in the first of several
Furnished rooms, head cocked for the kind of sound
That is recognized only when heard.
A fresh snowfall muffled the road, unplowed
To leave blanker and brighter
The bright, blank page turned overnight.

A yellow pencil in midair
Kept sketching unfamiliar numerals,
The 9 and 6 forming a stereoscope
Through which to seize the Real
Old-Fashioned Winter of my landlord's phrase,
Through which the ponderous *idées reçues*
Of oak, velour, crochet, also the mantel's
Baby figures, value told me
In some detail at the outset, might be plumbed
For signs I should not know until I saw them.

But the objects, innocent
(As we all once were) of annual depreciation,
The more I looked grew shallower,
Pined under a luminous plaid robe
Thrown over us by the twin mullions, sashes,
And unequal oblong panes
Of windows and storm windows. These,
Washed in a rage, then left to dry unpolished,
Projected onto the inmost wall
Ghosts of the storm, like pebbles under water.

And indeed, from within, ripples
Of heat had begun visibly bearing up and away
The bouquets and wreaths of a quarter century.

Let them go, what did I want with them?
It was time to change that wallpaper!
Brittle, sallow in the new radiance,
Time to set the last wreath floating out
Above the dead, to sweep up flowers. The dance
Had ended, it was light; the men looked tired
And awkward in their uniforms.
I sat, head thrown back, and with the dried stains
Of light on my own cheeks, proposed
This bargain with—say with the source of light:
That given a few years more
(Seven or ten or, what seemed vast, fifteen)
To spend in love, in a country not at war,
I would give in return
All I had. All? A little sun
Rose in my throat. The lease was drawn.

I did not even feel the time expire.

I feel it though, today, in this new room,
Mine, with my things and thoughts, a view
Of housetops, treetops, the walls bare.
A changing light is deepening, is changing
To a gilt ballroom chair a chair
Bound to break under someone before long.
I let the light change also me.
The body that lived through that day
And the sufficient love and relative peace
Of those short years, is now not mine.
Would it be called a soul?
It knows, at any rate,
That when the light dies and the bell rings
Its leaner veteran will rise to face
Partners not recognized
Until drunk young again and gowned in changing
Flushes; and strains will rise,

The bone-tipped baton beating, rapid, faint,
From the street below, from my depressions—

From the doorbell which rings.
One foot asleep, I hop
To let my three friends in. They stamp
Themselves free of the spring's
Last snow—or so we hope.

One has brought violets in a pot;
The second, wine; the best,
His open, empty hand. Now in the room
The sun is shining like a lamp.
I put the flowers where I need them most

And then, not asking why they come,
Invite the visitors to sit.
If I am host at last
It is of little more than my own past.
May others be at home in it.

Nights and Days

(1966)

NIGHTGOWN

A cold so keen,
My speech unfurls tonight
As from the chattering teeth
Of a sewing machine.

Whom words appear to warm,
Dear heart, wear mine. Come forth
Wound in their flimsy white
And give it form.

THE THOUSAND AND SECOND NIGHT

for Irma Brandeis

I / RIGOR VITAE

Istanbul. 21 March. I woke today
With an absurd complaint. The whole right half
Of my face refuses to move. I have to laugh
Watching the rest of it reel about in dismay

Under the double burden, while its twin
Sags on, though sentient, stupefied.
I'm here alone. Not quite—through fog outside
Loom wingèd letters: PAN AMERICAN.

Twenty-five hundred years this city has stood between
The passive Orient and our frantic West.
I see no reason to be depressed;
There are too many other things I haven't seen,

Like Hagia Sophia. Tea drunk, shaved and dressed . . .
Dahin! Dahin!

The house of Heavenly Wisdom first became
A mosque, is now a flame-
less void. The apse,
Militantly dislocated,
Still wears those dark-green epaulettes
On which (to the pilgrim who forgets
His Arabic) a wild script of gold whips
Has scribbled glowering, dated
Slogans: "God is my grief!" perhaps,
Or "Byzantine,
Go home!"
Above you, the great dome,
Bald of mosaic, senile, floated
In a gilt wash. Its old profusion's
Hypnotic shimmer, back and forth between
That of the abacus, that of the nebula,
Had been picked up from the floor,

The last of numberless handfuls,
By the last 18th-century visitor.
You did not want to think of yourself for once,
But you had held your head erect
Too many years within such transcendental skulls
As this one not to feel the usual, if no
Longer flattering kinship. You'd let go
Learning and faith as well, you too had wrecked
Your precious sensibility. What else did you expect?

Outdoors. Uprooted, turban-crested stones
Lie side by side. It's as I might have feared.
The building, desperate for youth, has smeared
All over its original fine bones

Acres of ocher plaster. A diagram
Indicates how deep in the mudpack
The real façade is. I want *my* face back.
A pharmacist advises

The Hamam

After the hour of damp heat
One is addressed in gibberish, shown
Into a marble cell and thrown
On marble, there to be scrubbed clean,

Is wrapped in towels and a sheet
And led upstairs to this lean tomb
Made all of panes (red, amber, green)
With a glass star hung in the gloom,

Here sits effaced by gemlike moods,
Tastes neither coffee nor loukoum,
And to the attendant who intrudes

(Or archeologist or thief)
Gravely uptilts one's mask of platinum
Still dripping, in a sign of life.

And now what? Back, I guess, to the modern town.
Midway across the bridge, an infantile
Memory promises to uncramp my style.
I stop in deepening light to jot it down:

On the crest of her wrist, by the black watered silk of the watchband, his
grandmother had a wen, a hard mauve bubble up from which bristled
three or four white hairs. How often he had lain in her lap and been lulled
to a rhythm easily the whole world's then—the yellowish sparkle of a
ring marking its outer limit, while in the foreground, silhouetted like the
mosque of Suleiman the Magnificent, mass and minarets felt by someone
fallen asleep on the deck of his moored caïque, that principal landmark's
rise and fall distinguished, from any other, her beloved hand.

Cold. A wind rising. An entire city
Dissolved by rhetoric. And out there, past
The mirror of the Bosporos, what black coast
Reflecting us into immobility?

On this side, crowds, a magic-lantern beam—
Belgians on bicycles, housewives with red hair,
Masts, cries of crows blown high in the rose-blue air,
Ataturk's tailcoat . . . It is like a dream,

The "death-in-life and life-in-death" of Yeats'
Byzantium; and, if so, by the same token,
Alone in the sleepwalking scene, my flesh has woken
And sailed for the fixed shore beyond the straits.

2 / THE CURE

The doctor recommended cortisone,
Diathermy, vitamins, and rest.
It worked. These months in Athens, no one's guessed
My little drama; I appear my own

Master again. However, once you've cracked
That so-called mirror of the soul,
It is not readily, if at all, made whole.
("Between the motion and the act

Falls the Shadow"—T. S. Eliot.)
Part of me has remained cold and withdrawn.
The day I went up to the Parthenon
Its humane splendor made me think *So what?*

One May noon in the Royal Park, among
The flora of l'Agneau Mystique—
Cypress, mimosa, laurel, palm—a Greek
Came up to name them for me in his tongue.

I thanked him; he thanked me, sat down. Peacocks
Trailed by, hard gray feet mashing overripe
But bitter oranges. I knew the type:
Superb, male, raucous, unclean, Orthodox

Ikon of appetite feathered to the eyes
With the electric blue of days that will
Not come again. My friend with time to kill
Asked me the price of cars in Paradise.

By which he meant my country, for in his
The stranger is a god in masquerade.
Failing to act that part, I am afraid
I was not human either—ah, who is?

He is, or was; had brothers and a wife;
Chauffeured a truck; last Friday broke his neck
Against a tree. We have no way to check
These headlong emigrations out of life.

Try, I suppose, we must, as even Valéry said,
And said more grandly than I ever shall—
Turning shut lids to the August sun, and all
Such neon figments (amber, green, and red)

Of incommunicable energy
As in my blindness wake, and at a blink
Vanish, and were the clearest hint, I think,
Of what I have been, am, and care to be.

3 / CARNIVALS

Three good friends in as many months have complained,
"You were nice, James, before your trip. Or so
I thought. But you have changed. I know, I know,
People do change. Well, I'm surprised, I'm pained."

Before they disappeared into the night
Of what they said, I'd make a stab at mouthing
Promises that meant precisely nothing
And never saved my face. For they were right.

These weren't young friends, what's more. Youth would explain
Part of it. I have kept somewhere a page
Written at sixteen to myself at twice that age,
Whom I accuse of having become the vain

Flippant unfeeling monster I now am—
To hear them talk—and exhorting me to recall
Starlight on an evening in late fall
1943, and the walk with M,

To die in whose presence seemed the highest good.
I met M and his new wife last New Year's.
We rued the cold war's tainted atmospheres
From a corner table. It was understood

Our war was over. We had made our peace
With—everything. The heads of animals
Gazed in forbearance from the velvet walls.
Great drifts of damask cleaned our lips of grease.

Then L—her "Let's be friends" and her clear look
Returned in disbelief. I had a herd

Of *friends*. I wanted love, if love's the word
On the foxed spine of the long-mislaid book.

A thousand and one nights! They were grotesque.
Stripping the blubber from my catch, I lit
The oil-soaked wick, then could not see by it.
Mornings, a black film lay upon the desk

. . . Where just a week ago I thought to delve
For images of those years in a Plain Cover.
Some light verse happened as I looked them over:

Postcards from Hamburg, Circa 1912

The ocelot's yawn, a sepia-dim
Shamelessness from nun's coif to spike heels,
She strokes his handlebar who kneels
To do for her what a dwarf does for him.
The properties are grim,

Are, you might want to say, unsexed
By use. A divan covered with a rug,
A flat Methusalem of Krug
Appear from tableau to tableau. The next
Shows him with muscle flexed

In resurrection from his underwear,
Gaining an underworld to harrow.
He steers her ankles like—like a wheelbarrow.
The dwarf has slipped out for a breath of air,
Leaving the monstrous pair.

Who are they? What does their charade convey?
Maker and Muse? Demon and Doll?
"All manners are symbolic"—Hofmannsthal.
Here's the dwarf back with cronies . . . oh I *say*!
Forget about it. They,

In time, in pain, unlearned their tricks.
Only the shrouded focusser of the lens

May still be chasing specimens
From his lone bathysphere deep in the Styx.
St. Pauli's clock struck six;

Sighing, "The death of sin is wages,"
He paid his models, bade them dress and go,
Earthlings once more, incognito
Down swarming boulevards, the contagious-
ly easy, final stages,

Dodged even by the faithful, one of whom
(Morose Great-Uncle Alastair)
Brought back these effigies and would shortly bear
Their doctrine unconfessed, we may assume,
Into his brazen tomb.

We found the postcards after her divorce,
I and Aunt Alix. She turned red with shame,
Then white, then thoughtful. "Ah, they're all the same—
Men, I mean." A pause. "Not you, of course."

And then: "We'll burn them. Light the fire." I must
Meanwhile have tucked a few into my shirt.
I spent the night rekindling with expert
Fingers—but that phase needn't be discussed . . .

"The soul, which in infancy could not be told from the body, came with
age to resemble *a body one no longer had,* whose transports went far
beyond what passes, now, for sensation. All irony aside, the libertine *was*
'in search of his soul'; nightly he labored to regain those firelit lodg-
ings . . . Likewise, upon the Earth's mature body we inflict a wealth of
gross experience—drugs, drills, bombardments—with what effect? A
stale *frisson,* a waste of resources all too analogous to our own. Natural
calamities (tumor and apoplexy no less than flood and volcano) may at
last be hailed as positive reassurances, perverse if you like, of life in the
old girl yet."

—GERMAINE NAHMAN

Love. Warmth. Fist of sunlight at last
Pounding emphatic on the gulf. High wails
From your white ship: The heart prevails!
Affirm it! Simple decency rides the blast!—
Phrases that, quick to smell blood, lurk like sharks
Within a style's transparent lights and darks.

The lips part. The plume trembles. You're afloat
Upon the breathing, all-reflecting deep.
The past recedes and twinkles, falls asleep.
Fear is unworthy, say the stars by rote;
What destinations have been yours till now
Unworthy, says the leaping prow.

O skimmer of deep blue
Volumes fraught with rhyme and reason,
Once the phosphorescent meshes loosen
And the objects of your quest slip through,
Almost you can overlook a risen
Brow, a thin, black dawn on the horizon.

Except that in this virgin hemisphere
One city calls you—towers, drums, conches, bells
Tolling each year's more sumptuous farewells
To flesh. Among the dancers on the pier
Glides one figure in a suit of bones,
Whose savage grace alerts the chaperones.

He picks you out from thousands. He intends
Perhaps no mischief. Yet the dog-brown eyes
In the chalk face that stiffens as it dries
Pierce you with the eyes of those three friends.
The mask begins to melt upon your face.
A hush has fallen in the marketplace,

And now the long adventure

Let that wait.
I'm tired, it's late at night.

Tomorrow, if it is given me to conquer
An old distrust of imaginary scenes,
Scenes not lived through yet, the few final lines
Will lie on the page and the whole ride at anchor.

I'm home, of course. It's winter. Real
Snow fills the road. On the unmade
Brass bed lies my adored Scheherazade,
Eight-ninths asleep, tail twitching to the steel

Band of the steam heat's dissonant calypso.
The wind has died. Where would I be
If not here? There's so little left to see!
Lost friends, my long ago

Voyages, I bless you for sore
Limbs and mouth kissed, face bronzed and lined,
An earth held up, a text not wholly undermined
By fluent passages of metaphor.

4

Now if the class will turn back to this, er,
Poem's first section—Istanbul—I shall take
What little time is left today to make
Some brief points. So. The rough pentameter

Quatrains give way, you will observe, to three
Interpolations, prose as well as verse.
Does it come through how each in turn refers
To mind, body, and soul (or memory)?

It does? Good. No, I cannot say offhand
Why this should be. I find it vaguely satis—

Yes please? The poet quotes too much? Hm. That is
One way to put it. Mightn't he have planned

For his own modest effort to be seen
Against the yardstick of the "truly great"
(In Spender's phrase)? Fearing to overstate,
He lets *them* do it—lets their words, I mean,

Enhance his—Yes, what now? Ah. How and when
Did he "affirm"? Why, constantly. And how else
But in the form. Form's what affirms. That's well
Said, if I do—[*Bells ring.*] Go, gentlemen.

5

And when the long adventure reached its end,
I saw the Sultan in a glass, grown old,
While she, his fair wife still, her tales all told,
Smiled at him fondly. "O my dearest friend,"

Said she, "and lord and master from the first,
Release me now. Your servant would refresh
Her soul in that cold fountain which the flesh
Knows not. Grant this, for I am faint with thirst."

And he: "But it is I who am your slave.
Free me, I pray, to go in search of joys
Unembroidered by your high, soft voice,
Along that stony path the senses pave."

They wept, then tenderly embraced and went
Their ways. She and her fictions soon were one.
He slept through moonset, woke in blinding sun,
Too late to question what the tale had meant.

MAISIE

1

One morning I shall find
I have slept with your full weight upon my heart,
Your motors and my breathing reconciled.
The edges of the blind,

The crack beneath the door will have blanched with day,
The walls will be about to jar apart
The sun to dust my lids deep in the opened flower.
And still I shall not have sent you away.

2

When you came home without your sex
You hid in the cupboard under the sink.
Its gasps and gurglings must have helped somehow.

The second noon you ventured forth,
A silent star, furred up to tragic eyes,
Hazarding recognition in a restaurant.

It was horrible to see how much
You honestly cared about food and comfort.
The dishes refused! The chairs tried one by one!

Eunuch and favorite both,
You loll about, exuding that old magic
There is mercifully no longer a market for.

3

For the good of the guest who has not yet looked over
The roof garden's brink to the eaves just below,
You shudder there long enough only to shriek

(If eyes could shriek, and if they were ever
Eyes, those chalcedony bonfires): *O
Scarpia! Avanti a Dio!*
                              —then plummet from view,
Leaving the newcomer aghast and weak.

THE FURNISHED ROOM

Blue boughs, green fruit—
That was our wallpaper.
Two doors, both shut;
Two windows, a mirror.

Against the walls
Table and divan stood,
Odd animals,
One pine, one cherry wood.

One bore the book, the bowl,
The lamp. Its four
Legs shook. Its soul
Slid out like an empty drawer.

The other: claw-foot, soft
Belly, striped hide.
Glad in its hug we laughed.
Time howled outside.

But central heat
Hissed back and kept us warm.
Come dusk, lamplight
Lit out into a storm

Determined, all that week,
To fill us with
What no one else could wreak
On the room's myth.

BETWEEN US

A . . . face? There
It lies on the pillow by
Your turned head's tangled graying hair:
Another—like a shrunken head, too small!
My eyes in dread
Shut. Open. It is there,

Waxen, inhuman. Small.
The taut crease of the mouth shifts. It
Seems to smile,
Chin up in the wan light. Elsewhere
I have known what it was, this thing, known
The blind eye-slit

And knuckle-sharp cheekbone—
Ah. And again do.
Not a face. A hand, seen queerly. Mine.
Deliver me, I breathe
Watching it unclench with a soft moan
And reach for you.

VIOLENT PASTORAL

Against a thunderhead's
Blue marble, the eagle
Mounts with the lamb in his clutch:
Two wings, four hooves,

One pulse pounding, pounding,
So little time being given
To feel the earth shrunken,
Gong-tilt of waters,

To be at once helplessly
Aching talon and bleating
Weight, both,
Lest the pact break,

To link the rut in dust
When the rope shortens
Between foreleg and stake
With the harder spiral of making

For a nest wrapped in lightnings
And quilted with their beaks who not yet,
As with their bones who no longer,
Are wholly brothers;

Beyond Arcadia at last,
Wing, hoof, one oriented creature,
Snake-scream of pride
And bowels of fright

Lost in the rainbow, to be one
Even with the shepherd
Still looking up, who understood
And was not turned to stone.

1 9 3 9

an American woman explores the estate
of friends who have fled France

for Grace

Madame!
And the earth opened
As in Perrault,
From an iron ring. I went by ladder
After the caretaker
Down to a buried chapel, Gallo-Roman,
A small, groined place—
One column, one rosette,
One woman without features peering
Up through the marble ripples
Of a capsized sarcophagus . . .
Madame!
Like an echo,
The second iron ring.
Down, deeper down,
A foot by now
For every year of mine,
Something remoter lay.
Over hewn walls
Trickled the lantern's shine.
And on an altar, perhaps Celtic, seemed
To stir, then stirred
This dirt-caked, geometric—
Heavens! A tortoise!
Madame!
But I stayed in the highest of spirits,
Tried on all next day, under a flowered ceiling,
Dresses by Alix and Chanel
My invisible hostess would not wear again.
I felt that I was steeling
Myself to bear what had to come.
Later, when that world fell,
I still could not help feeling . . .

TIME

for B. V. Winebaum

Ever that Everest
Among concepts, as prize for fruitful
Grapplings with which
The solved crossword puzzle has now and then
Eclipsed Blake's "Sun-Flower"
(Not that one wanted a letter changed in either)
And jazz believed at seventeen
So parodied the slopes
That one mistook the mountain for a cloud . . .

Or there was blessed Patience:
Fifty-two chromosomes permitting
Trillions of "lives"—some few
Triumphant, the majority
Blocked, doomed, yet satisfying, too,
In that with each, before starting over,
You could inquire beneath
The snowfield, the vine-monogram, the pattern
Of winged cyclists, to where the flaw lay
Crocus-clean, a trail inching between
Sheer heights and drops, and reach what might have been.

All day you had meant
To write letters, turn the key
In certain friendships, be ticked through at dusk
By hard, white, absent faces.

Let's say you went
So far as to begin: "It's me! Forgive . . ."
Too late. From the alcove came his cough,
His whimper—the old man whom sunset wakes.
Truly, could you bear another night
Keeping him company while he raved, agreeing
To Persia on horseback, just you two! when even
The garden path had been forbidden,
He was so feeble. Feeble!

He grasped your pulse in his big gray-haired hand,
Crevasses opening, numb azure. *Wait*
He breathed and glittered: *You'll regret*
You want to   Read my will first   Don't
Your old father   All he has   Be yours

Hours you raised the dark rum to his lips.
Your eyes burned. Your voice said:
"All right, we'll read Cervantes, we'll take trips.
She you loved lives. You'll see her in the morning.
You'll get well, you'll be proud of me. Don't smile!
I love you. I'll find work. You'll—I'll—"

It was light and late.
You could not remember
Sleeping. It hurt to rise.
There stood
Those features' ice-crowned, tanned—by what?—
Landmark, like yours, unwrinkled in repose.
Pouring tea strong and hot,
You swiftly wrote:

". . . this long silence. I don't know what's the matter with me. All winter
I have been trying to discipline myself—'Empty the mind,' as they say in
the handbooks, 'concentrate upon one thing, any thing, the snowflake, the
granite it falls upon, the planet risen opposite, etc., etc.'—and failing,
failing. Quicksands of leisure! Now summer's here, I *think*. Each morn-
ing a fog rolls in from the sea. It would lift, perhaps, if you were to come
and speak to it. Will you? Do! One catches the ferry at . . ."

The pen reels from your hand. Were you asleep?
Who were you writing to? Annette? Me? Jake?
Later, smoothing the foothills of the sheet,
You take up your worn pack.

Above their gay crusaders' dress
The monarchs' mouths are pinched and bleak.
Staggering forth in ranks of less and less
Related cards, condemned to the mystique

Of a redeeming One,
An Ace to lead them home, sword, stave, and ax,
Power, Riches, Love, a place to lay them down
In dreamless heaps, the reds, the blacks,

Old Adams and gray Eves
Escort you still. Perhaps this time . . . ?
A Queen in the discarded suit of Leaves,
Earth dims and flattens as you climb

And heaven, darkened, steams
Upon the trembling disk of tea.
Sixty or seventy more games
And you can go the rest alone maybe—

Arriving then at something not unlike
Meaning relieved of sense,
To plant a flag there on that needle peak
Whose diamond grates in the revolving silence.

Another evening we sprawled about discussing
Appearances. And it was the consensus
That while uncommon physical good looks
Continued to launch one, as before, in life
(Among its vaporous eddies and false calms),
Still, as one of us said into his beard,
"Without your intellectual and spiritual
Values, man, you are sunk." No one but squared
The shoulders of his own unloveliness.
Long-suffering Charles, having cooked and served the meal,
Now brought out little tumblers finely etched
He filled with amber liquor and then passed.
"Say," said the same young man, "in Paris, France,
They do it this way"—bounding to his feet
And touching a lit match to our host's full glass.
A blue flame, gentle, beautiful, came, went
Above the surface. In a hush that fell
We heard the vessel crack. The contents drained
As who should step down from a crystal coach.
Steward of spirits, Charles's glistening hand
All at once gloved itself in eeriness.
The moment passed. He made two quick sweeps and
Was flesh again. "It couldn't matter less,"
He said, but with a shocked, unconscious glance
Into the mirror. Finding nothing changed,
He filled a fresh glass and sank down among us.

THE ART DEALER

Because I hoped to come by, when you died,
Something of yours, a virtue or a view,
I would not go to let that other you
Ask who the stranger was at your bedside.
There were days I told myself *It's sheer pretense.*
Illness indeed. Besides, who'd mind the shop?
When finally word reached me, I hung up
And sat, revolted by my ornaments.

Of course I saw you at the funeral:
Youthful, restored expertly, but a fake.
I turned aside. The fat ubiquitous Sheik
Winked from his Cadillac to have you cased
And shipped to a gold house moated with oil—
Yet one more proof of his appalling taste.

THE BROKEN HOME

Crossing the street,
I saw the parents and the child
At their window, gleaming like fruit
With evening's mild gold leaf.

In a room on the floor below,
Sunless, cooler—a brimming
Saucer of wax, marbly and dim—
I have lit what's left of my life.

I have thrown out yesterday's milk
And opened a book of maxims.
The flame quickens. The word stirs.

Tell me, tongue of fire,
That you and I are as real
At least as the people upstairs.

My father, who had flown in World War I,
Might have continued to invest his life
In cloud banks well above Wall Street and wife.
But the race was run below, and the point was to win.

Too late now, I make out in his blue gaze
(Through the smoked glass of being thirty-six)
The soul eclipsed by twin black pupils, sex
And business; time was money in those days.

Each thirteenth year he married. When he died
There were already several chilled wives
In sable orbit—rings, cars, permanent waves.
We'd felt him warming up for a green bride.

He could afford it. He was "in his prime"
At three score ten. But money was not time.

When my parents were younger this was a popular act:
A veiled woman would leap from an electric, wine-dark car
To the steps of no matter what—the Senate or the Ritz Bar—
And bodily, at newsreel speed, attack

No matter whom—Al Smith or José María Sert
Or Clemenceau—veins standing out on her throat
As she yelled *War mongerer! Pig! Give us the vote!*,
And would have to be hauled away in her hobble skirt.

What had the man done? Oh, made history.
Her business (he had implied) was giving birth,
Tending the house, mending the socks.

Always that same old story—
Father Time and Mother Earth,
A marriage on the rocks.

One afternoon, red, satyr-thighed
Michael, the Irish setter, head
Passionately lowered, led
The child I was to a shut door. Inside,

Blinds beat sun from the bed.
The green-gold room throbbed like a bruise.
Under a sheet, clad in taboos
Lay whom we sought, her hair undone, outspread,

And of a blackness found, if ever now, in old
Engravings where the acid bit.
I must have needed to touch it
Or the whiteness—was she dead?
Her eyes flew open, startled strange and cold.
The dog slumped to the floor. She reached for me. I fled.

Tonight they have stepped out onto the gravel.
The party is over. It's the fall
Of 1931. They love each other still.

She: Charlie, I can't stand the pace.
He: Come on, honey—why, you'll bury us all!

A lead soldier guards my windowsill:
Khaki rifle, uniform, and face.
Something in me grows heavy, silvery, pliable.

How intensely people used to feel!
Like metal poured at the close of a proletarian novel,
Refined and glowing from the crucible,
I see those two hearts, I'm afraid,
Still. Cool here in the graveyard of good and evil,
They are even so to be honored and obeyed.

. . . Obeyed, at least, inversely. Thus
I rarely buy a newspaper, or vote.
To do so, I have learned, is to invite
The tread of a stone guest within my house.

Shooting this rusted bolt, though, against him,
I trust I am no less time's child than some
Who on the heath impersonate Poor Tom
Or on the barricades risk life and limb.

Nor do I try to keep a garden, only
An avocado in a glass of water—
Roots pallid, gemmed with air. And later,

When the small gilt leaves have grown
Fleshy and green, I let them die, yes, yes,
And start another. I am earth's no less.

A child, a red dog roam the corridors,
Still, of the broken home. No sound. The brilliant
Rag runners halt before wide-open doors.
My old room! Its wallpaper—cream, medallioned
With pink and brown—brings back the first nightmares,
Long summer colds, and Emma, sepia-faced,

Perspiring over broth carried upstairs
Aswim with golden fats I could not taste.

The real house became a boarding school.
Under the ballroom ceiling's allegory
Someone at last may actually be allowed
To learn something; or, from my window, cool
With the unstiflement of the entire story,
Watch a red setter stretch and sink in cloud.

Up beyond sense and praise,
There at the highest trumpet-blast
Of Fahrenheit, the sun is a great friend.
He is so brilliant and so warm!
Yet when his axle smokes and the spokes blaze
And he founders in dusk (or seems to),
Remember: he cannot change. It's earth, it's time,
Whose child you now are, quietly
Blotting him out. In the blue stare you raise
To your mother and father already the miniature,
Merciful, and lifelong eclipse,
Felix, has taken place;
The black pupil rimmed with rays
Contracted to its task—
That of revealing by obscuring
The sunlike friend behind it.
Unseen by you, may he shine back always
From what you see, from others. So welcome, friend.
Welcome to earth, time, others; to
These cool darks, of sense, of language,
Each at once thread and maze.
Finally welcome, if you like, to this
James your father's mother's father's younger son
Contrived with love for you
During your first days.

A CARPET NOT BOUGHT

World at his feet,
Labor of generations—
No wonder the veins race.
In old Kazanjian's
Own words, "Love that carpet.
Forget the price."

Leaving the dealer's,
It was as if he had
Escaped quicksand. He
Climbed his front steps, head
High, full of dollars.
He poured the wife a brandy—

And that night not a blessed
Wink slept. The backyard
Lay senseless, bleak,
Profoundly scarred
By the moon's acid.
One after another clock

Struck midnight; one. Up through
His bare footsoles
Quicksilver shoots overcoming
The trellis of pulse
—Struck two, struck three—
Held him there, dreaming.

Kingdom reborn
In colors seen
By the hashish-eater—
Ice-pink, alizarin,
Pearl; maze shorn
Of depth; geometer

To whom all desires
Down to the last silken
Wisp o' the will

Are known: what the falcon
Sees when he soars,
What wasp and oriole

Think when they build—
And all this could
Be bargained for! Lord,
Wasn't it time you stood
On grander ground than cold
Moon-splintered board?

Thus the admired
Artifact, like clock
Or snake, struck till its poison
Was gone. Day broke,
The fever with it. Merde!
Who wanted *things?* He'd won.

Flushed on the bed's
White, lay a figure whose
Richness he sensed
Dimly. It reached him as
A cave of crimson threads
Spun by her mother against

That morning in their life
When sons with shears
Should set the pattern free
To ripple air's long floors
And bear him safe
Over a small waved sea.

THE CURRENT

Down the dawn-brown
River the charcoal woman
Swept in a boat thin
As the old moon.
White tremblings darted and broke
Under her hat's crown.
A paddle-stroke
And she was gone, in her wake
Only miniature
Whirlpools, her faint
Ritualistic cries.

Now up the stream,
Urging an unwilling
Arc of melon-rind
Painted red to match
His wares, appeared
The meat-vendor.
The young, scarred face
Under the white brim
Glowed with strain
And flamelike ripplings.
He sat in a cloud of flies.

If, further on,
Someone was waiting to thread
Morsels of beef
Onto a green
Bamboo sliver
And pose the lean brochette
Above already glowing
Embers, the river,
Flowing in one direction
By moon, by sun,
Would not be going
To let it happen yet.

WATCHING THE DANCE

1 / BALANCHINE'S

Poor savage, doubting that a river flows
But for the myriad eddies made
By unseen powers twirling on their toes,

Here in this darkness it would seem
You had already died, and were afraid.
Be still. Observe the powers. Infer the stream.

2 / DISCOTHÈQUE

Having survived entirely your own youth,
Last of your generation, purple gloom
Investing you, sit, Jonah, beyond speech,

And let towards the brute volume VOOM whale mouth
VAM pounding viscera VAM VOOM
A teenage plankton luminously twitch.

THE MAD SCENE

Again last night I dreamed the dream called Laundry.
In it, the sheets and towels of a life we were going to share,
The milk-stiff bibs, the shroud, each rag to be ever
Trampled or soiled, bled on or groped for blindly,
Came swooning out of an enormous willow hamper
Onto moon-marbly boards. We had just met. I watched
From outer darkness. I had dressed myself in clothes
Of a new fiber that never stains or wrinkles, never
Wears thin. The opera house sparkled with tiers
And tiers of eyes, like mine enlarged by belladonna,
Trained inward. There I saw the cloud-clot, gust by gust,
Form, and the lightning bite, and the roan mane unloosen.
Fingers were running in panic over the flute's nine gates.
Why did I flinch? I loved you. And in the downpour laughed
To have us wrung white, gnarled together, one
Topmost mordent of wisteria,
As the lean tree burst into grief.

FROM THE CUPOLA

for H. M.

The sister who told fortunes prophesied
A love-letter. In the next mail it came.
You didn't recognize the writer's name
And wondered he knew yours. Ah well. That seed

Has since become a world of blossom and bark.
The letters fill a drawer, the gifts a room.
No hollow of your day is hidden from
His warm concern. Still you are in the dark.

Too much understanding petrifies.
The early letters struck you as blackmail.
You have them now by heart, a rosy veil
Colors the phrase repaired to with shut eyes.

Was the time always wrong for you to meet?—
Not that he ever once proposed as much.
Your sisters joke about it. "It's too rich!
Somebody Up There loves you, Psyche sweet."

Tell me about him, then. Not a believer,
I'll hold my tongue while you, my dear, dictate.
Him I have known too little (or, of late,
Too well) to trust my own view of your lover.

Oh but one has many, many tongues!
And you will need a certain smouldering five
Deep in the ash of something I survive,
Poke and rummage with as reluctant tongs

As possible. The point won't be to stage
One of our torchlit hunts for truth. Truth asks
Just this once to sleep with fiction, masks
Of tears and laughter on the moonstruck page;

To cauterize what babbles to be healed—
Just this once not by candor. Here and now,

Psyche, I quench that iron lest it outglow
A hovering radiance your fingers shield.

Renaissance features grafted onto Greek
Revival, glassed, hexagonal lookouts crown
Some of the finest houses in this town.
By day or night, cloud, sunbeam, lunatic streak,

They alternately ravish and disown
Earth, sky, and water—Are you with me? Speak.

SUNLIGHT   Crossfire
of rays and shadows each
glancing off a windowpane a stone
You alone my correspondent

have remained sheer
projection   Hurt   Not gravely   Not at all
Your bloodlessness a glaze
of thin thin varnish where I kneel

Were the warm drop
upon your letter oil and were that page
your sleeping person then
all would indeed be lost

Our town is small
its houses built like temples
The rare stranger I let pass with lowered
eyes   He also could be you

Nights the last red
wiped from my lips the harbor
blinking out gem by gem how utterly
we've been undressed

You will not come
to the porch at noon will you rustling your wings
or masked as crone or youth
The mouths behind our faces kiss

Kindlings of truth
Risen from the dawn mist
some wriggling silver in a tern's beak scrawls
joyous memoranda onto things

TODAY I have your letter from the South
where as a child I   but of course you know
Three times I've read it at my attic window
A city named for palms half mummy and half myth
pools flashing talking birds the world of my
first vision of you Psyche   Though it's May

that could be frost upon the apple trees
silvery plump as sponges above the pale
arm of the Sound and the pane is chill to feel
I live now by the seasons burn and freeze
far from that world where nothing changed or died
unless to be reborn on the next tide

You daylong in the saddles of foaming opal
ride   I am glad   Come dusk lime juice and gin
deepen the sunset under your salt skin
I've tasted that side of the apple
A city named for palms half desert and half dream
its dry gold settles on my mouth   I bloom

Where nothing died   Breaking on us like waves
the bougainvillea bloomed fell bloomed again
The new sea wall rose from the hurricane
and no less staunchly from the old freed slave's
ashes each night her grandchild climbed the stairs
to twitch white gauze across the stinging stars

City half dream half desert where at dawn
the sprinkler dervish whirled and all was crystalline
within each house half brothel and half shrine
up from the mirror tabletop had flown
by noon the shadow of each plate each spoon to float
in light that warbled on the ceiling   Wait

ALICE has entered talking

Any mirage if seen from a remote stand
point is refreshing   Yes but dust and heat
lie at its heart   Poor Psyche you forget
That was a cruel impossible wonderland

The very sidewalks suffered   Ours that used
to lead can you remember to the beach
I felt it knew and waited for us each
morning to trot its length in teardrop punctured shoes

when in fact the poor dumb thing lay I now know
under a dark spell cast from quite another
quarter the shadow of a towering mother
smooth as stone and thousandbreasted though

her milk was watery scant so much for love
false like everything in that whole world
However   This shadow that a royal palm hurled
onto the sidewalk from ten yards above

day night rustling and wrestling never shattered
except to mend back forth or lost its grip
the batwing offspring of her ladyship
Our orchid stucco house looked on greenshuttered

stoic   But the sidewalk suffered most
Like somebody I shall not name it lacked
perspective   It failed absolutely to detect
the root of all that evil   The clues it missed

Nights after a windstorm great yellow paper
dry branches lying on the curb in heaps
like fancy dress don't ask me whose someone who steps
forth and is changed by the harsh moonlight to vapor

the sidewalk could only grit itself and shift
Some mornings respite   A grisaille opaque

as poured concrete   And yet by ten o'clock
the phantom struck again in a first sunshaft

Off to the beach   Us nurse in single file
Those days we'd meet our neighbor veiled and hatted
tanagra leading home out of the sun she hated
a little boy with water wings   We'd smile

then hold our breaths to pass a barricade
of black smells rippling up from the soft hot
brink of the mirage past which sidewalks could not
follow   Ours stood there crumbling then obeyed

a whisper back of it and turned   The sea the loose
unshadowed sand too free white heterodox
ever to be congealed into sidewalks
ours never saw   GIVE ME THE SNAPPED SHOELACE

LIZARDS ANTS SCRAPS OF SILVER FOIL
hoarse green tongues begged from each new crack   No use
The shadow trod it as our nightmares us
Then we moved here where gray skies are the rule

What   Why not simply have cut down the tree
Psyche I can't believe my   Hush   You child
Cut down the   I've got gooseflesh   Feel   I'm chilled
My sister's hyperthyroid eyes fix me

The whites lackluster shot with miniature
red brambles abruptly glitter overspill
down powdered cheeks   Alice can weep at will
How to convey the things I feel for her

She is more strange than Iceland bathed all night
an invalid in sunshine   Lava cliffs
The geyser that erupts the loon that laughs
I move to kiss her but she hums a note

and licks her lips   *Well darling I must fly*
before you read what it does not intend

about yourself and your mysterious friend
say or some weird rivalry that I

may once have harbored though I harbor none
now nor does Gertrude not the tiniest pang
into this long but kindly meant harangue
She nods and leaves the room   And I am here alone

I place the ladder hoist from rung to rung
my pail and cloths into a cupola glassed
entirely with panes some tinted amethyst
it is my task to clean   Up here among

spatterings and reflections wipe as I will
these six horizons still the rain's dry ghost
and my own features haunt the roofs the coast
How does one get to know a landscape well

When did we leave the South   Why do we live indoors
I wonder sweating to the cadence   Even
on sunless days the cupola is an oven
Views blur   This thing we see them through endures

MIDNIGHT   I dream I dream   The slow moon eludes
one stilled cloud   Din of shimmerings   From across the Sound
what may have begun as no more
than a willow's sleepwalking outline quickens detaches
comes to itself in the cupola
panics from pane to pane and then impulsively
surrendering fluttering by now the sixteenfold
wings of the cherubim unclipped by faith or reason
stands there my dream made whole
over whose walls again
a red vine black in moonlight crawls
made habitable   Each cell of the concrete
fills with sweet light   The wave breaks
into tears   Come if it's you   Step down
to where I   Stop   For at your touch the dream

cracks the angel tenses flees

NOON finds me faced by a small troop of furies
They are my senses shrill and ominous
We who were trained they cry *to do your pleasure*
are kept like children   Is this fair to us

Dear ones I say bending to kiss their faces
trust me   One day you'll understand   Meanwhile
suppose we think of things to raise our spirits
and leading the two easiest to beguile

into the kitchen feed them shots of bourbon
Their brother who loves Brahms conceives a wish
for gems from L'Africana played at volumes
that make the dwarf palm shudder in its dish

The pale one with your eyes restively flashing
takes in the dock the ashen Sound the sky
The fingers of the eldest brush my features
But you are smiling she says coldly   *Why*

       STAR or candle being lit
           but to shed itself
           into blackness partly night's
sure that no less golden warm than it
                   is our love
           will have missed the truth by half
       We see according to our lights

       Eros   husband   names distort
           you who have no name
       Peace upon your neophytes
Help me when the christenings shall start
               o my love
           to defend your sleep from them
           and see according to our lights

Ah and should discernment's twin
        tyrants adamant
for their meal of pinks and whites
be who call those various torches in
            help me love
    This is nothing I shall want
    We see according to our lights

When as written you have lapsed
        back into the god
        darts and wings and appetites
what of him the lover all eclipsed
        by sheer love
    Shut my eyes it does no good
    Who will ever put to rights

Psyche, hush. This is me, James.
        Writing lest he think
Of the reasons why he writes—
Boredom, fear, mixed vanities and shames;
            Also love.
    From my phosphorescent ink
    Trickle faint unworldly lights

Down your face. Come, we'll both rest.
        Weeping? You must not.
All our pyrotechnic flights
Miss the sleeper in the pitch-dark breast.
            He is love:
    He is everyone's blind spot.
    We see according to our lights.

"What's that sound? Is it you, dear?"
"Yes. I was just eating something."
"What?"
"I don't know—I mean, an apricot . . ."
"Hadn't you best switch on the light and make sure?"
"No, thank you, Gertrude."
A hurt silence ensued.
"Oh, Psyche!" her sister burst out at length. "Here you you are, sur-
rounded by loving kin, in a house crammed with lovely old things, and

what do you crave but the unfamiliar, the 'transcendental'? I declare, you're turning into the classic New England old maid!"
. . . .

Psyche's hands dropped from her wet, white face. The time had come—except that Time, like Love, wears a mask in this story, whose action requires perhaps thirty-six hours of Spring, perhaps thirty-six Springs of a life—a moment nevertheless had come to take the electric torch and leave her sisters without a word. Later she was to recall a tear-streaked muzzle, the marvelous lashed golds of an iris reflecting her own person backed by ever tinier worlds of moonlight and tossing palms, then, at the center, blackness, a fixed point, a spindle on which everything had begun to turn. Piercing her to the brain.

Spelt out in brutal prose, all had been plain.

RAIN   Evening   The drive in   My sisters' gold sedan's
   eyes have gone dim and dark   windows are sealed
     For vision's sake two wipers wield
   the automatic coquetry of fans

In the next car young Eros and his sweetheart sit
   fire and saltwater still from their embrace
     Grief plays upon his sated face
   Her mask of tears does not exactly fit

The love goddess his mother overflows a screen
   sixty feet wide or seems to   Who can plumb
     those motes of rose and platinum
   At once they melt back into the machine

throbbing dry and dispassionate beyond our ken
   to spool her home whose beauty flabbergasts
     The nervous systems of her guests
   drink and drink the sparkling staleness in

Now in her element steam she looms up from a bath
   The hero's breastplate mirrors her red lips
     It burns and clouds   As waterdrops
   course down the monumental cheeks of both

they kiss   My sisters turn on me from either side
   shrieking with glee under the rainlight mask
     fondle and pinch in mean burlesque
of things my angel you and I once tried

In no time he alone is left of a proud corps
   That dustcloud hides triumphant fleeing Huns
     Lips parched by a montage of suns
he cannot taste our latter night's downpour

while she by now my sisters fatten upon fact
   is on location in Djakarta where
     tomorrow's sun illumines her
emoting in strange arms   It's all an act

Eros are you like her so false a naked glance
   turns you into that slackjawed fleshproud youth
     driving away   Was he your truth
Is it too late to study ignorance

These fictive lives these loves of the comedian
   so like so unlike ours which hurt and heal
     are what the gods know   You can feel
lust and fulfillment Eros no more than

ocean its salt depths or uranium its hot
   disintegrative force or I our fable
     My interest like the rain grown feeble
a film of sorrow on my eyes they shut

I may already be part god   Asleep awake
   some afterglow as of a buried heaven
     keeps flickering through me   I may even
learn to love it Eros for your sake

MORNING   The task is done   When my sisters wake
they will look once more upon pale water and clear sky
a fair far brow of land
with its fillet of Greek trees oak apple willow
and here below in the foreground
across a street finished down to the last detail

a red clapboard temple   The neat outlines
it's a warehouse really have been filled with colors
dull red flaking walls   white trim
and pediment   tar roof patched black on black
Greek colors   An effect I hope
not too much spoiled by a big yellow legend
BOAT WORKS on the roof which seagulls helicopters
the highup living and the happy dead
are in a position to read
Outside indeed a boat lies covered with tarpaulin
Old headlines mend a missing pane   The warehouse
seems but in the time it takes to say *abandoned*
a face male old molepale in sun
though blinded by the mullion's shadow
has floated to an eerie scale the rising
wind flutes out of the oaken depths
I look away   When I look back
the panic's over   It is afternoon
Now the window reflects my sisters' white
mock Ionic portico and me emerging
blinking   Too bright to bear or turn from
spring's first real sun burns on the numb blue Sound
Beyond the warehouse past the round GULF sign
whose warning it ignores a baby dock has waded
The small waves stretch their necks gulls veer and scold
I walk the length of our Greek Revival village
from library to old blind lighthouse
Like one entranced who talks as awake she cannot
a potpourri of dead chalkpetal dialects
dead anyhow all winter
lips caulked with faded pollen and dust of cloves
I find that I can break the cipher
come to light along certain humming branches
make out not only *apple blossom* and *sun*
but perfectly the dance of darker undertones
on pavement or white wall   It is this dance I know
that cracks the pavement   I do know
Finally I reach a garden where I am to uproot
the last parsnips for my sisters' dinner
Not parsnips mastodons   But this year's greens
already frill them and they pull easily

217

from the soft ground   Two of the finest
are tightly interlocked have grown that way   They lie
united in the grave of sunny air
as in their breathing living dark
I look at them a long while
mealy and soiled in one another's arms
and blind full to the ivory marrow
with tender blindness   Then I bury them
once more in memory of us
Back home   Gold skies   My basket full
Lifting it indoors I turn   The little dock
It is out there still on stilts in freezing water
It must know by now
that no one is coming after it that it must wait
for morning for next week for summer
by which time it will have silvered and splintered
and the whitewinged boats and the bridegroom's burning sandals
will come too late   It's dark   It's dinner time
Light the lamp my sisters call from where they eat
There follows a hushed preening and straining
wallpaper horsehair glass wood pewter glue
Now is their moment when all else goes black
and what is there but substance to turn to
Sister the lamp   The round
moon mallet has risen and struck   Of the warehouse pulverized
one faintest blueprint glimmers by which to build it
on the same spot tomorrow somehow right
Light your lamp Psyche dear
My hand is on the switch   I have done this
faithfully each night since the first
Tonight I think will not be different
Then soft light lights the room the furniture
a blush invades even the dropped lid
yes and I am here alone
I and my flesh and blood

Thank you, Psyche. I should think those panes
Were just about as clear as they can be.
It's time I turned my light on. Child, leave me.
Here on the earth we loved alone remains

One shrunken amphitheater, look, to moon
Hugely above. Ranked glintings from within
Hint that a small articulate crowd has been
Gathered for days now, waiting. None too soon,

Whether in lower or in upper case,
Will come the Moment for the metal of each
To sally forth—once more into the breach!
Beyond it, glory lies, a virgin space

Acrackle in white hunger for the word.
We've seen what comes next. There is no pure deed.
A black-and-red enchanter, a deep-dyed
Coil of—No matter. One falls back, soiled, blurred.

And on the page, of course, black only. Damned
If I don't tire of the dark view of things.
I think of your "Greek colors" and it rings
A sweet bell. Time to live! Haven't I dimmed

That portion of the ribbon—whose red glows
Bright with disuse—sufficiently for a bit?
Tomorrow mayn't I start to pay my debt,
In wine, in heart's blood, to la vie en rose?

This evening it will do to be alone,
Here, with your girlish figures: parsnip, Eros,
Shadow, blossom, windowpane. The warehouse.
The lamp I smell in every other line.

Do you smell mine? From its rubbed brass a moth
Hurtles in motes and tatters of itself
—Be careful, tiny sister, drabbest sylph!—
Against the hot glare, the consuming myth,

Drops, and is still. My hands move. An intense,
Slow-paced, erratic dance goes on below.
I have received from whom I do not know
These letters. Show me, light, if they make sense.

DAYS OF 1964

Houses, an embassy, the hospital,
Our neighborhood sun-cured if trembling still
In pools of the night's rain . . .
Across the street that led to the center of town
A steep hill kept one company part way
Or could be climbed in twenty minutes
For some literally breathtaking views,
Framed by umbrella pines, of city and sea.
Underfoot, cyclamen, autumn crocus grew
Spangled as with fine sweat among the relics
Of good times had by all. If not Olympus,
An out-of-earshot, year-round hillside revel.

I brought home flowers from my climbs.
Kyria Kleo who cleans for us
Put them in water, sighing *Virgin, Virgin*.
Her legs hurt. She wore brown, was fat, past fifty,
And looked like a Palmyra matron
Copied in lard and horsehair. How she loved
You, me, loved us all, the bird, the cat!
I think now she *was* love. She sighed and glistened
All day with it, or pain, or both.
(We did not notably communicate.)
She lived nearby with her pious mother
And wastrel son. She called me her real son.

I paid her generously, I dare say.
Love makes one generous. Look at us. We'd known
Each other so briefly that instead of sleeping
We lay whole nights, open, in the lamplight,
And gazed, or traded stories.

One hour comes back—you gasping in my arms
With love, or laughter, or both,
I having just remembered and told you
What I'd looked up to see on my way downtown at noon:

Poor old Kleo, her aching legs,
Trudging into the pines. I called,
Called three times before she turned.
Above a tight, skyblue sweater, her face
Was painted. Yes. Her face was painted
Clown-white, white of the moon by daylight,
Lidded with pearl, mouth a poinsettia leaf,
Eat me, pay me—the erotic mask
Worn the world over by illusion
To weddings of itself and simple need.

Startled mute, we had stared—was love illusion?—
And gone our ways. Next, I was crossing a square
In which a moveable outdoor market's
Vegetables, chickens, pottery kept materializing
Through a dream-press of hagglers each at heart
Leery lest he be taken, plucked,
The bird, the flower of that November mildness,
Self lost up soft clay paths, or found, foothold,
Where the bud throbs awake
The better to be nipped, self on its knees in mud—
Here I stopped cold, for both our sakes;

And calmer on my way home bought us fruit.

Forgive me if you read this. (And may Kyria Kleo,
Should someone ever put it into Greek
And read it aloud to her, forgive me, too.)
I had gone so long without loving,
I hardly knew what I was thinking.

Where I hid my face, your touch, quick, merciful,
Blindfolded me. A god breathed from my lips.
If that was illusion, I wanted it to last long;
To dwell, for its daily pittance, with us there,
Cleaning and watering, sighing with love or pain.
I hoped it would climb when it needed to the heights
Even of degradation, as I for one
Seemed, those days, to be always climbing

Into a world of wild
Flowers, feasting, tears—or was I falling, legs
Buckling, heights, depths,
Into a pool of each night's rain?
But you were everywhere beside me, masked,
As who was not, in laughter, pain, and love.

THE FIRE SCREEN

(1969)

For David Jackson

L O R E L E I

The stones of kin and friend
Stretch off into a trembling, sweatlike haze.

They may not after all be stepping-stones
But you have followed them. Each strands you, then

Does not. Not yet. Not here.
Is it a crossing? Is there no way back?

Soft gleams lap the base of the one behind you
On which a black girl sings and combs her hair.

It's she who some day (when your stone is in place)
Will see that much further into the golden vagueness

Forever about to clear. Love with his chisel
Deepens the lines begun upon your face.

THE FRIEND OF THE FOURTH DECADE

When I returned with drinks and nuts my friend
Had moved to the window seat, back to the view.

The clear central pane around which ran
Smaller ones stained yellow, crimson, blue,

Framed our country's madly whipping flag,
Its white pole above roofs, the sea beyond.

That it was time for the flag to be lowered shed
Light on my friend's tactful disinvolvement—

Or did he feel as chastening somehow
Those angry little stripes upon his shoulders?

A huge red sun flowed positively through
Him in spots, glazing, obscuring his person

To that of Anyman with ears aglow,
On a black cushion, gazing inward, mute.

After dinner he said, "I'm tired of understanding
The light in people's eyes, the smells, the food.

(By the way, those veal birds were delicious.
They're out of Fannie Farmer? I thought so.)

Tired of understanding what I hear,
The tones, the overtones; of knowing

Just what clammy twitchings thrive
Under such cold flat stones

As We-are-profoundly-honored-to-have-with-us
Or This-street-has-been-torn-up-for-your-convenience.

As for what I catch myself saying,
Don't believe me! I *despise* Thoreau.

I mean to learn, in the language of where I am going,
Barely enough to ask for food and love.

Listen," he went on. "I have this friend—
What's that face for? Did you think I had only one?

You are my oldest friend, remember. Well:
Karlheinrich collects stamps. I now spend mornings

With a bowl of water and my postcard box.
Cards from all over. God! Those were the years

I never used to throw out anything.
Each card then soaks five minutes while its ink

Turns to exactly the slow formal swirls
Through which a phoenix flies on Chinese silk.

These leave the water darker but still clear,
The text unreadable. It's true!

Cards from my mother, my great-uncle, you!
And the used waters deepen the sea's blue.

I cannot tell you what this does to me.
Scene upon scene's immersion and emergence

Rinsed of the word. The Golden Gate, Moroccan
Dancing boys, the Alps from Interlaken,

Fuji, the Andes, Titian's Venus, two
Mandrills from the Cincinnati zoo—

All *that* survives the flood, as does a lighter
Heart than I have had in many a day.

Salt lick big as a fist, heart, hoard
Of self one grew up prizing above rubies—

To feel it even by a grain dissolved,
Absolved I mean, recipient with writer,

By water holy from the tap, by air that dries,
Of having cared and having ceased to care . . ."

I nodded and listened, envious. When my friend
Had gone where he was going, I tried it, too.

The stamp slid off, of course, and the ink woke.
I watched my mother's *Dearest Son* unfurl

In blue ornate brief plungings-up:
Almost a wild iris taking shape.

I heard oblivion's thin siren singing,
And bore it bravely. At the hour's end

I had my answer. Chances are it was
Some simple matter of what ink she used,

And yet her message remained legible,
The memories it stirred did not elude me.

I put my postcards back upon the shelf.
Certain things die only with oneself.

"You should see Muhammed's taxi," wrote my friend.
"Pure junkyard Bauhaus, angular, dented white,

It trails a wedding veil of squawking dust.
Each ride is worth your life—except I'm just

Not afraid. I'm not.
Those chiefly who discern us have the juju

To take our lives. Bouncing beside Muhammed,
I smile and smoke, am indestructible.

Or else I just can't picture dying
On foreign soil. These years are years of grace.

The way I feel towards home is . . . dim.
Don't worry, I'll go back. Honeymoons end.

Nor does the just man cheat his native earth
Of its inalienable right to cover him."

Finally a dung-and-emerald oasis,
No place I knew of. "Here," he wrote on the back,

"Individual and type are one.
Do as I please, I *am* the simpleton

Whose last exploit is to have been exploited
Neck and crop. In the usual bazaar,

Darker, more crisscrossed than a beggar's palm,
Smell of money draws them after me,

I answer to whatever name they call,
Drink the sweet black condescending dregs,

Try on their hungers like a shirt of flame
(Well, a sports shirt of flame) whereby I've been

Picked clean, reborn each day increasingly
Conspicuous, increasingly unseen."

Behind a door marked DANGER
(This is a dream I have about my friend)

Swaddlings of his whole civilization,
Prayers, accounts, long priceless scroll,

Whip, hawk, prow, queen, down to some last
Lost comedy, all that fine writing

Rigid with rains and suns,
Are being gingerly unwound.

There. Now the mirror. Feel the patient's heart
Pounding—oh please, this once—

Till nothing moves but to a drum.
See his eyes darken in bewilderment—

No, in joy—and his lips part
To greet the perfect stranger.

16.IX.65

for Vassilis and Mimi

Summer's last half moon waning high
Dims and curdles. Up before the bees
On our friend's birthday, we have left him
To wake in their floating maze.

Light downward strokes of yellow, green, and rust
Render the almond grove. Trunk after trunk
Tries to get right, in charcoal,
The donkey's artless contrapposto.

Sunrise. On the beach
Two turkey gentlemen, heads shaven blue
Above dry silk kimonos sashed with swords,
Treat us to a Kabuki interlude.

The tiny fish risen excitedly
Through absolute transparence
Lie in the boat, gasping and fanning themselves
As if the day were warmer than the sea.

Cut up for bait, our deadest ones
Reappear live, by magic, on the hook.
Never anything big or gaudy—
Line after spangled line of light, light verse.

A radio is playing "Mack the Knife."
The morning's catch fills one straw hat.
Years since I'd fished. Who knows when in this life
Another chance will come?

Between our toes unused to sandals
Each step home strikes its match.
And now, with evening's four and twenty candles
Lit among stars, waves, pines

To animate our friend's face, all our faces
About a round, sweet loaf,
Mavríli brays. We take him some,
Return with honey on our drunken feet.

Unjeweled in black as ever comedienne
Of mourning if not silent star of chic,
You drift, September nightwind at your back,
The half block from your flat to the Bon Goût,
Collapse, order a black
Espresso and my ouzo in that Greek
Reserved for waiters, crane to see who's who
Without removing your dark glasses, then,
Too audibly: "Eh, Jimmy, qui sont ces deux strange men?"

Curiosity long since killed the cat
Inside you. Sweet good nature, lack of guile,
These are your self-admitted foibles, no?
My countrymen, the pair in question, get
Up, glance our way, and go,
And we agree it will not be worthwhile
To think of funny nicknames for them yet,
Such as Le Turc, The Missing Diplomat,
Justine, The Nun, The Nut—ah now, speaking of that,

I'm calling *you* henceforth The Lunatic.
Today at 4 a.m. in a snack bar
You were discovered eating, if you please,
Fried squid; alone. Aleko stood aghast.
"Sit down, try some of these,"
You said and gave your shrug, as when, the car
Door shutting on your thumb, a faint sigh passed
Uninterpreted till Frederick
At table glimpsed your bloodstained Kleenex and was sick.

Sapphó has been to your new flat, she *says*.
Tony, who staggered there with the Empire
Mirror you wanted from his shop, tells how
You had him prop it in a chair and leave
That instant. Really now!
Let's plan a tiny housewarming. "My dear,
Impossible with L'Eternel Convive."

Tall, gleaming, it could sit for years, I guess,
Drinking the cool black teas of your appearances.

Not that you're much at home this season. By
Ten you are being driven to the shore—
A madness known as Maria's Gardening Phase.
I went along once, watched you prune, transplant,
Nails ragged, in a daze
Of bliss. A whitewashed cube with tout confort
You'd built but would not furnish. "Bah, one can't
Spend day and night in Eden. Chairs, beds—why?
Dormir, d'ailleurs, this far from the Bon Goût? I'd die!"

In smarter weeds than Eve's (Chanel, last year's)
You kneel to beds of color and young vines.
The chauffeur lounges smoking in the shade . . .
Before you know it, sunset. Brass-white, pink-
Blue wallowings. Dismayed
You recollect a world in which one dines,
Plays cards, endures old ladies, has to think.
The motor roars. You've locked up trowel and shears.
The whole revived small headland lurches, disappears

To float pale black all night against the sea,
A past your jasmines for the present grow
Dizzyingly from. About what went before
Or lies beneath, how little one can glean.
Girlhood, marriage, the war . . .
I'd like once (not now, here comes Giulio)
Really to hear—I mean—I didn't mean—
You paint a smiling mouth to answer me:
"Since when does L'Enfant care for archaeology?"

"Some people are not charmed. I'm among those,"
Sapphó said, livid. "Fond of one? Pure myth.
Fond of her chauffeur—period. I refuse
Flatly to see her." As for me, I've come
To take you for the muse
Of my off-days, and tell you so herewith
If only to make you smile, shrug, run a comb
Through foam-grayed hair the wind from Egypt blows
Across a brow of faint lines powdered tuberose.

MORE ENTERPRISE

A sideways flicker, half headshake of doubt—
Meaning, confusingly, assent—fills out
The scant wardrobe of gesture I still use.
It clings by habit now. The old strait swank
I came in struts the town on local heirs.
Koula's nephew has the suit she shrank,
Andreas coveted my Roman shoes . . .
Into the grave I'll wear that Yes of theirs.

KOSTAS TYMPAKIANÁKIS

Sit, friend. We'll be drinking and I'll tell you why.
Today I went to Customs to identify
My brother—it was him, all right, in spite of both
Feet missing from beneath his Army overcoat.

He was a handsome devil twice the size of me.
We're all good-looking in my family.
If you saw that brother, or what's left of him,
You'd understand at once the kind of man he'd been.

I have other brothers, one whose face I broke
In a family quarrel, and that's no joke:
I'm small but strong, when I get mad I fight.
Seven hundred vines of his were mine by right

And still are—fine! He's welcome to them.
I'm twenty-two. It's someone else's turn to dream.
I liked our school and teacher till they made me stop
And earn my living in a welder's shop.

Cousins and friends were learning jokes and games
At the Kafeneíon behind steamed-up panes.
I worked without a mask in a cold rain of sparks
That fell on you and burned—look, you can still see marks.

The German officer stubbed his *puro* out
On my mother's nipples but her mouth stayed shut.
She lived to bear me with one foot in the grave
And they never found my father in his mountain cave.

He died last year at eighty. To his funeral
Came a NATO Captain and an English General.
Our name is known around Herakleion
In all the hill towns, just ask anyone.

Outside our village up above Knossós
A railed-in plot of cypresses belongs to us,

238

Where we'll put my brother, and if there's room
One day I'll lie beside him till the crack of doom.

But I'd rather travel to a far-off land,
Though I never shall, and settle, do you understand?
The trouble here is not with sun and soil
So much as meanness in the human soul.

I worked a time in Germany, I saw a whore
Smile at me from inside her little lighted door.
She didn't want my money, she was kind and clean
With mirrors we submerged in like a submarine.

The girl I loved left me for a Rhodiot.
I should be broken-hearted but it's strange, I'm not.
Take me with you when you sail next week,
You'll see a different cosmos through the eyes of a Greek.

Or write my story down for people. Use my name.
And may it bring you all the wealth and fame
It hasn't brought its bearer. Here, let's drink our wine!
Who could have imagined such a life as mine?

OUZO FOR ROBIN

Dread of an impending umptieth
Birthday thinning blood to water, clear
Spirits to this opal-tinted white—
Uncle, the confusion unto death!

Last night's hurled glass. On the wall a mark
Explored by sunlight inching blindly
Forth from the tavern onto tree-tarred
Heights of gilt and moleskin, now gone dark.

Thorn needle launched in spinning grooves' loud
Black. A salt spray, a drenching music.
Each dance done, wet hawklike features cling
To one more tumblerful of numb cloud.

Joy as part of dread, rancor as part.
Lamplit swaying rafters. Later, stars.
Case presented, point by brilliant point,
Against the uncounselable heart.

Ground trampled hard. Again. The treasure
Buried. Rancor. Joy. Tonight's blank grin.
Threshold where the woken cherub shrieks
To stop it, stamping with displeasure.

TO MY GREEK

Dear nut
Uncrackable by nuance or debate,
Eat with your fingers, wear your bloomers to bed,

Under my skin stay nude. Let past and future

Perish upon our lips, ocean inherit
Those paper millions. Let there be no word
For justice, grief, convention; *you* be convention—
Goods, bads, kaló-kakó, cockatoo-raucous

Coastline of white printless coves

Already strewn with offbeat echolalia.
Forbidden   Salt   Kiss   Wardrobe   Foot   Cloud   Peach
—Name it, my chin drips sugar. Radiant dumbbell, each

Noon's menus and small talk leave you

Likelier, each sunset yawned away,
Hair in eyes, head bent above the strummed
Lexicon, gets by heart about to fail
This or that novel mode of being together

Without conjunctions. Still

I fear for us. Nights fall
We toss through blindly, drenched in her appraising
Glare, the sibyl I turn to

When all else fails me, when you do—

The mother tongue!
Her least slip a mirror triptych glosses,
Her automation and my mind are one.
Ancient in fishscale silver-blue,

What can she make of you? Her cocktail sweats

With reason: speech will rise from it,
Quite beyond your comprehension rise
Like blood to a slapped face, stingingly apt

If unrepeatable, tones one forgets

Even as one is changed for life by them,
Veins branching a cold coral,
Common sense veering into common scenes,
Tears, incoherent artifice,

Altar upset, cut glass and opaline

Schools ricocheting through the loud cave
Where lie my Latin's rusted treasure,
The bones, picked clean, of my Italian,

Where some blue morning also she may damn

Well find her windpipe slit with that same rainbow
Edge a mere weekend with you gives
To books, to living (anything to forego
That final drunken prophecy whereby,

Lacking her blessing, you my siren grow

Stout, serviceable, gray.
A fishwife shawled in fourth-hand idiom
Spouting my views to earth and heaven)—Oh,

Having chosen the way of little knowledge,

Trusted each to use the other
Kindly except in moments of gross need,
Come put the verb-wheel down
And kiss my mouth despite the foot in it.

Let schoolboys brave her shallows. Sheer

Lilting azure float them well above
Those depths the surfacer
Lives, when he does, alone to sound and sound.

The barest word be what I say in you.

THE ENVOYS

The scurrier of the courtyard
Forth from whitewashed cranny
Behind the trumpet vine into lamplight
Frozen awaits your swooping hand.

It holds him gently, humorously.
The gullet pulses. The eye fixes on nothing.
Released, he darts from sight.
A smaller one emerges: Me! Now me!

Today you entered joyous. Not a joke.
There, patient on our very doorstep—
One moment. Had I thread?

You knotted the frail harness, spoke,
Revolved. Eureka! Round your head
Whirred a living emerald satellite.

Times, there may be some initial misunderstanding.
Phaedra, extracted from your jacket lining,
Flung herself like a bird against the glass—
Who that same night lay on your heart and purred.

The total experience depending, as it does,
Upon modulation into a brighter key
Of terror we survive to play,
I too have deeply feared.

Teach me, lizard, kitten, scarabee—
Gemmed coffer opening on the dram
Of everlasting life he represents,

His brittle pharoahs in the vale of Hence
Will hear who you are, who I am,
And how you bound him close and set him free.

"LIGHT OF THE STREET, DARKNESS OF YOUR OWN HOUSE"

Fused wires of wit, benighted attic
Whose owl, by day unseeing, glares
Down now into haloed vacancy
There precisely where the street has given

Way to some original crooked and narrow
Cascade of refuse, cactus, rock
The struggler upward must negotiate

To get beyond those final hovels clustered
Beneath their final bulb condemned
To hang revealing *nothing* till daybreak
When it can lose itself in you,

You woken smoking, reds and greens, godsped

Along a six-lane boulevard's hard ease,
Sun of my life in your dumb horses' power
Shining drunk, the siren, the migraine,
Pigeon-throat stains, fleet bodies, love oh love—

The street, if it ends at all, ends here.
This figure watching falls asleep,
On hands and knees continues the ascent

Into ignorance forever steeper
Hooting starless until a twitch of limbs
Betrays your lodging I am dreaming yet
From the windows, from the yawning door

Beams of the first unquenchable luster pour.

. . . shrinking to enter, did. Your heart
Was large—you'd often told me—large but light,
Ant palace, tubercular coral sponge amazed
With passages, quite weightless in your breast.
(Or did my entrance weigh? You never said.)
In sunlit outer galleries I pondered
Names, dates, political slogans, lyrics,
Football scores, obscenities too, scrawled
Everywhere dense as lace. How alike we were!
More than pleased, I penetrated further.
Strung haphazard now through the red gloom
Were little, doorless, crudely lighted chambers:
Four waxen giants at supper; the late king;
A dust-furred dog; a whore mottled with cold,
Legs in air; your motorbike; a friend,
Glass raised despite the bandage round his head,
His eyes' false shine. What had happened to them all?
Yet other cells appeared empty but lit,
Or darkly, unimaginably tenanted.
From one, a word sobbed over, "Waste . . . the waste . . ."
Where was the terrace, the transparency
So striking far away? In my fall I struck
An iron surface (so! your heart was heavy)
Hot through clothing. Snatched myself erect.
Beneath, great valves were gasping, wheezing. What
If all you knew of me were down there, leaking
Fluids at once abubble, pierced by fierce
Impulsions of unfeeling, life, limb turning
To burning cubes, to devil's dice, to ash—
What if my effigy were down there? What,
Dear god, if it were not!
If it were nowhere in your heart!
Here I turned back. Of the rest I do not speak.
Nor was your heart so cleverly constructed
I needed more than time to get outside—

Time, scorned as I scorned the waiting daylight.
Before resuming my true size, there came
A place in which one could have scratched one's name.
But what rights had I? Didn't your image,
Still unharmed, deep in my own saved skin
Blaze on? You might yet see it, see by it.
Nothing else mattered.

AN ABDICATION

First I looked at water. It was good.
Blue oblongs glinted from afar. From close
I saw it moving, hueless, clear
Down to a point past which nothing was clear
Or moving, and I had to close
My eyes. The water had done little good.

A second day I tried the trees. They stood
In a rich stupor, altogether
Rooted in the poor, the hard, the real.
But then my mind began to reel—
Elsewhere, smoother limbs would grow together.
How should the proffered apple be withstood?

One dusk upon my viewless throne
I realized the housecat's tyrant nature,
Let her features small and grave
Look past me as into their shallow grave.
No animal could keep me from a nature
Which existed to be overthrown.

Man at last, the little that I own
Is not long for this world. My cousin's eye
Lights on a rust-red, featherweight
Crown of thoughts. He seems to wait
For me to lift it from my brow (as I
Now do) and place it smartly on his own.

NIKE

The lie shone in her face before she spoke it.
Moon-battered, cloud-torn peaks, mills, multitudes
Implied. A floating sphere
Her casuist had at most to suck his pen,
Write of *Unrivalled by truth's own*
For it to dawn upon me. Near the gate
A lone iris was panting, purple-tongued.
I thought of my village, of tonight's *Nabucco*
She would attend, according to the lie,
Bemedalled at the royal right elbow. High
Already on entr'acte kümmel, hearing as always
Through her ears the sad waltz of the slaves,
I held my breath in pity for the lie
Which nobody would believe unless I did.
Mines (unexploded from the last one) lent
Drama to its rainbow surface tension.
Noon struck. Far off, a cataract's white thread
Kept measuring the slow drop into the gorge.
I thought of his forge and crutch who hobbled
At her prayer earthward. What he touched bloomed.
Fire-golds, oil-blacks. The pond people
Seemed victims rather, bobbing belly-up,
Of constitutional vulnerability
Than dynamite colluding with a fast buck.
Everywhere soldiers were falling, reassembling,
As we unpacked our picnic, she and I.
No wiser than the ant. Prepared to die
For all we knew. And even at the end,
Faced with a transcript bound in sunset
Of muffled depositions underground,
She offered wine and cookies first. She asked,
Before the eyes were bandaged, the bubble burst
And what she uttered with what I held back
Ran in red spittle down the chin,

Asked why I could not have lived the lie.
Flicking a crumb off, diffident, asked why
I thought my loved ones had been left to dream
Whole nights unbridled in the bed's brass jail
Beneath a ceiling washed by her reflected snows.

FLYING FROM BYZANTIUM

I

The hour has come. I'm heading home.
We take a cab to the airdrome
In time for the last brandy.
I've kept my Kodak handy
To snap the last unfocused Kodachrome.

Our linen's at the laundromat.
What will become of the gray cat
I'd rather not conjecture.
As for my regular lecture
—Kindness to Animals—I'll spare you that.

But a near lightning sheets the brain.
I cannot take your hand for pain.
Your brows knit above lonely
Filling eyes. If only
I thought that I would look in them again!

Crack! Mountain lurches, villas tilt,
Pale green coves right themselves unspilt
But smaller oh and faster,
Pace of the young ringmaster
Whipping to shreds of cloud a world he built.

Now to say something I'll regret—
It's not true, it's not true, and yet—
God save me from more living.
I loved you, I am leaving.
Another world awaits me? I forget.

You, you whose animal I am,
My senses' mage and pentagram,

Look, listen, miles above you
I love you still, I love you . . .
Then get in line to board the long slow tram.

2

Up spoke the man in the moon:
"What does that moan mean?
The plane was part of the plan.
Why gnaw the bone of a boon?"

I said with spleen, "Explain
These nights that tie me in knots,
All drama and no dream,
While you lampoon my pain."

He then: "Lusters are least
Dimmed among the damned.
The point's to live, love,
Not shake your fist at the feast.

So up from your vain divan,
The one on which you wane.
I've shown you how to shine—
Show me the moon in man!"

I rose to an old ruse,
Prepared to sell my soul
If need be. North winds neighed,
A blaze of silver blues

Flooded the scene, no sign
That either heart had been hurt.
The years shone back on yours
Free and immune from mine.

3

The priceless metal bird came down
At last. On either side were harsh
Foothills and an endless marsh.
He did not take the bus to town.

Suns rose and set in crimson dust.
Mountain lion, watersnake—
As if the choice were his to make,
Kneeling there on the earth's crust.

"Mother, I was vain, headstrong,
Help me, I am coming back."
He put his lips along a crack,
Inhaled the vague, compliant song.

"That I may be born again
Lead the black fly to my flesh."
Far off a young scribe turned a fresh
Page, hesitated, dipped his pen.

LAST WORDS

My life, your light green eyes
Have lit on me with joy.
There's nothing I don't know
Or shall not know again,
Over and over again.
It's noon, it's dawn, it's night,
I am the dog that dies
In the deep street of Troy
Tomorrow, long ago—
Part of me dims with pain,
Becomes the stinging flies,
The bent head of the boy.
Part looks into your light
And lives to tell you so.

Into the flame Godmother put her hand,
Lulling the olive boughs.
Lymph welled from them. I too in her strange house
Kindled and smoked and did not understand.

Followed the Cyclopean meal:
Loaves, rice, hens, goats, gallons of sweet red wine.
I mellowed with the men
Who now waxed crackling, philosophical

—For all I knew—but then
Were on their feet, with flashlights, tramping out
In ancient Air Force overcoats
After the small birds roosting roundabout.

Chains glowing strong
Had bound me to her hearth. Photograph time!
A whole boxful explained in pantomime,
One by one. The string

Retied, warm-hearted questioning
Could start, in mime, about my life.
Each offhand white lie gladdened her, good queen
In whose domain the rueful

Dream was fact. Subdued
Came back her hunters. The lone ortolan,
Head lolling from a sideboard out of Oudry,
Would be my very own to breakfast on.

Bedtime. Inconceivable upper room
Ashiver in lamplight.
Bed clean as ice, heavy as ice
Its layers of coarsely woven pink and white

Woken at once to struggle out from. Bitter
Closet reeking welcome. Wind, moon, frost.
Piebald hindquarters of another guest.
Fowl's nervous titter.

Relieved of wine's last warmth, to lie and freeze . . .
Day would break, never fear;
Rime-sparkling courtesies melt into blue air
Like dew. One hour more? Two? Goodbye! Write please!

The road would climb in bracelets toward the pass,
The sun be high but low,
Each olive tree shed its white thawing shadow
On sallow grass,

Myself become the stranger who remembers
Fire, cold, a smile, a smell,
One tiny plucked form on the embers,
Slow claw raised in blessing or farewell.

ANOTHER AUGUST

Pines. The white, ocher-pocked houses. Sky unflawed. Upon so much
former strangeness a calm settles, glaze of custom to be neither shattered
nor shattered by. Home. Home at last.

Years past—blind, tattering
wind, hail, tears—my head was in those clouds
that now are dark pearl in my head.

Open the shutters. Let variation
abandon the swallows one by one.
How many summer dusks were needed
to make that single skimming form!
The very firefly kindles to its type.
Here is each evening's lesson. First
the hour, the setting. Only then
the human being, his white shirtsleeve
chalked among treetrunks, round a waist,
or lifted in an entrance. Look for him.
Be him.

Envoi for S.

Whom you saw mannerless and dull of heart,
Easy to fool, impossible to hurt,
I wore that fiction like a fine white shirt
And asked no favor but to act the part.

REMORA

This life is deep and dense
Beyond all seeing, yet one sees, in spite
Of being littler, a degree or two
Further than those one is attracted to.

Pea-brained, myopic, often brutal,
When chosen they have no defense—
A sucking sore there on the belly's pewter—
And where two go could be one's finer sense.

Who now descends from a machine
Plumed with bubbles, death in his right hand?
Lunge, numbskull! One, two, three worlds boil.
Thanks for the lift. There are other fish in the sea.

Still on occasion as by oversight
One lets be taken clinging fast
In heavenly sunshine to the corpse a slight
Tormented self, live, dapper, black-and-white.

A FEVER

Two nights with her and I have caught the virus.
She leaves—for an hour? for ever? There is no knowing. I rouse
A chattering self. The thermometer quickly allows
It is not the least susceptible of her admirers.

Pull down the blind, crawl back to bed in gloom
Bright points keep being made through, monocle on black
Cord twirling—whose parchment dandy now with a merciless crack
Up and disappears. Delirium.

Where are the chimneys, the traffic? Instead come strange
Horizons of ink, and livid treetops massing raggedly
Beyond the sill like poor whites in a study
Of conditions we must one day seriously try to change.

Enter the moon like a maid in silence unsheeting the waste
Within, of giant toys, toy furniture.
Two button eyes transfix me. A voice blurred and impure
Speaks through lips my own lips have effaced:

"Back so soon? Am I to wish you joy, as usual,
Of a new friend? For myself, not quite the nice
Young thing first given to your gentleness,
These visits are my life, which is otherwise uneventful."

I touch her snarled hair and contrive to answer:
"Dear—" but have forgotten her vary name!—"dear heart,
How do you do? Speak freely, without art.
You have in me a sympathetic listener."

"I have in you nothing. Look at me. I am yours
Merely, as you've been told dozens of times already—
Though you may need reminding now that this season's lady
Deploys her pearl or coral apertures."

"You dolls who talk of broken faith," I say in fun,
"Yield to the first comer, to the twentieth."
But she: "I cannot vouch for others here on earth.
Le coeur n'est point, Seigneur, un don qui se redonne."

"Ah, so we know French? I congratulate—"
"What you know I know. That alone. No deeper thread,
Blacker, tougher, needles this soft head.
Such knowledge is its own forgiveness and my fate."

"Bravo! Asleep in a chest you kept informed of the middle-aged
Me who loves Verdi and Venice, who registers voters?"
"I woke always to music. A wake of waters
Dipped in brass your weakness for the underprivileged.

Look at me! How much do I sleep? Neglect and damage
Aren't dreams. Their dry dews fall. Their webs exhaust.
The point was to be one on whom nothing is lost,
But what is gained by one more random image

Crossed with mine at one more feast of crumbs?
The mirror wrinkles and wears, the drink undoes like a shirt.
Dream stain, the tears, the mendings—they all hurt;
The last, I have heard and believe, entirely consumes.

In time, in time . . ." Her voice dies away, singsong:
"When the mice ate my sugar heart what did you feel . . . ?"
Now only do I look, and see the wound, and kneel
Beside her on the dream's bare boards. A long

Spell seems to pass before I am found in a daze,
Cheek touching floor. From a position so low
Colors passionate but insubstantial fill the window.
Must it begin and end like this always?

My girl has come back as promised from the seashore, young,
Blithe in some latest fashion, and her face
Freshly made up bends down to evening's deep embrace.
I savor the thin paints upon my tongue.

And still at dawn the fire is lit
By whom a cold man hardly cares,
Reflection gliding up the legs of chairs,
Flue choking with the shock of it.

Next a frozen window thaws
In gradual slow stains of field,
Snow fence and birches more or less revealed.
This done, the brightness sheathes its claws.

The worst is over. Now between
His person and that tamed uprush
(Which to recall alone can make him flush)
Habit arranges the fire screen.*

Crewelwork. His mother as a child
Stitched giant birds and flowery trees
To dwarf a house, *her* mother's—see the chimney's
Puff of dull yarn! Still vaguely chilled,

Guessing how even then her eight
Years had foreknown him, nursed him, all,
Sewn his first dress, sung to him, let him fall.
Howled when his face chipped like a plate,

He stands there wondering until red
Infraradiance, wave on wave,
So enters each plume-petal's crazy weave,
Each worsted brick of the homestead,

That once more, deep indoors, blood's drawn,
The tiny needlewoman cries,
And to some faintest creaking shut of eyes
His pleasure and the doll's are one.

---

*Days later. All framework & embroidery rather than any slower looking into things. Fire screen—screen *of* fire. The Valkyrie's baffle, pulsing at trance pitch, godgiven, elemental. Flames masking that cast-iron plaque—"contrecoeur" in French—which backs the hearth with charred Loves & Graces. Some such meaning might have caught, only I didn't wait, I settled for the obvious—by lamplight as it were. Oh well. Our white heats lead us on no less than words do. Both have been devices in their day.

Angrier than my now occasional
Rum-blossom, to adolescence come
Deep buds of pain. The bloodstained butcher-boy
And Laure at the clavier who would not smile
Were sufferers no less than the Sun King
Spots on whose countenance, the theory goes,
Must answer for that August
Of dry electric storms, of leaves'
Incendiary pamphlets fluttering.
History's lesson? What is young and burns,
Complexion of the boy, the star, the age,
Invites disfigurement. Too late
The shepherdess, her peach-bloom criminal,
Was recognized as queen. Too soon
The cleaver glittered and the chord was struck,
And in the dark that mercifully fell
You had arisen, gibbous moon,
Lit by such laws as exile both of us
From the eruptions of a court whose pageants
These deeply-pitted features chronicle.

THE OPERA COMPANY

I

The impresario
Consigned to the pit

Energy, mass. He was prouder
Of effects that called for

The voice like a green branch
Lifted in gales,

The fat, scaled voice aflicker
From a cleft, the soaring,

Glancing fountain-voice, the voice
Of stone that sank;

This afternoon's effulgence,
Last night's crystallizations.

Season after season, swallowtail,
Unborn seal, pearl stomacher,

We flowed through slow red vestibules
To hear the great ones in their prime and ours.

Now if, of a night, our box is empty
And Chinese students fill the impresario's,

His cosmos wheezes into bloom regardless,
The seal outwits the airhole, and the all-star casts

Of polar ice break up, shining and drowning
Unconscionably in the summer sea.

2

The rival sopranos sang on alternate evenings.
The maid of one was sent
To fumigate the prima donna's dressing room
After the other had used it—who retaliated
By praising everything about the first:
Technique, beauty, age.

From the one's throat
Spurted into darkness
Gouts of adamant, a panoramic ramp
Lit and ascended in cold blood.
Those heights attacked, she struck
One ravishing blank attitude
Against the dead composer's starry mind.

The other's eyelids shut,
An autumn-rose hallucination rippled
Over waves, inward. Rock would blush
And seed swell, yes, and rapture flaw itself.
Another season, and the very song
Had forked, had broken
Flowing into clay.

Came the inevitable war. The one
Married a copper magnate and performed
Before the enemy. The other
Opened a ranch for divorcées.

Dependably for either, every night
Tenors had sobbed their hearts out, grates
Fluttering with strips of red and orange paper.
Such fires were fiction? Then explain
These ashes, if you please.

Less and less I rake them. Of the rivals
One is old now, one dead.
And I had never heard before today

The LP on whose cover my two loves
Wonderfully smiling have linked arms.
It's of some Brahms duets cut lord knows when
And issued with regrets for low fidelity.
What is my happiness, my dismay?
Lightly the needle touches my spinning heart,
The voices soar and mix, will not be told apart.

3

After the war
No jewel remained but feeling.
The head held itself high beneath
Instinct red and branchy, torn from depths,
The bleached jaws of the serpent or the cat.
No more tiaras. Joys, humiliations,
Greed's bluewhite choker, guilt beading the brow—
Thus we arrayed
Our women, and were proud.
The actual stones were kept or not, like Bibles,
Never used.
Meanwhile an old pitfall came to light.
When hadn't there been counterfeit
Emotions? But these now
Went undetected at the gala nights,
And "lumps of primal pain"
Were worn by daylight in resorts.
So much so, that many are preferring
To sit dry-eyed through the opera, to climb down
From the shabby rafters, having watched
Merely, and listened.
How beautiful these last performances
That fail to move us! Even as I write
They have broken ground for the new house
Whose boxes will be poured concrete emplacements,
Whose chandelier the roots of a huge tree.
On opening night
I shall be standing with others in the rain

As, one by one, skills, memories,
Prompter, electrician, negro star,
In street clothes, disappear
Through the unmarked stage door, rust-wreathed and massive.
Addio, one or two will say, *leb' wohl,*
And press my hand as if I, not they, were leaving.
Look for us. We have chosen—no—*You chose* . . .
(The point will be to close
With their exact words—only by luck, however,
Reconstructable in dim suspense
Before the curtains part.)

MATINÉES

for David Kalstone

A gray maidservant lets me in
To Mrs. Livingston's box. It's already begun!
The box is full of grown-ups. She sits me down
Beside her. Meanwhile a ravishing din

Swells from below—Scene One
Of *Das Rheingold*. The entire proscenium
Is covered with a rippling azure scrim.
The three sopranos dart hither and yon

On invisible strings. Cold lights
Cling to bare arms, fair tresses. Flat
And natural aglitter like paillettes
Upon the great green sonorous depths float

Until with pulsing wealth the house is filled,
No one believing, everybody thrilled.

Lives of the Great Composers make it sound
Too much like cooking: "Sore beset,
He put his heart's blood into that quintet . . ."
So let us try the figure turned around

As in some Lives of Obscure Listeners:
"The strains of Cimarosa and Mozart
Flowed through his veins, and fed his solitary heart.
Long beyond adolescence [One infers

Your elimination, sweet Champagne
Drunk between acts!] the aria's remote
Control surviving his worst interval,

Tissue of sound and tissue of the brain
Would coalesce, and what the Masters wrote
Itself compose his features sharp and small."

Hilariously Dr. Scherer took the guise
Of a bland smoothshaven Alberich whose age-old
Plan had been to fill my tooth with gold.
Another whiff of laughing gas,

And the understanding was implicit
That we must guard each other, this gold and I,
Against amalgamation by
The elemental pit.

Vague as to what dentist and tooth "stood for,"
One patient dreamer gathered something more.
A voice said in the speech of birds,

"My father having tampered with your mouth,
From now on, metal, music, myth
Will seem to taint its words."

We love the good, said Plato? He was wrong.
We love as well the wicked and the weak.
Flesh hugs its shaved plush. Twenty-four-hour-long
Galas fill the hulk of the Comique.

Flesh knows by now what dishes to avoid,
Tries not to brood on bomb or heart attack.
Anatomy is destiny, said Freud.
Soul is the brilliant hypochondriac.

Soul will cough blood and sing, and softer sing,
Drink poison, breathe her joyous last, a waltz
Rubato from his arms who sobs and stays

Behind, death after death, who fairly melts
Watching her turn from him, restored, to fling
Kisses into the furnace roaring praise.

The fallen cake, the risen price of meat,
Staircase run ten times up and down like scales

(Greek proverb: He who has no brain has feet)—
One's household opera never palls or fails.

The pipes' aubade. Recitatives.—Come back!
—I'm out of pills!—We'd love to!—What?—*Nothing,*
Let me be!—No, no, I'll drink it black . . .
The neighbors' chorus. The quick darkening

In which a prostrate figure must inquire
With every earmark of its being meant
Why God in Heaven harries him/her so.

The love scene (often cut). The potion. The tableau:
Sleepers folded in a magic fire,
Tongues flickering up from humdrum incident.

When Jan Kiepura sang His Handsomeness
Of Mantua those high airs light as lust
Attuned one's bare throat to the dagger-thrust.
Living for them would have been death no less.

Or Lehmann's Marschallin!—heartbreak so shrewd,
So ostrich-plumed, one ached to disengage
Oneself from a last love, at center stage,
To the beloved's dazzled gratitude.

What havoc certain Saturday afternoons
Wrought upon a bright young person's morals
I now leave to the public to condemn.

The point thereafter was to arrange for one's
Own chills and fever, passions and betrayals,
Chiefly in order to make song of them.

You and I, caro, seldom
Risk the real thing any more.
It's all too silly or too solemn.
Enough to know the score

From records or transcription
For our four hands. Old beauties, some
In advanced stages of decomposition,

Float up through the sustaining
Pedal's black and fluid medium.
Days like today

Even recur (wind whistling themes
From *Lulu,* and sun shining
On the rough Sound) when it seems
Kinder to remember than to play.

Dear Mrs. Livingston,
I want to say that I am still in a daze
From yesterday afternoon.
I will treasure the experience always—

My very first Grand Opera! It was very
Thoughtful of you to invite
Me and am so sorry
That I was late, and for my coughing fit.

I play my record of the Overture
Over and over. I pretend
I am still sitting in the theater.

I also wrote a poem which my Mother
Says I should copy out and send.
Ever gratefully, Your little friend . . .

POLA DIVA

after Christian Ayoub

Sensational effects have subtle causes.
Whenever you sang Madame Butterfly
    At the Pera
    Opera
The crowd inhaled the garlic of your high
Flat C's, and therefore pelted you with roses.

Ah how your salad fragrances afloat
One fine day over doldrums canvas blue
    In the Pera
    Opera
Would merge with bosomy undulation to
Defray the steep expenses of each note.

Years later, in the dive where ends our tale,
You loll, mute queen (a lame divan for throne)
    Of the Pera
    Opera,
Whom evening's client, by your breath alone,
Knows to have been the Phanar's nightingale.

THE SUMMER PEOPLE

. . . et l'hiver resterait la saison intellectuelle créatrice.
—MALLARMÉ

On our New England coast was once
A village white and neat
With Greek Revival houses,
Sailboats, a fishing fleet,

Two churches and two liquor stores,
An Inn, a Gourmet Shoppe,
A library, a pharmacy.
Trains passed but did not stop.

Gold Street was rich in neon,
Main Street in rustling trees
Untouched as yet by hurricanes
And the Dutch elm disease.

On Main the summer people
Took deep-rooted ease—
A leaf turned red, to town they'd head.
On Gold lived the Portuguese

Whose forebears had manned whalers.
Two years from the Azores
Saw you with ten gold dollars
Upon these fabled shores.

Feet still pace the whaler's deck
At the Caustic (Me.) Museum.
A small stuffed whale hangs overhead
As in the head a dream.

Slowly the fleet was shrinking.
The good-sized fish were few.
Town meetings closed and opened
With the question what to do.

Each year when manufacturers
Of chemicals and glues
Bid to pollute the harbor
It took longer to refuse.

Said Manuel the grocer,
"Vote for that factory,
And the summer people's houses
Will be up for sale, you'll see.

Our wives take in their laundry.
Our kids, they cut the grass
And baby-sit. The benefit
Comes home to all of us."

Someone else said, "Next winter
You'll miss that Chemical Plant."
Andrew breathed in Nora's ear:
"Go, grasshopper! Go, ant!"

These two were summer neighbors.
They loved without desire.
Both, now pushing fifty,
Had elsewhere played with fire.

Of all the summer people
Who dwelt in pigeonholes,
Old Navy or Young Married,
The Bad Sports, the Good Souls,

These were the Amusing,
The Unconventional ones—
Plus Andrew's Jane (she used a cane
And shook it at his puns)

And Nora's mother Margaret
With her dawn-colored hair,
Her novels laid in Europe
That she wrote in a garden chair.

"Where's Andrew?" Margaret queried
As Nora entered the room.
"Didn't he want to come over?
It seems to be my doom

To spend long lonely evenings.
Don't we *know* anyone?"
"Dozens of people, Mother."
"But none of them are fun!

The summer already seems endless
And it's only the first of July.
My eyes are too weak for reading
And I am too strong to cry.

I wish I weren't a widow,
I wish you weren't divorced—
Oh, by the way, I heard today
About a man named Frost

Who's bought the Baptist church
And means to do it over."
"Mother, he sounds like just the type
I don't need for a lover."

Andrew at the piano
Let the ice in his nightcap melt.
Mendelssohn's augmentations
Were very deeply felt.

Jane cleaned her paintbrushes
With fingers rheumatic and slow.
Their son came back from the movies,
She called a vague hello

But he'd bounded upstairs already,
Jarring three petals loose
From today's bunch of roses
Not dry yet—pink, cream, puce.

A young man spoke to Margaret
At a party: "Don't be bored.
I've read your books, I like your looks"—
Then vanished in the horde.

Her hostess said when questioned,
"Why, that's Interesting Jack Frost.
He's fixing up that eyesore
With no regard for cost.

Don't ask me where he comes from
Or why he settled here.
He's certainly attractive,
To judge by the veneer."

One thing led to another,
And long before summer's end,
Margaret, Nora, Andrew, Jane
Had found them a new friend.

Jack Frost was years older
Than his twenty-year-old face.
He loved four-hand piano
And gladly took the bass,

Loved also bridge but did not play
So well as to offend,
Loved to gossip, loved croquet,
His money loved to spend

On food and drink and flowers,
Loved entertaining most.
The happy few who'd been there knew
Him as a famous host.

The church was now a folly
Cloud-white and palest blue—
Lanterns, stained glass, mirrors,
Polar bear rugs, bamboo,

Armchairs of gleaming buffalo-horn,
The titter of wind chimes,
A white cat, a blue cushion
Stitched with the cat's name, Grimes.

"Proud Grimes, proud loyal kitty,"
Jack said, "I love you best."
Two golden eyes were trimmed to slits,
Gorgeously unimpressed.

Ken the Japanese "houseboy"
(Though silver-haired and frail)
Served many a curious hot hors d'oeuvre
And icy cold cocktail.

The new friends, that first evening,
Sat on till half past two.
"This man," said Andrew on the street,
"Is too good to be true.

One views with faint misgivings
The bounty of the young."
"Speak for yourself," said Nora
Or the Cointreau on her tongue.

"Well, *I* think he's enchanting,"
Said Margaret, "and what's more
In the long run he'll find, for fun,
No one to match us four."

October came too quickly,
The leaves turned red and sere,
Time for the summer people
To pack up and call it a year.

In the mind's mouth summers later
Ken's farewell banquet melts.
Where would Jack spend the winter?
Why, here of course—where else?

"Stay here all winter? Really,
The things some people do!"
"Whither thou goest, Margaret,
To thee I will be true."

"Come see us in the city."
"My lovely Nora, no.
Too full of dull, dull people
And dirty, dirty snow."

"Come see *us* in Barbados."
"Forgive me, dearest Jane.
I've planned a Northern winter."
So they cajoled in vain.

The next days Jack lay drowsing,
Grimes in the bend of his knees.
He woke one dusk to eat a rusk
And smile at the bare trees.

The first huge flakes descended
Hexagonal, unique.
The panes put forth white leafage.
The harbor froze in a week.

The shrieking children skated
Upon its harsh white jewel,
Whose parents stayed indoors and paid
Outrageous bills for fuel.

Great lengths of gnarled crystal
Glittered from porch and eave.
It was, in short, a winter
You had to see to believe.

Whole nights, a tower window
Threw light upon the storm.
"Jack's sure artistic," Manuel said,
"But how does he keep warm?"

Ken climbed the stair one March dusk.
"Dear Jack-san, now am ord,
Dream of my Kyushu virrage
Where nobody catch cord."

"Together, Ken, we'll go there,
But for the moment stay.
What would I do without you?"
Ken bowed and turned away.

Jack stood up. The cat scuttled
Discreetly out of sight.
Jack's eyes were wet. Pride and regret
Burned in his heart all night.

A mild sun rose next morning.
The roofs began to steam
Where snow had melted. Winter
Was ending like a dream.

Alerted and elated
The summer friends came back.
Their exile had been tiresome,
Each now confessed to Jack.

His garden made them welcome;
Ken had spent May on his knees
Among the plots. From Chinese pots
On the church porch small trees

Rose thick with purple blossoms
Pendulous as Turks.
Said Andrew gravely, "I have seen
The fuchsia, and it works."

That summer was the model
For several in a row—
High watermarks of humor
And humankindness, no

Discord at cards, at picnics,
Charades or musicales.
Their faces bright with pleasure might
Not have displeased Frans Hals.

Jane, speaking of pictures,
Had started one of Grimes
Drugged on Jack's lap. Those sessions
Made for the merriest times.

Margaret brought out her gripping
Stories of love and war,
Peking and Nice. They held their peace
Who'd heard them told before.

Nora, one August afternoon,
Burst in with currant fool
Enough for the whole village.
Its last sweet molecule

Eaten, they blushed like truants.
"Shame on us every one,"
Jane sighed, "we've got no fiber."
And Margaret: "Oh, the fun!

Let's stay for Christmas. Andrew,
You can play Santa Claus!"
Jack gave a cry. Into his thigh
The cat had dug its claws.

Jane's canvas, scarred and peeling
Turned up at the village fair
The other day. I'm sad to say
It found a customer.

The Chemical Plant director
Bought it for his wife
To overpaint with symbols
Flat as her palette knife.

They're a perfectly nice couple
So long as you steer clear
Of art and politics and such—
But to resume. That year

Jack's friends did stay for Christmas,
The next year into Lent,
A third year stayed all winter
To their own astonishment.

Logs burned, the sparks flew upward.
The whiteness when they woke
Struck them as of a genius
Positively baroque,

Invention's breast and plumage,
Flights of the midnight Swan . . .
The facts are in Margaret's journal
To be published when she's gone.

I should perhaps have trusted
To dry-eyed prose like hers.
The meter grows misleading,
Given my characters.

For figures in a ballad
Lend themselves to acts
Passionate and simple.
A bride weeps. A tree cracks.

A young king, an old outlaw
Whose temperament inclines
To strife where breakers thunder
Bleeds between the lines.

But I have no such hero,
No fearful deeds—unless
We count their quiet performance
By Time or Tenderness.

These two are the past masters
Of rime, tone, overtone.
They write upon our faces
Until the pen strikes bone.

Time passes softly, scarcely
Felt by me or you.
And then, at an odd moment,
Tenderness passes, too.

That January midday
Jack's head fell to his knee.
Margaret stopped in mid-sentence—
Whatever could it be?

"He's sound asleep," said Nora.
"So clever of him. If
Only I were! Your stories
Bore everybody stiff."

"What can she mean," said Margaret,
"Speaking to me like that?"
"I mean you're gaga, Mother."
"And you, my child, are fat."

Jack murmured in his slumber,
"I didn't sleep a wink
All during last night's blizzard.
Where am I? Where's my drink?"

His eyes flew wide. "I'm sorry,
I'm sick, I have to go."
He took his coat and tottered
Out into windless snow.

The dogwood at the corner,
Unbending in a burst
Of diamond levity, let drop:
Old friend, think! First things first,

Not June in January—
"Be still!" cried Jack, and bit
His stupid tongue. A snowflake stung
Silence back into it.

Ken helped him up the tower stair,
"Rie down, Jack-san, now rest."
He fell among white blankets,
Grimes heavy on his chest.

Margaret went round next morning
And rang. No one replied.
She found Ken sleeping on the stair,
A wineglass at his side.

A white blur sped to meet her—
Was it that ghastly cat?
Grimes spat, crouched, sprang and sank a fang
Into her, just like that!

She screamed. A stern young doctor,
Summoned out of the void,
Dressed her wound, then telephoned
To have the cat destroyed.

Jack flew to the Police Chief,
Called the SPCA,
Despairing thought that Margaret
Herself might save the day.

She kept him standing, coldly
Displayed her bandaged calf.
He spoiled it all by failing
To check a thoughtless laugh.

Two men with gloves were waiting.
They caught Grimes in a sack.
Two good whiffs of ether
And his gold eyes shut on Jack.

That same night, Grimes in ermine
And coronet of ice
Called him by name, cried vengeance,
Twitching his long tail twice.

Jack woke in pitch dark, burning,
Freezing, leapt dry-lipped
From bed, threw clothes on, neither
Packed nor reflected, slipped

Money between pages
Of Ken's dog-eared almanac,
Then on the sleeping village
Forever turned his back.

He must have let a month go by
Before he sent them all
Postcards of some Higher Thing—
The Jungfrau, white and tall.

"Well, that answers our question,"
Said Margaret looking grim.
They dealt with Jack from then on
By never mentioning him.

Languid as convalescents,
Dreading the color green,
They braced themselves for summer's
Inexorable routine.

Andrew at the piano,
Six highballs gone or more,
Played Brahms, his "venerable beads"
Fixed on the flickering score.

Kneeling in her muggy
Boxwood garden Jane

Stopped weeding, tried to rise
But could not move for pain.

She saw her son's tanned fingers
Lowering the blind
Of an attic window.
She did not know his mind.

Croquet and hectic banter
From Margaret's backyard
Broke up her twinges.
"*En*," shrieked Nora, "*garde!*"

"Oh God, this life's so pointless,
So wearing," Margaret said.
"You're telling me," Andrew agreed.
"High time we both were dead."

"It *is*. I have pills—let's take them!"
He looked at her with wit.
"Just try. You know we'd never
Hear the end of it."

Their laughter floated on the dusk.
Ken thought of dropping in,
But his nails were cracked and dirty
And his breath smelled of gin.

"Missed you at Town Meeting
Last night," said Manuel
As Nora fingered honeydews.
"Things didn't go too well.

Fact is, the Plant got voted in.
I call it a downright
Pity you summer people
Didn't care enough to fight."

"Manuel, there have been winters
We stayed here," Nora said.

"That makes us year-round people."
The grocer scratched his head.

"I guess I don't mean season
So much as a point of view."
It made her mad. She'd meant to add,
"And we do care, we *do*,"

But it was too late, she didn't,
Didn't care one bit.
Manuel counted out her change:
". . . *and* ten. Will that be it?"

"Insufferable rudeness!
Of course by now it's clear,"
Said Margaret, laying down her trumps,
"We must all get out of here."

"We go next week," admitted
Jane with a guilty air.
"Old friends in Locust Valley
Keep asking us down there."

"Besides," said Andrew quickly,
"This climate's bothersome.
I may take Jane to Port-of-Spain—
All *my* roads lead to rum."

"So they do. Well, that's lovely,
Leaving us in the lurch,"
Said Nora, "just like what's-his-name
Who had the Baptist church."

"The summer's over," said Margaret.
"But you misunderstood:
I meant this town was ruined.
We must all get out for good."

Ken wrapped some Canton saucers
Like a conspirator,

To be exchanged for credit
At the corner liquor store.

September. Dismal rainstorms
Made everything a blur,
Lashed Margaret into action—
City life for her!

"I'll stay up here," said Nora,
"A month or two. I need
Time to think things over,
Listen to records, read."

She drove home from Caustic
Where Margaret caught her plane.
The windshield streamed in silence,
The wipers thrashed in vain.

October. Early twilights.
To the wharf came a blue
And silver haul of fish too small
For anything but glue.

The boatyard was a boneyard,
Bleached hull, moon-eaten chain.
The empty depot trembled
At the scream of a passing train.

Nora long past midnight
Lay rereading *Emma*,
Unmoved for once by a daughter's
Soon-to-be-solved dilemma.

And late dawns. The first victim
Of Main Street's seventeen
Doomed elms awoke and feebly shook
Its sparrow-tambourine.

In the November mildness
Rose delicate green spears—
Spring flowers Ken had planted.
His small eyes filled with tears:

They were coming up too early!
He sniffed and went indoors.
He dusted all the objects,
Polished the bare floors,

Bathed and oiled his person;
Now put on his best clothes,
Thought up a huge sweet cocktail,
And sipping at it chose

The first words of a letter
He had long meant to write.
But wait, his glass was empty—
A foolish oversight.

Nora heard him coughing.
She stopped her evening stroll
And went to see. With courtesy
Both sinister and droll

Ken bowed low, made her welcome,
Concocted a new drink.
Darkly hilarious he said,
"Rong rife!" and gave a wink.

One didn't need to be Nora
To see that things weren't right.
In his brown silk kimono
Ken sat there high as a kite.

His talk was incoherent:
Jack—his mother's loom—
The weather—his green island—
Flowers he'd not see bloom—

The dead cat—a masked actor—
Ghosts up in the hills . . .
And then those frightful spasms
Followed by small white pills.

Nora thought food might help him
And ran back for a cup
Of homemade soup. He took a sip,
Set down the cup, got up:

"Dear Missy-san, too sorty.
Night-night now. Kissing hand."
This done, Ken headed for the stair,
Though hardly able to stand.

Next day she found him lying
Cold on his bed. "I knew,
I *knew*!" sobbed Nora over the phone.
"But what was there to do?

He wasn't kin or even friend,
Just old and sick, poor dear.
It was his right to take his life,
Not mine to interfere."

"Exactly," said her mother.
"I'll come tomorrow. Jack?
Try the address on Ken's letter.
A wire may bring him back."

It did not. The two ladies
Arranged the funeral,
Then sat at home in silence
Deeper than I can tell.

Jack sent a check weeks later
And wrote them from Tibet
A long sad charming letter,
But friendship's sun had set.

December. "I think sometimes,"
Said Margaret dreamily,
"That Jack was a delusion
Of the whole community.

No reasonable adult
Starts acting like a child.
How else can you explain it?
He had us all beguiled."

Nora looked up. The mirror
Struck her a glancing blow.
Her hair once blonde as summer
Was dull and streaked with snow.

"Oh tell me, Mother, tell me
Where do the years go?
I'm old, my life is ending!"
"Baby, I know, I know."

As soon as they were calmer,
"I also," Margaret said,
"Know what to do about it.
So get up from that bed.

I know a clever fairy
Who puts gold back in hair.
I know of jets to Rio.
It will be summer there."

Come May, Ken's garden blossomed
In memory of him—
Hyacinth, narcissus
White as seraphim.

Jane and Andrew saw it.
They'd driven up to sell

Their house at a tidy profit
To the Head of Personnel.

It had grown so big, so empty.
Their lawn was choked with weeds,
Their son in California
Barefoot, all beard and beads.

They stood among Ken's flowers
Gazing without a word.
Jane put her hand in Andrew's.
The cat in heaven purred.

And then a faint piano
Sounded—from where? They tried
The door, it floated open,
Inviting them inside.

Sitting at the keyboard
In a cloud of brilliant motes
A boy they'd both seen somewhere
Was playing random notes.

He rose as if uncertain
Whether to speak or run.
Jane said, "I know who you are,
You're Joey, Manuel's son,

Who used to cut the grass for us.
Look at you, grown so tall!"
He grinned. "I won a scholarship
At M.I.T. this fall

To study cybernetics
And flute—it's worth a try.
I used to come and talk to Ken.
I miss that little guy."

"One by one, like swallows . . ."
Said Andrew in the gloom

That fell when Joe departed.
"Dear God, look at this room."

Full ashtrays, soft-drink bottles
Told an artless tale
Of adolescent revels.
Tan stacks of ninth-class mail

Lay tumbled helter-skelter.
A chill in the stirred air
Sent Jane outdoors and Andrew
To brave the tower stair.

Moon after moon had faded
The papers on Jack's desk:
Unfinished calculation,
Doodle and arabesque.

One window framed the sunset
Transfiguring Main Street,
Its houses faintly crimson
But upright in defeat.

The other faced the harbor.
Lights of the Chemical Plant
Gloated over water.
"The grasshopper, the ant,"

Breathed Andrew, recollecting
His long ago remark,
Then shut both views behind him
And felt his way down in dark.

BRAVING THE ELEMENTS

(1972)

For my mother

LOG

Then when the flame forked like a sudden path
I gasped and stumbled, and was less.
Density pulsing upward, gauze of ash,
Dear light along the way to nothingness,
What could be made of you but light, and this?

AFTER THE FIRE

Everything changes; nothing does. I am back,
The doorbell rings, my heart leaps out of habit,
But it is only Kleo—how thin, how old!—
Trying to smile, lips chill as the fallen dusk.

She has brought a cake "for tomorrow"
As if tomorrows were still memorable.
We sit down in the freshly-painted hall
Once used for little dinners. (The smoke cleared
On no real damage, yet I'd wanted changes,
Balcony glassed in, electric range,
And wrote to have them made after the fire.)
Now Kleo's eyes begin to stream in earnest—
Tears of joy? Ah, troubles too, I fear.
Her old mother has gone off the deep end.

From their basement window the yiayia, nearly ninety,
Hurls invective at the passing scene,
Tea bags as well, the water bill, an egg
For emphasis. A strange car stops outside?
She cackles *Here's the client! Paint your face,
Putana!* to her daughter moistening
With tears the shirt she irons. Or locks her out
On her return from watering, with tears,
My terrace garden. (I will see tomorrow
The white oleander burst from its pot in the rains.)
Nor is darling Panayióti, Kleo's son,
Immune. Our entire neighborhood now knows
As if they hadn't years before
That he is a *Degenerate!* a *Thieving
Faggot!* just as Kleo is a *Whore!*

I press Kleo's cold hand and wonder
What could the poor yiayia have done
To deserve this terrible gift of hindsight,
These visions that possess her of a past
When Kleo really was a buxom armful

And "Noti" cruised the Naval Hospital,
Slim then, with teased hair. Now he must be forty,
Age at which degeneration takes
Too much of one's time and strength and money.
My eyes brim with past evenings in this hall,
Gravy-spattered cloth, candles minutely
Guttering in the love-blinded gaze.
The walls' original old-fashioned colors,
Cendre de rose, warm flaking ivory—
Colors last seen as by that lover's ghost
Stumbling downstairs wound in a sheet of flame—
Are hidden now forever but not lost
Beneath this quiet sensible light gray.

Kleo goes on. The yiayia's *warm,*
What can it mean? She who sat blanketed
In mid-July now burns all day,
Eats only sugar, having ascertained
Poison in whatever Kleo cooks.
Kill me, there'll be an autopsy,
Putana, matricide, I've seen to that!
I mention my own mother's mother's illness,
Querulous temper, lucid shame.
Kleo says weeping that it's not the same,
There's nothing wrong, according to the doctor,
Just that she's old and merciless. And warm.

Next day I visit them. Red-eyed Kleo
Lets me in. Beyond her, bedclothes disarrayed,
The little leaden oven-rosy witch
Fastens her unrecognizing glare
Onto the lightest line that I can spin.
"It's me, yiayia! Together let us plumb
Depths long dry"—getting no further, though,
Than Panayioti's anaconda arms:

"Ah Monsieur Tzim, bon zour et bon retour!
Excuse mon déshabillé. Toute la nuit
Z'ai décoré l'église pour la fête
Et fait l'amour, le prêtre et moi,

Dans une alcove derrière la Sainte Imaze.
Tiens, z'ai un cadeau pour toi,
Zoli foulard qui me va pas du tout.
Mais prends-le donc, c'est pas volé—
Ze ne suis plus voleur, seulement volaze!"

Huge, powerful, bland, he rolls his eyes and r's.
Glints of copper wreathe his porcelain brow
Like the old-time fuses here, that blow so readily.
I seem to know that crimson robe,
And on his big fat feet—my slippers, ruined.
Still, not to complicate affairs,
Remembering also the gift of thumb-sized garnet
Bruises he clasped round Aleko's throat,
I beam with gratitude. Meanwhile
Other translated objects one by one
Peep from hiding: teapot, towel, transistor.
Upon the sideboard an old me
Scissored from its glossy tavern scene—
I know that bare arm too, flung round my shoulder—
Buckles against a ruby glass ashtray.
(It strikes me now, as happily it did not
The insurance company, that P caused the fire.
Kleo's key borrowed for a rendezvous,
A cigarette left burning . . . Never mind.)
Life like the bandit Somethingopoulos
Gives to others what it takes from us.

Some of those embers can't be handled yet.

I mean to ask whose feast it is today
But the room brightens, the yiayia shrieks my name—
It's Tẓimi! He's returned!
—And with that she returns to human form,
The snuffed-out candle-ends grow tall and shine,
Dead flames encircle us, which cannot harm,
The table's spread, she croons, and I
Am kneeling pressed to her old burning frame.

PIECES OF HISTORY

1

Depressions visible from the air
Even today help you locate Qatum—
Huge red sandbox somewhere at whose heart
Twin-chambered lay the royal pair

How long equipped for a fantastic trek
Back to the sun and moon they had to be.
Time would have undressed them to the teeth,
Sucked their bones but spared their filigree.

I broke in with Daud. Taboos
Were for the old. Harp, harper, palanquin and groom,
The brittle ores of dagger-clasp, of wreath,
Pell-mell, hers, his, theirs, ours—by evening, what was whose?

2

I was only nine when an emotional war,
The Spanish one, streaked with powder, entered our house.
What right had she to arouse me, child that I was?
Yet she tried to. Wars are whores, they have no shame.

And how about the issue of female suffrage,
Dead now, but ripe enough in her heyday to be my mother?
Thinking of her, I peek at your ballot box
And you burn with aversion. Young people are all the same.

These eyes have turned Aunt Tom into a vegetable
And my godfather into sepia and ormolu.
Old women I hardly remember come up to say my name
And kiss me. One day you will love me, even you.

3

Up from wrinkled headlands see her loom
Enlarged by emanations, white as pearl or lime.
The lone surveyor working overtime
Puts away his useless pendulum.

Dream: A letter comes from Miss Thyra Reese
Who drummed the credenda of progress into some of us
And knew by heart "The Chambered Nautilus,"
Asking what have I done with her pince-nez and teeth.

There on the moon, her meaning now one swift
Footprint, a man my age with a glass face
Empty of insight signals back through space
To the beclouded cortex which impelled his drift.

IN MONUMENT VALLEY

One spring twilight, during a lull in the war,
At Shoup's farm south of Troy, I last rode horseback.
Stillnesses were swarming inward from the evening star
Or outward from the buoyant sorrel mare

Who moved as if not displeased by the weight upon her.
Meadows received us, heady with unseen lilac.
Brief, polyphonic lives abounded everywhere.
With one accord we circled the small lake.

Yet here I sit among the crazy shapes things take.
Wasp-waisted to a fault by long abrasion,
The "Three Sisters" howl. "Hell's Gate" yawns wide.
I'm eating something in the cool Hertz car

When the shadow falls. There has come to my door
As to death's this creature stunted, cinder-eyed,
Tottering still half in trust, half in fear of man—
Dear god, a horse. I offer my apple-core

But she is past hunger, she lets it roll in the sand,
And I, I raise the window and drive on.
About the ancient bond between her kind and mine
Little more to speak of can be done.

DAYS OF 1935

Ladder horned against moonlight,
Window hoisted stealthily—
That's what I'd steel myself at night
To see, or sleep to see.

My parents were out partying,
My nurse was old and deaf and slow.
Way off in the servants' wing
Cackled a radio.

On the Lindbergh baby's small
Cold features lay a spell, a swoon.
It seemed entirely plausible
For my turn to come soon,

For a masked and crouching form
Lithe as tiger, light as moth,
To glide towards me, clap a firm
Hand across my mouth,

Then sheer imagination ride
Off with us in its old jalopy,
Trailing bedclothes like a bride
Timorous but happy.

A hundred tenuous dirt roads
Dew spangles, lead to the web's heart.
That whole pale night my captor reads
His brow's unwrinkling chart.

Dawn. A hovel in the treeless
Trembling middle of nowhere,
Hidden from the world by palace
Walls of dust and glare.

A lady out of *Silver Screen*,
Her careful rosebud chewing gum,
Seems to expect us, lets us in,
Nods her platinum

Spit curls deadpan (I will wait
Days to learn what makes her smile)
At a blue enamel plate
Of cold greens I can smell—

But swallow? Never. The man's face
Rivets me, a lightning bolt.
Lean, sallow, lantern-jawed, he lays
Pistol and cartridge belt

Between us on the oilskin (I
Will relive some things he did
Until I die, until I die)
And clears his throat: "Well, Kid,

You've figured out what's happening.
We don't mean to hurt you none
Unless we have to. Everything
Depends on, number one,

How much you're worth to your old man,
And, number two, no more of this—"
Meaning my toothprints on his hand,
Indenture of a kiss.

With which he fell upon the bed
And splendidly began to snore.
"Please, I'm sleepy too," I said.
She pointed to the floor.

The rag rug, a rainbow threadbare,
Was soft as down. For good or bad
I felt her watching from her chair
As no one ever had.

Their names were Floyd and Jean. I guess
They lived in what my parents meant
By sin: unceremoniousness
Or common discontent.

"Gimme—Wait—Hey, watch that gun—
Why don't these dumb matches work—
See you later—Yeah, have fun—
Wise guy—Floozie—Jerk—"

Or else he bragged of bygone glories,
Stores robbed, cars stolen, dolls betrayed,
Escape from two reformatories.
Said Jean, "Wish you'd of stayed."

To me they hardly spoke, just watched
Or gave directions in dumb show.
I nodded back like one bewitched
By a violent glow.

Each morning Floyd went for a ride
To post another penciled note.
Indignation nationwide
Greeted what he wrote.

Each afternoon, brought papers back.
One tabloid's whole front page was spanned
By the headline bold and black:
FIEND ASKS 200 GRAND.

Photographs too. My mother gloved,
Hatted, bepearled, chin deep in fur.
Dad glowering—was it true he loved
Others beside her?

Eerie, speaking likenesses.
One positively heard her mild
Voice temper some slow burn of his,
"Not before the child."

The child. That population map's
Blanknesses and dots were me!
Mine, those swarming eyes and lips,
Centers of industry

Italics under which would say
(And still do now and then, I fear)
Is This Child Alive Today?
Last Hopes Disappear.

Toy ukelele, terrorstruck
Chord, the strings so taut, so few—
Tingling I hugged my pillow. *Pluck,*
Some deep nerve went. I knew

That life was fiction in disguise.
My teeth said, chattering in Morse,
"Are you a healthy wealthy wise
Red-blooded boy? Of course?

Then face the music. Stay. Outwit
Everyone. Captivity
Is beckoning—make a dash for it!
It will set you free."

Sometimes as if I were not there
He put his lips against her neck.
Her head lolled sideways, just like Claire
Coe in *Tehuantepec.*

Then both would send me looks so heaped
With a lazy, scornful mirth,
This was growing up, I hoped,
The first flushed fruits of earth.

One night I woke to hear the room
Filled with crickets—no, bedsprings.
My eyes dilated in the gloom,
My ears made out things.

Jean: The kid, he's still awake . . .
Floyd: Time he learned . . . Oh baby . . . God . . .
Their prone tango, for my sake,
Grew intense and proud.

And one night—pure *Belshazzar's Feast*
When the slave-girl is found out—
She cowered, face a white blaze ("Beast!")
From his royal clout.

Mornings, though, she came and went,
Buffed her nails and plucked her brows.
What had those dark doings meant?
Less than the fresh bruise

Powdered over on her cheek.
I couldn't take my eyes away.
Let hers meet them! Let her speak!
She put down *Photoplay*:

"Do you know any stories, Kid?
Real stories—but not real, I mean.
Not just dumb things people did.
Wouldja tell one to Jean?"

I stared at her—*she* was the child!—
And a tale came back to me.
Bluebeard. At its end she smiled
Half incredulously.

I spun them out all afternoon.
Wunspontime, I said and said . . .
The smile became a dainty yawn
Rose-white and rose-red.

The little mermaid danced on knives,
The beauty slept in her thorn bower.
Who knows but that our very lives
Depend on such an hour?

The fisherman's hut became Versailles
Because he let the dolphin go . . .
Jean's lids have shut. I'm lonely. I
Am pausing on tiptoe

To marvel at the shimmer breath
Inspires along your radii,
Spider lightly running forth
To kiss the simple fly

Asleep. A chance to slip the net,
Wriggle down the dry stream bed,
Now or never! This child cannot.
An iridescent thread

Binds him to her slumber deep
Within a golden haze made plain
Precisely where his fingertip
Writes on the dusty pane

In spit his name, address, age nine
—Which the newspapers and such
Will shortly point to as a fine
Realistic touch.

Grown up, he thinks how S, T, you—
Second childhood's alphabet
Still unmastered, it is true,
Though letters come—have yet

Touched his heart, occasioned words
Not quickened by design alone,
Responses weekly winging towards
Your distance from his own,

Distance that much more complex
For its haunting ritornel:
Things happen to a child who speaks
To strangers, mark it well!

Thinks how you or V—where does
It end, will *any*one have done?—
Taking the wheel (cf. those "Days
Of 1971")

Have driven, till his mother's Grade
A controls took charge, or handsome
Provisions which his father made
Served once again as ransom,

Driven your captive far enough
For the swift needle on the gauge
To stitch with delicate kid stuff
His shoddy middle age.

Here was Floyd. The evening sun
Filled his eyes with funny light.
"Junior, you'll be home real soon."
To Jean, "Tomorrow night."

What was happening? Had my parents
Paid? pulled strings? Or maybe I
Had failed in manners, or appearance?
Must this be goodbye?

I'd hoped I was worth more than crime
Itself, which never paid, could pay.
Worth more than my own father's time
Or mother's negligée

Undone where dim ends barely met,
This being a Depression year . . .
I'd hoped, I guess, that they would let
Floyd and Jean keep me here.

We ate in silence. He would stop
Munching and gaze into the lamp.
She wandered out on the dark stoop.
The night turned chill and damp.

When she came in, she'd caught a bug.
She tossed alone in the iron bed.
Floyd dropped beside me on the rug;
Growled, "Sleep." I disobeyed.

Commenced a wary, mortal heat
Run neck by nose. Small fingers felt,
Sore point of all that wiry meat,
A nipple's tender fault.

Time stopped. His arm somnambulist
Had circled me, warm, salt as blood.
Mine was the future in his fist
To get at if I could,

While his heart beat like a drum
And *Oh baby* faint and hoarse
Echoed from within his dream . . .
The next day Jean was worse

—Or I was. Dawn discovered me
Sweating on my bedroom floor.
Was there no curbing fantasy
When one had a flair?

Came those nights to end the tale.
I shrank to see the money tumble,
All in 20s, from a teal
Blue Studebaker's rumble

Down a slope of starlit brush.
Sensed with anguish the foreseen
Net of G-men, heard the hush
Deepen, then Floyd's voice ("Jean,

Baby, we've been doublecrossed!")
Drowned out by punctual crossfire
That left the pillow hot and creased.
By three o'clock, by four,

They stood in handcuffs where the hunt
Was over among blood-smeared rocks
—Whom I should not again confront
Till from the witness-box

I met their stupid, speechless gaze.
How empty they appeared, how weak
By contrast with my opening phrase
As I began to speak:

"You I adored I now accuse . . ."
Would imagination dare
Follow that sentence like a fuse
Sizzling towards the Chair?

See their bodies raw and swollen
Sagging in a skein of smoke?
The floor was reeling where I'd fallen.
Even my old nurse woke

And took me in her arms. I pressed
My guilty face against the void
Warmed and scented by her breast.
Jean, I whispered, Floyd.

A rainy day. The child is bored.
While Emma bakes he sits, half-grown.
The kitchen dado is of board
Painted like board. Its grain

Shiny buff on cinnamon
Mimics the real, the finer grain.
He watches icing sugar spin
Its thread. He licks in vain

Heavenly flavors from a spoon.
Left in the metallic bowl
Is a twenty-five-watt moon.
Somewhere rings a bell.

Wet walks from the east porch lead
Down levels manicured and rolled
To a small grove where pets are laid
In shallow emerald.

The den lights up. A Sazerac
Helps his father face the *Wall
Street Journal*. Jules the colored (black)
Butler guards the hall.

Tel & Tel executives,
Heads of Cellophane or Tin,
With their animated wives
Are due on the 6:10.

Upstairs in miles of spangled blue
His mother puts her make-up on.
She kisses him sweet dreams, but who—
Floyd and Jean are gone—

Who will he dream of? True to life
He's played them false. A golden haze
Past belief, past disbelief . . .
Well. Those were the days.

MANDALA

"I advise you to meditate upon the Third Eye."
—LETTER FROM T

OK. I see a whirlpool
Yawning at the heart of things.
In grave procession seasons, elements, creatures, kings
Ride the slowly sinking carrousel

From which they will never, not in ten million
Years, nor in any form, return. They are about to merge
With Nothing mirrored as a demiurge
Vaguely Mongolian.

Outside that circus, trivia.
Everyone else must redo his clumsy exercise
Life after life. No wonder the third eye's
Lid grows heavier.

All the same, I am setting my cat
Sights on two or three
More flings here in the dark. A certain ingenuity
Goes into meriting that.

One wants, to plot the boomerang curve
That brings one back,
Beyond the proper coordinates of Have and Lack,
A flair for when to swerve

Off into utter pointlessness—
Issues that burn like babies, furrows of grief and sloth
Sown with sperm, no talent glinting forth
Except for how to dress

At those last brunches on the yacht
While the pearly trough kept pace and the martini pitcher
Sweated and swirled, becoming second nature
—And oh yes, not

To return as a slug or a mayfly, plus one's GI pair
Shortsighted brown, should carry, as I do,
A peasant "eye" of blue
Glass daubed with yellow. Turkish work. So there,

Your point's made, I'm an infidel.
But who needs friends
To remind him that nothing either lasts or ends?
Garrulous as you, dear, time will tell.

18 WEST 11TH STREET

In what at least
Seemed anger the Aquarians in the basement
Had been perfecting a device

For making sense to us
If only briefly and on pain
Of incommunication ever after.

Now look who's here. Our prodigal
Sunset. Just passing through from Isfahan.
Filled by him the glass

Disorients. The swallow-flights
Go word by numbskull word
—Rebellion . . . Pentagon . . . Black Studies—

Crashing into irreality,
Plumage and parasites
Plus who knows what of the reptilian,

Till wit turns on the artificial lights
Or heaven changes. The maid,
Silent, pale as any victim,

Comes in, identifies;
Yet brings new silver, gives rise to the joint,
The presidency's ritual eclipse.

Take. Eat. His body to our lips. The point
Was anger, brother? Love? Dear premises
Vainly exploded, vainly dwelt upon.

Item: the carpet.
Identical bouquets on black, rose-dusted
Face in fifty funeral parlors,

Scentless and shaven, wall-to-wall
Extravagance without variety . . .
That morning's buzzing vacuum be fed

By ash of metropolitan evening's
Smoker inveterate between hot bouts
Of gloating over scrollwork,

The piano (three-legged by then like a thing in a riddle)
Fingered itself provocatively. Tones
Jangling whose tuner slept, moon's camphor mist

On the parterre compounding
Chromatic muddles which the limpid trot
Flew to construe. Up from camellias

Sent them by your great-great-grandfather,
Ghosts in dwarf sateen and miniver
Flitted once more askew

Through *Les Sylphides*. The fire was dead. Each summer,
While onto white keys miles from here
Warm salt chords kept breaking, snapping the strings,

The carpet—its days numbered—
Hatched another generation
Of strong-jawed, light-besotted saboteurs.

A mastermind
Kept track above the mantel. The cold caught,
One birthday in its shallows, racked

The weak frame, glazed with sleet
Overstuffed aunt and walnut uncle. Book
You could not read. Some utterly

Longed-for present meeting other eyes'
Blue arsenal of homemade elegies,
Duds every one. The deed

Diffused. Your breakfast *Mirror* put
Late to bed, a fever
Flashing through the veins of linotype:

NIX ON PEACE BID   PROPHET STONED
FIVE FEARED DEAD IN BOMBED DWELLING
—Bulletin-pocked columns, molten font

Features would rise from, nose for news
Atwitch, atchoo, God bless you!
Brought to your senses (five feared? not one bit)

Who walking home took in
The ruin. The young linden opposite
Shocked leafless. Item: the March dawn.

Shards of a blackened witness still in place.
The charred ice-sculpture garden
Beams fell upon. The cold blue searching beams.

Then all you sought
No longer, B came bearing. An arrangement
In time known simply as That June—

Fat snifter filled with morbidest
Possibly meat-eating flowers,
So hairy-stemmed, red-muscled, not to be pressed.

Pinhead notions underwater, yours,
Quicksilvered them afresh.
You let pass certain telltale prints

Left upon her in the interim
By that winter's person, where he touched her.
Still in her life now, was he, feeling the dim

Projection of your movie on his sheet?
Feeling how you reached past B towards him,
Brothers in grievance? But who grieves!

The night she left ("One day you'll understand")
You stood under the fruitless tree. The streetlight
Cast false green fires about, a tragic

Carpet of shadows of blossoms, shadows of leaves.
You understood. You would not seek rebirth
As a Dalmatian stud or Tiny Tim.

Discolorations from within, dry film
Run backwards, parching, scorching, to consume
Whatever filled you to the brim,

Fierce tongue, black
Fumes massing forth once more on
Waterstilts that fail them. The

Commissioner unswears his oath. Sea serpent
Hoses recoil, the siren drowns in choking
Wind. The crowd has thinned to a coven

Rigorously chosen from so many called. Our
Instant trance. The girl's
Appearance now among us, as foreseen

Naked, frail but fox-eyed, head to toe
(Having passed through the mirror)
Adorned with heavy shreds of ribbon

Sluggish to bleed. She stirs, she moans the name
Adam. And is *gone*. By her own
Broom swept clean, god, stop, behind this

Drunken backdrop of debris, airquake,
Flame in bloom—a pigeon's throat
Lifting, the puddle

Healed. To let:
Cream paint, brown ivy, brickflush. Eye
Of the old journalist unwavering

Through gauze. Forty-odd years gone by.
Toy blocks. Church bells. Original vacancy.
O deepening spring.

ANOTHER APRIL

The panes flash, tremble with your ghostly passage
Through them, an x-ray sheerness billowing, and I have risen
But cannot speak, remembering only that one was meant
To rise and not to speak. Young storm, this house is yours.
Let your eye darken, your rain come, the candle reeling
Deep in what still reflects control itself and me.
Daybreak's great gray rust-veined irises humble and proud
Along your path will have laid their foreheads in the dust.

IN NINE SLEEP VALLEY

1

Trying to read in Nature's book
The pages (canyon forest landslide lake)
Turn as the road does, the stock characters
Come and (marmot mallard moose)

Go too quickly to believe in. Look,
I'm told, but many of the words have wings
Or run to type in small fleet herds
No question of retaining—what's the use!

Coming meanwhile to believe in you,
Fluent and native. Only read aloud
Do the words stay with me, through
Whose roots those flat clear vowels flow

To mirror, surfacing, the things they mean:
Blue heron, mountain, antelope, spruce, cloud.

2

Yesterday's flower, American Beauty
Crimson and sweet all night in the city,
Limp now, changed in import as in color,
Floats behind us in the tinkling cooler.

Yesterday also Robert Kennedy's
Train of refrigerated dignitaries
Last seen on TV burying Dr. King
Wormed its way to Arlington Cemetery.

The beauty I mean to press fading
Between these lines is yours, and the misleading
Sweetness, leaves and portals of a body
Ajar, cool, nodding at the wheel already.

3

Dawn, the muted chirr and squeal—dream axle
Grinding your jaws? I mind for you
Prematurely.
In our roof are swallows,
Young ones breast to breast.

4

Next a high pool deep blue very hot
Illumination of the brimstone text
Beyond your windburned face panted and steamed
As did the spring left far below with death,

Its green rank to which we should return,
Two good men in high places out of breath
Less now than ant or tick the noon's cold bird
Lured to cast its ravenous milligram

Into the scale, and the small window steamed
Where I sat alone high blue
Taking stock of wing and wishbone stewed
At giddily low temperature—

Ice in the marrow of a star so pure
So beyond history, the eye-searing water
Onion or headline or your fine print drew
Dried in a wink, quick sleights of altitude.

5

Each day at dusk we roam the sage.
Heavenly repertory, bleakest rage

Bleeding to sour gleams, hard-edge jubilance,
All encompassed by one lariat glance.

The peaks turn baseless as the fear
That you will tell me what I live to hear.

Look, is all. The cabin. Look. The river.
Aspens glowing, site gloomed over.

Look. Out of thin air old gods (plume, hide, bead)
Appear to weigh your offerings of seed.

A leathery prospector god's pans fill
With fool's gold facets of my blackbird's trill.

Then all take umbrage in a blue
The silence positively ripples through.

6

From glade by river to a further day's
Thirst-crazed hilltop the abandoned cabin
Kept wandering like a mind with its few same
Obsessions, robin's nest and dish of rust,
Cracked pane dingily festooned,
Roof leaking sky, the same forty-year-old
Illustrated fictions sticking to its ribs

Where once again, the flask uncorked, two rooms
Are won back to this world,
Book by loaf a whole life dreams itself
From the foundation, from that withered rose
Mounted in antlers, up past the first morning
Glory's grasp of lightning rod,
Labor, cost, frostbite, bedazzlement,
Down to the last friend's guitar and stories,
Name called in sleep, fingers unclenching
In a long bath, its tepid amber inch
And dry bouquet—the future, gentlemen!

Tomorrow's cabin, who knows where, will seem
A shade sobered, abler to comprehend
How much, how little it takes to be thought worth
Crossing the threshold of, a place to dwell,
Will suffer once again the flashlight painless
Piercing of your dream, beam upon beam,

And its old boards before they turn to earth
Drink the mirage, the dreamer's volatile
Here all would have been well.

7

Sit then, draped in a sheet whose snowy folds
Darken in patches as when summer comes
And sun goes round and round the melting mountain.
Smiling debonair

You maybe wait for some not seen till now
Aspect of yours to blaze from the alembic
While one of mine in robe and slippers cries
Ah stay! Thou art so fair!

Or else are smiling not to wince recalling
Locks the grave sprang open. Blind, untrimmed,
Sheeted with cold, such rot and tangle must
In time be our affair.

But should you smile as those who doubt the novice
Hands they entrust their beautiful heads to,
I want to show you how the clumsiest love
Transfigures if you let it, if you dare.

There was a day when beauty, death, and love
Were coiled together in one crowning glory.
Shears in hand, we parted the dark waves . . .
Look at me, dear one. There.

8

Geode, the troll's melon
Rind of crystals velvet smoke meat blue
Formed far away under fantastic
Pressures, then cloven in two
By the taciturn rock shop man, twins now forever

Will they hunger for each other
When one goes north and one goes east?

I expect minerals never do.
Enough for them was a feast
Of flaws, the molten start and glacial sleep,
The parting kiss.

Still face to face in halfmoonlight
Sparkling comes easy to the Gemini.

Centimeters deep yawns the abyss.

9

Master of the ruined watercolor,
Citizen no less of the botched country
Where shots attain the eagle, and the grizzly
Dies for pressing people to his heart,

Truster, like me, of who (invoked by neither)
Hovered near the final evening's taper,
Held his breath to read his flickering nature
By our light, then left us in the dark,

Take these verses, call them today's flower,
Cluster a rained-in pupil might have scissored.
They too have suffered in the realm of hazard.
Sorry things all. Accepting them's the art.

WILLOWWARE CUP

Mass hysteria, wave after breaking wave
Blueblooded Cantonese upon these shores

Left the gene pool Lux-opaque and smoking
With dimestore mutants. One turned up today.

Plum in bloom, pagoda, blue birds, plume of willow—
Almost the replica of a prewar pattern—

The same boat bearing the gnat-sized lovers away,
The old bridge now bent double where her father signals

Feebly, as from flypaper, minding less and less.
Two smaller retainers with lanterns light him home.

Is that a scroll he carries? He must by now be immensely
Wise, and have given up earthly attachments, and all that.

Soon, of these May mornings, rising in mist, he will ask
Only to blend—like ink in flesh, blue anchor

Needled upon drunkenness while its destroyer
Full steam departs, the stigma throbbing, intricate—

Only to blend into a crazing texture.
You are far away. The leaves tell what they tell.

But this lone, chipped vessel, if it fills,
Fills for you with something warm and clear.

Around its inner horizon the old odd designs
Crowd as before, and seem to concentrate on you.

They represent, I fancy, a version of heaven
In its day more trouble to mend than to replace:

Steep roofs aslant, minutely tiled;
Tilted honeycombs, thunderhead blue.

BANKS OF A STREAM WHERE CREATURES BATHE

Through slits in the plantain leaf,
Celestial surge!
The fabulous old Goat
Extends nightlong

Ancien régime
Propositions. Stick with him
And you'll be wearing diamonds . . .
Barely relenting

You of the cool breast
Unclasp the rivière.
Facets reassembled
Pulse and scatter.

The courts of heaven
In sparkling shambles
Struggle against you
Like a shack on poles.

I can't compete.
Giving of my very
Self, I've seen you
Clouded by the gift.

You want diversions
Deeply pure, is that it?
Trust me. I keep trying
Not to break down.

I know the hoof
Imprinted on my clay,
His bulk and poise
Who drinks you, enters you;

And hold you close,
Too close to make the best
Of that recurrently
Real beast in you.

At dawn asleep
In fairness take these colors.
Do not sweep me
Downstream with the stars.

UNDER MARS

Cricket earphones fail us not
Here in the season of receptions

One prism drips ammonia still
Penknife-pearl-and-steel ripples

Paring nobody's orchard to the bone
Cut both ways the pond believes

And boulders' heavy sighs appear
Out of mown meadows and inside a head

Laid on the block you half erase
Chiefly to yourself antagonist

Our light fantastic fills the barn
Turning the Model A's stripped body gold

Turning it nightfall nothing space
Become emotion ball in full career

Frog-footmen croak those highnesses
Of empty sleeve and battle star

Who wither at a glance us gentlefolk
Though such as we have made them what they are

YAM

Rind and resurrection, hell and seed,
Fire-folia, hotbeds of a casserole
Divinely humble, it awaits your need.
Its message, taken in by you,

Deep reds obliterate. Be glad they do.
Go now by upward stages, fortified,
Where an imaginary line is being
Drawn past which you do not melt, you suffer

Pure form's utter discontent, white waste
And wintry grazing, flocks of white
But with no shepherd-sage, no flute, no phrases;
Parchment frozen, howling pricksong, mute

Periods that flash and stun—
Hit on the head, who brought you to this pass?
Valleys far below are spouting
Baby slogans and green gripes of spring,

Clogged pools, the floating yen . . .
You feel someone take leave, at once
Transfiguring, transfigured. A voice grunts
MATTER YOU MERELY DO I AM

Which lies on snow in dark ideogram
—Or as a later commentary words it,
One-night's-meat-another-morning's-mass-
Against-inhuman-odds-I-celebrate.

THE BLACK MESA

So much is parchment where I gloom,
Character still sharp enough to prick
Into the hide my igneous
Old spells and canticles of doom.
The things that shape a person! Peace.
Depth therapy in early stages crowned
One fuming anchorite with river stones.

Remember, though, how in *Thaïs*
The desert father falls for the land's lie—
That "grande horizontale" (blown shawls
Shining and raveling to this day
Above erosions in her pot of rouge)
Whom any crossing cloud turns dim,
Ascetic, otherworldly, lost to him.

By way of you a thousand human
Frailties found in me their last refuge.
The turquoise lodged for good one night
In a crevice where the young blood drummed.
Discharge, salvo, sulphur ringed me round
Below the waist. I knew thirst. Dawns,
The viceroy's eagle glittered like a gnat.

Sieges like that come late and end
Soon. And we are friends now? Funny friends.
Glaringly over years you knit
A wild green lap robe I shake off in tears.
I steal past him who next reclaims you, keep
Our hushed appointments, grain by grain . . .
Dust of my dust, when will it all be plain?

UNDER LIBRA:
WEIGHTS AND MEASURES

for David McIntosh

The stones of spring,
Stale rolls or pellets rather, rounded
By a gorgon's fingers, swept to the floor,

Dragged south in crushing folds,
Long dirty tablecloth of ice,
Her feast ended, her intimates dispersed

Where certain curious formations
Dwindle in the red wind like ice in tea,
These stones, these poor scarred loaves

Lichen-crusted mould-gray or burnt orange
Stop doors and rest on manuscripts.
Backbreaking it was to haul them home.

Home. That winter's terrible storms,
Apartment shivering, whistling through its teeth,
Throb of a furnace fit to burst—

To go in the small hours from room to room
Stumbling onto their drugged stubborn sleep.

The heaviest dream
Gets told to the sunrise. The ditch
Hides its rapid and self-seeking nature

Beneath a blown glass simulacrum.
Mist and fire, tomorrow's opal
Defying gravity, inspiring it,

The sun will float across thin ice
To where two swans are dozing, swansdown quilts
Drawn over heads, feet tucked on top,

And snow be light as plumage upon theirs.
Paper windflowers like things possessed
Will dance upon Angel Ortiz

Leaving whose raw grave in the churchyard
The peacock, blue snake-neck zigzag
Through biscuit everlastings twice its height,

Will pass the shower window and not scream
Inward at a nude gone up in steam.

There then, his peacock
Past, the dreamer dries and gazes
Into the dormant crystal of himself,

A presence oval, vitrified—
That without warning thaws, trickles, and burns!
Frightened he looks away. He learns

To live whole days in another
Tense, avoid the bathroom scales or merely
Sing them. Wipe lather from his lip. Dress. Drive

Until the trees have leaves again
And the tanner's colors change to those of the mint,
Copper, silver, green

Engraved by summer's light, by spring's.
The riverbend's great horseshoe print
Where time turned round at last, drew rein,

Glints through a windshield blazing dust and wings,
Scum of the earth rebuffed upon the pane.

Warm afternoons
In his son's truck, Angel, both quick and dead,
Awaited judgment and suspended it.

His right side like a thing possessed
Danced, light birdclaw fast upon the guest.
The left had long let go—its tear

Oozed as from stone. It seemed
Both sides of the old character knew best.
In, out the unhinged doors

White coma'd spores were drifting, shining.
Flies lit, cudgeled quarter-carat wits,
Then washed their wings of him.

Blanca, too, who used to leap
Reeking of rain, licking his face like fire,
Lay back. Her coat caked red and speaking eyes

Clear as the baby's or the priest's
Wondered could he last another night.

For see, by dusk
A crescent jaw, a sudden frost of stubble
Yesterday's Gem will float across,

Enters the rear-view mirror. There was one
Direction only, after all?
How many more nights will that double-headed

Friend woven, wings outspread,
Into the dreamer's blanket keep him warm?
Here now's a little mesa set for two—

Over purple places, intimate
Twinklings, early stones, wide open spaces,
And soon on the horizon the "necklace of death,"

Los Alamos' lights where wizards stay up late
(Stay in the car, forget the gate)
To save the world or end it, time will tell

—Mentioned for what it's worth in hopes
Of giving weight to—Brr! It's freezing!

Clay room. Firelight.
No measures taken, no words weighed—
As next morning, pen in hand, the whole

House sown by the prism on the sill
With arcs of spectral seed, a peacock's tail—
Or ten years from next morning, pen in hand,

Looking through saltwater, through flames,
Enkindlings of an absent *I* and *you*,
Live, spitting pronouns, sparks that flew

And were translated into windiest
Esperanto, zero tongue of powers
Diplomatic around 1 a.m.'s

Undripping centerpiece, the Swan . . .
Days were coming when the real thing
No longer shrugged a wing, dipping its mask

Where any surface thawed and burned.
One learned. The heavy stones of spring.
These autumn feathers. Learned.

KOMBOLOI

the Greek "worry-beads"

Begin. Carnation underfoot, tea splashing stars
Onto this mottled slab, amber coherences,

Unmatched string of the habitué
Told and retold, rubbed lucid, quick with scenes . . .

That face—fire-slitted fur, whip fury, slate iced over!
Click. An early life. The warrior's

Came late, enchanted brief. Then, gem on brow
And far-eyed peregrine on wrist,

One life in profile brushed so fine
You felt no single stroke until the last of thousands.

All that while, the bed had flowed, divided,
Deepened and sung in sparkling attacks

None but whose woman brought her warm specific,
Her tongue unspeakable. Click. Taxis

Yoked together floors below were making
Summer hell. Yet from her pupil streamed

Radii such as gall the ferry's shadow
Plunging like my pen past shoals of shilly-shally

Into fathomless gentian. Or into
Some thinnest "shade" of blue

Juniper berries fallen on this far bank
Of now no river. Wingbeats echo where its ghost

Forks. Focus the half mile down
Upon snapped golds—if not a corn plantation

Then a small ill-strung harp which dead hands pluck
And pluck. No sound. No issue. The wheel

Founders in red rainwater, soul inchdeep in pain,
Charred spokesman of reflections grimly

Sanguine with siftings from the great
Cracked hourglass. Click. Will . . . ? Click.

Will second wind come even to the runners
Out of time? These beads—O marble counter—Done.

STRATO IN PLASTER

στῆθος μάρμαρο καὶ καρδιὰ πατάτα

Out of the blue, in plaster from wrist to bicep
Somebody opens a beer, pretending to be
My friend Strato. Years or minutes—which?—
Have passed since we last looked upon each other.
He's in town for his sister's wedding
To this elderly thin-lipped sonofabitch
Who gets the house for dowry—enough to make
A brother break with the entire family.
Considering it, his eyes fairly cross
With self-importance. That, I recognize.

Here at hand is a postcard Chester sent
Of the Apollo at Olympia,
Its message *Strato as he used to be.*
Joy breeds in the beautiful blind gaze,
The marble mouth and breastbone. I look hard
At both the god and him. (He loves attention
Like gods and children, and he lifts his glass.)
Those extra kilos, that moustache,
Lies found out and letters left unanswered
Just won't do. It makes him burst out laughing,
Curiously happy, flecked with foam.

At present he is living far from home,
Builder by day and autocrat by dark,
Athenian among peasants. Fine Athenian
Whose wife learns acquiescence blow by blow.
That strikes a nerve. "I haven't married her!
Am I a fool to marry before thirty?
Who trusts a woman anyhow?
The nurse that set my elbow, filthy crone,
I cried out, it hurt so—but did she care?"
He goes on quickly, looking proud:

"I'm full of spite. Remember what you wrote
In answer to my asking for a loan?

336

I tore up your address—though you were right!—
Then sold the cufflinks and the black trenchcoat."

Now that he wants to go to El Dorado
His brother there has given up urging him.
"OK. I fuck his Virgin.
Bad son, bad father, and bad friend to you,
I might as well be a bad brother, too."
The little boy is three and "delicate"
But still "a devil, full of fight!"
My guest drinks up. Twin jewels unsold somehow,
His eyes are sparkling with delight.

Three winters, playing backgammon
At the café for stakes that pierce the heart,
One cigarette or dram of burning mud,
And never losing ("dice are in my blood")—
Marika sleeping, her cheeks ice,
Where oil smoke sickens and a chicken's cough
Wakes the child who dashes to the floor
Any red elixir *he* might pour—

Three winters. Trowels of frigid white
Choke the sugar-celled original
That once stayed warm all night with its own sun.
The god in him is a remembered one.
Inflexibility through which twinges shoot
Like stars, the fracture's too complex,
Too long unmended, for us to be friends.
I, he hazards, have made other friends.
The more reason, then, to part like friends.

Today at least a cloud of rice and petals
Aimed at others will envelop him.

Risen, he wonders—almost saying what.
I take his swollen hand in both of mine.
No syllable of certain grand tirades
One spent the worse part of a fall composing,
Merely that word in common use
Which means both *foolishness* and *self-abuse*

Coming to mind, I smile:
Was the break caused by too much malakía?
Strato's answer is a final burst
Of laughter: "No such luck!
One day like this the scaffold gave beneath me.
I felt no pain at first."

UP AND DOWN

"The heart that leaps to the invitation
of sparkling appearances is the heart
that would itself perform as handsomely."
—JOHN H. FINLEY, JR.,
Four Stages of Greek Thought

I / SNOW KING CHAIR LIFT

Prey swooped up, the iron love seat shudders
Onward into its acrophilic trance.
What folly has possessed us? Ambulance!
Give me your hand, try thinking of those others'

Unhurt return by twos from June's immense
Sunbeamed ark with such transfigured faces.
We sought admission on the shaky basis
That some good follows from experience

Of anything or leaving it behind,
As now, each urchin street and park sent sprawling
By the mountain's foot—why, this is fun, appalling
Bungalows, goodbye! dark frames of mind,

Whatever's settled into, comfort, despair,
Sin, expectation, apathy, the past,
Rigid interiors that will not outlast
Their decorator or their millionaire,

Groaning of board and bed of ruses, oh
I've had it up to here, fiftieth story
Glass maze, ice cube, daybreak's inflammatory
Montage subsiding into vertigo

Till, with their elevations all on file,
Joys, now demolished, that I used to live in,
This afternoon I swear halfway to heaven
None housed me—no, not style itself—in style.

Risen this far, your ex-materialist
Signs an impetuous long lease on views
Of several states and skies of several blues
Promptly dismantled by the mover mist

—What's going on? Loud ceiling shaken, brute
Maker of scenes in lightning spurt on spurt—
How did those others, how shall we avert
Illuminations that electrocute!

Except that suddenly the danger's gone.
Huge cloudscapes hang in the sun's antechamber.
Somebody takes our picture, calls a number.
We've done it. Reached the heights and quit our throne.

While knowing better, now, than to repeat
Our sole anabasis, unless in rhyme,
I love that funny snapshot from a time
When we still thought we were each other's meat.

The very great or very fatuous
Complicate the pinnacles they reach,
Plant banners, carve initials, end a speech,
"My fellow Texans, let us pray . . ." Not us.

You merely said you liked it in that chill
Lighthearted atmosphere (a crow for witness)
And I, that words profaned the driven whiteness
Of a new leaf. The rest was all downhill.

Au fond each summit is a cul-de-sac.
That day at least by not unprecedented
Foresight, a Cozy Cabin had been rented.
Before I led you to the next chair back

And made my crude but educated guess
At why the wind was laying hands on you
(Something I no longer think to do)
We gazed our little fills at boundlessness.

Hearing that on Sunday I would leave,
My mother asked if we might drive downtown.
Why certainly—off with my dressing gown!
The weather had turned fair. *We* were alive.

Only the gentle General she married
Late, for both an old way out of harm's,
Fought for breath, surrendered in her arms,
With military honors now lay buried.

That week the arcana of his medicine chest
Had been disposed of, and his clothes. Gold belt
Buckle and the letter from President Roosevelt
Went to an unknown grandchild in the West.

Downtown, his widow raised her parasol
Against the Lenten sun's not yet detectable
Malignant atomies which an electric needle
Unfreckles from her soft white skin each fall.

Hence too her chiffon scarf, pale violet,
And spangle-paste dark glasses. Each spring we number
The new dead. Above ground, who can remember
Her as she once was? Even I forget,

Fail to attend her, seem impervious . . .
Meanwhile we have made through a dense shimmy
Of parked cars burnished by the midday chamois
For Mutual Trust. Here cool gloom welcomes us,

And all, director, guard, quite palpably
Adore her. Spinster tellers one by one
Darting from cages, sniffling to meet her son,
Think of her having a son—! She holds the key

Whereby palatial bronze gates shut like jaws
On our descent into this inmost vault.

The keeper bends his baldness to consult,
Brings a tin box painted mud-brown, withdraws.

She opens it. Security. Will. Deed.
Rummages further. Rustle of tissue, a sprung
Lid. Her face gone queerly lit, fair, young,
Like faces of our dear ones who have died.

No rhinestone now, no dilute amethyst,
But of the first water, linking star to pang,
Teardrop to fire, my father's kisses hang
In lipless concentration round her wrist.

Gray are these temple-drummers who once more
Would rouse her, girl-bride jeweled in his grave.
Instead, she next picks out a ring. "He gave
Me this when you were born. Here, take it for—

For when you marry. For your bride. It's yours."
A den of greenest light, it grows, shrinks, glows,
Hermetic stanza bedded in the prose
Of the last thirty semiprecious years.

I do not tell her, it would sound theatrical,
Indeed this green room's mine, my very life.
We are each other's; there will be no wife;
The little feet that patter here are metrical.

But onto her worn knuckle slip the ring.
Wear it for me, I silently entreat,
Until—until the time comes. Our eyes meet.
The world beneath the world is brightening.

ELECTRA: A TRANSLATION

Cold step by step
Shoulders between sweating
Walls their way. The candle staying lit,
Eyes meet elated.

Or has he been misled?
"Patience, wanderer to this place.
My dead are everywhere,
Don't tread on them."

Twelve thousand souls
Prickle with recognition
The plot to slaughter meter radiates.
"I thought I was

Myself. I'm not. I am
The sun, the sea
Urchin. Black needles fester hot at heel,
Sister! the ax—"

"Before the weapons of his yawn, his laughter,
Are drilled for gold,
Are blunted, drawn,
Before in us the god grows old—"

The autarch sinks:
Dark red groaning table
Set for the housefly. Flat by wing by leaf
A forest scene's

Unities snake-haired and ember-eyed
From root or treetop hoot
Palace to hovel, hone the queen to crone,
Her larder all

But bare. Baked crumbling meets
The children's hands. They've stumbled. It's nightfall.

"Come, Brüderlein,
The more living, the less truth.

On high till now obscured
Slow-stabbing instruments together
Sound their A.
Face the first music. Sleep."

DREAMS ABOUT CLOTHES

for John and Anne Hollander

In some, the man they made
Penetrates the sunlit fitting room,
Once more deciding among bolts of dark.
The tailor kneels to take his measure.
Soon a finished suit will be laid out
By his valet, for him to change into.
Change of clothes? The very clothes of change!
Unchecked blazers women flutter round,
Green coverts, midnight blues . . .
My left hand a pincushion, I dispose,
Till morning, of whole closets full of clues.

What ought I in fact to do with them?
Give away suits worn six, eight times?
Take them to the shrink until they fit?
Have them mothproofed at least
(Arturo's Valet Service, one block east,
Picks up, delivers)—or just let them be,
Still holding sway above me, Harvard Law's
Loyal sons of 'oo hanging by claws
On their slow shuttle to the sea.

Sure enough, a waterfront
Glides into place on small, oiled waves.
Taverns are glittering and the heavens have cleared.
(Far inland lie the crossroads,
Oxcart overturned, graybeard
Lamented by his slaves.)
From whom did I inherit these shirtsleeves
And ancient, sexy jeans?
Fingers of a woman I am with
Tease through holes made by the myth.
Bad music starts in ⅝ time.
I order drinks and dinners. I'm
Being taken, her smile means
Once more to the cleaners.

Sleeping clean through those August afternoons
Whose Prospero, on shuttles quick as play,
Was weaving rainy spells—
Warp of physics, woof of whim;
Feeling him under some new pressure thunder
Forth in loud black surges to outsweat
Until the lightning twinkling of an eye
Dissolved his corporation,
The tempest used to be my cup of tea.
(Come in, Mme. de Garments called,
You'll be soaked to the skin! I never woke.)
Relief poured through me shining wet,
Lining of purest silver.

But now, his baby face unlined and bald,
The old-clothes man comes down the street,
Singing the little song he sings.
His overcoat is all humped up in back
To hide his powerful wings.
Snow melts at the touch of his bare feet.
He passes me unseeing, yet how much
Of mine's already in his sack!

Tell me something, Art.
You know what it's like
Awake in your dry hell
Of volatile synthetic solvents.
Won't you help us brave the elements
Once more, of terror, anger, love?
Seeing there's no end to wear and tear
Upon the lawless heart,
Won't you as well forgive
Whoever settles for the immaterial?
Don't you care how we live?

FLÈCHE D'OR

Windowglass, warmed plush, a sneeze
Deflected by the miracle
Into euphoria's
Authoritative gliding forth,
The riddle of the rails
Vitally unmoved in flight
However fast
I run racing that arrow
Lodged in my brain
Down the board platform beyond hurt or hope
Once more, once more
My life ended, having not,
Veils lifted, words from the page
Come to my senses
Eased of that last arrivederci deep
In book or view, my own
Fleet profile calmer catapulted due
North a pane floats off, desire sinks
Red upon piercing stubble—"Traveler,
Turn back!" the tracks
Outcry, din flash fade, done,
Over forever, done I say, now yet
Might somebody
Seeing it all (for once not I or I)
Judge us wisely in whose heart of
Hearts the parallels
Meet and nothing lasts and nothing ends

DAYS OF 1971

Fallen from the clouds, well-met.
This way to the limousine.
How are things? Don't tell me yet!
Have a Gauloise first, I mean.

Matches now, did I forget—
With a flourish and no word
Out came the sentry-silhouette
Black against a big, flame-feathered bird,

Emblem of your "new" regime
Held, for its repressive ways,
In pretty general disesteem

Which to share just then was hard,
Borne up so far on a strategic blaze
Struck by you, and quite off guard.

In Paris you remark each small
Caged creature, marmoset, bat, newt, for sale;
Also the sparkling gutters, and the smelly
Seine this afternoon when we embark.

And the Bateau Mouche is spoiled by a party of cripples.
Look at what's left of that young fellow strapped
Into his wheelchair. How you pity him!
The city ripples, your eyes sicken and swim.

The boy includes you in his sightseeing,
Nodding sociably as if who of us
Here below were more than half a man.

There goes the Louvre, its Egyptian wing
Dense with basalt limbs and heads to use
Only as one's imagination can.

Can-can from last night's *Orphée aux Enfers*
Since daybreak you've been whistling till I wince.
Well, you were a handsome devil once.
Take the wheel. You're still a fair chauffeur.

Our trip. I'd pictured it another way—
Asthmatic pilgrim and his "nun of speed,"
In either mind a music spun of need . . .
That last turnoff went to Illiers.

Proust's Law (are you listening?) is twofold:
(a) What least thing our self-love longs for most
Others instinctively withhold;

(b) Only when time has slain desire
Is his wish granted to a smiling ghost
Neither harmed nor warmed, now, by the fire.

Stephen in the Pyrenees—our first
Real stop. You promptly got a stomachache.
Days of groans and grimaces interspersed
With marathon slumbers. Evenings, you'd wake

And stagger forth to find us talking. Not
Still about poetry! Alas . . .
So bottles were produced, and something hot.
The jokes you told translated, more or less.

Predictably departure cured you. Stephen
Investing me with a Basque walking stick,
"How much further, James, will you be driven?"

He didn't ask. He stood there, thin, pale, kind
As candlelight. Ah, what if *I* took sick?
You raced the motor, having read my mind.

Sucked by haste into the car,
Pressing his frantic buzzer, Bee!
Suppose he stings—why such hilarity?
These things occur.

Get rid of him at once
While we can! His wrath
Is almost human, the windshield's warpath
Dins with a song and dance

In one respect unlike our own:
Readily let out into the open.
There. Good creature, also he had known
The cost of self-as-weapon;

Venom unspent, barb idle, knows
Where they lead now—thyme, lavender, musk-rose,

Toulouse, Toulon, the border. Driven?
At ease, rather among fleeting scenes.
The O L I V E T T I signs
Whiz by, and azure Lombardy is given

Back, as the Virgin of Officialdom
Severely draped twists on her throne to peek
At the forbidden crags of kingdom come
Before resuming her deft hunt and peck.

One V sticks. Venice. Its vertiginous pastry
Maze we scurry through like mice and will
Never see the likes of in our lives.

It is too pink, white, stale to taste,
Crumbling in the gleam of slimy knives.
Have your cake and eat it? Take the wheel.

Wait—now where are we? Who is everyone?
Well, that's a princess, that's the butler . . . no,
Probably by now the butler's son.
We were stopping till tomorrow with Umberto

Among trompe l'oeil, old volumes, photographs
Of faded people wearing crowns and stars.
Welcome to the Time Machine, he laughed
Leaning on us both up its cold stairs.

At table the others recalled phrases from
Homer and Sappho, and you seemed to brighten.
Your sheets would entertain the "priest" that night
(Dish of embers in a wooden frame)

And eyes glaze on the bedside book, remote
But near, pristine but mildewed, which I wrote.

Take the wheel. San Zeno will survive
Whether or not visited.
Power is knowledge in your head.
(Sorry, I must have been thinking aloud. Drive, drive.)

Time and again the novel I began
Took aim at that unwritten part
In which the hero, named Sebastian,
Came to his senses through a work of art.

O book of hours, those last
Illuminated castles built
In air, O chariot-motif

Bearing down a margin good as gilt
Past fields of ever purer leaf
Its burning rubric, to get nowhere fast . . .

The road stopped where a Greek mountain fell
Early that week. Backed-up cars glared in the dusk.
Night fell next, and still five stupid slack-
Jawed ferries hadn't got their fill of us.

Tempers shortened. One self-righteous truck
Knocked the shit out of a eucalyptus
Whose whitewashed trunk lay twitching brokenly—
Nijinsky in *Petrouchka*—on the quai.

Later, past caring, packed like sheep,
Some may have felt the breathless lounge redeemed
By a transistor singing to the doomed

At last in their own tongue. You fell asleep
Life-sentenced to the honey-cell of song,
Harsh melisma, torturous diphthong.

Strato, each year's poem
Says goodbye to you.
Again, though, we've come through
Without losing temper or face.

If care rumpled your face
The other day in Rome,
Tonight just dump my suitcase
Inside the door and make a dash for home

While I unpack what we saw made
At Murano, and you gave to me—
Two ounces of white heat
Twirled and tweezered into shape,

Ecco! another fanciful
Little horse, still blushing, set to cool.

THE VICTOR DOG

for Elizabeth Bishop

Bix to Buxtehude to Boulez,
The little white dog on the Victor label
Listens long and hard as he is able.
It's all in a day's work, whatever plays.

From judgment, it would seem, he has refrained.
He even listens earnestly to Bloch,
Then builds a church upon our acid rock.
He's man's—no—he's the Leiermann's best friend,

Or would be if hearing and listening were the same.
Does he hear? I fancy he rather smells
Those lemon-gold arpeggios in Ravel's
"Les jets d'eau du palais de ceux qui s'aiment."

He ponders the Schumann Concerto's tall willow hit
By lightning, and stays put. When he surmises
Through one of Bach's eternal boxwood mazes
The oboe pungent as a bitch in heat,

Or when the calypso decants its raw bay rum
Or the moon in *Wozzeck* reddens ripe for murder,
He doesn't sneeze or howl; just listens harder.
Adamant needles bear down on him from

Whirling of outer space, too black, too near—
But he was taught as a puppy not to flinch,
Much less to imitate his bête noire Blanche
Who barked, fat foolish creature, at King Lear.

Still others fought in the road's filth over Jezebel,
Slavered on hearths of horned and pelted barons.
His forebears lacked, to say the least, forbearance.
Can nature change in him? Nothing's impossible.

The last chord fades. The night is cold and fine.
His master's voice rasps through the grooves' bare groves.
Obediently, in silence like the grave's
He sleeps there on the still-warm gramophone

Only to dream he is at the première of a Handel
Opera long thought lost—*Il Cane Minore*.
Its allegorical subject is his story!
A little dog revolving round a spindle

Gives rise to harmonies beyond belief,
A cast of stars . . . Is there in Victor's heart
No honey for the vanquished? Art is art.
The life it asks of us is a dog's life.

SYRINX

Bug, flower, bird of slipware fired and fluted,
The summer day breaks everywhere at once.

Worn is the green of things that have known dawns
Before this, and the darkness before them.

Among the wreckage, bent in Christian weeds,
Illiterate—X my mark—I tremble, still

A thinking reed. Who puts his mouth to me
Draws out the scale of love and dread—

O ramify, sole antidote! Foxglove
Each year, cloud, hornet, fatal growths

Proliferating by metastasis
Rooted their total in the gliding stream.

Some formula not relevant any more
To flower children might express it yet

Like $\sqrt{\left(\frac{x}{y}\right)^{n}} = I$
—Or equals zero, one forgets—

The y standing for you, dear friend, at least
Until that hour he reaches for me, then

Leaves me cold, the great god Pain,
Letting me slide back into my scarred case

Whose silvery breath-tarnished tones
No longer rivet bone and star in place

Or keep from shriveling, leather round a stone,
The sunbather's precocious apricot

Or stop the four winds racing overhead
                  Nought
            Waste   Eased
                  Sought

FROM

DIVINE COMEDIES

(1976)

THE KIMONO

When I returned from lovers' lane
My hair was white as snow.
Joy, incomprehension, pain
I'd seen like seasons come and go.
How I got home again
Frozen half dead, perhaps you know.

You hide a smile and quote a text:
Desires ungratified
Persist from one life to the next.
Hearths we strip ourselves beside
Long, long ago were x'd
On blueprints of "consuming pride."

Times out of mind, the bubble-gleam
To our charred level drew
April back. A sudden beam . . .
—Keep talking while I change into
The pattern of a stream
Bordered with rushes white on blue.

LOST IN TRANSLATION

for Richard Howard

Diese Tage, die leer dir scheinen
und wertlos für das All,
haben Wurzeln zwischen den Steinen
und trinken dort überall.

A card table in the library stands ready
To receive the puzzle which keeps never coming.
Daylight shines in or lamplight down
Upon the tense oasis of green felt.
Full of unfulfillment, life goes on,
Mirage arisen from time's trickling sands
Or fallen piecemeal into place:
German lesson, picnic, see-saw, walk
With the collie who "did everything but talk"—
Sour windfalls of the orchard back of us.
A summer without parents is the puzzle,
Or should be. But the boy, day after day,
Writes in his Line-a-Day *No puzzle.*

He's in love, at least. His French Mademoiselle,
In real life a widow since Verdun,
Is stout, plain, carrot-haired, devout.
She prays for him, as does a curé in Alsace,
Sews costumes for his marionettes,
Helps him to keep behind the scene
Whose sidelit goosegirl, speaking with his voice,
Plays Guinevere as well as Gunmoll Jean.
Or else at bedtime in his tight embrace
Tells him her own French hopes, her German fears,
Her—but what more is there to tell?
Having known grief and hardship, Mademoiselle
Knows little more. Her languages. Her place.
Noon coffee. Mail. The watch that also waited
Pinned to her heart, poor gold, throws up its hands—
No puzzle! Steaming bitterness
Her sugars draw pops back into his mouth, translated:

"Patience, chéri. Geduld, mein Schatz."
(Thus, reading Valéry the other evening
And seeming to recall a Rilke version of "Palme,"
That sunlit paradigm whereby the tree
Taps a sweet wellspring of authority,
The hour came back. Patience dans l'azur.
Geduld im . . . Himmelblau? Mademoiselle.)

Out of the blue, as promised, of a New York
Puzzle-rental shop the puzzle comes—
A superior one, containing a thousand hand-sawn,
Sandal-scented pieces. Many take
Shapes known already—the craftsman's repertoire
Nice in its limitation—from other puzzles:
Witch on broomstick, ostrich, hourglass,
Even (surely not just in retrospect)
An inchling, innocently branching palm.
These can be put aside, made stories of
While Mademoiselle spreads out the rest face-up,
Herself excited as a child; or questioned
Like incoherent faces in a crowd,
Each with its scrap of highly colored
Evidence the Law must piece together.
Sky-blue ostrich? Likely story.
Mauve of the witch's cloak white, severed fingers
Pluck? Detain her. The plot thickens
As all at once two pieces interlock.

Mademoiselle does borders— (Not so fast.
A London dusk, December last.
Chatter silenced in the library
This grown man reenters, wearing gray.
A medium. All except him have seen
Panel slid back, recess explored,
An object at once unique and common
Displayed, planted in a plain tole
Casket the subject now considers
Through shut eyes, saying in effect:
"Even as voices reach me vaguely
A dry saw-shriek drowns them out,
Some loud machinery—a lumber mill?

363

Far uphill in the fir forest
Trees tower, tense with shock,
Groaning and cracking as they crash groundward.
But hidden here is a freak fragment
Of a pattern complex in appearance only.
What it seems to show is superficial
Next to that long-term lamination
Of hazard and craft, the karma that has
Made it matter in the first place.
Plywood. Piece of a puzzle." Applause
Acknowledged by an opening of lids
Upon the thing itself. A sudden dread—
But to go back. All this lay years ahead.)

Mademoiselle does borders. Straight-edge pieces
Align themselves with earth or sky
In twos and threes, naive cosmogonists
Whose views clash. Nomad inlanders meanwhile
Begin to cluster where the totem
Of a certain vibrant egg-yolk yellow
Or pelt of what emerging animal
Acts on the straggler like a trumpet call
To form a more sophisticated unit.
By suppertime two ragged wooden clouds
Have formed. In one, a Sheik with beard
And flashing sword hilt (he is all but finished)
Steps forward on a tiger skin. A piece
Snaps shut, and fangs gnash out at us!
In the second cloud—they gaze from cloud to cloud
With marked if undecipherable feeling—
Most of a dark-eyed woman veiled in mauve
Is being helped down from her camel (kneeling)
By a small backward-looking slave or page-boy
(Her son, thinks Mademoiselle mistakenly)
Whose feet have not been found. But lucky finds
In the last minutes before bed
Anchor both factions to the scene's limits
And, by so doing, orient
Them eye to eye across the green abyss.
The yellow promises, oh bliss,
To be in time a sumptuous tent.

Puzzle begun I write in the day's space,
Then, while she bathes, peek at Mademoiselle's
Page to the curé: ". . . cette innocente mère,
Ce pauvre enfant, que deviendront-ils?"
Her azure script is curlicued like pieces
Of the puzzle she will be telling him about.
(Fearful incuriosity of childhood!
"Tu as l'accent allemand," said Dominique.
Indeed. Mademoiselle was only French by marriage.
Child of an English mother, a remote
Descendant of the great explorer Speke,
And Prussian father. No one knew. I heard it
Long afterwards from her nephew, a UN
Interpreter. His matter-of-fact account
Touched old strings. My poor Mademoiselle,
With 1939 about to shake
This world where "each was the enemy, each the friend"
To its foundations, kept, though signed in blood,
Her peace a shameful secret to the end.)
"Schlaf wohl, chéri." Her kiss. Her thumb
Crossing my brow against the dreams to come.

This World that shifts like sand, its unforeseen
Consolidations and elate routine,
Whose Potentate had lacked a retinue?
Lo! it assembles on the shrinking Green.

Gunmetal-skinned or pale, all plumes and scars,
Of Vassalage the noblest avatars—
The very coffee-bearer in his vair
Vest is a swart Highness, next to ours.

Kef easing Boredom, and iced syrups, thirst,
In guessed-at glooms old wives who know the worst
Outsweat that virile fiction of the New:
"Insh'Allah, he will tire—" "—or kill her first!"

(Hardly a proper subject for the Home,
Work of—dear Richard, I shall let *you* comb
Archives and learned journals for his name—
A minor lion attending on Gérôme.)

While, thick as Thebes whose presently complete
Gates close behind them, Houri and Afreet
Both claim the Page. He wonders whom to serve,
And what his duties are, and where his feet,

And if we'll find, as some before us did,
That piece of Distance deep in which lies hid
Your tiny apex sugary with sun,
Eternal Triangle, Great Pyramid!

Then Sky alone is left, a hundred blue
Fragments in revolution, with no clue
To where a Niche will open. Quite a task,
Putting together Heaven, yet we do.

It's done. Here under the table all along
Were those missing feet. It's done.

The dog's tail thumping. Mademoiselle sketching
Costumes for a coming harem drama
To star the goosegirl. All too soon the swift
Dismantling. Lifted by two corners,
The puzzle hung together—and did not.
Irresistibly a populace
Unstitched of its attachments, rattled down.
Power went to pieces as the witch
Slithered easily from Virtue's gown.
The blue held out for time, but crumbled, too.
The city had long fallen, and the tent,
A separating sauce mousseline,
Been swept away. Remained the green
On which the grown-ups gambled. A green dusk.
First lightning bugs. Last glow of west
Green in the false eyes of (coincidence)
Our mangy tiger safe on his bared hearth.

Before the puzzle was boxed and readdressed
To the puzzle shop in the mid-Sixties,
Something tells me that one piece contrived
To stay in the boy's pocket. How do I know?

I know because so many later puzzles
Had missing pieces—Maggie Teyte's high notes
Gone at the war's end, end of the vogue for collies,
A house torn down; and hadn't Mademoiselle
Kept back her pitiful bit of truth as well?
I've spent the last days, furthermore,
Ransacking Athens for that translation of "Palme."
Neither the Goethehaus nor the National Library
Seems able to unearth it. Yet I can't
Just be imagining. I've seen it. Know
How much of the sun-ripe original
Felicity Rilke made himself forego
(Who loved French words—verger, mûr, parfumer)
In order to render its underlying sense.
Know already in that tongue of his
What Pains, what monolithic Truths
Shadow stanza to stanza's symmetrical
Rhyme-rutted pavement. Know that ground plan left
Sublime and barren, where the warm Romance
Stone by stone faded, cooled; the fluted nouns
Made taller, lonelier than life
By leaf-carved capitals in the afterglow.
The owlet umlaut peeps and hoots
Above the open vowel. And after rain
A deep reverberation fills with stars.

Lost, is it, buried? One more missing piece?

But nothing's lost. Or else: all is translation
And every bit of us is lost in it
(Or found—I wander through the ruin of S
Now and then, wondering at the peacefulness)
And in that loss a self-effacing tree,
Color of context, imperceptibly
Rustling with its angel, turns the waste
To shade and fiber, milk and memory.

McKANE'S FALLS

The great cold shoulders bared,
The last great masts grown rich with moss, the slow-to-topple
Pilings, amassings of a shadily

Conservative nature—Balzac alone
Could have "done" this old salon,
Its airs, its tediums. The more astounding, then,

To be led by laughter out onto the sunny balcony
Where somebody quite dashing for a change
Ran on about banks broken and weights lifted,

Dorsals, laterals, pure and simple
Ripplings of a soul
—Lost, mon père? Well . . . savable, who knows?

They knew. The two dirt-caked prospectors
Rubbed their eyes and squatted within earshot:
A Yankee ornery enough to seek

Unfluctuating values, and a meek
Rebel, an embittered dreamer
Out of Balzac. For what it was worth, God loved them—

His 12 oz. rainbow sizzled in their pan;
Next morning, the first nugget.
The creek, a crystal tendon strained,

Tossed on its couch, no longer freely associating
Hawk with trout, or cloud with pebble white as cloud.
Its mouth worked. The history began.

I

Since being gelded of my gold,
Gray moods, black moods come over me.
Where's my old sparkle? Of late
I've felt so rushed, so cold.

Am I riding for another fall?
Will I end up at the power station
On charges, a degenerate?
Have my spirit broken in a cell?

Must I grow broad- and dirty-minded
Serving a community, a nation
By now past anybody's power to shock?

Doctor of locks and dams, the delta's blinded,
The mudfish grins, how do I reach the sea?
Help me. No! Don't touch me! Let me be!

2

Time was, time was a handful of gold dust
Fought for like breath, though it was only time.
Grain by grain sifting to a slender waist
Inevitably, the climber gave
Up on those slopes so sheer they seemed concave.

Here below, the campsite—second growth,
Charred beams, a skillet dew gnaws bottomless.
Of our two actors, which one surfaced then
In the casino mirrors of Cheyenne?
Why was his partner not apparent? Guess.

Listen. We must be near. And look, the currant
Berries—how their scarlets drip
Into clear conscience from a fingertip,
Or shrivel, tiny redskins, where next spring
Will rise big ghost-white scentless violets.

Senseless violence! Our quarrels, friend,
Have been, how shall I say,
Mortal as theirs, but less material.
You played your part in a Far Eastern theater.
I stayed home with Balzac, and meditated.

Red shelter from the blizzard thought, bloodshed . . .
No hands are washed clean in the same stream twice.

And in the novel which was to have ended the *Comédie*
Little Hanno Nucingen is lost at sea,
A figure of angelic sacrifice.

3

Come live within me, said the waterfall.
There is a chamber of black stone
High and dry behind my stunning life.
Stay here a year or two, a year or ten,
Until you've heard it all,
The inside story deafening but true.

Or false—I'm not a fool.
Moments of truth are moments only,
Eyes burning on the brink of empty beds.
The years wink past, the current changes course.
Ruined by tin-pan blues
The golden voice turns gravelly and hoarse.

Now you've seen through me, sang the cataract,
A fraying force, but unafraid,
Plunge through my bath of plus and minus both,
Acid and base,
The mind that mirrors and the hands that act.
Enter this inmost space

Its lean illuminations decompose.
Sun's rose wash on the wall,
Moon clinging like the Perils of Pauline—
God knows I haven't failed her yet!
And yet how far away they seem, how small.
Get me by heart, my friend,

And then forget. Forgive
These bones their hollow end, this amulet
Its wearer who atones.
All things in time grow musical.
How can you live without me? While I live
Come live within me, said the waterfall.

CHIMES FOR YAHYA

I

Imperiously ringing, "Νὰ τὰ ποῦμε;
(Shall we tell it?)" two dressy little girls inquire.
They mean some chanted verse to do with Christmas
Which big homemade iron triangles
Drown out and a least coin silences
But oh hell not at seven in the morning
If you please! and SLAM the frosted glass
Spares me their tidings and themselves
Further inspection of the foreigner
Grizzled and growling in his flannel robe.
All day children will be prowling loose
Eager to tell, tell, tell what the angel said.
So, having gagged the mechanism with a towel,
Washed hands and face, put on the kettle—
But bells keep ringing in my head.
Downhill too, where priests pace in black dresses,
Chignons and hats, like Chekhov's governesses,
Their toy church on a whole block of bare earth
In central Athens (what it must be worth!)
Clangs like a locomotive—well, good lord,
Why not? Tomorrow's Christmas. All aboard.

2

Another memory of Mademoiselle.
We're in a Pullman going South for Christmas,
She in the lower berth, I in the upper
As befits whatever station we pass through.
Lanterns finger our compartment walls.
At one stop, slipping down into her dream
I lift the blind an inch. Outside, some blanketed
Black figures from a crèche, part king,
Part shepherd and part donkey, stamp and steam
Gliding from sight as rapturous bells ring.

Mummy and Daddy have gone ahead by sleigh
Packard piled with gifts I know too well.
Night after autumn night, Mademoiselle
Yielding to endearments, bringing down
From the attic, lion by tiger, acrobat by clown,
Tamer with her little whips and hoops,
The very circus of my wildest hopes,
I've seen it, memorized it all. *Choo-choo*
Goes the train towards the déjà-vu.
Christmas morning, in a Mandarin suit—
Pigtail and fan, and pipe already staled
By the imaginary stuff inhaled—
I mimed astonishment, and who was fooled?
The treasure lay outspread beneath the tree.
Pitiful, its delusive novelty:
A present far behind me, in a sense.
And this has been a problem ever since.

3

While I carry tea up to the terrace
—The day is ravishingly mild and fair—
Thirty years pass. My train of thought
Stalls near a certain tunnel's end—despair
Lit by far-off daylight . . . Isfahan.
Change of scene that might, I thought, be tried
First, instead of outright suicide.
(Looked back on now, what caused my sufferings?
Mere thwarted passion—commonest of things.)
I had been shown into a freezing room
Belonging to a man I didn't know.
"What does that matter? Simply go,"
The friend of friends had said. (These friends of friends
Were better company, that year, than real ones.)
Surrendering his letter with my shoes,
Was taking what cold comfort one can take
When one's heart is breaking, on the carpet.
The carpet? Carpet overlapping carpet,
Threadbare, opulent. Enormous carpet-

Covered cushions. On the wall a carpet
Portrait of an old forbidding man
Correct in carpet cutaway, tarboosh
And deep white pile moustache: my host's grandfather,
As I would learn, who founded the carpet works.
Rose trees in such bloom they looked unreal
(Odorless also, or had I caught cold?)
Stood in the four corners. Nearby squatted
A brazier wheezing like a bronchitic old
Bulldog, ash-white, garnet-eyed.
Smoke curled, cardings from the comb of light,
Between me and a courtyard still in shadow.
A well. A flowering tree. One tethered goat,
Her face both smug and martyred, giving suck
To a white puppy's warm, incarnate mess
Of instincts only the pure in heart confess.
Back and forth, grimly eyebrowed under shawls,
Humans passed jacketed in sheepskin.
Was that a gentle summons from within?
The person entering, as I made to rise,
Sketched a rapid unrepeatable gesture
Perfectly explicit. "I," it said,
"Am an old retainer. By these eyes
I would not have you see me otherwise—
Unless you cared to sample my poor graces,
Lampblack and henna, on a hazier basis."
Kneeling, he arranges full black trousers
To hide his striped socks full of holes,
And fusses with the kettle on the coals.

4

"Ah, you have met Hussein," the gentle voice
Just heard says at my shoulder. There
In your corduroy jumpsuit, knotting a foulard
Of camouflage greens-and-browns, you are. You are
No older or younger than I've pictured you,
No handsomer, no simpler—only kinder.
Lover, warrior, invalid and sage,

Amused, unenvious of one another,
Meet in your face. Hussein pours cups too full.
"Our friend is fidgeting. Time for his pipe.
You don't object? I used to smoke myself,
Before my father died and I became
What—the prince? the chieftain of our tribe?
We're smiling but it's serious. One belongs
To the working class of prince. The feuds alone—
Tribesmen at one's gate from miles away,
Needing a doctor or a judgment. Summers, though,
We all live *their* life, high in the foothills,
A world you wouldn't dream. Perhaps one day . . ."
Meanwhile Hussein, positioning the tar
Pearl upon his cloudy blue-green globe,
Applies a coal, is sucking peacefully
At the long polished stem. Peculiar
Sweetness—so I *can* smell—fills the air.
As for the roses, you apologize,
"Roses in Isfahan don't bloom till May.
These are imitation, from Times Square."

5

You kept me by you all that day.
I never had to think why I was there.
Figures materialized, obeyed, unraveled.
One young man brought you his smooth breast
Like an heirloom to unwrap, to probe and dress.
Hussein brought omelets, brandy, cake, fruit, lamb.
A barber shaved you. A tall blonde from Berkeley,
Gloria, doing fieldwork in the tribe,
Got asked back that evening for dinner.
After she left: "Or don't you like
The company of your compatriots?"
I liked whatever you would ask me to,
Wanted to get so many lines a week
Of you by heart. Would want tomorrow
When, to senses sharpened by the pipe
Shared with Hussein once you had gone to bed,

Jets of rigid color—the great mosque—
Rose from a pure white carpet, snowlight flowing
Through every vein and duct, would want to spend
One lifetime there as a divinity
Student niched in shallowest faience,
Pilaf steaming while the slow air
Dried his turban's green outfloating prayer.
Had there perhaps already been
Lives at your side? A paperback I read
Compares the soul to a skimmed stone
Touching the waters of the world at points
Along a curve—Atlantis, Rome, Versailles—
Where friends arrange to be reborn together.
Absurd? No more than Freud or Chemistry
To explain the joy, the jolt that had set wheels
Rolling toward some vapor-tasseled view
—And, incidentally, away from you.

6

Not a year later, ink-blue stains
Would spell the worst—a "letter" of Hussein's:

A boyhood skirmish, a (word blotted) slug
Lodged in your skull, which must . . . which finally must . . .

Prince, that the perennial gift (remember)
Unroll another time beneath your feet,

That, red with liability to bloom
And blow, the rose abstainer of your loom

Quicken a pattern ever incomplete,
Dear Prince in whom I put my trust,

Away with pipe and ember,
The real thing's dark and malleable drug;

Withdrawal rendering, as we know, more strict
Our buried craving for the habit kicked.

375

7

Dinner was over. Hussein spoke in your ear.
You nodded him away. We drained our beer.
Gloria went right on theorizing
About "relationships within the tribe"
I now appeared to be a member of—
Dressed by you in the black ballooning trousers,
White vest, coarse sherbet-colored shirt
And brimless derby hat your people wore.
(I wore them here once during Carnival
With burnt cork eyebrows. Nobody was fooled.)
Time for a highball? But a piercing scream
Somewhere in the household interrupted
Our flow of spirits. What on earth . . . ?
"Ah, it's too tiresome," you sighed.
"These mountain women *will* give birth
Under one's roof. They wait until their labor's
So far advanced we've no way to prepare—"
The girl from Berkeley lit up like a flare:
"In two whole years I've—oh I've told and told you—
Never seen a childbirth! Can't we just—"
You shook your head. "Ah no. The stranger
Brings bad luck, we think. Best let her be.
A doctor? No. Hussein knows an old woman.
He's gone to fetch her." "But I must, must, must!
Think of my thesis, Yahya, let me please!"
Gloria had risen to her knees.
Counterpoint of screams and argument
Making you disdainfully relent,
"All right. But quietly. Into your coats."
And into the cold courtyard black with goats.

Across, a glimmering shutter stood ajar.
Come-and-go of oil lamps, moans and shadows.
As far as we could tell on tiptoe, there
In the small room's dissolving shabbiness
Lay this veiled figure writhing on a carpet.
Gloria found the bench, I climbed beside her.
Elbows on sill, we presently were staring

While you chuckled back against the wall,
Staring like solemn oxen from a stall
Upon the mystery. "Wow," breathed Gloria,
"Smell that smell. They gave her opium."
Women were chanting. The midwife had come.
Maternal invocations and convulsions
Reaching a pitch—did I detect
In all that pain an element of play?
You also seemed convulsed, with laughter, why?—
Reaching a pitch, an infant's feeble cry
From underneath dark swathings clove the night.
These totteringly picked themselves erect.
Made for Gloria. Into her credulous
Outstretched arms laid—*not* a wriggling white
Puppy! Horrors twinkled through the brain.
Then the proud mother bared her face: Hussein.

8

Cooling tea and clouding day . . .
Over the neighborhood prevailing
Bells, triangles, tuneless treble voices
Of children one imagines. Little boys
Whose rooster tessitura, plus ça change,
Will crow above the cradle of a son.
Little girls each with her Christmas doll
Like hens a china egg is slipped beneath.
Voices so familiar by now
It might as well be silence that I sit in,
Reliving romps with my animal nature. Its ecstasy
Knocking me over, off the leash at last
Or out of the manger at least; tongue, paw and pelt,
Loyal fearless heart—the vipers it saved us from;
Unlikeness to myself I knelt embracing.
Times, too, it turned on me, or on another—
Squawks, feathers—until the rolled-up *Times*
Imposed obedience. Now by its own scale
Older than I am, stodgy, apprehensive,
For all I know, of what must soon . . .

Yet trustful, setting blurred sights on me still.
What were five or six half playful bites?
Deep no doubt, but the pain so long forgiven
It might as well be pleasure I rise in,

9

Grazing music as I do so—my bells,
Silent all this while, my camel bells
From Isfahan. Their graduated brass
Pendant hangs on the awning-frame, discolored
Shades of dully wintering
Oleander. Verdigris on fingertip
And sleeve dew-wet, to make them ring
Together, reach down for the smallest. Shake.
A tingling spine of tone, or waterfall
Crashing pure and chill, bell within bell,
Upward to the ninth and mellowest,
Their changes mingle with the parish best,
Their told tale with the children's doggerel.

MANOS KARASTEFANÍS

Death took my father.
The same year (I was twelve)
Thanási's mother taught me
Heaven and hell.

None of my army buddies
Called me by name—
Just "Styles" or "Fashion Plate."
One friend I had, my body,

And, evenings at the gym
Contending with another,
Used it to isolate
Myself from him.

The doctor saved my knee.
You came to the clinic
Bringing *War and Peace*,
Better than any movie.

Why are you smiling?
I fought fair, I fought well,
Not hurting my opponent,
To win this black belt.

Why are you silent?
I've brought you a white cheese
From my island, and the sea's
Voice in a shell.

YÁNNINA

for Stephen Yenser

*"There lay the peninsula stretching far into the dark gray water, with its
mosque, its cypress tufts and fortress walls; there was the city stretching
far and wide along the water's edge; there was the fatal island, the
closing scene of the history of the once all-powerful Ali."*

—EDWARD LEAR

Somnambulists along the promenade
Have set up booths, their dreams:
Carpets, jewelry, kitchenware, halvah, shoes.
From a loudspeaker passionate lament
Mingles with the penny Jungle's roars and screams.
Tonight in the magician's tent
Next door a woman will be sawed in two,
But right now she's asleep, as who is not, as who . . .

An old Turk at the water's edge has laid
His weapons and himself down, sleeps
Undisturbed since, oh, 1913.
Nothing will surprise him should he wake,
Only how tall, how green the grass has grown
There by the dusty carpet of the lake
Sun beats, then sleepwalks down a vine-festooned arcade,
Giving himself away in golden heaps.

And in the dark gray water sleeps
One who said no to Ali. Kiosks all over town
Sell that postcard, "Kyra Frossíni's Drown,"
Showing her, eyeballs white as mothballs, trussed
Beneath the bulging moon of Ali's lust.
A devil (turban and moustache and sword)
Chucks the pious matron overboard—
Wait—Heaven help us—SPLASH!

The torch smokes on the prow. Too late.
(A picture deeply felt, if in technique slapdash.)

Wherefore the Lion of Epirus, feared
By Greek and Turk alike, tore his black beard
When to barred casements rose the song
Broken from bubbles rising all night long:
"A ton of sugar pour, oh pour into the lake
To sweeten it for poor, for poor Frossíni's sake."*

Awake? Her story's aftertaste
Varies according to the listener.
Friend, it's bitter coffee you prefer?
Brandy for me, and with a fine
White sandy bottom. Not among those braced
By action taken without comment, neat,
Here's how! Grounds of our footnote infiltrate the treat,
Mud-vile to your lips, crystal-sweet to mine.

Twilight at last. Enter the populace.
One little public garden must retrace
Long after school its childish X,
Two paths that cross and cross. The hollyhock, the rose,
Zinnia and marigold hear themselves named
And blush for form's sake, unashamed
Chorus out of *Ignoramus Rex*:
"What shall the heart learn, that already knows

Its place by water, and its time by sun?"
Mother wit fills the stately whispering sails
Of girls someone will board and marry. Who?
Look at those radiant young males.
Their morning-glory nature neon blue
Wilts here on the provincial vine. Where did it lead,
The race, the radiance? To oblivion
Dissembled by a sac of sparse black seed.

* "Time was kind to the reputation of this woman who had been unfaithful to her husband, vain, and grasping. She came to be regarded as a Christian martyr and even as an early heroine in the struggle for Greek independence. She has been celebrated in legend, in poetry, in popular songs and historical fiction, and surrounded with the glamour which so often attaches to women whose love affairs have been of an intense nature and have involved men of political or historical importance."
—WILLIAM PLOMER, *The Diamond of Jannina*

Now under trees men with rush baskets sell
Crayfish tiny and scarlet as the sins
In any fin-de-siècle villanelle.
Tables fill up. A shadow play begins.
Painted, translucent cut-outs fill the screen.
It glows. His children by a jumping bean
Karaghiózi clobbers, baits the Turk,
Then all of them sing, dance, tell stories, go berserk.

Tomorrow we shall cross the lake to see
The cottage tumbling down, where soldiers killed
Ali. Two rugless rooms. Cushions. Vitrines
In which, to this day, silks and bracelets swim.
Above, a painting hangs. It's him,
Ali. The end is near, he's sleeping between scenes
In a dark lady's lap. Vassilikí.
The mood is calm, the brushwork skilled

By contrast with Frossíni's mass-produced
Unsophisticated piece of goods.
The candle trembles in the watching god's
Hand—almost a love-death, höchste Lust!
Her drained, compliant features haunt
The waters there was never cause to drown her in.
Your grimiest ragamuffin comes to want
Two loves, two versions of the Feminine:

One virginal and tense, brief as a bubble,
One flesh and bone—gone up no less in smoke
Where giant spits revolving try their rusty treble,
Sheep's eyes pop, and death-wish ravens croak.
Remember, the Romantic's in full feather.
Byron has visited. He likes
The luxe, and overlooks the heads on pikes;
Finds Ali "Very kind . . . indeed, a father . . ."*

* Letter to his mother, November 12, 1809. Plomer observes: ". . . even allowing for Oriental effu-
siveness, it seems doubtful whether [Ali's] interest in Byron was exactly as paternal as he pretended,
for a father does not give his son sweets twenty times a day and beg him to visit him at night. It is
worth remarking that Ali was a judge of character and a connoisseur of beauty, whether male or
female, and that the like of Byron, and Byron at twenty-one, is not often seen."

Funny, that is how I think of Ali.
On the one hand, the power and the gory
Details, pigeon-blood rages and retali-
ations, gouts of fate that crust his story;
And on the other, charm, the whimsically
Meek brow, its motives all ab ulteriori,
The flower-blue gaze twining to choke proportion,
Having made one more pretty face's fortune.

A dove with Parkinson's disease
Selects *our* fortunes: TRAVEL AND GROW WISE
And A LOYAL FRIEND IS MORE THAN GOLD.
But, at the island monastery, eyes
Gouged long since to the gesso sockets will outstare
This or that old-timer on his knees
Asking the candlelight for skill to hold
The figures flush against the screen's mild glare.

Ali, my father—both are dead.
In so many words, so many rhymes,
The brave old world sleeps. Are we what it dreams
And is a rude awakening overdue?
Not in Yánnina. To bed, to bed.
The Lion sets. The lights wink out along the lake.
Weeks later, in this study gone opaque,
They are relit. See through me. See me through.

For partings hurt although we dip the pain
Into a glowing well—the pen I mean.
Living alone won't make some inmost face to shine
Maned with light, ember and anodyne,
Deep in a desktop burnished to its grain.
That the last hour be learned again
By riper selves, couldn't you doff this green
Incorruptible, the might-have-been,

And arm in arm with me dare the magician's tent?
It's hung with asterisks. A glittering death
Is hefted, swung. The victim smiles consent.
To a sharp intake of breath she comes apart
(Done by mirrors? Just one woman? Two?

A fight starts—in the provinces, one feels,
There's never that much else to do)
Then to a general exhalation heals

Like anybody's life, bubble and smoke
In afterthought, whose elements converge,
Glory of windless mornings that the barge
(Two barges, one reflected, a quicksilver joke)
Kept scissoring and mending as it steered
The old man outward and away,
Amber mouthpiece of a narghilé
Buried in his by then snow white beard.

VERSE FOR URANIA

Through the dimness, curtains drawn, eyes closed,
Where I am composing myself before tonight's excitement
(It's not quite five, yet outdoors the daylight
Will have begun to ripple and deepen like a pool),
Comes your mother's footstep, her voice softly,
Hesitantly calling. She'll have come upstairs
To borrow something for the evening, cups or chairs,
But it can't be urgent, and the footsteps fade
Before I've made my mind up, whether to answer.

Below, where you live, time will be standing cowed
Among the colors and appliances.
What passionate consumers you've become!
Second washing machine, giant second TV,
Hot saffron, pink, eyeshadow ultramarine—
Rooms like those ghostly ones behind the screen
With just the color tuned to Very Loud.
Your father's out in his new Silver Cloud
Delivering invitations. You've all been
Up since dawn—not you, of course, you're a baby,
But your mother and your sister. Between chores
Teasing each other's hair like sisters, touching
Rouged indexes to one another's cheek.
The lamb will have cooled nicely in its fat now,
Cake been iced to match the souvenir
Rosettes (two ribbons with your name and mine),
Whiskey and set-ups set up like tenpins.
According to tradition I'm affecting
Ignorance of, the post-baptismal party
Ought to be given by the godfather.
But this is your godfather speaking, calling halt.
I have already showered you with garments
Priced inversely to their tininess.
Have been shown rushes of what else my doom
Is to provide you with, world without end:
Music lessons from beyond the tomb,

Doll and dentist and dowry, that 3-D
Third television we attain so far
Exclusively in dreamland, where you are.
Would that *I* were. All too soon I'll place
Round your neck a golden chain and cross
Set with stones watery as the stars at noon;
And don't forget the fancy sheet you'll want
The moment you are lifted, born anew
Squalling and squirming out of the deep font,
While the priest lifts only his deep baritone
That makes the skull a vault of melismatic
Sparklings, and myself groan with your weight—
Renunciation of the vanities
In broken Byzantine on your behalf,
Or your father's flashbulbs popping, or your mother's eyes
Laughing to see salvation's gas inflate
Their fat peach-petal bébé-Michelin,
Not having made you, on me, a lighter burden.

Time drawing near, a clock that loses it
Tells me you must wake now, pagan still.
Slowly the Day-Glo minnow mobile twirls
Above you. Fin-glints ripple in the glass
Protecting an embroidery—your great-
Grandmother's? No one remembers. Appliquéd
On black: cross-section of a pomegranate,
Stem and all. The dull gold velvet rind
Full as a womb with flowers. Their faded silks entwine
The motto ΚΙ ΑΥΤΟ ΘΑ ΠΕΡΑΣΗ—This too will pass.

You're being named for yet another
Science whose elements cause vertigo
Even, I fancy, in the specialist.
A sleepless and unlettered urban glow
On everyone's horizon turns to gist
That rhetoric of starry beasts and gods
Whose figures, whose least phoneme made its fine
Point in the course of sweeping periods—
Each sentence thirty lives long, here below.

From out there notions reach us yet, but few
And far between as those first names we knew
Already without having to look up,
Children that we were, the Chair, the Cup,
But each night dimmer, children that we are,
Each night regressing, dumber by a star.
Still, fiction helps preserve them, those old truths
Our sleights have turned to fairy tales (or worse:
Look at—don't look at—your TV).
The storybooks you'll soon be reading me
About the skies abound with giants and dwarfs.
Think of the wealth of pre-Olympian
Amber washed up on the shores of Grimm—
The beanstalk's tenant-cyclops grown obese
On his own sons; the Bears and Berenice.
Or take those masterfully plotted high
Society conjunctions and epicycles
In a late fable like *The Wings of the Dove.*
Take, for that matter, my beanstalk couplet, above,
Where such considerations as rhyme and meter
Prevail, it might be felt, at the expense
Of meaning, but as well create, survive it;
For the first myth was Measure. Finally take
Any poor smalltown starstruck sense of "love
That makes the world go round"—see how the phrase
Stretches from Mystic to Mount Palomar
Back to those nights before the good old days,
Before the axle jumped its socket so
That genes in shock flashed on/off head to toe,
Before mill turned to maelstrom, and IBM
Wrenched from Pythagoras his diadem.

Adamant nights in which our wisest apes
Met on a cracked mud terrace not yet Ur
And with presumption more than amateur
Stared the random starlight into shapes.

Millennia their insight had to flee
Outward before the shaft it had become
Shot back through the planetarium
Cathodic with sidereality,

As ^{mul}KAK.SI.DI (in Sumerian)
Saw through haphazard clay to innermost
Armatures of light whereby the ghost
Walks in a twinkling he has learned to scan.

≈

Where has time flown? Since I began
You've learned to stand for seconds, balancing,
And look away at my approach, coyly.
My braincells continue to snuff out like sparks
At the average rate of 100,000 a day—
The intellect suspiciously resembling
Eddington's universe in headlong flight
From itself. A love I'd been taking nightly
Readings of sets behind the foliage now;
I wonder what will rise next from the sea—
The heart, no less suspiciously,
Remaining geocentric. Of an evening
I creak downstairs, unshaven in my robe,
Jaw with your father in his undershirt.
He's worn out by a day of spreading tar
Overtime upon America.
The TV off, you and your sister sleeping,
Your mother lifts from needlework a face
Lovelier, I find, without make-up,
Even as worry stitches her white brow:

She's written twice, and sent the photographs.
Silence from her people, weeks of it.
I've asked myself how much the godfather
They picked contributes to imbroglio.
Someone more orthodox . . . ? I'll never know.
Who ever does? From the start, his fine frank grin,
Her fine nearsighted gaze said *Take us in.*
Let them make anything they liked of me
From personal effect to destiny.
Now should he reappraise or she regret,
Fly back, why don't they? We've a daily jet.

Ah but time lost, missed payments—they're in deep.
Listen. Your sister whimpering, her sleep
Dislocated, going on three years.
Some days the silver cloud is lined with tears.
(Another day, when letters thriftily
Stamped for surface mail arrive,
Connecticut is heaven once again.)
And what if I'd done nothing, where would *you* be?
"One more baby back there in the Greece,"
Your father firmly putting his best face
On pros and cons, "when every day make seven
Bucks at the foundry? Never in my life.
Why I say to mean, this kid, she yours!"
Let's hope that my expression reassures.

Finding a moment, I've written: *Rose from bed*
Where I'd begun imagining the baptism
(In my old faith bed *was* the baptism)
To dress for it. Then all of us were racing
The highway to a dozen finishing lines
Every last one unquotable, scored through,
You bubbling milk, your sister in my lap
Touching her rhinestone treble-clef barrette
—Made-up touches. Lately I forget
The actual as it happens (Plato warns us
Writing undermines the memory—
So does photography, I should tell your father)
And have, as now, less memory than a mind
To rescue last month's Lethe-spattered module
From inner space—eternal black-on-white
Pencilings, moondusty palindrome—
For splashdown in the rainbow. Welcome home.

Let evening be at its height. Let me have stolen
Past the loud dance, its goat-eyed leader steadied
By the bull-shouldered next in line,
And found you being changed. Let your mother, proudly
Displaying under the nightie's many-eyeleted
Foam a marvelous "ripe olive" mole
Beside your navel, help me to conceive

That fixed, imaginary, starless pole
Of the ecliptic which this one we steer by
Circles, a notch each time the old bring golden
Gifts to the newborn child, whose age begins.
Nothing that cosmic in our case, my dear—
Just your parents' Iron Age yielding
To some twilight of the worldly goods.
Or myself dazed by dawnings as yet half sheer
Lyric convention, half genetic glow
("May she live for you!" guests call as they go)
Which too will pass. Meanwhile, à propos of ages,
Let this one of mine you usher in
Bending still above your crib enthralled,

Godchild, be lightly taken, life and limb,
By rosy-fingered flexings as by flame.
Who else would linger so, crooning your name,
But second childhood. When time came for him . . .

For me, that is—to go upstairs, one hitch
Was that our ups and downs meant so much more
Than the usual tralala from floor to floor.
Now I was seeing double—which was which?

No thing but stumbled toward its heavenly twin,
No thought but helped its subject to undress . . .
(Mother of that hour's muse, Forgetfulness,
Hold me strictly to the might-have-been.)

Each plate shattered below, each cry, each hue,
Any old composer could fix that
(Purcell? His "Blessed Virgin"? Strauss's "Bat"?)
Unless my taste had gone to pieces, too.

Well, light a lamp, but only long enough
To put the former on the turntable.
Head back, feet up, watch dark revolving fill
With coloratura, farthingale and ruff,

A schoolgirl's flight to Egypt, sore afraid,
Clasping the infant, thorn against her breast,
Through dotted quaver and too fleeting rest
The clavecin's dry fronds too thinly shade.

The text she sang was hackwork—Nahum Tate—
Yet ending: *Whilst of thy dear sight beguil'd,*
I trust the God, but O! I fear the Child.
Exactly my own feelings. It was late

And early. I had seen you through shut eyes.
Our bond was sacred, being secular:
In time embedded, it in us, near, far,
Flooding both levels with the same sunrise.

THE WILL

I am standing among the coal black
Walls of a living room that is
Somehow both David the Wise's and not his.
Outside, the dead of winter, wailing, bleak.

Two men and a woman, dressed in black,
Enter with a will. A will of mine?
They nod encouragement. I sign,
Give each my hand in parting. Now to pack

This canvas tote-bag. I have wrapped in jeans
With manuscript on either side for wadding
Something I'm carrying to a . . . to a wedding . . .

Then, wondering as always what it means
And what else I'm forgetting,
On my cold way. A car is waiting.

(Only last night a person more urbane
Than usual was heading for the Seine.

Here was one façade he seemed to know
From times he'd seen it all aglow

And heard its old chronologist pronounce
It not the present but the thought that counts.

He rang impulsively. No bell
Resounded from within the dark hotel.

Its front door, Roman-numeralled,
Still said, "I" in white-on-emerald.

Some humbler way into the edifice
Was chalked just legibly "*Ibis.*"

Steam from a sudden manhole bore
Wetness to the dream. I woke heartsore.)

I'm at an airport, waiting. The scar itches.
Carving, last month I nearly removed my thumb.
Where was my mind? Lapses like this become
Standard practice. Not all of them leave me in stitches.

In growing puzzlement I've felt things losing
Their grip on me. What's done is done, dreamlike;
Clutches itself too late to stop the oozing
Reds, the numbing inward leak

Of pressures we have effortlessly risen
Through on occasion to a brilliant
Ice blue and white sestet

Six lines six miles above, if not rhyme, reason.
Its wingèd shadow tiny as an ant
Keeps up far down, state after sunnier state,

Or grown huge (have we landed?)
Scatters into human shadows all
Underfoot skittering through the terminal
To greet, lulled, blinded,

The mild, moist South. Che puro ciel . . .
I'm riding in a taxi. The lightskinned
Driver steering me through scenery skeined
With twitterings, flutterings, scrim of shell

Pink, shell ivory—O dogwood days—
Fleet against unutterably slow
Dynastic faces of a portico,

These float from view, lids quiver, the air dies
Upon my lips, the bag's bulk at my feet
Gone underwater-weightless, tempting fate.

My burden is an old wall-eyed stone-blond
Ibis. Over the years (I bought it with
A check my father wrote before his death)
I took to heart its funerary chic

Winged like a sandal, necked like the snakes on a wand,
Stalker that spears *and* spares . . .
Which passing into a young, happy pair's
Keeping could stand for the giver. Now, next week

I mean to remember to take
David the Fair's acrylics
And turn the wooden base to baked blue brick
With lotus frieze, blossom and pad and calyx,

Abstraction of a river, eau de Nil
Arrested by the powerful curving bill.

Gliding to a halt, the prodigal stirs.
Pays the driver. Gives himself up to home.
His mother, a year younger, kisses him.
Maids are wafting suitcases upstairs.

While sirens over seventy, with names
Like Myra, Robin, Rosalie and Midge,
Call from the sun porch, "Come play bridge!"
They love their sweetly-sung bloodthirsty games.

He is sitting at the table, dealing,
When a first tentative wrong note
Is quickly taken up ("What is it, darling?")

By the whole orchestra in unison.
The unbid heart pounds in his throat—
The bag, the bird—left in the taxi—gone!

Gone for good. In the first shock of
Knowing it he tries
To play the dummy, dreads to advertise,
"Drinks water" like a character in Chekhov.

Life dims and parches. Self-inflicted
Desolation a faint horselaugh jars.
Property lies toppled, seeing stars
Nowhere in the dry dreambed reflected.

So that tonight's pint-size amphibian
Wriggler from murky impulse to ethereal act
Must hazard the dimensions of a man

Of means. Of meanings. Codicil
And heir alike. White-lipped survivor hacked
Out of his own will.

U DID WELL JM TO DISINHERIT
YR SELF & FRIENDS OF THAT STONE BIRD
—It's June, we're at the Ouija board,
David the True and I and our familiar spirit—

SACRED TO THOTH NOW AT 310 KNOX DRIVE
MACON GA IT HAS BROUGHT DISASTER
COMME TOUJOURS PARALYZED THE DRIVERS SISTER
MAXINE SHAW BORN 1965

THESE BALEFUL PRESENCES SHAPED FOR THE DEAD
WHEN THEY CHANGE HANDS EXACT A SACRIFICE
REMEMBER ITS FIRST YEAR CHEZ VOUS YR FACE
TURNED VOTIVE GOLD JAUNDICE THE DOCTOR SD

GODS BEAK SAY I EMBEDDED IN YR SIDE
HARDLY THE BIBELOT TO GIVE A BRIDE

Ephraim, we take you with a grain of salt,
Protagonist at best of the long story
Sketches and notes for which were my missing bag's
Other significant cargo, by the way.

BY THE WAY SINCE U DID NOT CONSULT
THEIR SUBJECT YR GLUM PAGES LACKED HIS GLORY
That stings. The guide and I lock horns like stags.
What is *his* taste? Aquinas? Bossuet?

SOIS SAGE DEAR HEART & SET MY TEACHINGS DOWN
Why, Ephraim, you belong to the old school—
You think the Word by definition good.

IF U DO NOT YR WORLD WILL BE UNDONE
& HEAVEN ITSELF TURN TO ONE GRINNING SKULL
So? We must write to save the face of God?

With which the teacup pointer goes inert.
Ephraim, are you still there? Angry? Hurt?

Long pause. YR SPIRIT HAS BEEN CAUGHT REDHANDED
IT IS HIS OCCUPATIONAL FAIBLESSE
TO ENTER & POSSESS REPEAT POSSESS
L OBJET AIME   Who, me?   WELL I HAD PLANNED IT

WITHOUT SO MANY DAVIDS TO COMBAT
MY GIANT DESIGNS UPON YR ART MON CHER
SHRINK TO THIS TOPSYTURVY WILLOWWARE
IGLOO WALTZING WITH THE ALPHABET

So what is the next step?   LIVE MORE LIVE MOST
EXPECTING NO RETURN   To earth?   IT SEEMS
U WILL NOT   Hush, don't tell us— PLEASANT DREAMS
GIVE UP EVERYTHING EXCEPT THE GHOST

I'm at my desk. Paralysis.
No headway through the drafts
Before me—bleaching wastes and drifts
Of time spent writing (or not writing) this.

Then a lucky stroke unearths the weird
Basalt passage of last winter,
Tunneling black. The match struck as I enter
Illuminates . . . My word!

(At someone's bidding smooth white plaster
Had been incised with mourning slave and master

And pets with mystic attributes
In profile among goblets, fans and fruits.

Here was a manuscript. Here were
Five catgut stitches laid in lusterware.

And here in final state, where lost was found,
The ibis sat. Another underground

Chamber made ready. If this one was not
Quite the profoundest or the most ornate,

Give it time. The bric-a-brac
Slumbered in bonds that of themselves would break

One fine day, at any chance unsealing,
To shining leaf and woken shades of feeling.)

Already thickskinned little suns
Are coming back, and gusts of sharp cologne
—Lemon trees bearing and in bloom at once—

And rings exchanged for life,
And one high jet that cut to the blue's bone
Its healing hieroglyph,

While briefly over the house
A dirtbrown helicopter
Like the bad fairy Carabosse, its clatter
Drowning out the vows,

Drowning out the sweet
Voices of doves and finches
At home among the branches
In the bright, cool heat,

Hovered close, then, seeing
That it would not eclipse
The sunniness beneath it, up and went

As much had, without saying—
Leaving to lovers' lips
All further argument.

Indigo, magenta, color of ghee,
An Indian summer boiling where he sat
Put ours to shame. Six decades in the vat
Had turned his fingers emerald. Ah me.

For everyone's dirty linen here was *the*
Detergent. Zoom to combed snows on his line
—But not so fast! How fast were the colors of mine?
Was I mere printed personality

Or the real stuff, handwoven, deep-dyed Soul?
Wasn't, as he spoke, some vital red
Already running like madras, while the whole
System churned with . . . dread? hilarity?

Bless the old fool. The rustic lecture hall
Held still. Mosquitoes dipped their needle straws
And drank our blood in perfect peace because,
Along with being holy, life was hell.

LATE SETTINGS

(1985)

For my sister Doris and my brother Charles

I

GRASS

The river irises
Draw themselves in.
Enough to have seen
Their day. The arras

Also of evening drawn,
We light up between
Earth and Venus
On the courthouse lawn,

Kept by this cheerful
Inch of green
And ten more years—fifteen?—
From disappearing.

CLEARING THE TITLE

for DJ

Because the wind has changed, because I guess
My poem (what to call it though?) is finished,
Because the golden genie chafes within
His smudged-glass bottle and, god help us, you
Have chosen, sight unseen, this tropic rendezvous
Where tourist, outcast and in-groupie gather
Island by island, linked together,
Causeways bridging the vast shallowness—

Through the low ceiling motors rip.
Below me, twisting in the asphalt grip
Of mall and pancake house, boatel and bank,
What's left of Nature here? Those trees five thousand tin
Roofs, like little mirrors in distress,
Would flash up from if the sun were out . . .
Oh for the lucid icebound book of winter
I gave up my rapt place in for this trip!

Such a mistake—past fifty and behaving
As if hope sprang eternal. At the baggage claim
Armed with *The Power and the Glory* (Greene),
I notice, finger-drawn in a soaped pane,
One black sun only, spokes in air
Like legs of a big bug flipped on its back,
Above a clumsy WELLCOME TO THE KEYS
—Then see the open car. You in it, waving.

Couldn't one have gone into the matter
Before succumbing? Easier said than done,
What with this tough white coral skeleton
Beneath a crop of shanties built on blocks,
On air, on edge for, any day,
Water and wind to sweep them clean away—
Ill-braced like me, capricious chatterbox,
Against your blasts of horn and floods of casual patter.

Sales patter? The appalling truth now bores
Into my brain: you've *bought* a house
And pass, en route to it, the peeling white
Five-story skyscraper in which "our" title
Is being cleared!—activity no more
Thinkable (you park, fling a green-painted door
Open onto a fresh white hall)
Than what the termites do, look! to these floors

Between the muddy varnish of whose lines
(But can you picture *living* here? Expect
Me to swelter, year by sunset year,
Beneath these ceilings?—which at least aren't low.
What about houses elsewhere, rooms already packed
With memories? That chiffonier
Would have to go, or else be painted white . . .)
More brightly with each word the daylight shines.

And fresh as paint the bare rooms, if you please,
Having consumed whatever came before,
Look up unblinking: will *we* bring
Their next meal—table, mirror, bed, lamp, chair?
Serve the ravenous interior
With real-life victuals, voices, vanities
Until it lolls back purring?—like our slum
Garden zonked by milk-bombs from two old bent trees.

Presuming, then, tripod and pendulum
Tell truly, and the freckled county clerk
Completes, adds to the master file
A Gothic-lettered "title" with your name—
What happens next? Behind a latticework
Of deeds no one has time or patience to undo
We cultivate our little lot, meanwhile
Waiting companionably for kingdom come?

Close-ups: hibiscus broad as garden hats.
Large-winged but nameless insect excavated
By slaves; the abdomen's deep strata

Primitive-intricate, like macramé.
Then from beneath the house, fee fi fo fum!
Caller the color of good smoke blown through the years
Into this dumb scarred mug he lifts to say:
"Huh? Not want *me*? Man, the whole world wants *cats*!"

No. No, no, no. We can't just cast
Three decades' friendships and possessions out.
Who're our friends here? (In fact I recognize
Old ones everywhere I turn my eyes—
Trumpet-vine, cracked pavement, that faint sulphur smell,
Those see-through lizards, quick as a heartbeat . . .)
But people? (Well, the Wilburs live downstreet . . .)
Of course, if shutting doors onto the past

Could damage *it* . . . Wherever that thought led,
Turning the loose knob onto better-late-
Than-never light, we breast its deepening stream
Along with others who've a date
With sunset. Each day's unspent zinc or red brass penny
—Here at land's end not deposited
In winter palisades crowned by antennae,
Fuel for the all-night talk shows of the dead—

Inflates to moidore, melts toward an oblivion
Alone, its gravity unspecified,
The far-off mangrove islet saves
From being wholly formed of air and waves,
Of light and birdcry, as with each step less
Divides the passer-through from, what to call
Such radiance—creative? terminal?
Day's flush of pleasure, knowing its poem done?

Our poem now. It's signed JM, but grew
From life together, grain by coral grain.
Building on it, we let the life cloud over . . .
Time to break through those clouds, for heaven's sake,
And look round. Any place will do
(Remember, later at the discothèque)

And what at first appall precisely are the changes
That everybody is entitled to.

Here at the end's a landing stage swept clean
Of surplus "properties" and "characters."
Gone the thick banyan, the opaque old queen.
Only some flimsiest human veil
Woven of trickster and revivalist,
Musician and snake-charmer (and, yes, us as well)
Pot- and patchouli-scented floats between
The immense warm pink spotlight and the scene.

Here's the Iguana Man, from lands
"Beneath the world." Dragons, withered like him,
Unwinking drape his fishnet singlet. Here
Balloons are straining for release; we pick
A headstrong silver one. And here a clown
Cat-limber, white-lipped with a bright cerulean tear
On one rouged cheek, rides unicycle, hands
Nonchalantly juggling firebrands.

Circles round every act form, or to groans
Disperse. This portion of the dock's been cleared
By the Salvation Army. (They're
Nine strong, a family; beneath the same
Grim visor glowers, babe to grandmother,
The same grim love.) "Y'all give!" our deadpan clown
Yells brandishing a hammer fit for Thor,
"Give or Ah'll clobber yew!" and *grunt* go the trombones.

Though no one does, no thunder strikes. Because—
Say, because a black girl with shaved skull
Sways on the brink: flexed knee and ankle-bell
And eyes that burn back at the fiery ball
Till it relenting tests with one big toe
Its bath, and Archimedean splendors overflow.
As the sun sets, "Let's hear it for the sun!"
Cry voices. Laughter. Bells. Applause

(Think of the dead here, sleeping above ground
—Simpler than to hack a tomb from coral—
In whitewashed hope chests under the palm fronds.
Or think of waking, whether to the quarrel
Of white cat and black crow, those unchanged friends,
Or to a dazzle from below:
Earth visible through floor-cracks, miles—or inches—down,
And spun by a gold key-chain round and round . . .)

Whereupon on high, where all is bright
Day still, blue turning to key lime, to steel
A clear flame-dusted crimson bars,
Sky puts on the face of the young clown
As the balloons, mere hueless dots now, stars
Or periods—although tonight we trust no real
Conclusions will be reached—float higher yet,
Juggled slowly by the changing light.

ISLAND IN THE WORKS

From air seen fathom-deep
But rising to a head—
Abscess of the abyss
Any old night letting rip
Its fires, yearlong,
As roundabout waves hiss—

Jaded by untold blue
Subversions, watered-down
Moray and Spaniard . . .
Now to construe
In the original
Those at first arid, hard,

Soon rootfast, ramifying,
Always more fruitful
Dialogues with light.
Various dimwit under-
graduate types will wonder
At my calm height,

Vapors by then surmounted
(Merely another phase?)
And how in time I trick
Out my new "shores" and "bays"
With small craft, shrimpers'
Bars and rhetoric.

Darkly the Old Ones grumble
I'll hate all that. Hate words,
Their schooling flame?
The spice grove chatted up
By small gray knowing birds?
Myself given a name?

Waves, as your besetting
Depth-wish recedes,
I'm surfacing, I'm home!

Open the atlas. Here:
This dot, securely netted
Under the starry dome.

(Unlike this page—no sooner
Brought to the pool than wafted
Out of reach, laid flat
Face-up on cool glares, ever
So lightly swayed, or swaying . . .
Now who did that?)

DEVELOPERS AT CRYSTAL RIVER

Elysian glade—
Roilings, upshudderings
Of tinsel, mirror-sycamores in wind . . .
No, we are underwater.
These are the Springs:
From deep below the bottom of white sand
Mercurial baubles effervesce
To aerate
A glassed-in bower of bliss
They keep at 74 degrees.

The mother manatees,
Brought here as babies, bring their babies here
To see the year-round decorations
And revel in each "tree's"
Renewing fruitlessness.
Muses of sheer
Indolence they are, and foes
To nothing in creation
—Least of all, those
Luscious undulating lawns downstream

Plowing through which, a sudden
Tenor scream,
The power launch veers—on guard!
Paths widen blue, then redden . . .
The huge, myopic cows go unheard. Poor
Finely-wrinkled humps
Over and over scarred
By the propellers, gaffs and garden tools
The boatmen use on them for fun,
Each year are fewer.

Sweet heaven, here comes one—
No heavier than a sigh
Or small dirigible
Gone limp, or adipose

413

Naiad walking through murk, on knives. Unmarriageable
(Unless to the Prince of Whales)
In her backwater court
She'll have escaped our human hells—?
Look how the blades have cut
Even into her.

Intuiting the visitor,
She drifts closer;
Flippers held out, deprecative but lonely,
Makes to salute
Her long-lost cousin with *his*
Flippers, his camera and visor.
Time stops as, face to face,
She offers what he'll only
Back on Earth find words for—a rueful, chaste,
Unshaven kiss.

THINK TANK

Because our young were drab
And slow to grow, for Carnival we ate them,
Pennants of motley distancing the deed
In the dechlorinated crystal slab.

The harlequin all grace and greed
Made glancing mincemeat of the mirror kissed.
The scholar blotched with ich
Sank into lonely shudderings.

But at our best we were of one mind,
Did our own sick or vital things
Within a medium secured by trick

Reflections over which, day, night, the braille
Eraser glided of the Snail
Our servant, huge and blind.

The shallows, brighter,
Wetter than water,
Tepidly glitter with the fingerprint-
Obliterating feel of kerosene.

Each piling like a totem
Rises from rock bottom
Straight through the ceiling
Aswirl with suns, clear ones or pale bluegreen,

And beyond! where bubbles burst,
Sphere of their worst dreams,
If dream is what they do,
These floozy fish—

Ceramic-lipped in filmy
Peekaboo blouses,
Fluorescent body
Stockings, hot stripes,

Swayed by the hypnotic ebb and flow
Of supermarket Muzak,
Bolero beat the undertow's
Pebble-filled gourds repeat;

Jailbait consumers of subliminal
Hints dropped from on high
In gobbets none
Eschews as minced kin;

Who, hooked themselves—bamboo diviner
Bent their way
Vigorously nodding
Encouragement—

Are one by one hauled kisswise, oh
Into some blinding hell
Policed by leathery ex-
Justices each

Minding his catch, if catch is what he can,
If mind is what one means—
The torn mouth
Stifled by newsprint, working still. If . . . if . . .

The little scales
Grow stiff. Dusk plugs her dryer in,
Buffs her nails, riffles through magazines,
While far and wide and deep

Rove the great sharkskin-suited criminals
And safe in this lit shrine
A boy sits. He'll be eight.
We've drunk our milk, we've eaten our stringbeans,

But left untasted on the plate
The fish. An eye, a broiled pearl, meeting mine,
I lift his fork . . .
The bite. The tug of fate.

THE HELP

Louis Leroy, gentleman's gentleman
Among cashmeres and shantungs never quite
Caught smoking; shiftless Beulah with her fan,
Easing her dream books out of sight;
Jules all morning sharpening the bright
Kitchen knives, his one dull eye on Grace . . .
—The whole arranged so that *we* might,
Seeing nothing, say they Knew Their Place.

Gods they lived by, like the Numbers Man
Supremely dapper in the back porchlight,
Their very skins, cocoa and tan
Up the scale to glistening anthracite,
Challenged yet somehow smiled away the white
Small boy on Emma's lap: home base
Of common scents. Starch, sweat, snuff, they excite
Me still. Her arms round me, I knew my place.

James Madison, who chauffeured the sedan . . .
Shirt off in the garage after a fight
"At my friend's house," red streamers ran
Down his tall person, filling me with fright
—Or had I gained an abrupt, gasping height
Viewed from which pain shrugged and wore his face?
("We loved our darkies"—Cousin Dwight.)
I've since gone back up there. I knew the place.

Father and Mother, side by side tonight
Lax as dolls in your lit showcase,
Where are those poor souls now? Did they see right
Into our hearts at last, and know their place?

DOMINO

Delicious, white, refined
Is all that I was raised to be,
Whom feeling for the word
Plus crystal rudiments of mind
Still keep—however stirred—
From wholly melting in the tea.

Far, far away, men cut
The sea-wide, sea-green fields of cane.
Often a child's lament
Filled the infested hut.
Doña Pilar flew back for Lent
—Had she been inhumane?

The better to appraise his mess,
History's health freak begs
That such as we be given up.
Outpouring bitterness
Rewards the drainer of the cup . . .
He'll miss those sparkling dregs.

PALM BEACH WITH PORTUGUESE
MAN-OF-WAR

for Tony Parigory

A mile-long vertebrate picked clean
To lofty-plumed seableached incurving ribs

Poor white the soil like talcum mixed with grit
But up came polymorphous green

No sooner fertilized than clipped
Where glimmerings from buried nozzles rose

And honey gravel driveways led
To the perpetual readiness of tombs

Shellwhite outside or white-on-white
A dropping bird motif still wet

Pastel and madrepore the shuttered rooms'
Nacreous jetsam wave on wave

Having swept our late excrescences
The wens and wives away to mirrorsmoke

Place settings for the skin
Diver after dark the extra man

Drowning by candlelight whose two minds reel
How to be potent *and* unsexed

Worth a million *and* expendable
How to be everybody's dish

And not have seen through the glass visor
What would be made of him some night

By the anemone's flame chiffon gown
Like those downtown in the boutiques

By razor labia of hangers-on
To territories this or that

Tiny hideous tycoon stakes out
Empire wholly built upon albino

Slaves the fossil globules of a self-
Creating self-absorbing scheme

Giddy in scope pedantic in detail*
Over which random baby gorgons

Float without perception it would seem
Whom their own purple airs inflate

And ganglia agonizingly outlive
Look out! one has been blown ashore

For tomorrow's old wet nurse to come
Ease from the dry breast and sheet in foam

---

*"Exactly like Egypt in the thirties," you marvel. ("The Nile without Cleopatra," Henry James had said.) But across the lake West Palm Beach tells a different story. Here are garages, trailer camps, fruit stands, TV bars. Here people actually live year round, or die—my father's buried in that old cemetery off the Interstate. Such rudiments as these make up a flat prose text, which dented fender or gouged stucco or the slash in a black forearm help, like punctuation, to render fully, finally intelligible.

THE SCHOOL PLAY

"Harry of Hereford, Lancaster, and Derby,
Stands here for God, his country, and . . ." And what?
"Stands here for God, his Sovereign, and himself,"
Growled Captain Fry who had the play by heart.
I was the First Herald, "a small part"
—I was small too—"but an important one."
What was not important to the self
At nine or ten? Already I had crushes
On Mowbray, Bushy, and the Duke of York.
Handsome Donald Niemann (now himself,
According to the Bulletin, headmaster
Of his own school somewhere out West) awoke
Too many self-indulgent mouthings in
The dummy mirror before smashing it,
For me to set my scuffed school cap at him.
Another year I'd play that part myself,
Or Puck, or Goneril, or Prospero.
Later, in adolescence, it was thought
Clever to speak of having found oneself,
With a smile and rueful headshake for those who hadn't.
People still do. Only the other day
A woman my age told us that her son
"Hadn't found himself"—at thirty-one!
I heard in the mind's ear an amused hum
Of mothers and fathers from beyond the curtain,
And that flushed, far-reaching hour came back
Months of rehearsal in the gymnasium
Had led to: when the skinny nobodies
Who'd memorized the verse and learned to speak it
Emerged in beards and hose (or gowns and rouge)
Vivid with character, having put themselves
All unsuspecting into the masters' hands.

The loving cup was poisoned.
How is it that I knew?
Its drinkers before long—
Flagstad and Melchior
Or Fremstad and whoever,
Couple after couple
Drawn by the horseshoe magnet—
Lay quenched on the stage floor.
Small hands ached from applauding
A residue of song,
Highly pearly C's not wholly
Dissolved in that strong brew.

An old print: La Fenice
(The house burnt and rebuilt)
From center stage appears
Almost a bird—stalls each a
Copperplated feather;
Aisle a proud neck; the boxes
Blazing with glass and gilt
An outspread tail in tiers.
No "gods," no mortals—only
Those bright blank quizzing tracers
Anticipation aims
At the rekindled pair

For whom aigrette and shako
Climb tonight's torchlit stair,
To fan whose flames the posters
Torn off like Tristan's bandage
In his delirium
Are pasted with fresh names.
Soon throughout Western Europe
Until the First World War
In every garret room
A highly motivated

Young would-be Isolde
Takes up the fatal score.

What did I want? A golder,
Emptier cup, a grail
Quite plain within. Whoever
Lifted it would quail;
The fires of that iris
Focus and draw him down.
He now becomes *its* pupil,
Thirsty for the moment
When the parched gold abyss
Upheld amid the din
Swallows the human image
And huge wings clap in bliss.

DAYS OF 1941 AND '44

for David Mixsell

The nightmare shower room. My tormentor leers
In mock lust—surely?—at my crotch.
The towel I reach for held just out of reach,
I gaze back petrified, past speech, past tears.

Or Saturday night war games. Shy of the whole
Student body, and my own, I've hid
In the furnace room. His warning stokes my head:
This time, Toots, it's your pants up the flagpole!

And why, four-letter man, descend
To pick on me, in those days less than nothing,
A shaky X on panic's bottom line?

Imagine meeting now, here at the end—
You sheep-eyed, stripped of your wolf's clothing—
And seeing which came true, your life or mine.

At Silver Springs, that Easter break,
I'd noted "heavenly colors and swell fish"
—Mismarriage of maternal gush
To regular-guy. By evening: "Bellyache."

I was *fifteen?* Dear god. Page after page,
Fury and rapture, smudge and curlicue,
One ugly duckling waddled through
The awkward age.

A month of sundaes, gym excuses, play
("I got the part!!") and "long walk with S. J."
Locate the diarist away at school

Right after the divorce. Would brat-
tishness that ripe for ridicule
Ever be resorbed like baby fat?

"A lord of Life, a prince of Prose"—
Alliterations courtesy of Wilde.
Another year, with such as these to wield,
I won the Fourth Form Essay Prize.

In vain old Mr. Raymond's sky-blue stare
Paled with revulsion when I spoke to him
About my final paper. "Jim,"
He quavered, "don't, *don't* write on Baudelaire."

But viewed from deep in my initial
Aesthetic phase, brought like a lukewarm bath to
Fizzy life by those mauve salts,

Paradises (and if artificial
So much the better) promised more than Matthew
Arnold. Faith rose dripping from the false.

My dear—yes, let that stand: you were my first
True hate. You whispering, the sadist's glee.
You lounging, buried in my diary—
Each phrase a fuse. I wanted you to burst.

Your cubicle across from mine was bleak
As when school opened. Oh, *you* didn't need
Cushions, posters, cotton for nosebleed.
A mother caught by flash in Red Cross chic.

Or did you? Three more years and you would die,
For lack of them perhaps, in France, at war.
Word reached me one hot twilight. It was raining,

Clay spattering the barracks. I
Fell back onto my bunk, parched for décor,
With *Swann's Way*. Basic training . . .

I'd have my France at war's end. Over highballs
Back home, would show that certain of us *were* up

To the museums and cafés of Europe—
Those peeling labels!

Rich boy you called me. True, there'd be no turning
Back from the mixed blessings of a first-rate
Education exquisitely offset
By an inbred contempt for learning.

And true, when money traveled, talent stayed
Deep in the trunk, assuming it got packed.
Mine was a harmless figment? If you like.

Remember, though, how untrained eyes subtract
From the coin-glint of a summer glade
The adder coiled to strike.

The nothing you'd become took on a weight
No style I knew could lighten. The latrine
Mirrors that night observed what once had been
Your mortal enemy disintegrate

To multi-absent and bone-tired hoplite,
Tamed more than told apart by his dog-tags.
Up the flagpole with those rank fatigues
Bunched round his boots! Another night

Beneath unsimulated fire he'd crawl
With full pack, rifle, helmeted, weak-kneed,
And peeking upward see the tracers scrawl

Their letter of atonement, then the flare
Quote its entire red minefield from midair—
Between whose lines it has been life to read.

PAGE FROM THE KORAN

A small vellum environment
Overrun by black
Scorpions of Kufic script—their ranks
All trigger tail and gold vowel-sac—
At auction this mild winter morning went
For six hundred Swiss francs.

By noon, fire from the same blue heavens
Had half erased Beirut.
Allah be praised, it said on crude handbills,
For guns and Nazarenes to shoot.
"How gladly with proper words," said Wallace Stevens,
"The soldier dies." Or kills.

God's very word, then, stung the heart
To greed and rancor. Yet
Not where the last glow touches one spare man
Inked-in against his minaret
—Letters so handled they are life, and hurt,
Leaving the scribe immune?

TOPICS

1 / CASUAL WEAR

Your average tourist: Fifty. 2.3
Times married. Dressed, this year, in Ferdi Plinthbower
Originals. Odds 1 to 9^{10}
Against her strolling past the Embassy

Today at noon. Your average terrorist:
Twenty-five. Celibate. No use for trends,
At least in clothing. Mark, though, where it ends.
People have come forth made of colored mist

Unsmiling on one hundred million screens
To tell of his prompt phone call to the station,
"Claiming responsibility"—devastation
Signed with a flourish, like the dead wife's jeans.

2 / POPULAR DEMAND

These few deep strongholds. Each with generator,
Provisions, dossiers. It would seem the worst
Has happened, who knows how—essential data
Lost in the bright, chromosome-garbling burst.

You, Comrade, will indefinitely be resident
Of this one, with your disciplined women and staff;
You and yours of this one, Mr. President.
Grim huddles. Then a first, uncertain laugh

—Spirits reviving, as life's bound to do?
Not from dead land, waste water, sulphur sky.
Nowhere is anything both alive and blue
Except, inside your block heads, the mind's eye

Marveling up out of our common grave:
You never thought . . . Sincerely didn't think . . .

Who gave it clearance? It ransacks the cave
For you with cordial venom. Damn you, drink!

3 / CAESARION

A glow of cells in the warm Sea,
Some vaguest green or violet soup
Took a few billion days to loop
The loops we called Eternity.

Before the splendor bit its tail
Blake rendered it in aquatint
And Eddington pursued a glint—
Recoil, explosion—scale on scale.

What stellar hopefuls, plumed like Mars,
Sank to provincial rant and strut,
Lines blown, within the occiput?
Considering the fate of stars,

I think that man died happiest
Who never saw his Mother clasp
Fusion, the tiny naked asp,
By force of habit to her breast.

II

IDEAS

CHARLES *and* XENIA *are discussing them*
At her place. Interrupted solitaire,
Fern, teapot, humdrum harmonies from where
Blinks a green cat's-eye, the old FM.

XENIA: Now no. But when I am child my parents
Are receiving them. Emigrés I think very old,
Distinguished. Spectacles with rims of gold.
Clothes stained by acid of expérience.

Forever I am mixing them, although
My father explain, this one is physicist,
Archéologue, poet, so, down the list.
Tongues they are speaking sometimes I not know,

But the music! After dinner they are
Performing 18th century trio or quatuor
As how do French say digestif before
Mother is bringing in the samovar.

When they have finish tea they kiss, pif paf,
My father's both cheeks and my mother's hand—
Me too, if I go not yet to dreamland
So late bezaubert on my little pouf.

Maybe I visit Necropole in Queens
By underground with flowers once a year
To show respect. But they are buried here,
Here in my heart. CHARLES: Oh you Europeans . . . !

Mine by comparison are so, well, crude,
Self-pitying, opportunistic, young. Their gall
Is equaled only by that paradoxical
Need for acceptance the poor dears exude.

I'm sitting quietly? Up roars the motorbike
Cavalcade—horns, goggles, farts of flame.

They swagger in as if their very name
Implied a nature seminal, godlike.

One strips. One dials Biloxi. One assumes
The lotus position; and all, that I am who
Was put on earth to entertain them. As I do.
You simply wouldn't believe the state of my rooms,

And the racket, and the 6 × 18 psychedelic
Daubs. Weeks on end, I'll shut my doors to even
The few I fancy. Can you think what heaven
It is not to have to hear the syllables "Tillich,

Hesse, Marcuse," at least not from their lips?
Back they go to the glassy Automat
They thought was the Ritz, before we met.
Just picturing them there, though, their collapse,

Without me, into vacancy, the joint
Stubbed out in ketchup, I begin to feel,
Well, sorry. How long since their last real meal?
And am I all that fond of needlepoint?

Besides, the simplest can appear—once dressed
In things of mine, and keeping their mouths shut—
Presentable. Not in smart places, but
You know my soft spot for the second best.

Enfin, considering the lives they've led,
They're shaping up. Some of my polish must
Be rubbing off on them. Now if they'd just
Learn to stick to their side of the bed—

Midnight already? I've a date. Bye. *Goes.*
The music stops. XENIA *resumes her Patience.*
VOICE: This performance of the *Enigma Variations*
Has brought our evening concert to a close.

THE "METRO"

One level below street, an airless tank—
We'd go there, evenings, watch through glass the world
Eddy by, winking, casting up
Such gorgeous flotsam that hearts leapt, or sank.

Over the bar, in polychrome relief,
A jungle idyll: tiger, water hole,
Mate lolling on her branch, apéritif-
Green eyes aglare. We also lolled and drank,

Joking with scarface Kosta, destitute
Sotíri, Plato in his new striped suit . . .
Those tigers are no more now. The bar's gone,
And in its place, O memory! a bank.

THE HOUSE FLY

Come October, if I close my eyes,
A self till then subliminal takes flight
Buzzing round me, settling upon the knuckle,
The lip to be explored not as in June
But with a sense verging on micromania
Of wrong, of tiny, hazy, crying wrongs
Which quite undo her—look at that zigzag totter,
Proboscis blindly tapping like a cane.
Gone? If so, only to re-alight

Or else in a stray beam resume the grand toilette
(Eggs of next year's mischief long since laid):
Unwearying strigils taken to the frayed,
Still glinting wings; the dull-red lacquer head
Lifted from its socket, turned mechanically
This way and that, like a wristwatch being wound,
As if there would always be time . . .

Downstairs in this same house one summer night,
Founding the cult, her ancestress alit
On the bare chest of Strato Mouflouzélis
Who stirred in the lamp-glow but did not wake.
To say so brings it back on every autumn
Feebler wings, and further from that Sun,
That mist-white wafer she and I partake of
Alone this afternoon, making a rite
Distinct from both the blessing and the blight.

AN UPSET

Drowsing in bed alone, quite thoughtless of nights
When I didn't, an ominous crack, some loud low snaps
     Like river ice breaking up
From the next room (lit still—I hadn't retired)
  Swept me out there in time to watch my
       Grandfather's table,
    One of the pedestal's three
      Leonine hips
Disjointed under mounting stress,
      Collapse.

    It could have been
   The old man felled anew
    Seen through a thaw
Of pain—struck broadside, banks whose failure
    Sent slowly crashing full
Ashtray, lamp, magnifying glass and—no!—
Lisʒt; *Les Dieux*; *The Japanese Tattoo*;
  Babel's *Collected Stories*; *Last*
Poems; *Thinking* and *Willing* (boxed together);
Animal Farm; *A Little Boy Lost*—to name just a few.

   Whew. A disaster zone
Facing therapy: sandpaper, clamps and glue,
Jetsam and overflow's diversion to shelves
    Unbuilt, if not to plain
     Oblivion . . .
   Another "flood" behind us,
    Now to relearn
  Uprightness, lightness, poise:
First things—the lamp supposes, prone
    Yet burning wildly on.

MONTH

Sun-up off easterly casings prints a first
Sheet of pink, soon-to-be-cancelled commemoratives:
Liner with tugs, the old king's midair medallion
Balancing a new moon's in the next frame.
Or it's an edifice of frames and valances,
Noons, twilights, seven to a floor, arranging
For views (*12:30—G at the Flèche d'Or*)
Of someone permanently opposite,
Whose wallpaper is change; thin rain, the tinsel
Flocking of today's. Antagonist
And tenant both, across this neutral grid
Green and red forces monitor
She'd meet your eye. But names, claims, fleet o'clocks
(*Pick up opera tickets before 6*)
Forming between you like a frost,
Or like the TV's electronic blizzard
Phasing to terror in a ski-mask
Whatever cozy personality,
White out all glow of her interior,
All recollection that on high
Reigns cloudless glory, moon just past the full,
And stars. Unfelt, they even so
Strike through cover to the date. Tomorrow's
Four edges flush with a great furnace door
Go dark. Already the last act? One fugitive
Beam from that first, half-mythic dawn
Degenerates to limelight Dalibor
Falls bleeding in. Check. Don't make his mistake
And wish on the wrong crescent, lest her pawn
Turn queen and—Thunder scores. You've just this moment
Left to unriddle her new name, and wake.

SANTO

for Peter Hooten and Alan Moss Reverón

Francisco on his shelf,
Wreathed in dusty wax
Roses, for weeks and weeks
Hadn't been himself—

Making no day come true
By answering a prayer,
Just dully standing there . . .
What did our Grandma do?

She painted his beard black
And rinsed the roses clean,
Then hid his rags in half
A new red satin cloak,

Renaming him Martín.
Next week the baby spoke,
Juan sent a photograph
On board his submarine,

Aunt Concha went to cook
Downtown at the hotel,
The sick white dog got well
—And that was all it took!

PETER

1 / TATTOOS

Right arm: a many-splendored
Korean dagger-and-heart
Wound in a scroll, or banner—
DEATH BEFORE DISHONOR.

(Between the H and O
One barely audible
Stammer of skin,
DISH ONOR—so.)

Then left: italic *Lillia,* herself
Far out in Venice West
With the car and the children, sinking
Painlessly in

Under a BB shot
Probed to this white star
Through deepening north woods where "Spring was best"
And "never human foot . . ."

But your chest, a boy's no longer,
Paler, leaner
From night shifts at the Mill:
Across it still, over your real heart—rainbow

Fixes of plumage all that while postponed—
The USA's storm-blue
Project of an eagle
Glides, with nothing in its claws but you.

2 / BAD TRIP

Gray light. A cautious tread.
Your weight
On the bedside, shuddering—
Eighty million comets in your head!

Walking all night
Beach after beach, surfstrafe,
Starknout, clockwise flailings of the dark . . .
I want to think we're safe,

Each of us, in each day's golden scales.
From your unwinking stare
A juice of pain
Trickles between knuckles. There,

The tranquilizer's working. There, lie back,
Hush. Tears
Wetting the pillow touch
Its featherbrain

And soon enough a suite for solo pharynx
Clumsily bowed and scraped will find me bent,
A room away, on putting words
Into an angel's mouth. Thirty-eight years

No less the waif
Afraid of dark? Sunshine
Spread over hurt feet, snore to your heart's content
And mine.

3 / FUTURE APPLES INC.

You've fallen on work.
Luck smiles her little smile, by legerdemain
Those knuckles turn to outcrop,
Those tricklings to a wind-creased pool,

And here's your form
Reflected in a farm!—
Gaunt, lightly, chronically stoned
Latterday Eden with its absentee

Landlord, its wary creatures. The mud-caked brush-hog
Loves no man yet, neither (to judge by scratches
On wrists and calves)
Do the blackberry patches.

441

Some trees then, old as wives,
But bearing. And uphill, a beard
Of second growth, fruitless perplexities,
Dead roots, bygone

Entanglements *away* from light
Beg to be cleared.
It's winter wheat, clover and timothy,
Seasons of sweetening

If young limbs are to climb
Where a brow's furrowed, and the first-born so deftly
Hefts his bushel that you blink astonished
From time to time.

4 / THE FIRST-BORN

—Of *this* union.
Fact is, you've children everywhere,
Vermont, Korea, some
Grown-up enough to have kids of their own,

For misspelt pleas to come—
Illness, abortion, welfare and parole.
They all need help.
You're sorry and would like to help

But figure you help them more in the long run
By not helping now.
And so you grin and shrug
As at the mention of vasectomy—

Genetic litterbug!
This latest batch is "different"—still unscarred
By life, you mean?
In drifts the six-year-old

Wearing his mother's blouse (where's she?
Oh, "off on a rampage"),
Red polish on the fingernails
Of one hand. Drawn to me,

He lolls between my knees, asks *why* and *why,*
But listens also, much as if the die
Hadn't been cast. Will he have you—will I—
When all else fails?

5 / *FIDELIO* FROM THE MET

Upon a certain rock
—Glacial warden over "dreams come true"—
You kept on building castles, no,
Dungeons in air,

Unspeakable, unvisitable glooms
Whose guiltless prisoner,
Wasted beyond recognition, was alive
Just barely, just because you were.

(How often in the city
I'd see you—boots, jeans, glasses, hair—
And shout. As if you could do better than
To look like everyman.)

Yet when that boulder you'd go sit on,
Peter, come night,
To smoke and watch the constellations
For its dislodging needed dynamite

And like the heaviest heart at freedom's trumpet
Leapt awkwardly an inch, and broke,
There was no question whose
Whole life, starwise along its faults, had started

To set the musical
Crystals, feldspar and quartz,
Aglow down pristine faces only now
Seeing the light.

The billionth-or-so dawn,
And yet how primitive
The little factory looks, upstream,
Its brickwork that of "early man"

Launched and paddling through creation's
At-a-stroke venerable inventory
Baked into clay banks, bedded onto stone,
The day meanwhile our own.

Tire after scuttled tire
Glides under the canoe,
Manholes of a twilit avenue.
Better admire

The tannin-tinted clarity
—An opal freckle? A bug's wing—
Dimpled, asway, working
Cures for singularity,

Each view, to its least defect,
Flawlessly duplicated, healed . . .
Or was that last cornfield
Greener in reflection than in fact?

Duck! Museum
Skylight lowers
Like a boom. Through bowers
Of the no-see-um

One broad-bowed solo
Chord subtending, now,
Brindled cow,
Barn and silo,

Carries the Ur-
Conceptualist further

Into mimesis:
Life ever truer

To life, begun
Afresh with a few like-minded species,
While the rest of *ours* whizzes
Down Route 91

Whose traffic drone
(Or falls ahead?
Stay, reconnoiter
This white water—)

Yields to the eternal
Drumming of bees
In a noon tree's
Bleached bone.

Ah but, our zenith passed, my friend,
Two galley slaves, retracing a dead end
Of scum-glaze, lilypad, Atari dragonfly,
We're cuffed alert by headwind—empty sky—

Miles from a landing—every pulse a mean
Swipe of the palette knife—painstaking sheen
In jeopardy—the master's touch lost—sun
Cross-questioned, mutely reddening—damage done:

What good's "eternity" if it won't get
Us anywhere in time to build a fire
And pitch the tent and heat our stew before
Night falls, and share a final cigarette

Whereby new-smelted leads of the moonrise
Nonplus the prowling far-off headlight eyes,
And twin dreams fumble, ember and earth chill,
Shadow and cave, for one another—? Still

Once more in the event
All came to pass.
First light. Then, piece by piece,
Exact scales weigh the fortune lent

On such fair terms. From clay,
Cuneiform cliff swallows whistling dart—
Transaction noted here, in part—
Up and away.

Another misty one. These opaline
Emulsions of world and self. Paulette high up
In eucalyptus uttering her sun cry.
Arms reaching for the glimmer coming, going.

Tan shingle house, its hearth out cold, its tenant
Likewise, under patchwork. Fortune told
In Cups, a child on whom the Sun sweats fire,
The cards inverted, strewn, and his wild words

"Fool that one was and Hermit one now is,
Simple Death we'll both feel like tomorrow—"
Screwdrivers flecking the carpet with damp rust.
Of late a Guest, a further figure

Almost himself thanks to some B Complex
Taken in time, sits in the ferny alcove
Leafing a book of words Paulette appears to have learned
Never, never again to climb trees with.

She turns magnificent sane eyes upon this other's
Apparition. Strokes its grizzled beard
With gray-gloved fingers. Nearly gets to share
Its Danish when—a rent in air, the day's first

Thudding shudder (little hornet jet
Lonesome for Asia) sends the lemur flying
Into her master's limbs. His features dim and brighten
Working their way through night school. Every morning

The rip widens. At its edge a sun
Great white cloths equip will be wiping grime
From the tinted blue plate glass of fifty stories.
Perilous task. You wouldn't dare look down

On meditation center or shopping plaza.
One hard glance at the fault so many out here built on

And who knows? by noon another scarp upcoast,
Gilt broom and giant antennae, could be toppling

Dream material into some profounder
Pacific state—sea-boom, its thunder stolen
By the sleeper's softly breathing cave. Carnation
Pink to bone-white snippet stitched,

Laved past bleeding. Just one head, one tail
Protruding. Loud gin stilled and dyer's blues broadcast
On the spent wavelengths of the quilting bee . . .
Instead, the reader looks up "eucalyptus"

(From the Greek, *well-hidden*). Or if the sun has slipped
This once from its mile-high, breakneck ledge
To land somehow unhurt, all smiles,
Square in the suitcase he is living out of,

Goes—the cards have had him coming and going—
And kneels before the radiant disarray,
Clothing for days to come. On any one of them
Shutting the lid in a twinkling he'll be gone.

BRONZE

In August 1972 a skin-diver off Riace, on the Calabrian coast, saw at a depth of seven or eight meters an arm upthrust from the sandy bottom. Having made sure that it was not of flesh, and remarking nearby a second, sanded-over form, he notified the local Archeological Museum. Frogmen easily raised the two figures. Even encrusted with silica and lime, they were from the start felt to be Greek originals. Their restoration, in Florence, would take nine years.

I

Birdsong. May. Tuscany. A house. Sunset
Through red or green panes falling on small print
Pored over by two figures: my companion
("David the Fair") still, after all these years,
Marvelously young, gentle in manner—yet
A certain eager bloom is lost, like wax,
To earn a new, inexorable glint;
Umberto then, our host, gnarled round his cane,
Long freckled hands refolding the timetable
Dense as himself with station and connection.
Triumphant stumps of silver light
His austere satyr's face. The morning train
To Florence will allow us, he opines,
Forty minutes with them, "all one needs.
The next train down will have you back for lunch."

Perfection—they won't be in such easy reach
Ever again. But guess who hesitates!
"Close connections," says too quiet a voice,
"Harm the soul." I stare (indeed,
So he has always thought) and check a groan.
He's been unwell—one must remember that;
Has no resistance to cold, heat, fatigue,
Or anything, apparently, but me.
Fine! Say we never see them. I'm already
Half resigned. Half fuming also. These
Two halves, a look exchanged, now choose their weapons—
Notebook and cigarette—then step outside
To settle their affair beneath the trees.

The trees! Tall domed communicating chambers,
A dark flight above ground. One duellist
Writes blind: *my piano nobile*. The other
Levels his lighter, fires into the air,
Panicking the nearest green room where
Starlings by now have joined—safety in numbers—
Forces against the Owl. A twittering dither
Fills no less the wisdom-threatened mind . . .
The starlings, though, seem rather to rewind
Our day of human speech, erasing it
At treble speed from the highstrung cassette.
If one could do as much— A last drag. Wrong
To be so—so— Saved by the dinner gong.
I run to dip my hands in water first.
How pale they turn, how innocent, immersed.

2

Umberto's meal: a tablespoon of wine
Stirred into his minestra. While we cope
With eggs and spinach, fruit and cheese, he talks.
The life inside him's like a local clay
Gritty with names, Montale, Berenson,
Edith Wharton making our eyes flash
—Mario's too, who waits in his white jacket.
Plates gleam dimly from the walls' high gloom.
Our host's gaze lidded, voice a purr,
Out comes the story long heard *of.* I wash
It down tonight a shade too greedily—
Hence this impression in blurred chalk:
The famous story of Umberto's walk.

When Italy surrendered to the Allies
In 1943, September 3rd,
The proclamation was five days deferred
Until their main force landed at Salerno.
It was imperative that liaison
Be made with them, in those five days, by (word
Meaning to me anything but certain) "certain

Anti-fascist groups." And as there were no
Lines of communication safe from the Germans,
"Withdrawn," but smelling Naples' every rat,
Umberto offered to get through alone.
The train he boarded, one warm dusk in Rome,
Left after midnight, crept an hour down
The unlit coast; sniffed peril, backed away;
Returned its passengers to Rome at dawn.

Next . . . a bus? a jeep? a peasant's cart?
The vehicle evaporates. Our friend
(To be imagined half a lifetime spryer,
Credentials drily folded to his heart,
Correct as now in city clothes—
Whatever garment, that surreal year,
Betrayed its wearer like an epithet,
Skewfoot, fleet of spirit, dressed in whose very
Visibility to glide unseen
Across a poppied or a blackened field,
A bullet- or a fullmoon-pitted square)
Kept haltingly advancing. Hillsides rang
With the cicada of one sunny parasang.

The social fabric and his place in it
Were such that he knew people everywhere—
People the war had sent like snails
Into their shells, to feed on books and air.
So the stale biscuit and tea-tainted water
Served by a scholar's maiden aunt or sister
Brought him, through a last long stretch of dark,
Face to face with—tree-tall in lamplight—
"A type of Roman hero, your Mark Clark,
Beside whom on the Prefettura balcony,
His forces having landed overnight,
I megaphoned next morning—as my one
And only 'moment' on a balcony—
The terms of peace, translated, to the crowd."

"You were the hero," David murmurs, wowed.

3

Now Florence? But a stratagem
We only later analyze—
Bared shoulder and come-hither shrug
Of hill, the spread of golden thighs—
Lures our rented Fiat bug
Away from Them.

And soon enough, to two ecstatic
Oh's, on the horizon shines
Then vanishes, then shines again,
One of those metaphysical lines
Blue-penciled through the pilgrim's brain—
The Adriatic.

Our spirit-level, salt of life!
(Unpack the picnic here?) Above
Lie field and vineyard, castle built
To nurture intellect, art, love
Together with, let's face it, guilt,
Deception, strife.

Below, in brilliant aquarelle,
Undulating dullness fans
Itself to tatters. Bubble-streamers
Betray the scuba-superman's
Downward bent or Jungian dreamer's
Diving bell.

Here at my desk, but fathoms deep,
I've known the veer and shock of schools,
The kiss of inky Mafiosi;
Perusing stanzas like tide pools,
Have seen the stranger flex a rosy
Mussel heap,

And shaken myself clear. The break
Of glib, quicksilver levity,
The plunge of leaden look or phrase

Thudding to rest where none can see . . .
I name just two of the world's ways
Picked by mistake.

Sheathed in a petrifying mitt,
A hand took mine on the sea floor.
That detour (we'll reach Florence yet)
Had to be structural before
Heroes tomorrow stripped of threat
Could rise from it.

4

—Not a moment, poor babies, too soon!
For the Mediterranean will in
Another few decades have perished,
And with it those human equivalents,
Memory, instinct, whatever
In you the first water so joyously
Answered to. These you have fed
To your desktop computers—e basta.
Yes, hard on the heels of God's death,
As reported in Nietzschean decibels,
Follows (writes Mary McCarthy
In Birds of America*) one*
Far more ominous bulletin: Nature
Is dead, or soon will be. And we
Are well out of it, who in the tempest—
Exultantly baring through coppery
Lips the carnivorous silver—
Knew best how to throw around weight
And go overboard. Thus we arrived
At the couch of the green-bearded ancient
To suffer the centuries' limpet
Accretions unwelcome as love
From a weakling, cold lessons imparted
Through waves of revulsion, yet taken
How deeply to heart! From their oozy
Sublime we have risen. Dissolving

The clay at our core, sonar probe and
Restorative poultice have brought
The high finish in which we began
Back to light. Your nostalgia completes the
Illusion with flickering tripods,
Where feasters, fastidious stucco
Pilasters, and vistas of shimmering
Water red roses rope off
Make us objects of art. We dislike it
As women in your day dislike
Being sexual objects, but were not
Consulted. To fictive environments
Blood is the fee. And this light,
This pink gel we peer out through (not gods
Like the hurler of levin in Athens,
Not tea-gowned ephebes like the driver
At Delphi, but men in their prime
With the endocrine clout so rebarbative
To the eternally boyish
Of whichever sex) is the shadow of
Light we once lived by, dealt death in,
Dividing the spoils. And it burns
But to spangle the gulf that expires
Between you—still crusted with appetite,
Armed to the teeth by your pitiful
Wish not to harm—and ourselves
Whose much-touted terribilità
Is at last this articulate shell
Of a vacuum roughly man-sized. We
Should rather be silent. Rhetorical
Postures, the hot line direct
To the Kremlin or out of Hart Crane,
Leave us cold. It's for you to defuse them.
For us, in our Dämmerung swarming
With gawkers, what trials of mettle
Remain?—short of meltdown your fantasies
Trigger, then grandly shrug off
With a sangfroid our poor old heroics
Were child's play beside. Go. Expect no
Epiphany such as the torso
In Paris provided for Rilke. Quit

454

Dreaming of change. It is happening
Whether you like it or not,
So get on with your lives. We have done.

5

Let's do. From the entropy of Florence, dead
Ends, wrong turns, *I told you so*'s, through rings
First torpid then vertiginous, our route
Leads outward into the bright spin of things.
Our separate routes. A month. A year.
Time for Umberto, hobbling under plane
Trees now, now cypressed-in by memory,
To take a last step, crumple, disappear.
Time for Fair David to regain
A small adobe fortress where, beset
By rodent insurrections, howl and hoot,
He turns his skylit oils to the wall rain
Exorbitantly gutters. Time for me,

Who off and on had idolized these two,
To heed a sympathetic twinge.
The doctor probes and listens. Powers failing?
A shot of hormone? The syringe he fills,
At tip one shining droplet, pure foreplay,
Sinks into muscle. And on the third day
Desire floods the old red studio.
A figure reincarnate, wings outspread,
Full quiver, eager lips, from years ago—
My Eros to the life—awaits unveiling.
Friends, here is salvation! Are you blind?
Here, *under* the dumb layers which unwind
I somehow cannot. Tanglingly opaque,
They're nothing if not me. The hidden god,
Unknelt-to, feels himself to be a fake,

The poorest jerky newsreel of dead forces
Breast-deep in waves, that strained for shore,
Bayonets flashing, helmeted young faces
Mad to provoke from the interior
Those attitudes assumed in love and war—

All fair, till peace limps forward on a cane.
The Axis fell. Its partners rose again.
Up came from vaults, for light to kiss awake,
The groggy treasures of the Glyptothek.
Out came war babies. Only the lost life
Held back, reduced to skeletal belief,
Coils of shot film, run-down DNA.
Earth saw to it as usual, clay to clay.

6

All fair? Precisely what, fair friend, umpteen
Stanzas your distance tinges haven't been.
You whom night strips to armature, whom day
Equips with tones to brush desire away,
Painting as much of sheer Experience
(Your holy mountain, that sea-born, immense
Magnet, its fatalities untold)
As one tall window facing north can hold,
Raptly, repeatedly have scaled it, if
Only to canvas. Metamorphs of cliff,
Quarry and timberline, you understand,
Haunt me, too. Come then, "because they're there,"
On with our stories. Make the telling fair.
But first, in all but liaison—this hand.

7

Off the record, but as everyone
Perfectly knew, Umberto was the son
Of his father's friend the King, whose name he bore.
A discreet match, the death of the young bride,
This phantom parentage on either side . . .
Rumor? Yet the King's bust, I recall,
Kept reigning, on its trophied pedestal,
Head and shoulders over a salon
Never in use (gilt horrors, plush, veneer),
The single, token room to have been done
Up for the Contessa. Her demise

Preserved in prelapsarian Empire
And Biedermeier the enchanting rest:
Stained glass and goat-foot chair, blue willows peeling
From gesso'd wall, tent-stripes or clouds from ceiling.

Blows that set our braver products clanging
Level categorically these hanging-
By-a-thread gardens of the West.
Umberto first intended the estate
As a "retreat for scholars." His last will
Left it intact to Mario the butler,
So long devoted and his brood so great.
The house sighed. It had entertained the subtler
Forms of discourse and behavior. Still,
There'd be the baby's tantrum, the wife's laugh,
The old man's groan. New blood. How else redeem
Spells of such cast and temper as to seem
Largely the stuff of their own cenotaph?

8

For in the odd hour made even
Odder as it dawns,
I too exist in bronze.
We were up on the deck, drinking
With summer friends, when Fred
Asked who the bust was of.
Year-round sentinel
On the domestic ramparts,
Acquiring pointlessness
As things we live with do,
It gave me a look back:
The famous, cold, unblinking
Me at six, I said—
Then drifted from his side
To stand by it. Ah yes.

Slowly the patina
Coarsened, paled—no perch
For owl or nightingale.

The local braggart gull
Flaps off and up, its shriek
Leaving a forelock white.
Where the time's flown I wonder.
A deeply-bored eye sees,
Or doesn't, the high trees
Waving in vain for sundry
Old games like Hide and Seek
Or Statues to be played,
Come evening, in their shade.

Losses of the foundry!
As chilling aftermath
Laszlo—my sculptor—made
Headlines one morning: QUEENS
MAN AXED BY SONS. Had they
Also posed for him,
Two trustful little boys . . . ?
Smoothing their brows, the maker's
Hypnotic fingertips
(I still feel my scalp crawl)
Were helpless to forestall
The molten, grown-up scenes
Ahead, when ire and yearning,
Most potent of alloys
Within us, came to grips.

Here Augie, seeing me absent,
Ambled up to rest
Tanned forearms easily
On my unruffled hair.
A tilted beer, a streak
Staining bluegreen my cheek—
Bless him, he couldn't care
Less for the Work of Art!
The stubborn child-face pressed,
Lips parted, to the heart
Under his torn T-shirt
Telling the world *Clean Air
Or Else,* was help and hurt
As much as I could bear.

III

CHANNEL 13

It came down to this: that merely naming the creatures
        Spelt their doom.
Three quick moves translated camelopard, dik-dik, and
        Ostrich from
Grassland to circus to Roman floor mosaic to
        TV room.

Here self-excusing voices attended (and music,
        Also canned)
The lark's aerobatics, the great white shark's blue shadow
        Making sand
Crawl fleshwise. Our ultimate "breakthrough" lenses took it
        In unmanned.

Now the vast shine of appearances shrinks to a tiny
        Sun, the screen
Goes black. Anaconda, tree toad, alpaca, clown-face
        Capuchin—
Launched at hour's end in the snug electronic ark of
        What has been.

THE BLUE GROTTO

for Mona Van Duyn

The boatman rowed into
That often-sung impasse.
Each visitor foreknew
A floor of lilting glass,
A vault of rock, lit blue.

But here we faced the fact.
As misty expectations
Dispersed, and wavelets thwacked
In something like impatience,
The point was to react.

Alas for characteristics!
Diane fingered the water.
Don tested the acoustics
With a paragraph from Pater.
Jon shut his eyes—these mystics—

Thinking his mantra. Jack
Came out with a one-liner,
While claustrophobiac
Janet fought off a minor
Anxiety attack.

Then from our gnarled (his name?)
Boatman (Gennaro!) burst
Some local, vocal gem
Ten times a day rehearsed.
It put us all to shame:

The astute sob, the kiss
Blown in sheer routine
Unself-consciousness
Before one left the scene . . .
Years passed, and I wrote this.

Thanks, Dr. Williams, my throat feels better already.
ANY TIME. I WASN'T IN THE AUDIENCE
WHEN YOU READ YR OPUS   Oh dear—   PLEASE   DE NADA!
NEITHER WAS WHITMAN. WE SULKED IN OUR TENTS:
'BILL, I MADE DO WITH A DOORWAY IF IT HAD A
LILAC OR A HANDSOME LAD IN IT,
YOU WITH A SMALL TOWN & BABIES. GUESS WE MISSED
THE TRAIN?' But you were . . . America! LAND OF THE FREE
SAMPLE, HOME OF THE (GRADE B) RAVE. FADS, FADS:
WHAT HAPPENED TO THE BEATNIKS? KEROUAC
WAS HERE, MADE A BRIEF TRUCKER'S STOP   Then? BACK.
WHAT WOULD HAVE KEPT HIM? I ENVIED BODENHEIM
HIS HOUR OF FAME. WHERE'S OLD MAX NOW? A BLACK
CANE WORKER IN CUBA. *Your* star, though, would seem
Fixed in our skies. YOU KNOW WHY? WHITMAN. 'BY GOD
(HE SAID) BILL STAYS OR I GO BACK WITH HIM!'
Good for you both! I MISS LIFE. LIFE WAS GOOD.
Well, can't we always botch our lives in order
Just to be born again, time after time?
NOT IF THE STAR CHUGS OFF & LEAVES ITS BOARDER.

≈

I felt your presence yesterday, Miss Moore,
But lost you in the crush. TOM ELIOT
GAVE ME YOUR KIND THOUGHTS. We had hoped to hear
Your own. May we? O? WELL! THERE'S SUCH A NEED
FOR CHLOROPHYLL, SOME OF US WORK AT HUMUS DEPOTS
TRYING TO EVEN OUT THE 'GOOD' AND 'BAD'.
BACTERIAL MOULDS ARE SAVAGE, LIVE, MINUTE
WORLDS GOING FIERCELY AT EACH OTHER. WE
TRY FOR, O YOU KNOW, PEACE CONFERENCES?
TOM LAUGHS. WELL, LANGUAGE, LOVELY HOW IT RUNS
AWAY WITH YOU. AH NOW HE DOESN'T LAUGH.
HERE IT'S A VELVET BLACKNESS GIVEN TO THOUGHT,
BUT WE'VE OUR LITTLE GET-TOGETHERS. YOU
FINISH A WORK, OR PLATO LEAVES, OR YOUNG
MR LOWELL ARRIVES: A PARTY. OTHERS FAR

LESS FORMAL: SAY I'M BENT OVER A SLIDE
SUGGESTING . . . TROUBLE? THINGS AT ODDS? & THINK
SOMETHING THERE IS THAT TRULY NEEDS A WALL,
& THERE'S RF: 'YOU CALLED ME, MARIANNE?'
'YES, ROBERT, YOUR POEM'S WRONG.' DON'T WE GO AT IT!
You always need the live occasion, then—
A death, a poem, a bacterial strain.
HERE, YES, WE BOUNCE OFF LIFE. IT'S OUR TELSTAR.
BUT ALSO, WE WHOSE LIVES WERE SPENT 'CREATING'
(O WEARY WORD) SEEM BUT A TOUCH AWAY.
From? LIFE. EACH OTHER. OFTEN I THINK, WHY NOT
JUST ASK M LAFONTAINE TO HELP WITH THAT?
'CHERE MADEMOISELLE, ME VOICI' AND WE CHAT.
In French? MINE'S BAD. HIS ENGLISH WORSE. WE TALK
IN PERFECT THOUGHT, FAR EASIER THAN TALK.

THIS HOUR IS A REFRESHMENT. WHEN I SAT
WITH DJUNA THE RESULTS WERE TERRIFYING!
DJUNA OF COURSE LIKED A LOW CROWD. SHE REVELLED
IN STRANGLED MESSAGES: 'THEY HADN'T OUGHT
TO'VE HUNG ME' ETC. 'DJUNA, ENOUGH!'
RAT SQUEAKS, I TOLD HER. You were right, I fear.
I FEAR SO TOO. WITH ONLY NOW & THEN
THE GENTEEL MOUSE. Funny . . . pure La Fontaine.
ISN'T IT ODD? I WONDER NOW AT ALL
THAT MAKING-HUMAN OF THE ANIMAL.
And its reverse, as feral natures roam
Our ever dimmer human avenue.
GERTRUDE CRIED OUT TO ME AS WE LEFT YOUR DO:
'CAREFUL, MY DEAR, DON'T GET MUGGED GOING HOME!'

≈

Elvis Presley "meets the press"
In Heaven. Hostess, Gertrude Stein—
Expatriate Mother of Them All.
YOU FROM THE PAPERS HUH he wonders. She:
(POOR BLOATED BOOBY   WHAT A MESS,
AT LEAST MY EMBONPOINT WAS MINE)
PITY YOUR TIME'S SHORT   NICE OF YOU TO CALL!
B4 YOU GO, A CUP OF NULLITY?

464

He hates this: WHERE R THE CAMERAS   IT'S LIKE
NOTHING HERE   NO DRESSINGROOM   LIKE WHERE
AM I   WHERE R THE FANS   Thin air
Manages to coax from the dead mike
Aksel Schiøtz singing a Schubert song.
LISTEN   NO WAY   LIKE WHAT THE FUCK IS WRONG

≈

AS WITH THE HOUSE CAT THE HOUSE PLANT DRINKS U IN. THAT RUBBER
TREE NEAR YR GOLD FRAME IS NOW QUITE DENSE WITH LONG
    REMEMBRANCE
    —Of our neglect. How small its leaves have grown!
    Why didn't we repot it years ago?
YET THIS CONTRACTED OLD NUMBER LONG IN THE TOOTH WILL GO
ON SHRINKING/THINKING. HAS IT SHRUNK BACK OUT OF OUR WAY?
    Back from the mirror's door ajar, aglow,
    Into your realm—an old, old image, no?
                                      OLD
AS THE LEGEND OF NARCISSUS FALLEN INTO THE DEATH
OF HIS OWN IMAGE. FOR THE IMAGE IN YR MIRROR IS
NOT YOU BUT REVERSED, TIMELESS: ONLY ONE MOMENT IN 10,
000 DO YOU NOTE THE CHANGE IN TIME. THE MIRROR WORKS TO
DECEIVE. IT MUST. FOR THE VANISHT FAERY FOLK ARE NO MORE
ELUSIVE THAN THE VANISHING YOU. AS MERCURY WE
HOLD FAST & HYPNOTIZE THOSE CERTAIN VALUABLE ONES
PEERING AT US WITH INCREASED DESPAIR SAYING 'CURIOUS,
THE EYE'S CLEAR WOODLAND POOL CLOUDED WHERE A FAUN DRANK
    & FLED,
THAT TEMPLE GONE FROM ONYX TO MARBLE, YES, PASSING STRANGE.'

    GREAT MAGIC, EH ENFANTS? FASCINATION'S UNBLINKING
    RABBIT PULLED FROM THE OPERA HAT OF CHANGE

≈

. . . BUT DRAT, I'VE QUITE FORGOTTEN   Robert, shame!
No mind left, there in the realm of Total Recall?
MIND ON THE THRESHOLD OF A NEW LIFE KEEPS
THE DEATHWATCH OVER ITS REMAINS OR NOT
AS IT SEES FIT. MINE'S RATHER LIKE THE FAMOUS

RUSTY-BOTTOMED COLANDER. The famous what?
ISN'T IT FAMOUS? (Voices: MR ROBERT,
WHAT FAMOUS RUSTY-BOTTOMED COLANDER?)
NOW NOW, JUST BECAUSE I'M GIRT BY DIMMER WITS . . .
I GIVE YOU WALLACE STEVENS, AN AUTHORITY
ON THE WHOLE SUBJECT *If* he remembers. JM
A CIVIL TONGUE BEHIND THOSE TEETH!

                        AHEM:
THIS OBJECT WAS DISCOVERED WHEN A CLUMP
OF ROYALTIES RISING FROM LUNCH AT SANDRINGHAM
PRAISING THE CURRY, ITS UNIQUE FLAVOR, ITS RICH
COLOR, FOLLOWED THEIR HOSTESS INTO THE KITCHEN
TO THANK (A SIGNAL HONOR) THE INDIAN COOK.
'I'VE BROUGHT IT FROM MY VILLAGE, MAM'   THE SPICE?
'NO MAM, THE INSTRUMENT'   & TO SICKLY PLUMP
RESPONSES OUT CAME THE FAMOUS R B C!
So our corroding minds give *these* concoctions
Their je ne sais quoi? AND MANY A MAJESTY
UP HERE AT LEAST, MANY A NASTY SHOCK

(And so forth. An antacid tone like Tums.
We hang on those lips, two flaky mediums.)

                        ≈

One evening in April '79
At table, mulling over cuts and changes
I have in mind—though DJ disagrees—
To make before the *Pageant* goes to press,
We ask our Lord of Light to arbitrate.

FROM HALF ACROSS THE WORLD, SCRIBE, HAND,
LIGHTING GAUNT LIVES IN JAIPUR, KINDLING THAT PEAK
OF POLISH ON A HOUSEWIFE'S BRASS TEAKETTLE,
OPENING A BABY'S (NO, NOT THAT ONE'S) EYES,
I SAY: HAND, YOU ARE WRONG. WE LIGHTERS-UP
KNOW THE MIND'S COBWEBS. IN THAT BALLROOM SCENE
O GLORY WHERE I PLAYED OUR MISTRESS' FOOL,
THE POINT WAS, LET THE (BLURRED) BRIGHT POINT REMAIN.
OUR AUDIENCE, REMEMBER, WERE THE DEAD.
WHO AMONG THEM, OF A SUNNY DAY,

COULD TOTTER TO THE POSTBOX: 'CHER CONFRERE,
ABOUT YR SECTION 6 I MEANT TO ADD . . .'
NO, IN THE BALLROOM A LATE CONGREGATION
SAT CONGRATULATING ITSELF UPON
(FACE IT, DEAR HAND) AN ARDUOUS TASK DONE.
THE BALLROOM, AH! COULD I BUT KISS ONCE MORE
THOSE DIMWIT FACES WITH THE DAWN!
BUT THEY HAVE HAD THEIR DAY (& SAY). THEREFORE
CHANGE AND CHANGE, O SCRIBE! COME UP TO THIS
INSTANT (FOR YOU INKY) AT MY HEIGHT
AS TOUCHING THE HIMALAYAS I DEFINE,
MORE, REFINE THEM, FOLD ON FOLD, FOREVER
GETTING AT THEIR BONE OF MEANING. CHANGE!
REVISE, RISE, SHINE! GOOD AH MY CHILDREN NIGHT!

ARCLIGHT

By day unlit, the magic helmet keeping
Its lord invisible, now at dusk leaps forth,
Air darkens round, less after all (despite
Ambit and atomies magnesium-bright)
A person than a presence of sheer mind
Which, in itself however genial,
Brought once more to bear upon the scene—
Glassglint, palmetto, crabgrass between cracks,
And, glowering feebly at its pale, five shacks—
Arrays our dim old crossroads in a dread
Exceeding dark's own. This discourager
Alike of stealth and star has come to do
By night. The dog it dusts asleep or dead.
Wings battering the naught it makes to shine.

RADIOMETER

At sunrise on a pin
Upright within a globe
No bigger than your frontal lobe
Four little blades of tin begin to spin.

One side of each is white
And one side black—
White knowing only to fend off,
Black only to drink in, drink in the light

At first with circumspection, then be hurled
Backwards by noon at dizzying speed
Through the revolving door that gives onto the world;

While forward, just as helplessly,
Ghost-faces hurtle—Yang and Yin?
Phlegm and fervor? You/me?

World without end?
Not this one. Look: the setting sun, my friend.

Overture. A shutter opens. Down
Goes light. The Norfolk Island pine
Potted in peatmoss breathes
Deeply once; resigns itself on cue.
Under the dimming dervish crown
Extend now four, no, five fringed limbs
(Twelve more hang downward barely skirting trance)
In stills—in stills that—yes! inspired
Revolve and quicken. As though fingers flew,
Each organ point's plump quiver
Already stitching, radiance
Turning to raiment and back, forth steps a spine
Threadbare in seams picked out by the moonrise.

Wonders who'll itemize? Why, the jade tree,
Budding collector grown
Roundshouldered from its decade in the shade,
A shut-in life. Though short on fun,
It takes note, missing none.
Some nine score pitch-pure, stone-smooth lobes
Store the Courante, the Sarabande's grave strobes.
Exact dynamics are its law,
And juicy, time-consuming pedantry
Its lesson. Fluke or flaw,
Dust in a groove, temptation to emote
And blot performance leaving it unswayed,
Its roc's claw grips a base that creeps clockwise.

Not so two chestnuts in the streetlamp's glow
Champing, manes tossing. No
Obstacle brooked: RUSH to developer
These multiple exposures, bring the sheaf,
Or by now trunkful, up to date
As if their whole belief
Racing each night a green cross-country inch
Depended on it. Time—do they suspect?—

Is changing signature and only stable
These random moments ridden, then reined in,
As now, foam-petal-flecked,
Splattering triplets . . . Here the Gigue dismounts.
The stillness reaches "to the skies."

On the used plate a wash of silver dries.

PAUL VALÉRY: *PALME*

Veiling, barely, his dread
Beauty and its blaze,
An angel sets warm bread
And cool milk at my place.
His eyelids make the sign
Of prayer; I lower mine,
Words interleaving vision:
—Calm, calm, be ever calm!
Feel the whole weight a palm
Bears upright in profusion.

However its boughs yield
Beneath abundance, it
Is formally fulfilled
In bondage to thick fruit.
Wonder and see it grow!
One fiber, vibrant, slow,
Cleaving the hour fanwise,
Becomes a golden rule
To tell apart earth's pull
From heaven's gravities.

Svelte arbiter between
The shadow and the sun,
It takes much sibylline
Somnolent wisdom on.
Unstintingly to suffer
Hails and farewells, forever
Standing where it must stand . . .
How noble and how tender,
How worthy of surrender
To none but a god's hand!

The lightest gold-leaf murmur
Rings at a flick of air,

Invests with silken armor
The very desert. Here
This tree's undying voice
Upraised in the wind's hiss,
As fine sand sprays and stings,
To its own self is oracle
Complacent of the miracle
Whereby misfortune sings.

Held in an artless dream
Between blue sky and dune,
Secreting, dram by dram,
The honey of each noon,
What is this delectation
If not divine duration
That, without keeping time,
Can alter it, seduce
Into a steady juice
Love's volatile perfume?

At moments one despairs.
Should the adored duress
Ordain, despite your tears,
A spell of fruitlessness,
Do not call Wisdom cold
Who readies so much gold,
So much authority:
Rising in solemn pith
A green, eternal myth
Reaches maturity.

These days which, like yourself,
Seem empty and effaced
Have avid roots that delve
To work deep in the waste.
Their shaggy systems, fed
Where shade confers with shade,
Can never cease or tire,

At the world's heart are found
Still tracking that profound
Water the heights require.

Patience and still patience,
Patience beneath the blue!
Each atom of the silence
Knows what it ripens to.
The happy shock will come:
A dove alighting, some
Gentlest nudge, the breeze,
A woman's touch—before
You know it, the downpour
Has brought you to your knees!

Let populations be
Crumbled underfoot—
Palm, irresistibly—
Among celestial fruit!
Those hours were not in vain
So long as you retain
A lightness once they're lost;
Like one who, thinking, spends
His inmost dividends
To grow at any cost.

LENSES

1 / CONTACTS

Light as parentheses, your scales
(If not quite true so far
For weighing things "exactly as they are,"
OK for skills

And situations) float
Insensibly on unshed tears . . .
One spark of dust? Quick, the extinguishers!
A stare afire, an entire flight

—Out, out! Their little drum's
Twin lids unscrew to let them soak.
And (look) here comes the Sandman with his sack
Of love and dreams.

2 / MICROSCOPIC

The club is tiny, hard to locate. No
Neon sign, no noise.
You need immense focus and poise
To catch its minstrel show:

Nonstop cakewalk of multiple-jointed
Carbon-featured end-
Man enzymes, each with mirror friend
And high on his personal acid. Disappointed?

Still out to bridge the chasm?
But the strict program will not cease to size
You up, enucleate your inmost eye's
Nostalgie du protoplasme.

3 / TELESCOPE

Mark tonight's variation *Maggiore. Lento.*
Clear. Cold. The heavens' hushed, centrifugal evasion
Of the bungled hospitality we call vision.
Even should one of their company, entering the lean-to

Cloaked in a darkness bygone splendors break through,
Begin—O my swineherd!—the retelling, his itinerary
Is simply too complicated, too remote and solitary
For any human mind to stay awake through.

Yes, it was more than you or I could have imagined
Without the sense that made an old black pointer
Dozing by your embers twitch upright, and know the Hunter
And earn this dusty corner of his legend.

4 / CAMERA

Eyes wild, hair midnight-tangled, robe in disarray,
Convulsed by sobs, or laughter:
Once again they've photographed her,
That everlasting woman led away

From—flash! As background blurs,
Hands out of nowhere reach for tomorrow's saint.
Which terrible, which heaven-sent
Passion was hers—

Stark grief, stark frenzy, stark
Helpless amusement? All of these? All of these?
Not to be outfaced by journalese,
Print her next likeness in your own red dark.

IN THE DARK

Come, try this exercise:
Focus a beam
Emptied of thinking, outward through shut eyes
On X, your "god" of long ago.

Wherever he is now the photons race,
A phantom, unresisting stream,

For nothing lights up. No
Sudden amused face,
No mote, no far-out figment, to obstruct
The energy—
                    It just spends
And spends itself, and who will ever know

Unless he felt you aim at him   and ducked

Or you before the session ends
Begin to glow

MIDSUMMER EVENING ON THE PRINSENGRACHT

for Hans

It's late. The sun
Gone down, the scene remains—
Lintel, cornice, roof
Annealed in proof;

Idle each block-and-tackle
There at the apex of so many panes;
Cloud and clock tower one
With counterpremises the moon

Sleepwalks, and arches (doubled now to black
Silver-rimmed lenses of the blind) festoon . . .
Friend at last young, indeed
Almost a son,

Here it's your poems I can't read
That light lamps, fling up sashes, row beneath
Quickened, this quarter hour,
By the old tower,

Chime on chime on chime
—Percussions unresolved, conciliatory,
As if, still thinking out their story,
To ask for time.

SANTORINI: STOPPING THE LEAK

Five sessions of God willing lethal x
Rays on a live target purple-inked
For isolation, and the plantar wart
(Girt by its young, one throbbing multiplex
Neither knife nor acid could abort)
Active half my adult life's extinct
—Whereupon, sporting a survivor's grin,
I've come by baby jet to Santorin.

Inches overhead, a blue that burns,
That all but blackens—heaven as a flue?—
Against this white that all but calcifies.
Behind, a breakneck mile of hairpin turns,
The Golden Climb—mule dung and reek, whips, flies—
Lurches and jolts. Each moment someone new
Arrives at this despaired-of-from-below
Village unmelted on the crest like snow.

A gentler view, south from my balcony:
Past cubes and domes the baked vine terraces
Descend to beaches' black volcanic sand
And pewter glare of the September sea.
Mechanically a pencil guides my hand,
Then bells ajangle through the diocese
Bring the next balcony to life. Who's there?
Nelláki toweling her short silver hair.

She's not been idle, not our girl. It seems
We come provided with an introduction
To three old maiden sisters here, who set
A table that exceeds her wildest dreams
Of gourmandise. The ladies must be met,
And to that end I fear she's taken action:
Dispatched a note. A day or two should bring
Their summons. Meanwhile, homework, sightseeing!

The reason I've not made this trip before
Is that it would be—is—magnificent.
One wanted the companion who might
Act on a hushed injunction, less to ignore
The worst than stroll through it by evening light,
Made into courtyards (whitewashed, some for rent)
Where even stone-deaf Nelly hears her name
Spoken by mute bursts of nasturtium-flame.

Which color added, I've prepared my palette—
White, silver, black, night purple, dab of lake
For cliff-coagulations that regress
To null mist at a blow from the moon mallet.
Brushes? These five of mine with nothingness
Threatening forever to unmake
The living form it sees through in a trice—
A challenge to hold steady, these suffice.

Innermost chaos understood at first
As Gaia's long-pent-up emotions crippling
Her sun-thrilled body, spun to the great Lyre;
Pent up, but all too soon unleashed—outburst
Savage enough to bury in its fire
The pendant charms she wore, palace and stripling,
A molten afterbirth transmuting these
Till Oedipus became Empedocles—

Leaper headlong into that primal scene
And deafening tirade. The mother tongue
At which his blood boiled, his brain kindled. Ash
Of afterthought where once the sage had been,
Louse in a log . . . Or else, supposing flesh
Withstood temptation, could a soul that clung
To its own fusing senses crawl at last
Away unshriveled by the holocaust?

The curtain on a universal hiss
Would fall; steam cover all; millennia pass.
An island surface. Two. Three. Vineyards wax.
The plume of smoke with airier emphasis

Slant from the inky crater. Paperbacks
About Atlantis map the looking-glass
Rim of that old disaster, deep salt blue
Unrippling oval noon sun peers into.

Apart from the volcano and the wine,
The place, I read, was famous for its vampires.
People we inquire of shrug and stare—
No matter. Clearly, as the gods decline,
An eerie radiation fills the air
And eats their armor. The Byzantine Empire's
Avian-angelic iridescence
Shrank to black flitterings in the lymph of peasants.

Nelly agrees, but wears a child's gold cross
One hadn't seen, and wants to start with snails
Smothered in garlic. She's put in her hearing
Aid—we can talk. Out of the blue the loss,
Young, of her twin brother flickers, searing
Us both an instant; then her gaze drops. Veils
Of sheer belated comprehension blur
This little tumbler lifted, drunk to her.

Dear soul. Maria called her La Petite.
She has a modesty of scale and scope,
No use for buried motives, double vision:
Not one, beyond the voltage that a sweet
Dessert infuses, or a street musician,
To draw the lightning. Yet her isotope
Perished forever in it. As the waiter
Brings fresh wine, the grim, drowned point breaks water.

Not that I've lost or am about to lose
More than on the one hand (or one foot)
An ingrown guest, and on the other, well,
Greece itself. Corrupted whites and blues,
Taverns torn down for banks, the personnel
Grown fat and mulish, marbles clogged with soot . . .
Things just aren't what they were—no more am I,
No more is Nelly. The good word's goodbye

—Or so at least the radiologist's
Black box thought, humming it for all prognosis.
Goodbye. One smelt it as a scorching, read
The heat in shielded eyes and sausage wrists
Throughout his waiting room, where each was fed
Terror and time in exact, equal doses.
As for our meal tonight—which far-out lab
Prepares and serves it: Gemini? the Crab?

We must be light, light-footed, light of soul,
Quick to let go, to tighten by a notch
The broad, star-studded belt Earth wears to feel
Hungers less mortal for a vanished whole.
Light-headed at the last? Our lives unreal
Except as jeweled self-windings, a deathwatch
Of heartless rhetoric I punctuate,
Spitting the damson pit onto the plate?

And if (weeks later, Athens) life still weighs
Too heavily, why, leave the bulk behind.
Give M the bed. Let what was done in it
Parch at a glance from certain killing rays,
And the trunk-oubliette's black yawn admit
Such pictures, records, books as we've consigned,
Poor well-bred things in panic, to the freighter
(Bound for yet more life) Prestidigitator.

On this last evening, once tiny flames
Have danced within my pupils to consume
Letters and photographs, once M, dead drunk,
Muttering of bad faith, though he "names no names,"
Has sobered up enough to lift the trunk,
Alone I've stretched out in a rifled room,
Aching for sleep. There comes to me instead
—Brilliantly awake but cased in lead—

A cinéma-mensonge. Long, flowing fits
Of seeing—whose? Utterly not my own:
Bayonet fixed, one olive-skinned Iraqi
Guarding the stairwell of a wartime Ritz;

The look outflashing from his brass and khaki,
That single living cell needed to clone
In depth a double, phantom yet complete
With skills and jokes, cradle to winding-sheet;

His moonbaked slum, muezzin cry and tank
Rumble, the day Grandfather plucked the goose,
The sore in bloom on a pistachio-eyed
Tea-shop girl above the riverbank
—Vignettes as through a jeweler's loupe descried,
Swifter now, churning down the optic sluice,
Faces young, old, to rend the maître d's
Red cord, all random, ravenous images

Avid for inwardness, and none but driven
To gain, like the triumphant sperm, a table
Set for one—wineglass, napkin, and rosebud?
Or failing that, surrender to blue heaven
Its droplet of pure ego, salt as blood?
The warm spate bears me on, helpless, unable
Either to sink or swim, though knowing whence
My trouble springs. Psychic incontinence.

A ghost-leak in the footsole. Fighting free
Of sheets that flap off spectral over tiles,
Like bats in negative, sobbing for air
I hobble to the mirror, wordlessly
Frame this petition to its oval, where
Behind a twitching human curtain smiles
Those revels' Queen, in easy ownership,
Sated, my vigor coloring her lip:

I whose demotic commune at your kiss
Took on new senses, snowflake-singular
Facets and symmetries, even as I fall
Back out of mind, yours, anyone's to this
Upsteaming human thaw, babble and brawl
Of now no thought, O that the shattered star,
The music-maker, broadcast limb from limb,
Be made whole, Lady—hear and remember him!

No answer. Or—? In gloom the peevish buzz
Of a wee wingèd one-watt presence short-
Circuiting compulsively the panes
Gone white. *My* drained self doesn't yet . . . yet does!
From some remotest galaxy in the veins
A faint, familiar pulse begins. The wart,
Alive and ticking, that I'd thought destroyed.
No lasting cure? No foothold on the void?

Its tiny secret agent watchful still,
Just where I'd counted on—say an oblivion
That knew its limits. Here was Santorini
Once more, blue deeps, white domes, in imbecile
Symbiosis with the molten genie.
I hear the ferrous, feather-light diluvian
Lava clink at a knife-tap from our guide;
Once more attain, Nelláki at my side—

Grumpy all day because a civil note
Had come by hand, before the morning mail,
Professing the three sisters "desolate"
(One with lumbago, one with a sore throat,
The third with friends in Athens—well, that's Fate)
Not to receive us. So goodbye, roast quail,
French wines and pastries briefer than a bubble . . .
We must be light!—once more attain the double

Site of our last excursion: Prophet Elias'
Radar-crowned monastery, reached by mule.
(Oven, winepress, lentil boutique, and loom.
A sunken door. We rose from hand and knee as
Oil lamps awoke an underground classroom.
Here, throughout centuries of Turkish rule,
Small pupils widening, their abbot set
Before them bread and wine—the Alphabet

Pruned of meaning to dry glottal kernel,
Gaunt root and stock that, quickened, resurrect
Sibyl and scribe's illuminated leaves—
Food for thought even now in this nocturnal

Limbo of straw children, scarecrow sleeves
Lifting their Book of Life mute with neglect,
While overhead a flickering in fetters
Descended on the office of dead letters.)

Behind us then. Next, down and up the gorge,
To gain, past a toy chapel to Saint Michael,
The precinct of Apollo of the Herds
—Of tourists? Not that day. A heavenly forge,
Hammer and tongs, our solitude, our words
Snapped up by North Wind, bellowed to recycle
The bare, thyme-tousled world we'd stumbled on,
Its highbrow wholly given to the Sun

Who beamingly returned the gift. We felt
A stone heart quicken, a deep fault made whole.
Far and wide round us infant waters laughed.
But He meant business also. Having knelt
In amused piety, and photographed
Our Friend, *and* fingered, open-mouthed, the hole
Burnt through my film—by one split-second glance!—
I drew a breath. So much for radiance.

Here, finally, music that would take Satie
Twenty-five hundred years to reinvent
Put naked immaturity through paces
Of a grave dance—as if catastrophe
Could long be lulled by slim waists and shy faces.
Our "worst" in part lived through, part imminent,
We made on sore feet, and by then *were* made,
For a black beach, a tavern in the shade.

AFTER THE BALL

Clasping her magic
Changemaking taffeta
(Old rose to young spinach
And back) I'd taken

Such steps in dream logic
That the Turnstile at Greenwich
Chimed with laughter—
My subway token.

THE INNER ROOM

(1988)

For Peter Hooten

I

LITTLE FALLACY

Chamber of blossom, not a petal spilled,
Yesterday's Japanese cherry
—You and I charmed inside the glow—
By evening had borne fruit:

A whole day in Beirut
—According to the radio,
The first since January—
With no one killed.

DECLARATION DAY

Shiners dance counter to the tide.
The dragon kite, all wagging tail,
    Hangs fire in a fair gale.
No trace of knowledge called inside,

Where after daybreak, as a gust
Of radiance unsealed its doom,
    An entire fresco'd gloom
Crumbled gratefully to dust.

The pool. Drowned leaves beset the drain:
Crown-deep how long in pale cement,
    Poor laureate?—till blent
With flash and ripple from your brain

Up swim two figures, surfacing.
Crosslight of blue flares, hazel flares.
    Noon bells. The garden chairs
Simply keel over in a ring.

A rose. The two as one. To wit,
Petals encompassed and exact,
This heart that opens to contract,
And, beating time, grows out of it.

The bower. Shadow of a space
    For picture-taking. Each
Foiling the sun in turn, they teach
His brightness to the smitten face.

And now the moment. The house tried
    To warn them. It's of hard
White pine stained dark as a lifeguard,
With lips and brows of zinc oxide.

Down even the dim hall they burn.
    A door just floats ajar.

The stillness trembles like a star.
A wish. Come true? Here's where to learn.

Unnoticed, evening falls. Night falls.
   In one another's glow
Foreshadowed attributes take slow
Possession of the old, primed walls.

MORNING GLORY

for Howard Moss

I

The *bud* a foreskin? More so as it wilts—
The vine of any afternoon
Drooping with once radiant antennae,
Now purplish, drained, the rite of passage done,
That generation's at-a-blow adults
Going obediently to seed.

As if a plant could disobey!
—In whose encyclicals ego alone
Is sacrilege. Why, even among the blue
Tuareg of the Atlas foothills a certain few
Will have remained, like you and me,
True to the miracle, or its memory:

The single day, at six or seven,
When each was little but a wide-ribbed heaven
Tuned wholly to the cosmic one
Of pulsing depths, blue deepest overhead,
And where, though busy Eros visited,
All we knew, all we lived for, was the Sun.

2

That talent scout
Meanwhile kept untold millions in view.
Intending everyone (as you know who
Posited deadpan) to be famous
Precisely for his hour in the sun,
The roving eye alit, over and out,

Cast through taut silk the shadowplay
Of lives-to-be. Yet how one given day

Allowed for Byzantine intrigue
With many a new twist
As the ascending tangle of spotlights
Became itself protagonist—

Art nouveau poster: August, matinée
Idol whose averted
Gaze the atavistic Greeks
Lament on dancefloors, in their Sulka-shirted
Nightmare of lucre: *The sun*
Hasn't seen me for weeks!

3

From afternoon shade
Where the others, sated and bruised, have called it quits,
A virgin frill emits
Wrong signals. Able neither, caught in vines,
To open and espouse
The world nor (consequently) to fade,

What have we here? Well, well!
Eye-shadow on an old maid? A clear case,
Dear colleague, of that syndrome—Down's—
In which the fontanel
Forecloses early on its full
Quota of intelligence. *Not all there,*

Yet touching, even gay,
It strikes a note sadly malapropos
—Or so, shaking our gray
Heads, we agree.
Its very dying is suspect,
Flaunted. A last shred of indecency.

4

Crete, 1975. Edward, one's friend,
Alcoholic but a gentleman—
Stabbed on the stair in his elegant shell of a house
Twenty-six times. The "other American,"
Pierce, blue-eyed novelist, nastily bright,
Owing him money—out of town that night.

The killer was *his* friend:
Village blade whose mutant tendencies
Village manners might have held in check.
Instead, the daily session
Up on Pierce's cantilevered deck
Was teaching Spiro to Release Aggression.

Sober for once (affirmed the weeping cook
At the taverna where the foreigners ate)
Edward had gone home early. There he found
Spiro hunting for the IOUs.
Fierce ultra-violet shone to saturate
All three. A form gone limp. The midnight news.

5

Every day the line of bloom gets higher,
And now the topmost flares
Go off, sky-bright in bright sky. There's
No last-ditch rescue for—or from—our own
Natures, who so aspire
To the unknown.

Any charring from those bursts of fire?
Open just one
Tiny bronze-purple thurible: briquettes!
Black as coal next year, they'll catch, they'll climb,
Repeating their tribe's miniature
Resurrection myth, where seed is savior.

For like the Sun, behavior that begets
Calls for a camera obscura
To distance, or domesticate, it in.
It's the unknown,
Here in these stanzas, in your lover's eyes—
The radiant pinhole shadows fertilize.

6

But, Howard, at eighteen,
When first in bud, half open to the world,
What prompted us? And flowers—what were they?
The "thought" wired home on Mother's Day.
Who'd have conceived
A god's arrival by such idling green

Machines as ours, all veinwork, exhibition;
A Poem's giving up its throne
For Life, the commoner,
At her messy vanity—disposable issues
And cleansing screams, her latest instrument
To curl the hair . . .

Now more and more we furl asleep
Waking into the next blue "lighted tent"
Of song and story
Nicely made up, like her. For her!
The world at last our own to reinvent,
This or that bit gets titled "Morning Glory."

7

Violet, the sinister of blue . . .
Frost killed the vine. That morning it
Swung man-high
Where four winds crossed. I also felt the stab.

Our local Color Lab
Came up with images. My favorite—

(Remember the roof-garden, its lamppost
Crowned with a rusted fixture
First holding gaslight, now just sky?
Year-round ring for clouds to tumble in
Or tedium to blow
Great bubbles through—)

Anyhow, my favorite
Has "green hearts" and pristine cornets
Twining until the iron aureole
Drew to its vacancy for once a face
So human, so in focus, word
Went flashing, pole to pole:

CONNECTICUT MAN FOUND IN STATE OF GRACE

SERENADE

Here's your letter the old portable
Pecked out so passionately as to crack
The larynx. I too dream of "times
We'll share." Across the river: MUTUAL LIFE.

Flush of a skyline. Owning up to past
Decorum, present insatiety,
Let corporate proceedings one by one
Be abstracted to mauve onionskin,

Lit stories rippling upside down in thought
Be stilled alike of drift and personnel,
Then, only then, the lyric I-lessness
At nightfall banked upon renew

Today's unfolder. Whose lips part. Heard now
In his original setting—voice and reeds—
As music for a god, your page
Asks to be held so that the lamp shines through

And stars appear instead of periods.

WATERSPOUT

Where foam-white openwork
Rumples over slate,
Flash of a fork, the first
Wild syllables in flight,
The massive misty forces
Here to be faced are not
Of wind or water quite
So much as thought uptwisted
Helplessly by thought,
A fullblown argument
Sucked racing through whose veins
Whitebait and jellyfish
Repeat the lacy helices
Threaded into the stem
Of a Murano—wait:
Spirits intoxicate
The drinker, not the glass;
Yet *goblets*—three of them—
Weave up to be counted
Like drunks in the stormlight.
Self-dramatizing scene
That cries and reels and clouds . . .
From somewhere above clouds,
Above thunder and levin
And the herring gull's high scream
(At which one glass may seem
To shatter), from this heaven
Slaked by the spinal fluid,
A bright-eyed reveller
Looks down on cloth outspread,
Strewn silver, fruits de mer,
The lighthouse salt-cellar—
A world exhausted, drained
But, like his word, unbroken;
Looks down and keeps his head.

DAVID'S WATERCOLOR

Dusk. The old cloaked shepherd of terracotta
standing guard, front center. A weak, unshaded
bulb you worked by throws, from offstage, his shadow
onto the blue wall.

Shutter flung wide. Glow from my downstairs desk-lamp
shows how close we are to our neighbor. Further
up the dark street, luminous rifts distinguish
household from household,

flat from flat, each climbing the common hill, each
lit its own way. Wires like birdflight swoop in
insulated pairs—they've been mates so long now—
gracefully skyward.

Restless late last night, I switched on your Key West
guestroom light. There, dead to the world, my young love
lay. The scene hung over his head, its message
sweet, unemphatic:

Fifteen years this hillside was home. Let someone
else's eye be grazing those Greek horizons.
High in space, sunlit (the one source we still trust)
glimmers a new moon.

ARABIAN NIGHT

Features unseen embers and tongs once worried
bright as brass, cool, trim, of a depth to light his
way at least who, trusting mirages, finds in
them the oasis,

what went wrong? You there in the mirror, did our
freshest page get sent to the Hall of Cobwebs?
Or had Rime's Emir all along been merely
after your body?

No reply. Then ("there" of course, also) insight's
dazzle snaps at gloom, like a wick when first lit.
Look! on one quick heartstring glissando, stranger
kindles to father

thirty years a shade, yet whose traits (plus others
not so staring—loyalty, cynicism,
neophyte's pure heart in erotic mufti
straight out of Baghdad)

solve the lifelong riddle: a face no longer
sought in dreams but worn as my own. Aladdin
rubs his lamp—youth? age?—and the rival two beam
forth in one likeness.

TWO FROM FLORIDA

1 / GREEN COVE SPRINGS

Aqua concrete has girdled this inveterate
Uppouring from Earth's heart, at 3000 gallons per minute.
A sign recounts the excellent things in it,
Among them calcium, iron, magnesium sulfate.

Thus fortified, it proceeds to fill the municipal
Plunge, free to the public from May through November.
(Limbs in my father's day flashed, as he liked to remember,
From a now-defunct, excitingly "private" pool.)

With almost professional quickness and tact it takes
The imprint of some dozen random figures, then
—Goodbye to that small floating world of women and men,
Their upside-down stucco hotel rechristened ANTIQUES—

Having arrived at a lucid, babbling sufficiency
White sand and green grass pave, between banks of grass
Yellowed by frost's dispassionate coup de grâce,
It joins the St. Johns River to the Sea.

2 / THE DRESDEN DOLL

Mis' Annie looks just like a Dresden doll,
People would say about my mother's mother
All her life, particularly after
She came back from Europe *with* a Dresden doll.

That must have been around 1930?
The doll, of porcelain like her little chair,
Had panniered skirts and piled-up, powdered hair,
But sat, as women did by 1930,

Legs crossed, with a pert smile—the platitudes
Of rotogravure—bewildering unless
From someone I ought to have known, in fancy dress.
Would we all harden into attitudes?

Painted more pertly each decade, my grandmother
Crossed her short-skirted legs and sipped her toddy,
Chatting about everything and everybody,
Even what it was to be poor, and a young mother,

In Jacksonville at the beginning of the century.
People, as it were, kept brightly dusting some dull
Irrevocability from the living doll,
Dead nonetheless this quarter century,

While the other perches on my bureau, here to stay
Little as I now want it, under its glass bell,
A smiling figure—punishment as well—
For what I simply can no longer say.

THE FIFTEENTH SUMMER

Scrambling with a book
The hundred-or-so feet
Up the Australian pine
To a slung-rope seat—
The nerve it took!

Small wonder, often as not
He never read a line,
Flaubert or Howard Fast,
Just pondered earth and ocean,
The odd car's crawling dot:

Why were we here?
To flow. To bear. To be.
Over the view his tree
In slow, slow motion
Held sway, the pointer of a scale so vast,

Alive and variable, so inlaid
As well with sticky, pungent gold,
That many a year
Would pass before it told
Those mornings what they weighed.

A ROOM AT THE HEART OF THINGS

Two rooms, rather, one flight up, half seen
Through the gilt palm-fronds of rue Messaline.

Sparse furnishings: work table, lamp, two chairs,
Double bed, water closet, fourteen stairs;

Six windows, breathing spaces in the plot,
Between its couplings, to enjoy or not.

A poster—Carnival's white eyeless faces.
The ceiling fan. The floor the actor paces

From room to room, getting by heart the lines
Of boards washed ruddier as day declines,

Of fate upon the palm slapped to his brow,
Of verse the instant they are written (*now*)—

His shadow anyman's, chalk walls a trite
Clown-camouflage all comers penetrate.

≈

The role he studies—a Young Man in love—
Calls upon self and the eclipse thereof

By second nature. Evenings, dazed from sun,
Earth buries her worn faces one by one

Deeper in fleecy quilts, dusk atmospheres,
Then high-up quivering Hesperus appears.

Just so, the actor, deep in middle age,
Assumes a youth till now unknown. On stage

Within a stanza to be somehow first
Turned inside out and only then rehearsed,

508

It's this one's pen he seizes, and lamplit
Page he corrects. Soon he may read from it

Tonight's draft of the curtain line (Act II):
"Light of my life, I've made a play for you!"

≈

Reduce, said Malraux, to the minimum
In every man the actor. Brave bonhomme,

Coming from him—! Beret and cigarette,
The worldwide field-reporter style was set

By how he posed, key witness to his time,
Questions of moment, face a paradigm.

We plain folk who believed what we were told
Had seen our crops burnt and our wives grown old

In one same night. Malraux alone took note,
As all who could read, would. Neat, was it not?

Life gave the palm—much the way God once did—
For "living biographically" amid

Famines, uprisings, blood baths, hand to heart,
Saved by a weakness for performance art.

≈

Those ivory towers were bric-a-brac. One flight
Of wooden steps, one slapdash coat of white,

Sets the room hovering like a UFO
At treetop level. Spellbound by the glow,

Moth hallucinates and cat outstares
The glamour of dimensions never theirs.

Its tenant treads a measure, lights a joint,
Drawing perspective to the vanishing point

Inside his head. Here vows endure beyond
Earshot of lovers who dissolved their bond;

Whitewash keeps faith with tenements of dew
Already atomized to midnight blue;

And Gravity's mask floats—at Phase XV
Oblivion-bright—above the stolen scene.

≈

Actor and lover contemplate the act
So-called of darkness: touch that wrestles tact,

Bedsprings whose babble drowns the hearing, sight
That lids itself, gone underground. Torchlight

Gliding down narrow, redly glimmering veins,
Cell by cell the celebrant attains

A chamber where arcane translucences
Of god-as-mortal bring him to his knees.

Words, words. Yet these and others (to be "tarred"
And "set alight" crosswise by "Nero's guard")

Choreograph the passage from complex
Clairvoyance to some ultimate blind x,

Raw luster, rendering its human guise.
The lover shuts, the actor lifts his eyes.

≈

By twos at moonset, palm trees, up from seeds
Big as a child's heart, whisper their asides—

Glittery, fanlike, alternating, slow
Pointers in the art of how to grow!

They have not relished being strewn before
Earth-shaking figures, Christ or Emperor.

Profoundly unideological
Wells of live shadow, they are no less tall

Pillars of strength when—every twenty-six
Millennia, say—their namesake the Phoenix

Comes home to die. (Stylite and columnist
Foretell the early kindling of that nest

—Whence this rustle, this expectant stir?)
The actor robed as priest or birdcatcher

≈

Steps forth. The room at heart is small, he smiles,
But to the point. Innumerable aisles

Converge upon its theater-in-the-round's
Revolving choirs and footlit stamping grounds.

Only far out, where the circumference
Grazes the void, does act approach nonsense

And sense itself—seats cramped, sightlines askew—
Matter not a speck. Out there the *You*

And *I*, diffracted by the moiré grid
Have yet to meet (or waffled when they did!),

But here, made room for, bare hypothesis
—Through swordplay or soliloquy or kiss

Emitting speed-of-light particulars—
Proves itself in the bright way of stars.

II

THE IMAGE MAKER

A Play in One Act

CHARACTERS

The SANTERO *(Manuel)*
His MOTHER
JUANITA, *his niece*
FRANCISCO ⎫
MIGUEL   ⎬ *santos*
BARBARA   ⎭

The santos are puppets and may if necessary be operated, and their lines spoken, by the actors themselves from backstage. As the MOTHER *never appears, her lines may be spoken by* JUANITA *in the voice of an old woman.*

The Santero's workshop in a Caribbean village. Two finished santos stand in a recess behind him. To his right, a door open onto the street. To his left, the curtained entrance to an inner room. A cot, a chair, a tiny stove. Three or four logs stacked in a corner, for future carving. A caged bird hangs cooing in the morning light. A calendar on the wall says clearly: MAY.

SANTERO   I am the Santero Manuel.
It's I who make the images
For the entire community.
My works are in the mountain villages
And in the little boats far out at sea.
Wherever people work or dwell
Some figure that I've made
Keeps them and theirs
Safe and sound and unafraid.
The santo works, too, to dispel
The dark within them, hears their prayers,
Then maybe says a word on high
To the old Image Maker in the sky.

I'm getting famous! Down at the Hotel,
An English tourist wants to buy
Anything I make. But I say, why
Go to such trouble if it's just to sell?

It's never easy! First I choose
My wood and age it. Laurel, oak,
Rosy cedar or the capa wood
That, kindled, gives out fragrant smoke,
Proving its nature sweet and good.
And then my different dyes and glues,
Metallic powder, colored clay,
Red, blue and ocher, black and white—
All these must be at hand.
Before each job I fast a day
Until my head is light,
Until my hand is true.
Certain other things, you understand,
I am required to do
At moonrise on the final night,

515

But may not speak of that to anyone.

At last the figure is begun.
And never mind how well
I know my saint, I'm in for a surprise
Or two before I'm done—
A crafty smile, a new, hard-pressed
Look in the eyes . . .
I clean my tools, and while the last coat dries,
Lie down and try to rest.
It's never easy.

MOTHER   *(from the inner room)* Manuel!

SANTERO   Mamá?

MOTHER   Have I drunk my sweetened milk today?

SANTERO   Yes, Mamá, not an hour ago.

MOTHER   What about Pepé? Have you fed Pepé?

SANTERO   Of course, Mamá. *(explains)* Our dove, Pepé.
          Of course I fed him. Don't I love him, too?

MOTHER   And what's to eat at noon?

SANTERO   Cornbread. Enough bean soup left in the pot
          At least for one.

MOTHER   A mother's blessing on you, faithful son!
          Make sure it's good and hot.

SANTERO   *(resuming)* Now if you wish
          I'll show you two I finished just last week.
          Francisco, there, knows how to speak
          With birds and wolves and fish.
          Therefore he is the go-between
          Who keeps alive good will
          Among all creatures, and the hunter clean

In spirit for the kill.
And over here's Miguel
Who cast the Devil down
From Heaven's citadel.
He's a great angel. See his crown?
See his gold scales? In them he weighs
The light of all our days.

JUANITA   *(in the doorway with a bundle)* Uncle . . . ?

SANTERO   Juanita, child, come in. What have we here?
Why it's a friend from years ago,
Saint Barbara. Her dress I made
Out of the wide red sash my mother wore
In the first Independence Day parade.
Your mother's her namesake.
What's wrong? Did something break?
Architecture and artillery
Are Barbara's double specialty.
When thunder dances on the roof rough-shod,
She's better than a lightning rod.
You've brought her back, though.

JUANITA   She's always taken care of us, but . . . Well,
First the milk turned sour, you know?
And then the sugar box got filled with salt.
Concha pretends it was my fault.
And then Antonio—
He told me that he'd be away
On business until Saturday,
But Concha saw him last night late
Downtown with Rosa. Now I'm full of hate!
Then Concha—my own sister—gave a sneer
And said, "Go ask our Uncle Manuel
For a true-love spell
And get your boyfriend back, Juanita dear—
Or try!"
I hate her too! I want to die!

SANTERO   Nothing else?

JUANITA   Well, the mule's lame.
I don't believe the Saint's to blame,
And told our Grandma so,
But she looked in the mirror and said, "Go.
There's always something, to our shame,
Wrong with the world. So take her to Manuel."

SANTERO   *(standing the figure between the other two)*
Leave her with me. She looks worn out.

JUANITA   Then Grandma grumbled—she's lame, too, with gout—
And said, "Look for bad news beneath the paint
Even of the household saint."
Uncle, what did she mean?

SANTERO   Why, just that God has many faces,
And different names in different places.
Come,
I'll walk you home.

JUANITA   And my love spell?

SANTERO   Brown cheeks, green eyes,
Love is its own spell, don't you realize?

They go out. The santos come to life.

BARBARA   This god with faces—has he powers
Like ours?

MIGUEL   He made the Earth, the Stars and Sun.

BARBARA   How should we know?

MIGUEL   He made the Man.

BARBARA   The man says so.
He also says in tones
That chill

My bones,
"God's will be done."

MIGUEL   The man made us.

BARBARA   You see now? Without further fuss
Let's have some fun—
Let's do man's will!

Blackout. Then moonlight. A cloth drapes the birdcage. The Santero lies sleeping. In this scene Barbara speaks with the Mother's voice.

BARBARA   Bad son, bad son—
Where's my bad, lazy son?

SANTERO   Me lazy? Bad? When all I do
Is cook your meals and make your bed?

BARBARA   And leave me in it! Ha! Confess it's true
You wish me ill, you want me dead!

SANTERO   Mamá, you're dreaming! Or am I?

BARBARA   You never married—why?
Am I supposed to die
Without grandchildren? What a life!

SANTERO   My work, Mamá. That's *my* whole life. Admit
I'd have no time for child or wife.
But don't I love you? Don't I care for you?

BARBARA   Care for me? Care for *me*!
Ha! If you cared one bit
You'd throw these dolls out no one pays you for,
And get work at the factory.

SANTERO   Mamá, I beg you, I implore—

BARBARA   Be still! I'll have a fit!
If you were half the son that you pretend,

Gold would come out of you as soon as shit,
And with the money in my purse
I'd take a first-class train to the world's end!

SANTERO   What have I done?

BARBARA   I'll tell you what, halfwit—
You've made me ill!
A mother's curse
Upon you! Ay, ay, ay!
Run, wake the pharmacist! I'll die
Without a stomach pill!

Fully awake by now, the Santero sits up, slips on his sandals, and without thinking to look in the other room, rushes into the street. The light changes to include all three santos and the birdcage.

BARBARA   This god—is he a master
Black or white?

MIGUEL   He made the bat, the rooster,
The black she-goat.

BARBARA   He made the priest.

MIGUEL   The priest tells wrong from right.

BARBARA   Or only sees by full-moon light
Which beast
To kill.
He draws the blade across the throat—
A floor of blood!

MIGUEL   Our sawdust vitals drink their fill.

BARBARA   Why shouldn't God?
Brother, do his will!

The third santo, Francisco, throws back his head and utters several loud, hawklike cries. Under its cloth the dove calls, flutters in panic, falls silent with a small thud.

BARBARA   Bravo! Now, Brother, stealer of fire, your turn.
                  Something to burn?

MIGUEL   First be it understood:
                  No man shapes *me*
                  From a block of wood,
                  Paints *my* face with white clay,
                  Dresses *my* mind in dimity.
                  I am the Light of Day,
                  I entered the forbidden Tree,
                  And every other tree since then.
                  I am the generator.
                  By reason's lamp or fever's flickering ray
                  I make the Image Maker.
                  Whatever god is magnified by men,
                  I, I stare through their glass until
                  He does my will!

The calendar on the wall bursts into flame. Consternation.

BARBARA   Oh, no! A book, a chair—
                  Never the calendar!

MIGUEL   There go our holy days
                  Up in a flash!

FRANCISCO   Caw! Caw!

BARBARA   The month of May's
                  Already ash!

MIGUEL   What was to come, ablaze!

BARBARA   Keep it away from my skirt!

MIGUEL   Don't let it melt my scales!

BARBARA   So bright—my eyes hurt!

MIGUEL   So hot—my heart fails!
          Save us before we expire!

ALL   Save us! Caw! Caw! Help! Fire!

They break off as the Santero returns. He tears down the calendar and stamps out the fire. Calmer now, recalling his mother, takes the pills and a cup of water to her door, but does not enter.

SANTERO   Sleeping . . . She slept right through . . .

Only now thinks to check the birdcage.

          Pepé! Ah so.
          This is your work, Changó.

Behind him, Barbara twitches to attention. The Santero lays the dead bird at her feet, and assembles within reach: necklaces, spices, a candle, a cigar, etc. A small drum or bell he will strike at intervals.

          Changó, no more! Drop your disguise,
          Or pick on someone your own size.
          Work through the Popes, the Presidents,
          Figures of influence.
          Work through a poor santero if you must,
          But spare these simple clods
          Of paint and dust.
          Don't tempt them to distress—
          As man does Earth and Air and Sea—
          The houses they were made to bless,
          Or, when they've drawn like poultices
          A thousand lifelike fears and fantasies,
          To act like gods.
          Changó, away! Take your artillery
          To Addis Ababa or Zanzibar.
          Away! Our dove Pepé has died.
          Drink up its blood. Be satisfied.
          Changó, away! I've lit

522

The strong cigar
You love. Inhale the smoke. Vanish like it!

Begins to chant.

CHANGÓ MANI COTE CHANGÓ MANI COTE
OLLE MASA CHANGÓ OLLE MASA CHANGÓ
ARA BARI COTE CHANGÓ ARA BARI COTE
ADA MANI COTE ADA MANI COTE
ARA BASONI COTE CHANGÓ MANI COTE
OYE CHANGÓ ARA BASONI COTE
ARA BARI COTE CHANGÓ ARA BARI COTE
CHANGÓ MANI COTE CHANGÓ MANI COTE
OYE CHANGÓ ARA BASONI COTE
ARA BARI COTE OYE CHANGÓ

*Throughout the above, which may be freely varied or prolonged, the figures—
Barbara in particular—struggle. On the final convulsion there comes a feeble
pop and flash in the air above their heads. Five beats. A roll of distant thunder.
The santos stand in a row, chastened. Day is breaking.*

*The Santero tidies up. Out goes the dead bird, on goes milk to warm. He
arranges his tools, takes Barbara from the recess, and, after a reassured glance
into the next room, sets to work.*

Forgive me, Lord, if I presume
To show You how to do Your work.
From Your high, starry room
You overlook the murk—

Interrupting his prayer to talk to himself.

Look at this bad scar,
See how the color cracks and chips.
No wonder fumes eclipse
The morning star.

—The murk that clogs the mind
And eats away its godlike face.

Take us in hand, as I do these.
Lord, change mankind!—

A wash of alcohol,
A touch of healing gum . . .
There now. A final crumb
Of white on the eyeball . . .

—Take us in hand, as I do these.
Repair, freshen, efface,
So that unswerving grace
Flows through Your images.—

We'll hide that angry red
Under a cloak of blue.
Now, Barbara, maybe you
Will keep your head?

No more explosions, understand?
—And, Lord, make us unlearn
The skills that wound us, blind and burn.
Take us in hand.

MOTHER   *(from within)* Manuel!

SANTERO   Mamá?

MOTHER   Have I drunk my milk today?

SANTERO   Not yet, Mamá. Good morning! Are you well?

MOTHER   How can I tell?
           Always the same. Forgetful, fat and old.
           Ready for breakfast anyway.

SANTERO   Milk's warming now. You wouldn't want it cold.

MOTHER   Good son. And have you fed Pepé?

SANTERO   Mother, our poor Pepé . . .

MOTHER   And what's to eat at noon, eh? Something nice?

SANTERO   Well, if the Englishman at the Hotel
             Keeps his word, meets my price
             And buys Francisco and Miguel—
             Chicken and beans and rice?

Takes the milk in to her. Francisco and Miguel exchange a look, and shrug.
Returning, the Santero removes and begins to wrap them.

MOTHER   *(cackling)* Chicken and beans and rice . . .

SANTERO   If I can pay,
             Chicken and beans and rice.

JUANITA   *(at the door)* Uncle, good day!

SANTERO   Well, well. Come in.
             Do I see a change?

JUANITA   Don't tease me! It's the true-love spell.
             Grandma knew exactly what to do.
             You hollow out a gourd
             And put inside
             Your lover's name—Antonio—
             With something that he's given you—
             A flower I'd kept and dried.
             Then five drops of perfume,
             Five peppercorns and . . .

SANTERO   *(resigned)* Cinnamon.

JUANITA   Pepper and cinnamon, a rooster's comb—
             They sell them at the corner, cured—
             Then light a candle in the room
             And say a prayer to . . .

SANTERO   To all the saints in Rome.

JUANITA   Saint *Clara*. As if you didn't know!
           And then Antonio's sister came today,
           Just now. He *was* away.
           Faced with the truth, Concha admitted she
           Was only teasing me!
           The ferry-boat arrives at ten o'clock.
           I want to be there at the dock.
           Goodbye!

SANTERO   You've time. First take this home.

Hands her the figure of Barbara.

JUANITA   Oh, Uncle! Look, she's changed her dress!
           She's beautiful—like an actress.
           Aren't her eyes bigger? That's not her old smile.
           Will she be good now?

SANTERO   Yes.
           Well, for a while.
           You be good, too, child—or I'll have you hexed!

Juanita runs off, laughing. Ready to leave with his two bundles, the Santero pauses, puts them down. He selects an uncarved log and sets it upright in the empty recess. Studies it a long moment. Sighs.

           What next? What next?

III

THE PARNASSIANS

Theirs was a language within ours, a loge
Hidden by bee-stitched hangings from the herd.
The mere exchanged glance between word and word
Took easily the place, the privilege
Of utterance. Here therefore all was tact.
Pairs at first blush ill-matched, like *turd* and *monstrance*,
Tracing their cousinage through consonants,
Communed, ecstatic, through the long entr'acte.

Without our common meanings, though, that world
Would have slid headlong to apocalypse.
We'd built the Opera, changed the scenery, trod
Grapes for the bubbling flutes mild fingers twirled;
As footmen, by no eyelid's twitch betrayed
Our scorn and sound investment of their tips.

MENU

Dawn. Mist for the grill. As our visual purple
Unfurls to usher in another day,
Highnesses of Appearance are discovered
Touring—with us—the Smokies. Dubious figures,
Like all their subjects. That bearded and bandanna'd
Kid outside the laundromat could be
Nature's nobleman, a local dirtbag,
Or one disguised as the other. Smell this coffee.
Its molecules, as you bend your head to them,
Outwhiz the edge of space. Exciting, but
Why the incognito, and will it never
Be seen through? Is my dread of the electorate
Justified or fatally naive?
What relation has the mother cat
To (a) her litter, (b) the barrio
Women who corner her, and (c)
The TV coverage of their meal? To what
Degree was Gandhi neither fish nor fowl,
The War of the Roses an innocuous masque,
The brook our supper table? (Ragged white
Cloud-cloth, blue plates of calm, courses in swift
Succession chattering on to pebble mints . . .)
Mental sleights and tints and taints untold,
Only perhaps reflected in a dewdrop
Or viewed from Venus do they concentrate
Into a single beam, though it too flickers.
Satiety meanwhile, or something not
Unlike it deep in things, calls for the check.
That's why the cabin floor was strewn with petals,
And the brook, backsliding helplessly all night,
Clutched its bed for dear life, knuckles white.

FOR A BESTIARY

I / CARP

"Bread on the waters." Would
Such literary crusts
Do for their thrash of lusts?
Half fiction was the food

Too many times already
Snapped up in expectation.
Simply to keep the ashen-
Filmy, flame-gilt eddy

Banked in its grate of reeds—
An underwater fire,
How lit?—might prove desire
Itself the fast that feeds.

Yet, alchemy beyond
Fresh lapses into gold
Having made blood run cold
Throughout the pivot-pond,

Come winter, seal them in,
Unplug the glittery nerves,
Lidding those red preserves
With rime's white paraffin

On which a skater writes
(Ah, loop and curlicue
Of letters we once knew)
Here sleep the appetites.

2 / SPELL

Three times a triple strand
Of quietly ticking wire
Is wound about what were
Acres of wonderland

Cropped bare now. One prize ox
Gazes in mute appeal
At grass beyond the pale:
Terrestrial paradox,

Which drawn-to-by-degrees,
Weird, rough-and-tumble veldt
Of voltage, jolt on jolt,
He'll sooner starve than graze.

The vignette touches you?
Be my guest, let him out!
—And yourself in, no doubt,
For a shock or two.

3 / MONDAY MORNING

Hot sun on Duval Street.
Bicycling very slowly
I see, by all that's holy,
An acute blur of fleet

Parrot-green plumage coast
Onto the bus-stop bench:
Less bird, after all, than mensch
"Free as a bird"—its ghost

Face cocked. Now Daddy Kaiser
Of Angelo's Cut 'n Comb
Waddles forth, spry gnome
Waving his atomizer,

Diamonding with spray
One instant hedonist!
Pure whim? Fair-weather tryst?
Already a block away,

I keep risking collision
(In each year's crazier traffic)
To fix that unseraphic
Duo within my vision.

HINDU ILLUMINATION

T loping down the stairs at Mellifont.
That end-of-March, half-mad, half-mocking
Duel with O. NR's
Forearms, who taught me pinochle at ten.
E's glow of pure seduction as it stole
Throughout a nature presently
To be reviled by it. (Reviled? Revealed.)
P's helpless laughter. H's body heat . . .
Remembering all these and more, I smile.

Likewise an artist made his elephant
Entirely of interlocking
Animal and human avatars:
Antelope, archer, lion, duck, each then
Reborn as portion of the whole
Proverbial creature—wisdom, memory—
Shown dancing on a crimson field.
Now, reaching for you in pitch dark, to meet
The mahout's gaze, upon me all this while.

GINGER BEEF

Soon to attain its famous afterglow,
The mountain drinks late sun. Below and early,
Shown to the terrace, we two pause, as always
Silenced by green fields, cottonwoods, the pond,
The two (same?) swans, their nest
Empty at this season. Close beyond's
The low clay house my friend—twelve years ago?—
Rented, only to move. And move again,
A painter's eye in quest
Of the ideal arrangement. While this scene
Didn't quite serve his purposes, no less
Radiant, forgiving and serene,
It takes him in as always, head to foot
—Where a new six-month puppy plays the fool.

They'll have found other tenants for that house—
Two rooms—in which I came to see him first:
House where, cold evenings, he and I, the dog,
Gazed, all three, into the blazing log;
Where he and I drained the last drop of red
Before he and the dog went off to bed;
From which, excited mornings, we'd all pile
Into the truck—we two in the front seat,
The dog behind us—and drive mile on mile,
Vast backdrop rippling heat . . .
When the run ended, did the cast forget
Those properties, that unstruck, sunstruck set?

Creak, offstage, of a screen door
—Our hosts? Instead, impossibly, appears
(As when "for charity" a legend acts
Despite old age, arthritis, cataracts,
The role that made her famous) who
But . . . Ouspenskaya in a dog suit? Or
Who herself! The very dog, those years
Imprinted by her master raptly crooning
"Who are you? *Who* are *you?*"
(Mix of coyote, shepherd, malamute)

Till Who at last was all she'd answer to.
Slowly now she limps the length of terrace,
Lashes gone white beneath the widow's peak,
To kiss—no prompting now or ever—
His palm, then mine: *Yes, here's*
That friend of His I grew
To tolerate, let stroke me, soul and senses
Fixed on the roadside store
He'd presently, if I kept faith, once more
Emerge from. As He did, at first. But then . . .

But then life's thrifty. Every day a bit
Gets put aside, the why and where of it
A puzzle, till the nest egg hatches—wings
Whistling through us as the pieces knit.

Isn't the right place everywhere, and found
By everyone? Some, though, turn round and round—
Ever about to settle, never quite
Able to do so—on the faithful ground.

Fear of belonging, or inflicting harm?
Friends gestured from their niches. "Pure dull charm"
Kept at arm's length—no. Make the story short.
He gave the dog to these two, for their farm.

Of course it hurt. His reasons were austere
As rainlight, as the two-or-three-per-year
Landscapes he showed us. But with what wry phrase
Of mine shall I give *him* away? For here

Our hosts come. Bright-eyed lookalikes, hair shot
With silver, smiles of puckered apricot,
Their manners—all our manners—past reproach.
I wonder how we bear it. Who does not.

For her, it's more . . . more like tonight's pièce
De résistance.—Lift from the crock, let stand;
Then chill, trim, slice, and recompose
Within its essence, clarified topaz
(Afterwards, find a moment, thank the cook)

Of a deliciousness—
                    She comes to sniff,
But is too dignified to take,
The surreptitious morsel from my hand.

Fields green still, heights their celebrated red
Well after sunset, past the panes
Flashes the puppy yapping—in Who's stead?
With passion she recalls? Yes, and disdains:
Eyes nowhere, slumping down on stone
In mute, in mortal weariness, alone.

Nambé, 1981

EIGHT BITS

1 / LASER MAJESTY

Light show at the Planetarium.
Schlock music. Seven colors put through drum
Majorette paces. "We saw God tonight,"
Breathes Wendy. Yes, and He was chewing gum.

2 / IF U CN RD THS

u cn gt a gd jb w hi pa!
So thinks a sign in the subway.
Think twice when letters disappear
Into Commodity's black hole—
No turning back from that career.
This counterspell may save your soul.

3 / VOLTAIRE: A STATUE OF CHRIST IN JESUIT ATTIRE

Admire these monks' excessive art
And industry who've dressed you, dear
Lord, in their very robes for fear
Lest someone take you to his heart.

4 / ANAGRAM/ANAGRAMME

Here *Pasolini* lies, decorum's foil,
Writhing in PAIN and crumbling into SOIL.

Ci-gît *Pasolini*, après de longs effrois,
Son corps devenant PAIN, ses cris devenus LOIS.

5 / LIPSTICK, 1935

At Aunt Pearl's kiss the pointed head
Extruded glistening pale red
From the jet sheath where it was housed
Looked like our Labrador, aroused.

6 / SNAKE PIT

Uplands. The dead of winter. Yet you've seen
Mist rising from an April ring of green
(We're massed beneath, all moistly interlaced)
Whose self-engendered garden in the waste
Shows Eden as it were "by natural light,"
And Baptist ranchers where to dynamite.

7 / TO AN ACTOR ON LOCATION FOR A FILM
IN WHICH HE GETS KILLED

Who live a life so charmed, time and again
The spear goes through you but you feel no pain,
Who rise amused, even as Earth receives
A battered image and the housewife grieves,
Go forth to die, Adonis. Then let's dine
Your first night back in town. My place at nine?

8 / A BIT OF BLUE TILE ON THE BEACH

Fragments like this, my Sunshine, fall
When you flash from your shower stall.

DEAD CENTER

Upon reflection, as I dip my pen
Tonight, forth ripple messages in code.
In Now's black waters burn the stars of Then.

Seen from the embankment, marble men
Sleep upside down, bat-wise, the sleep bestowed
Upon reflection. As I dip my pen

Thinking how others, deeper into Zen,
Blew on immediacy until it glowed,
In Now's black waters burn the stars of Then.

Or else I'm back at Grandmother's. I'm ten,
Dust hides my parents' roadster from the road
Which dips—*into* reflection, with my pen.

Breath after breath, harsh O's of oxygen—
Never deciphered, what do they forebode?
In Now's black waters burn the stars. Ah then

Leap, Memory, supreme equestrienne,
Through hoops of fire, circuits you overload!
Beyond reflection, as I dip my pen
In Now's black waters, burn the stars of Then.

IV

PROSE OF DEPARTURE

For Donald Richie

IMAGING IT

Paul phones to say goodbye. He's back in New York two days early, but we are tied to our trip—departure this evening—and he, for his part, doesn't ask us over. (Can a single week have changed him? Surely not.) Our dear one sounded strong, unconcerned, above all glad to have left the Clinic. Famous and vast and complex as an ocean liner, it catered chiefly to elderly couples from the Plains. Whether both were ill, or just the husband or the wife, they'd chosen not to be separated. They slept (as did Paul) at the nearby hotel, then spent their waking hours together in lounges, the magazine unread, or strolling hand in hand the gleaming, scentless corridors from one text—one test, rather—to the next. Paul, though, was by himself, was perhaps not even "sailing." Waiting to hear over his own system the stern voice calling *Visitors ashore!* he would have begun to feel that, aside from the far too young and noncommittal crew, bona-fide passengers only were expected to circulate there, all in the same boat, their common dread kept under wraps, yet each of them visibly

> at sea. Yes, yes, these
> old folks grown unpresuming,
> almost Japanese,
>
> had embarked too soon
> —Bon voyage! Write!—upon their
> final honeymoon.

ARRIVAL IN TOKYO

Our section of town is Roppongi, where thirty years ago I dined in W's gloomy wooden farmhouse. The lanes and gardens of his neighborhood have given way to glitzy skyscrapers like this hotel—all crystal and brass, a piano and life-size ceramic Saint Bernard in the carpeted lobby. It is late when the revolving door whisks us forth, later yet when our two lengthening shadows leave the noodle shop to wander before bed through the Aoyama cemetery. Mishima is buried down one of its paths bordered by cherry trees in full, amazing bloom. Underneath, sitting on the ground—no, on outspread plastic or paper, shoes left in pairs alongside these instant "rooms"—a few ghostly parties are still eating and drinking, lit by small flames. One group has a transistor, another makes its own music, clapping hands and singing. Their lantern faces glow in the half-dark's black-beamed, blossom-tented

> dusk within the night.
> The high street lamp through snowy
> branches burns moon-bright.

DONALD'S NEIGHBORHOOD

Narrow streets, lined with pots: wistaria, clematis, bamboo. (Can that be syringa—with *red* blossoms?) Shrines begin. A shopkeeper says good day. Three flights up in the one ugly building for blocks around, Donald welcomes us to his bit of our planet. Two midget rooms, utilitarian alcoves, no trace of clutter. What he has is what you see, and includes the resolve to get rid of things already absorbed. Books, records. His lovers he keeps, but as friends—friends take up no space. He now paints at night. Some canvases big as get-well cards bedeck a wall. Before we leave he will give the nicest of these to Peter.

What are we seeing? Homages to Gris, Cornell, Hokusai, Maxfield Parrish. Three masters of compression and one of maple syrup. Without their example, where mightn't his own work have gone? (Would he have painted at all?) As for his album of lovers, without the archetypal Uncle Kenny to seek throughout the world, who mightn't he have loved? And what if he hadn't settled in Japan forty years ago? Living here has skimmed from his features the self-pity, cynicism and greed which sour his Doppelgänger in that all too imaginable jolly corner of Ohio.

Later—stopping first at a bookstore to buy what they have of Donald's in stock—we proceed to the projection room, where at our instigation we are to be shown six of his films. No clutter about them either. The program is over in just ninety minutes. What have we seen?

> Boy maybe eighteen
> bent over snapshots while his
> cat licks itself clean.

> Naked girl, leading
> suitors a merry chase: she'll
> leave them stripped, bleeding—

this last to courtly music by Rameau. And finally

> a dead youth. The shore's
> gray, smooth, chill curve. His flesh a
> single fly explores.

STRATEGIES

Halfway around the globe from Paul the worst keeps dawning on us. We
try to conjure him up as he was only last winter: hair silvered early, the
trustful, inquisitive, nearsighted face, the laugh one went to such lengths
to hear. His book was practically done, he'd quit biting his nails. Well,
now he knows, as do we; and the date line, like a great plateglass revolv-
ing door, or the next six-foot wave in an epic poem, comes flashing up to
face the music. I need a form of conscious evasion, that at best permits
odd moments when the subject

> looking elsewhere strays
> into a local muse's
> number-benumbed gaze

—fixed there, ticking off syllables, until she blinks and the wave breaks.
Coming to, once again drenched, a fugitive, one is after all saner for the
quarter-hour spent as a splotch of lichen upon that quaintest of stepping-
stones.

   Don't worry, I'm getting my share of fast food, TV news and tearjerk-
ers, police running toward the explosion, our sickeningly clear connec-
tions to New York, a boîte called Wet Dream, the taximeter advancing,
like history itself, by lifespans: 1880 to 1950 to 2020. Yet this automated
Japan tends chiefly to mirror and amplify a thousandfold the writhing
vocalist in my own red boîte, whom *I* want gagged, unplugged, shortcir-
cuited. If every trip is an incarnation in miniature, let this be the one in
which to arrange myself like flowers. Aim at composure like the target a
Zen archer sees through shut eyes. Close my borders to foreign devils.
Take for model a cone of snow with fire in its bowels.

KYOTO

Daybreak. Brightest air
left brighter yet by hairline
cracks of gossamer.

Temple pond—work of the mad priest who thought he was a beaver? In the foreground roots scrawl their plea for clemency upon a golden velvet scroll. *Granted*, breathe the myriad starlets of moss, the dwarf maple's inch-wide asterisks. The dead stump is tended as if it had never been more alive. "To die without assurance of a cult was the supreme calamity." (L. Hearn)

RIVER TRIP

Short walk through fields to soft-drink stand where boats wait—all aboard! Creak of rope oarlock. One man pulls the single oar, another poles, a third steers, a fourth stands by to relieve the first. High-up shrine, bamboo glade. Woodland a cherry tree still in bloom punctuates like gun-smoke. Egret flying upstream, neck cocked. Entering the (very gentle) rapids everyone gasps with pleasure. The little waves break backwards, nostalgia con moto, a drop of fresh water thrills the cheek. And then? Woodland, bamboo glade, high-up shrine. Years of this have tanned and shriveled the boatmen. For after all, the truly exhilarating bits

> were few, far between
> —boulders goaded past, dumb beasts
> mantled in glass-green
>
> gush—and patently
> led where but to the landing,
> the bridge, the crowds. We

step ashore, in our clumsiness hoping not to spill these brief impressions.

Plays of unself. Peel off the maiden pearl-diver to find her mother's ghost, the ghost to wake a dragon who, at the end of his dance, will attain Buddhahood. Masked as each of these in turn, the protagonist has the wattles and frame of

> a middle-aged man—
> but time, gender, self are laws
> waived by his gold fan.

Often depicted are the sufferings of poor people—woodcutters and fishermen, who nonetheless appear in uncommon finery. They've earned it. Each has entered the realm of legend and artifice, to become "a something else thereby." What glides before us is the ectoplasm of plot.

Enter today's ghost. Masked, longhaired and lacquer-bonneted, over his coral robe and white trousers he wears a coat of stiff apple-green gauze threaded with golden mazes. In life he was the warrior prince Tsunemasa. Before long, stirred by a votive lute *we* don't hear, he will relive moonlight, storm and battle, and withdraw, having danced himself to peace. At present the stage picture is static, a problem in chess. The eight-pawn chorus is chanting in antiphon with Tsunemasa—a droning, fluctuating,

> slowly-swelling hymn:
> the god's fingertip circling
> one deep vessel's rim

after another, until all the voices are attuned.

The drummer with a thimbled fingertap neat as a pool shot cuts short his vocalise at once resumed: a guttural growl that ends falsetto, hollow pearl balanced upon a jet of water,

> full moon kept at bay
> above Death Valley by the
> wolf-pack roundelay.

The music has no purpose, Professor Shimura insists, but to mark time for the actors. Blindfolded by their masks, oriented, if at all, by the peripheral pine tree or stage pillar, they need whatever help they can get. (Then why *this* music, so animal, so ghostly?)

Feet in white socks explore the stage like palms of a blind man. When they stamp it is apt to be without impact, the dancer having levitated unawares. Hands are held relaxed but gravely furled. Middle knuckles aligned with thumb unbent compose half a right angle. Into the hollow that results may be set a fan or willow-branch. Nothing easier than to withdraw it. Hands like these will never clench or cling or stupidly dangle or helplessly be wrung. They are princes to be served and defended with one's life. My own hand as I write, wielding this punctilious lance of blue, belongs to a lower caste.

A story Paul heard from an old Surrealist in Pau:

The Emperor's boyhood friend was convicted of treason and sentenced to death by decapitation. In honor of their former intimacy, the Emperor ordered the execution before dawn, after a banquet for his friend at which the Court dancers would appear. That legendary troupe could perform anything: the Spider Web, A Storm at Sea, the Nuptials of the Phoenix. On this occasion they outdid themselves. Yet well before the stars had set, the doomed man turned to his host: "The Son of Heaven has shown unmerited consideration, but really, can't we call it a night and conclude our business without further ado?" The Emperor raised his eyebrows: "My poor friend," he smiled, "haven't you understood? Your head was cut off an hour ago."

Oki Islands, a week later, after dinner. The maid, miming anticipation, slides open doors onto a little scrim of pine trees flat and black against the dazzle.

> Waves whisper. Tonight
> the netmender's deaf son reads
> their lips by moonlight,

but the real drama is due to go on elsewhere. Already owls and crickets are studying the program in silence. Long minutes pass. Imperceptibly the moon's ripeness comes to us bruised by some imminent "shadow of a thought." A dark thought that fills the psyche, leaving a bare brilliant cuticle, then nothing, a sucked breath, a pall. The stars crowd forward, like wizards round a sickbed. The goddess has donned her

> brownest mask: malign
> pomegranate, carbon-stifled
> ember—muss es sein?

                                                    Not this time. Watch:
Minim by scruple the high renaissance . . .
Celestial recovery. Doctors amazed. Altogether grander and more mysterious than anything at the Noh, yet from what lesser theater did we absorb the patience and piety needed to bring the moonlight back?

DOZEN

Circling the island. Fantastic volcanic forms, dragon-coil outcrops
nostril-deep in clear water—or so it might have been. But this stormy
noon we're alone in the boat, screens of mist enfold the heights, and the
famous drowned savannas, green-gold or violet-pink in travel posters,
come through as dim, splitsecond exposures during which

> one seaweed fan waves
> at another just under
> from above the waves.

KYOGEN INTERLUDE: AT THE BANK

It is by now clear that the poor flushed clerk—a trainee's badge on his lapel—knows nothing. Fifty minutes have passed, our travelers checks are still being processed, and we have missed our train to Koyasan.

Donald *(at the counter, smiling gleefully):* Excuse me, would you kindly ask your supervisor to step this way?

Clerk *(in sudden English):* No. Please, he. Today not here.

Donald *(still in Japanese):* Nonsense. It's Monday morning. Everyone's here.

Clerk: I. No. He.

Donald: Because if you do not fetch him I shall be obliged to go and ask for him myself.

The clerk pales and vanishes, returning accompanied by an older man in neat shirtsleeves—the supervisor—who asks how he can be of service.

Donald: Good morning. My name is R——. I am a writer and journalist living in Tokyo. Allow me to give you my card.

Manners require that a card be studied by its recipient with every show of genuine interest. The supervisor beautifully clears this first hurdle. Donald resumes. During his tirade his listener's breathing quickens, his eyes glitter. He and the red-faced clerk, side by side, are contemplating the abyss to whose brink we've led them. The younger man, slightly bent, hands clasped at his crotch, has braced himself like one about to be flogged.

Donald: . . . and furthermore I shall speak of this on my return to Tokyo.

Supervisor *(face carefully averted from the culprit):* See here, you've been trained. Are you still incapable of a simple transaction? Then find someone in the office to take over. This is Osaka, not your village. I hold you responsible for a great rudeness to these distinguished guests.

To every phrase the clerk winces assent. Trays of clean money appear, which having pocketed we take our leave.

Supervisor *(bowing us to the door):* There is no apology for such a mortifying affair.

Donald: Please, it is of no consequence. I mentioned it only to spare your bank any future embarrassment.

JM *(on the eventual slower train):* Will you really make a fuss in Tokyo?

Donald: Goodness, no. What do you take me for?

Eleanor *(hearing it told months later):* Yes, that's what Mother used to call The Scene. As a child I watched her make it all over the world. You begin by saying you're an intellectual. It strikes the fear of God into them, I can't think why. Not here in America, of course, but anywhere else—! How do you think I got on that air-conditioned bus in Peru? How do you think I got out of East Berlin that ghastly Christmas? I told them I was a writer and journalist. I made The Scene.

DJ *(amused in spite of himself):* That story wasn't nice. Even bank clerks have to live.

Eleanor: Darling boy, nobody has to live. It's what I came away from Paul's service thinking. Nobody has to live.

SANCTUM

Another proscenium. At its threshold we sit on our heels, the only audience. Pure bell notes, rosaries rattled like dice before the throw. Some young priests—the same who received us yesterday, showed us to our rooms, served our meal, woke us in time for these matins—surround a candlelit bower of bliss. The abbot briskly enters, takes his place, and leads them in deep, monotonous chant. His well-fed back is to us. He faces a small gold pagoda flanked by big gold lotus trees overhung by tinkling pendants of gold. Do such arrangements please a blackened image deep within? To us they look like Odette's first drawing room (before Swann takes charge of her taste) lit up for a party, or the Maison Dorée he imagines as the scene of her infidelities. Still, when the abbot turns, and with a gesture invites us to place incense upon the brazier already full of warm, fragrant ash, someone—myself perhaps—tries vainly

> to hold back a queer
> sob. Inhaling the holy
> smoke, praying for dear

life—

The very river has stopped during Koganosuke's dialogue with his father. All at once—heavens!—the young man takes up a sword and plunges it into his vitals. There is no blood. He cannot die. The act will end with his convulsive efforts to. Meanwhile the rapids that divide him from his beloved begin to flow again—blue-and-white cardboard waves jiggled up and down—so that the lacquer box containing her head may be floated across to where he quakes, upheld by three mortals in black.

> (Into the Sound, Paul,
> we'd empty your own box, just
> as black, just as small.)

The lovers neither spoke nor acted—how could they? Their words came from the *joruri*, or reciter, who shares with the samisen player a dais at the edge of the stage. Upon taking his place the *joruri* performs an obeisance, lifting the text reverently to his brow. It is a specialized art—what art is not?—and he glories in it. He has mastered Koganosuke's noble accents, the heroine's mewing, and the evil warlord's belly-laugh which goes on for minutes and brings down the house. To function properly each puppet requires three manipulators. These, with the *joruri*, are the flesh and blood of this National Theater, and come to stand for—stand *in* for—the overruling passions, the social or genetic imperatives, that propel a given character. Seldom do we the living, for that matter, feel more "ourselves" than when spoken through, or motivated, by "invisible" forces such as these. It is especially true if, like a puppet overcome by woe, we also appear to be struggling free of them. (Lesser personages make do with two manipulators, or only one.)

> "... wonderful today ...!"
> you yawned that night. It moved me:
> words began to play
>
> like a fountain deep
> in gloom. Did love reach out your
> arm then? Sorrow? Sleep?

GEIGER COUNTER

Pictures on a wall:
a *View of Fuji* challenged
by *The Dying Gaul.*

Syringe in bloom. Bud
drawn up through a stainless stem—
O perilous blood!

Tests, cultures . . . Weeks from
one to the next. That outer
rim of the maelstrom

hardly moved. Its core
at nightmare speed churned onward,
a devolving roar:

Awake—who? why here?
what room was this?—till habit
shaded the lit fear.

"You're not dying! You've been reading too much Proust, that's all! I could be dying too—have you thought of that, JM?—except that I don't happen to be sick, and neither do you. What we *are* suffering are sympathetic aches and pains. Guilt, if you like, over staying alive. Four friends have died since December, now Paul's back at the Clinic. You were right,"—the dying *Paul,* what else?—"we should have scrapped the trip as soon as we heard. But God! even if you and I *were* on the way out, wouldn't we still fight to live a bit first, fully and joyously?"

Such good sense. I want to bow, touch my forehead to the straw mat. Instead: "Fight? Like this morning? We can live *or* die without another of those, thank you." Mutual glares.

The prevailing light in this "Hiroshima" of trivial symptoms and empty forebodings is neither sunrise nor moonglow but rays that promptly undo whatever enters their path. They strip the garden to clawed sand. They whip the modern hotel room back into fatal shape: the proportions and elisions of centuries. In their haste to photograph Truth they eat through a blue-and-white cotton robe, barely pausing to burn its pattern onto the body shocked alert:

> "What's the story, Doc?"
> —dark, cloud-chambered negatives
> held to the light. Knock,

knock. Not dinnertime already? Donald, making his ghoul face, joins us for another feast less of real food than of artfully balanced hues and textures. "I'm sick," sighs the sunburnt maid who serves it, and whose kimono we think to please her by admiring, "sick of wrapping myself up like a dummy day after day." Has the radiation affected her, too? And what *about* this morning's blinding outburst?

ANOTHER CEMETERY

We pass it on our descent from the temple. The gravestones are vertically incised with the deceased's new name, the name assumed after death. Only by knowing it can a friend or kinsman hope to locate one's tomb among so many others. They all—untapering stone shafts on broad plinths—look exactly like scale models for skyscrapers in the 1930s. Intelligent intervals separate them. Light and air will have been of prime importance to whoever planned this "city of tomorrow," its little malls and avenues half-lost in foliage, and took care to place its ugly realities out of sight. In today's cold drizzle we feel he was not wholly successful. Oh for a glowing hearth to come home to!—as another name sputters, a

> last flickering shift
> of flame flutters off. The log's
> charred forked shape is left.

(Sold up at the temple, distant cousin to both the gravestone and the "Plant-Tab" stuck in a flowerpot to release nutrients over weeks to come: the incense stick. This brittle, narrow slab of dark green, set upright in the burner's ash-heap and lit, will also turn to ash. But in the process, as it whitens, a hitherto unseen character appears, below it a second, slowly a third, each traced by the finest penpoint of incandescence. They cool the way ink dries. Once complete and legible, their pious formula can be scattered by a touch. Any fragrance meanwhile eludes me. Have I caught cold?)

IN THE SHOP

Out came the most fabulous kimono of all: dark, dark purple traversed by a winding, starry path. To what function, dear heart, could it possibly be worn by the likes of—

Hush. Give me your hand. Our trip has ended, our quarrel was made up. Why couldn't the rest be?

Dyeing. A homophone deepens the trope. Surrendering to Earth's colors, shall we not *be* Earth before we know it? Venerated therefore is the skill which, prior to immersion, inflicts upon a sacrificial length of crêpe de Chine certain intricate knottings no hue can touch. So that one fine day, painstakingly unbound, this terminal gooseflesh, the fable's whole eccentric

> star-puckered moral—
> white, never-to-blossom buds
> of the mountain laurel—

may be read as having emerged triumphant from the vats of night.

V

Little has changed. Of the buildings—tufted clay,
Like tennis courts upended—
Some to this day won't see a dentist.
Others, robed in light green, head to toe,
For on-the-spot surgery, won't see us.
The senior ones, as when the family doctor
Closing the consultation
Doffs his white jacket for a chat or chess game,
Have stripped to the gruff brick. Those latterday
Sutures of iron hint
At the dramatically rose-lit
Martyrdom within, while the protruding giant
Veined foot reminds the patient that it's all
A dream. Only a dream?
If so, one we can walk the whole night through,

Arm in arm, like lovers in a story.
(Or can we?—"Amore! Tesoro!"—OK, wise guy!
—As the unerring Vespa whipping by
Takes the word out of my mouth. Amore.)

And walk whole days through rusty, falling leaves
Above the river racing still.
It will never grow up, suffer the frugal houseboat,
The coral barge. Better one dragonfly
Scull hovering in place. Better an Angel's
Bird-of-prey shadow rippling
Down from his ramparts. Yet once we descend, you and I,
To the cobbled embankment, push through gangling weeds,
Acne of burrs, to the brink,
Tiber, as usual instinctively
Sweeping itself from view, wakes the reflection:
It knows how to live! —
Current so debonair, so vital, why
Personified in sculpture with an urn,
Bearded, funereal, recumbent?
As I begin to follow, my eyes burn

The bridge of years. I feel in my old bones
A young man's dread. His longing. To be cast
Upon the waters! Pleasure sauntering past
Looked back? He sank into these very stones

Now gilt with mist. Our trattoria empties.
Tall in the Ptolemaic night
Houses red wine unsteadies reminisce.
That was Umberto's window, this was mine.
That bijou penthouse? Josie
Lived there one winter. Rome is a time exposure.
From his black square Orion cuts degrees
Of adamant whereby the here-below
Church, palace, obelisk,
Boarded-up flower stall, *our* square, all grow
Solider, and with each whispered nothing,
Each fading cry, more "eternal,"
While the cars, the people—? Just a human smear
About the Bocca della Verità,
Then eerie, disembodied shots of light
Down a late artery. It develops
We've all along had somewhere else to go.

The friends of 1986 are Swiss.
Italian men, discos and Art Deco,
Fashion and Hollywood are what they know.
Gowns by Hadrian?——Here Antinous,

Everyone's favorite,
Enters the strobe-lit crypt in shock. Despite
The warm blue honey of his glances,
Golden hair and mornings at the gym,
He didn't get the part. *Too old,* said Truth,
Adding lines left and right:
My monumental chronicles drag on.
Life glitters once, an epigram, and—gone.
Time now to walk him home?
Anything but! Tour instead the sedated
Fountains of 4 a.m.? Half awake, offer
Our balcony's coming attractions?——

Bells wrangling, cappucino,
Charioteers of the marble Typewriter
Driving their team through bare sky, winged with flame;
Dew-glazed below, the neighborhood Franciscans'
Kitchen garden. Not his scene,
He smiles, blowing a kiss

And gliding off—our cavalier of stealth
Turning the nearest corner, lest we see him
Make for that blackest mass, the Colosseum,
Whose faithful have stayed up to drink his health.

Chessboards, buried one beneath the other,
How slow, how fierce the contests
That foundered each . . . Yet a young pawn I spent
Two years as (if time kept
So to oneself was spendable) blinks round him,
Dazed. For the opponent—thank you, Angel? —
Whose "men" and "moves" he parried is no more.
Problem solved? If not, its weight commuted
To levels underfoot
Where now-classic solutions rest in pieces
Hard to pry loose. The new subway
Performed a bypass through them, but how slowly:
Checked by the bone bishop of a cell
Fetid with faith, or queen's encaustic chamber
Blossoming deep in the hive—
Work held up (two more years? porca Madonna!)
For fear that, looked too closely at by day,
The nectarine would peel,
And mote by mote the cupid fly away.

Malaise of airports. Even this morning's King
Charles spaniel knew his hour on Earth was done;
Kenneled as baggage, howled. I wrote: Dear One,
My westbound high noon is your evening,

You've climbed—you promised—to a certain sunny
Outlook above trees in shade.
Overhead, the choral molecules

Will have already formed, their least electron
Blackly twinkling. Starlings, little stars.
On a vast slide you'll study
The life in one gold drop of heaven's blood—
Rapidly overlapping rival circuses,
Like animated ink
Drawings by Miró—till a motif
Out of the ancient city comes alive:
Gladiators' nets, the mortal
Fling and pounce reborn, over the ages,
As play. The victims too
React good-humoredly. They are big trees now,
Used in their noble calling,
Night after night, to dreams of suffocation,
Chattering burdens—*nothing* (Truth to tell)
The sunrise won't dispel.
Remember that. Who loves you? Write. Keep well.

GRAFFITO

Deep in weeds, on a smooth chunk of stone
Fallen from the cornice of the church
(Originally a temple to Fortuna),
Appears this forearm neatly drawn in black,
Wearing, lest we misunderstand,
Like a tattoo the cross-within-a-circle
Of the majority—Christian Democrat.

Arms and the man. This arm ends in a hand
Which grasps a neatly, elegantly drawn
Cock—erect and spurting tiny stars—
And balls. One sports . . . a swastika?
Yes, and its twin, if you please, a hammer-and-sickle!
The tiny stars, seen close, are stars of David.
Now what are we supposed to make of that?

Wink from Lorenzo, pout from Mrs. Pratt.
Hold on, I want to photograph this latest
Fountain of Rome, whose twinkling gist
Gusts my way from an age when isms were largely
Come-ons for the priapic satirist,
And any young guy with a pencil felt
He held the fate of nations in his fist.

GRACE

"All this is very tiring,"
The old, old woman sighed:
"Another railroad station . . ."
Which one today? In her time
She'd traveled, seen the world
Forming its vast impression,
The Gare des Invalides,
The Termini in Rome—
A vault of groans and grime,
Triumphant engineering
Each dawn shone sicklier through.
Now clocks were striking, she'd be going home

   —But with an artful smile
Lay back in her hospital bed:
"This one I designed
Myself, though. Glassed-in wings
Overlook the Nile,
So you can lie back and read
Or sleep if at the last
Moment you decide
To take tomorrow's train instead."

The girders of the mind
Were twisting. Pane by pane
Her spattered sense of things
All autumn had been caving
Inward to this bead
Full of its own dry light,
With just room for a river,
One plume of smoke, one bird . . .
Tinier locomotives
Each afternoon kept leaving
Without her for the Valley of the Kings.
Each night's rain fell unheard.

ICECAP

Yes, melting changes
  the whole picture. That
once young republic tassled
sea to sea with golden wit
  has tattered to a
  wrack of towns, bubble
domes unpricked on the lagoon's
fogged mirror. Losses and debts
  are equally, now,
  past calculation,
resources (but for the odd
oil rig or artisan or
  lone—ah my dearest—
  body ardently
asleep beneath a sunset-
rippled vault of stucco) nil.
  Still, the shift from world
  power to tourist
mecca goes unmourned. People
appear relieved of the real
  embarrassment the
landscape had become
in those late decades. Dead roads
and deconsecrated malls,
  moth-eaten orchards
  far North, deep crops left
rotting on the Plains gave out
how the collective psyche
  shrugged off its future
  and despised its roots,
bent upon pleasures merely
of the here and now. Wherefore
  toward those gossamer
  centers all night long
causeways whip and barges throb.
By air—thanks to this morning's
  cold front, sharp enough,
  following weeks of

doggedly adolescent
weather, to wake reflection
    even in shallows—
    breeding grounds, rather,
for a small scavenger crab,
the local delicacy—
    by air on the hour
    arrive not only
the groups but: bonsai birches,
Brie, vaccines and lenses, out-
    of-date ensembles
    in tomorrow's shades,
correction fluid Mister
Magoo (the draftsman's cat) can,
    deft paw dipped, spatter
    across the blueprint;
neatest of all, a fine-gauge
20-carat wire, from which
    our morose goldsmith
    on the Bridge of Smiles
has already fashioned this
shimmering, cereal wand.
    Wear it, Milady,
    in your frosted hair.

CORNWALL

Wind clear and heavy as a paperweight,
Lead crystal in which flowerets are set,

Sunburst-, trumpet-, bell-, spire-, star-shaped choirs
That faintly shudder at the names we pluck

Out of the handbook: rupturewort, wild carrot,
Thrift, self-heal, and—recognized too late

From fairy tales—the nettle, freckling fiery
White your windburned knuckles. Over this whole

Knee-deep enchanted cliff-top forest spreads
Iseult's Hair (shall we call it?), fine and coppery

Proof against wind, as if in wind outstreaming.
The sea, too, has grown eerily placid. Seams

Ennoble features like a dreaming titan's,
Taken for shelter. Rarely are outsiders

Shown these cramped conditions. But now under lichened
Brows flash sudden mica-chip embrasures,

Into the living vein the raindrop snuggles,
Some least quartz kernel, grit of the homestretch,

Grows lucid. We're already there, and learning
Symmetry, obliqueness, breadth of beam,

Weight of quilt, and have glimpsed beyond mote and carat
Suspended in the weak, lead-crystal light

That tiny medicine chest where the two vials—
Put away long ago for us—are gleaming:

One of brown glass with skull-and-crossbones label,
The other frosted, near empty, exhaling Joy.

LOSING THE MARBLES

for John Malcolm Brinnin

I

Morning spent looking for my calendar—
Ten whole months mislaid, name and address,
A groaning board swept clean . . .
And what were we talking about at lunch? Another
Marble gone. Those later years, Charmides,
Will see the mind eroded featureless.

Ah. We'd been imagining our "heaven"s.
Mine was to be an acrobat in Athens
Back when the Parthenon—
Its looted nymphs and warriors pristine
By early light or noon light—dwelt
Upon the city like a philosopher,
Who now—well, you have seen.

Here in the gathering dusk one could no doubt
"Rage against the dying of the light."
But really—rage? (So like the Athens press,
Breathing fire to get the marbles back.)
These dreamy blinkings-out
Strike me as grace, if I may say so,
Capital punishment,
Yes, but of utmost clemency at work,
Whereby the human stuff, ready or not,
Tumbles, one last drum-roll, into thyme,
Out of time, with just the fossil quirk
At heart to prove—hold on, don't tell me . . . What?

2

Driving its silver car into the room,
The storm mapped a new country's dry and wet—
Oblivion's ink-blue rivulet.
Mascara running, worksheet to worksheet
Clings underfoot, exchanging the wrong words.
The right ones, we can only trust will somehow
Return to the tongue's tip,
Weary particular and straying theme,
Invigorated by their dip.

Invigorated! Gasping, shivering
Under our rough towels, never did they dream—!
Whom mouth-to-mouth resuscitation by
Even your *Golden Treasury* won't save,
They feel their claim
On *us* expiring: starved to macron, breve,
Those fleshless ribs, a beggar's frame . . .
From the brainstorm to this was one far cry.

Long work of knowing and hard play of wit
Take their toll like any virus.
Old timers, cured, wade ankle-deep in sky.

Meanwhile, come evening, to sit
Feverishly restoring the papyrus.

3

body, favorite
      gleaned,   at the
          vital
    frenzy—

act and moonshaft, peaks
         stiffening
     Unutter[able]
  the beloved's

          slowly
   stained in the deep   fixed
      summer nights
  or,

    scornful   Ch[arm]ides,
      decrepitude
   Now, however, that
 figures also

       body everywhere
     plunders and
what we cannot—from the hut's lintel
  flawed

         white as
sliced turnip   the field's brow.
   our old
  wanderings

home   palace, temple,
 having   of those blue foothills
  no further   clear
    fancy[.]

4

Seven ages make a crazy quilt
Out of the famous web. Yet should milk spilt
(As when in Rhetoric one's paragraph
Was passed around and each time cut in half,
From eighty words to forty, twenty, ten,
Before imploding in a puff of Zen)
White out the sense and mutilate the phrase,
My text is Mind no less than Mallarmé's.
My illustration? The Cézanne oil sketch
Whose tracts of raw, uncharted canvas fetch
As much per square inch as the fruit our cloyed
Taste prizes for its bearing on the void.
Besides, Art furnishes a counterfeit
Heaven wherein ideas escape the fate
Their loyal adherents—brainwashed, so to speak,
By acid rain—more diatribes in Greek—
Conspicuously don't. We diehard few
Embark for London on the *QE2*.
Here mornings can be spent considering ours
Of long ago, removed and mute, like stars
(*Un*like vociferous Melina, once
A star herself, now Minister of Stunts).
Removed a further stage, viewed from this high wire
Between the elegiac and the haywire,
They even so raise questions. Does the will-
To-structural-elaboration still
Flute up, from shifting dregs of would-be rock,
Glints of a future colonnade and frieze?
Do higher brows unknit within the block,
And eyes whose Phidias and Pericles
Are eons hence make out through crystal skeins
Wind-loosened tresses and the twitch of reins?
Ah, not for long will marble school the blood
Against the warbling sirens of the flood.
All stone once dressed asks to be worn. The foam-
Pale seaside temple, like a palindrome,

Had quietly laid its plans for stealing back.
What are the Seven Wonders now? A pile
Of wave-washed pebbles. Topless women smile,
Picking the smoothest, rose-flawed white or black,
Which taste of sunlight on moon-rusted swords,
To use as men upon their checkerboards.

5

The body, favorite trope of our youthful poets . . .
    With it they gleaned, as at the sibyl's tripod,
        insight too prompt and vital for words.
            Her sleepless frenzy—

cataract and moonshaft, peaks of sheer fire at dawn,
    dung-dusted violets, the stiffening dew—
        said it best. Unutterable too
            was the beloved's

save through the index of refraction a fair, slowly
    turned head sustained in the deep look that fixed him.
        From then on veining summer nights with
            flickering ichor,

he had joined an elite scornful—as were, Charmides,
    your first, chiseled verses—of decrepitude
        in any form. Now, however, that
            their figures also

begin to slip the mind—while the body everywhere
    with peasant shrewdness plunders and puts to use
        what we cannot—from the hut's lintel
            gleams one flawed image;

another, cast up by frost or earthquake, shines white as
    sliced turnip from a furrow on the field's brow.
        Humbly our old poets knew to make
            wanderings into

homecomings of a sort—harbor, palace, temple, all
    having been quarried out of those blue foothills
        no further off, these last clear autumn
            days, than infancy.

6

Who gazed into the wrack till
Inspiration glowed,
Deducing from one dactyl
The handmaiden, the ode?

Or when aphasia skewered
The world upon a word,
Who was the friend, the steward,
Who bent his head, inferred

Then filled the sorry spaces
With pattern and intent,
A syntax of lit faces
From the impediment?

                No matter, these belated
Few at least are back. And thanks
To their little adventure, never so
Brimming with jokes and schemes,
Fussed over, fêted
By all but their fellow saltimbanques—
Though, truth to tell,
Who by now doesn't flip
Hourly from someone's upper story
("That writer . . . no, on shipboard . . . wait . . . Charmides?")
And come to, clinging to the net?
And yet, and yet
Here in the afterglow
It almost seems
Death has forgotten us
—As the old lady said to Fontenelle.
                And he,
A cautionary finger to his lip:
"Shh!"

7

After the endless jokes, this balmy winter
Around the pool, about the missing marbles,
What was more natural than for my birthday
To get—from the friend whose kiss that morning woke me—
A pregnantly clicking pouch of targets and strikers,
Aggies and rainbows, the opaque chalk-red ones,
Clear ones with DNA-like wisps inside,
Others like polar tempests vitrified . . .
These I've embedded at random in the deck-slats
Around the pool. (The pool!—compact, blue, dancing,
Lit-from-beneath oubliette.) By night their sparkle
Repeats the garden lights, or moon- or starlight,
Tinily underfoot, as though the very
Here and now were becoming a kind of heaven
To sit in, talking, largely mindless of
The risen, cloudy brilliances above.

INVESTITURE AT CECCONI'S

for David Kalstone

Caro, that dream (after the diagnosis)
found me losing patience outside the door of
"our" Venetian tailor. I wanted evening
clothes for the new year.

Then a bulb went on. The old woman, she who
stitches dawn to dusk in his back room, opened
one suspicious inch, all the while exclaiming
over the late hour—

Fabrics? patterns? those the proprietor must
show by day, not now—till a lightning insight
cracks her face wide: *Ma! the Signore's here to
try on his new robe!*

Robe? She nods me onward. The mirror triptych
summons three bent crones she diffracted into
back from no known space. They converge by magic,
arms full of moonlight.

Up my own arms glistening sleeves are drawn. Cool
silk in grave, white folds—Oriental mourning—
sheathes me, throat to ankles. I turn to face her,
uncomprehending.

Thank your friend, she cackles, *the Professore!*
Wonderstruck I sway, like a tree of tears. You—
miles away, sick, fearful—have yet arranged this
heartstopping present.

FAREWELL PERFORMANCE

for DK

Art. It cures affliction. As lights go down and
Maestro lifts his wand, the unfailing sea change
starts within us. Limber alembics once more
make of the common

lot a pure, brief gold. At the end our bravos
call them back, sweat-soldered and leotarded,
back, again back—anything not to face the
fact that it's over.

You are gone. You'd caught like a cold their airy
lust for essence. Now, in the furnace parched to
ten or twelve light handfuls, a mortal gravel
sifted through fingers,

coarse yet grayly glimmering sublimate of
palace days, Strauss, Sidney, the lover's plaintive
Can't we just be friends? which your breakfast phone call
clothed in amusement,

this is what we paddled a neighbor's dinghy
out to scatter—Peter who grasped the buoy,
I who held the box underwater, freeing
all it contained. Past

sunny, fluent soundings that gruel of selfhood
taking manlike shape for one last jeté on
ghostly—wait, ah!—point into darkness vanished.
High up, a gull's wings

clapped. The house lights (always supposing, caro,
Earth remains your house) at their brightest set the
scene for good: true colors, the sun-warm hand to
cover my wet one . . .

Back they come. How you would have loved it. We in
turn have risen. Pity and terror done with,

programs furled, lips parted, we jostle forward
eager to hail them,

more, to join the troupe—will a friend enroll us
one fine day? Strange, though. For up close their magic
self-destructs. Pale, dripping, with downcast eyes they've
seen where it led you.

PROCESSIONAL

Think what the demotic droplet felt,
Translated by a polar wand to keen
Six-pointed Mandarin—
All singularity, its Welt-
Anschauung of a hitherto untold
Flakiness, gemlike, nevermore to melt!

But melt it would, and—look—become
Now birdglance, now the gingko leaf's fanlight,
To that same tune whereby immensely old
Slabs of dogma and opprobrium,
Exchanging ions under pressure, bred
A spar of burnt-black anchorite,

Or in three lucky strokes of word golf LEAD
Once again turns (LOAD, GOAD) to GOLD.

A Scattering of Salts

(1995)

For Stephen Yenser

I

A DOWNWARD LOOK

Seen from above, the sky
Is deep. Clouds float down there,

Foam on a long, luxurious bath.
Their shadows over limbs submerged in "air,"

Over protuberances, faults,
A delta thicket, glide. On high, the love

That drew the bath and scattered it with salts

Still radiates new projects old as day,
And hardly registers the tug

When, far beneath, a wrinkled, baby hand
Happens upon the plug.

BIG MIRROR OUTDOORS

Specter, inside with you where you belong!
Must the blond hibiscus be reminded
Of privileges tentatively won
From pay dirt? or our puppet selves grow pale
Here at their narrow lot's far end, beneath
Your glittering aplomb? Yes, yes, we know:
Artillery fern, chameleon, dinner guest,
Greens and blues, deck wreathed with fairy lights
Had begun, like us, to dodder and digress.
The realm of chance cried out for supervision.
One stroke, and the casino stood corrected—
A halfway house. Now yours, inviolate
Heart, is the last word, the cool view we shrink
To couple with. Yet breeding likenesses
That won't need food or shelter has become
(Given the hapless millions lured into
Our networks) an undertaking not entirely
Vain. Ah, even when it's death you deal—!
Puss lays the feathered fool at Uli's feet.
Too weak this year to set his easel up,
He'll render it in charcoal. Alone, later,
You will reflect the lighted pool while slowly,
Darkly in the pool revolves a float
On which two baby blots of dew reflect
Glimmerings of you. So that, much as the plot
Was to make do without us, sun and rain,
Reds and blacks, terrestrial roulette,
Nature grows strong in you. Again last night
Rustling forth in all her jewelry
She faced the glacial croupier: Double or nothing!
Again dawn hot and airtight found you sweating
Out that horrifying, harmless dream.

The ancient comic theater had it right:
A shuttered house, a street or square, a tree
Collect, life after life, the energy
To flood what happens in their shade with light.
A house in Athens does the trick for me—
Thrilling to find oneself again on stage,
In character, at this untender age.

I

[*Enters with DJ.*] . . . and the kitchen. Ours,
Along with all the rest. What are those headlines
Whose upper-case demotic holds the floor—
GET THE U.S. BASES OUT OF GREECE
—That old refrain, where's their imagination?
And what's outside?
                    [*A sullen, peeling door*
Wrenches open onto glare that weighs
So heavily on things, these August days
—And cats! The nursing mother stares appalled,
While one black kitten actually topples
Over in consternation before streaking
With three or four white siblings out of sight.]

That old shed houses them. The lilac shrub
Patient as a camel on its knees
Shades them. We used to water it—remember—
Magnanimously, with a warm, pulsing hose
From three flights up. Here in this basement flat
Lived old Miss Pesmazóglou and her cat,
Or cats. They seem to have made do without her.
Now we'll be on hand to mind them. Good of Gus
And Ab to rent the dear house back to us
While they're on tour. *You* take the upstairs. These
Half-buried rooms, so glimmeringly tiled—
The kittens also—keep me here, beguiled.

2

A dozen habits fostered by the scene
Spring back to life. Old troupers reemerge:
Tony and Nelly; from oblivion's verge
Strato himself, whose bloodshot eyes (once green)
And immense bulk confound the dramaturge.
There even comes an afternoon when, bored,
We sit down to a makeshift Ouija board.

A courtesy call merely. No big deal.
A way of letting our familiars share
In these old haunts. Instead: U MUST PREPARE
YRSELVES. It's David's and my turn to keel
Over in consternation. YES MES CHERS
A CERTAIN 8 YEAR DARLING LEAVES BOMBAY
BY PLANE FOR ATHENS ONE WEEK FROM TODAY.

I hate to say it, but the neophyte
Must take the full amazement of this news
(At least till he can purchase and peruse
A heavy volume called *The Changing Light
At Sandover*) on faith.—What? Oh. My muse,
Smiling indulgently upon the wretch,
Authorizes a quick background sketch.

Maria Mitsotáki (here in Greece
An adored, black-clad mentor) crossed the bar,
From then on dazzling our binocular
Lenses, the poem's astral Beatrice,
Its very Plato. Now—OK so far?—
This bit of doctrine vital to our text:
Souls bright as hers quit one life for the next

Conscious, to what degree I shan't here tell,
Of where they lived and whom they used to know.
Maria was reborn eight years ago
In India, as a future (male) Nobel
Prize-winning chemist. The spring overflow
Of Ganges glittering with daybreak pales
Beside our wonder. CALL BACK FOR DETAILS

3

TREMORS MES CHERS SHAKE THE SUBCON [*The teacup*
Pauses, collects itself, glides on.] TINENT
AS THE CHATTERJEE FAMILY SERVANTS BUSILY PACK.
FATHER MADLY HINDU & MADLY PUNJABI
MEMBER OF PARLIAMENT, BANKER, FIREBRAND
COMING TO ATHENS AS A MEDIATOR
IN (HO HUM) GOVT TRADE TALKS. FAMILY
STAYING AT INDIAN EMBASSY INCLUDES
PAPPA, MAMMA & YOUNG SHANTIHPRASHAD
The magic child!
       [*Concerning whom we've gleaned*
Such tantalizing facts. For instance, he
Was spoken to at five by TINKLING VOICES
From test-tubes in his Junior Chemistry Kit.
At six turned WINE INTO WATER. *Lit at seven,*
While gardeners looked on goggle-eyed, HIS FIRST
SMOKELESS FIRE.]
       That tongue-twister's a name?
CALL HIM SHANTY: THIN, INTENSE BLACK EYES,
WEARING A FLAT STRAW HAT WITH LONG BLACK RIBBON
HE WILL NOT BE PARTED FROM. THAT IS YR CUE:
HAT BLOWS OFF (WITH OUR HELP IF NEED BE)
LANDING LATE AFTERNOON SEPTEMBER 4
NEAR (IF NOT ON) YR TABLE   CAN U GUESS WHERE?

We can, of course. In Kolonáki Square,
At the Bon Goût, where we always met Maria.
TEATIME INDIAN FASHION MOTHER SLIM
IN PARIS CLOTHES, AYAH IN SARI. A LIMO
WILL WHISK THEM BACK TO PURDAH AFTER SHANTY
UTTERS THE SENTENCE HE HAS BEEN REHEARSING:
'WE WILL MEET AGAIN IN MY HOME CITY'

Well, it will be the proof we've never had
Or asked for. And if nothing happens, Ephraim?
If no hat sails our way? If D and I
Just wait like idiots?   THE WIND WILL DIE

4

[*The following midday.*] David calls the cats
Our latest Holy Family. Why not?
Urania and hers have long outgrown
The Stonington arrangements. And indeed
A kind of "flight into Egypt" air pervades
The backdoor scene. Athens is full of Herods
Ready to massacre those innocents
Now suckling under leaves, now playing tag
On what to them must seem a parapet.
[*A three-foot drop divides our narrow "courtyard"*
From that of the house immediately downhill.]
Just after sunrise, watching as I set
The scraps out, which they're coming to depend on,
An old white tom, responsible and scarred—
Saint Joseph to the life—was standing guard.
He took no food; devoutly our eyes met.
The mother, too, with speaking glances said:
"Take him, my blackest and my wiliest,
Teach him the table manners of the West."
Later, the door left wide as usual,
A little bold black heart-shaped face peered in
To where I wrote, but fled my eager start.
If I could touch him—! Hasn't someone proven
That just to stroke a kitten, make it purr,
Lowers the blood pressure, both yours and its?
These kittens maddeningly don't concur:
The sight of me still throws them into fits.

[*With that, strides through the kitchen on the slender*
Chance that they're learning. Pandemonium.
The same black kitten somersaults—oh no!—
Backwards into the cement court below,
There taking refuge under an oil drum
Mounted on venerable two-by-fours
Complex and solid as the Trojan Horse.
No way to lure him out. In the other direction
A long escape route to the street leads past
The neighbors' house, promiscuously open

594

For renovations. Workmen come and go,
Plaster-white faces, joke and song. JM
Intends to play it cool in front of them.
Meanwhile for his—for everybody's sins
A frantic mewing back and forth begins.]

5

[*Two nights later.*] Talcum, loopy names
In an address book, strand of fine blond hair
Flossing a comb—God! if the Dutch au pair
Could sleep here . . . But my firework stratagems
To save the kitten fizzle in black air.
Today was Sunday. Not a soul next door.
The mother cat, cool on that canyon floor,

Suckled her black one. Ways to house and street
Were blocked, the hose hooked up. I hissed. He fled
To his old shelter. Quick! full stream ahead:
Faucet on, nozzle thumbed, a fluid sheet
Sliding beneath the oil-drum, out he sped,
Black lightning, eyes like headlights of a hit-and-run
Driver, the raison d'être of my kitten run!

With nimbleness approaching the sublime,
Seizing a bathtowel against fangs and claws
And lunging like an avatar of Shaw's
Life Force, I overtook my prey in time
To see him scuttle—not the slightest pause
Or pity for one instant laughingstock—
Into a vine-wreathed hole I'd failed to block.

The roof next door is level with our own.
It's there, as in a déjà-vu, mater-
ialized a mother dolefully—night was near—
Mewing down the drainpipe-telephone.
Feeling our eyes, "Now just see what you've done!"
Hers shone back. Such communicable pain!
From being human we grow inhumane.

We have, it seems, methodically wrecked
Her world. Analogies are rife and various
To worlds like Strato's, now disaster areas
We helped create. Hopeless to resurrect
Cradles of original neglect.
Our tidbits teach the kittens how to shit,
And day by day we put our foot in it.

6

[*Late evening, September 3.*] DJ:
Let's get some sleep. Tomorrow's the big day.

JM: All I can think about's my kitten.
It's sixty hours since we saw him last.
By now he's dying of thirst, wedged in the drainpipe . . .
I never should have opened that back door.

DJ: At least he has eight lives to go!
Remember when the Nestlé Company
Shipped its formula to Ghana, free?
The babies thrived on it. Then one fine morning,
End of shipments. No thought for all the mothers
Who weaned their babies on the formula
And had no milk left. There in a nutshell's
American policy.
                    JM: Say no more.
Leave every little skeleton in peace.
I never should have opened that back door.

7

[*Wednesday, 4 o'clock at the Bon Goût.*
Much harder to determine is the year.
Decades have passed since our first coffees here,
Ordered in dumbshow. Ah, if youth but knew!
The sky was then a sacramental blue,
The café's two old waiters dignified,
The tourist rare, nose buried in the Guide.]

DJ: There's a free table. It'll do . . .

[*Today's Bon Goût is more a minipark*
Cars eddy round. Yet here's a little breeze,
Respite of awnings, rustle of plane trees.
Real action won't begin till after dark.
Our glances wander—it's in fact a lark
Revisiting this former commonplace—
With guarded carelessness from face to face.]

DJ: The big thing is, they've all made money.
These young men don't have waistlines any more.
Do they still dance in pairs on the dirt floor?
JM: Would they still think our jokes were funny?

[*Sealed with red labels, wrapped in cellophane,*
Aimed at some unsuspecting hostess, boom!
Off goes the florist's grand hydrangea bomb.
Green pinks, cream blues. Beneath its weight the vain
Eternal shopboy, scion of that swain
Who piped away the War of Independence,
Whistles egregiously for his descendants.]

Waiter: Caffé, Signori? Kein Problem.

[*Living familiars infiltrate the scene.*
The lottery man. Those two crème de la crème
Canasta-playing ladies. Trailing them,
The "Diplomat"?! Don't look, there's Fritz the Queen
From Chattanooga. But in olive-green
Cords and Chanel cloud a favorite Greek
Urbanely interrupts our hide-and-seek.]

Tony: Paidiá! In public? In the Square?
Mais c'est la fin du monde! I can't, I'm late—
I've found a buyer for that desk I hate.
Tomorrow noon, then? Nelly's cut her hair.

[*Tomorrow noon we meet aboard the white*
Boat to Spetsai, where a niece's villa
Is Nelly's all this month. The island's still a

Niche for the happy few. If they invite,
Who're we to be standoffish? Our first night
A widowed Gräfin hopes that we'll drop in
For camomile or cognac after din—]

DJ: A sari, look! JM: You're right—
No, look again. The company she's chosen
Disqualifies her—sideburns, Lederhosen . . .
Our ayah would be older, more soignée.
Besides, where's little Shanty? DJ [*sighing*]:
Delayed in traffic? Well, at least they're trying.

[*We look and look. Soon it's the absent faces*
We see. Mimí. Proud Chester. His evzone
"Of hollow bronze" from Thessaly. The crone—
Gray, toothless Papagena—hung with braces
Of snipe and quail. Called up from an oasis
Watered by Lethe, which no sun can warm,
They cower from our love like a sandstorm.]

JM: It's after five. My social graces
Are crumbling. Ten more minutes, would you say?

[*As shadows lengthen we prepare to pay,*
Collect ourselves, and bend our steps uphill.
Wait, though—how beautiful the light—sit still.
Now or never, as in the old play,
Its moonbeam-dappled feats performed by day,
Titania, Oberon, wake up! Employ
Your arts, produce that little Indian boy!

Long pause.] DJ: Well, let's be. On. Our. Way.

[*Giving the magic one last opportunity,*
Clutching at straws—if it should come to that,
We'd settle for a disembodied hat,
Flutter of black somewhere in the vicinity
To pin our hopes upon, if not our sanity—
We slowly get up. Eyes front. Dignified.
Two old ex-waiters. For the wind has died.]

8

[*Spetsai.*] The Gräfin: No, no, *I* am Greek,
My husband was a Hamburger. *He* spoke
The Ursprache. Oh later, perfect Greek,
But not our first year. I'm remembering—
Nelláki tells me you adored Maria—
Didn't we all—the party where Maria
And Helmut met for the first time. Without
A single word in common they communed.
They sat down on the sofa and *communed*
All evening long. Well, forty minutes. Thirty.
Quite long enough to make a bride of twenty
Run home in tears, and lock herself in the bathroom.
I'm ashamed *for* her to this day. I am!
Helmut was knocking, frantic . . . All at once—
We lived those first years in "a wood near Athens"
As my grandfather liked to call Kifissia *then*—
No loud cafés, no traffic—all at once
Came music, music from nowhere, at one a.m.!
—Ah, don't ask me. Say the "Liebestraum"
Or something Viennese. But in this *dream*
Helmut and I met on the balcony. There
Below, like an Embarkment for Cythère,
Musicians from the party: clarinet,
Guitar, two violins. It must have been
Full moon, the garden seemed electrified,
And from the fiacre they'd come in—Maria
Waving the coachman's whip like a conductor.
We waved back, back in love. The summer night
Was young again. And then? She blew a kiss
And off they went clop-clop into the night.

Nelly [*back at the villa*]: Bah, che dream!
Moonlight and roses, pitiful old cat—
As if Maria's genre were operetta . . .

DJ: Come on, she's not so—cat? The *cat*!
I saw him—yes—this morning, our black kitten!
Meaning to tell you but it slipped my—where?
Down in the neighbors' court. No worse for wear.

9

MES CHERS WE OVERESTIMATED OURSELVES
Please don't apologize. If I may borrow
The Gräfin's genial phrase, we feel ashamed
For you already. FATHER CHATTERJEE
WD NOT ALLOW THEM OUT: SECURITY!
EMBASSY GUARDS HAD WARNED AGAINST THAT SQUARE
Innocent Kolonáki? I'll just bet.
YET (AND WE WEEP) OUR BRAVE BOY ROSE FROM HIS NAP
AS IF SLEEPWALKING & STOLE OUT UNSEEN
INTO THE STRANGE CITY. HE WAS FOUND
IN HIS PAJAMAS BY AN ANXIOUS CROWD.
'HELLO? HELLO? (IN ENGLISH, BUT SO FAINTLY)
WHERE ARE YOU?' HE WAS CALLING Ephraim, spare—
FORGIVE US. WE GREW OVERCONFIDENT.
A GRIEF FOR YOU, FAR GREATER FOR LITTLE SHANTY
SOBBING & FLAILING OUT   JM   DEAR SCRIBE
[*From whom burst certain long-pent-up reproaches*
Ending:] . . . the proof. The proof we've never had
Or, mind you, sought. Proof that you act in our theater
Not for once purely in a manner of speaking,
No: word made flesh. Flesh wailing, wide-eyed, seeking
Us! THE KITTEN LIVES! DJ'S PLAN SOUND
[*A stopgap ramp connecting the two levels.*]
I didn't mean the *kitten*— [*Here our revels*
Grind to a halt on Ephraim's shifting ground.]

Like Wise Men we'd been primed to kneel in awe
At journey's end before that child whose nature
Proved Earth at one with Heaven, and past with future.
Instead, the perfect fools we still are saw
A manger full of emptiness, dust, straw . . .
AND LIGHT! Well, yes. Light also. We weren't blind,
The sun was out. THE PLAY OF H E A V E N ' S M I N D

10

There is a moment comedies beget
When escapade and hubbub die away,

Vows are renewed, masks dropped, La Folle Journée
Arriving star by star at a septet.
It's then the connoisseur of your bouquet
(Who sits dry-eyed through *Oedipus* or *Lear*)
Will shed, O Happiness, a furtive tear.

We've propped the rough hypotenuse of board
Between the pit to which his fall consigned
Our prodigal and the haven left behind.
Nature must do the rest. No coaxing toward
The haggard matriarch on high. A blind
Protecting us, we smile down through the slats
As our flyblown road company of *Cats*

Concludes its run. (Did T. S. Eliot
Devise the whole show from his sepulcher?)
By dusk—black, white—the kittens suck and purr.
Shanty will fly, we're told, ON MIDNIGHT'S DOT
BACK TO HIS WASTE LAND—back, if you prefer,
To our subconscious, this much being sure:
That black hole is three-quarters literature.

(Why otherwise, midway in my fifth section,
Didn't I forestall my rhyme scheme's lapse,
Its walk downtown in sleep? Although, perhaps
Thanks to a nagging sense of misdirection
Once HEAVEN'S MIND came out from under wraps,
I've caught up with it, shaken it awake,
These aren't the "risks" a poem's meant to take.)

To all, sweet dreams. The teacup-stirring eddy
Is spent. We've dropped our masks, renewed our vows
To letters, to the lives that letters house,
Houses they shutter, streets they shade. Already
Empty and dark, this street is. Dusty boughs
Sleep in a pool of vigilance so bright
An old tom skirts it. The world's his tonight.

MORNING EXERCISE

Poem, neat pseudonym
For thoughts in disarray,
Tell how we'd gone that day
Separately to the gym.

I did things on a mat
To make me flexible.
The room was bare and chill;
I could relate to that.

You must have waded straight
Into the billowing steam,
Wanting to sweat your frame
Till choler stored of late

Should sparkle in your hair
And trickle down your chest.
So neither would have guessed
His missing half was there

Except that someone sane
(Between "my" room's and "yours"
Respective temperatures)
Had set a small, fogged pane

Through which—quick to bemuse
Wits for a change wiped clear—
Our eyes met. Oh my dear!
Against such interviews

Each pressed a sorry nose
And made his goldfish face:
Not much of an embrace
But better, I suppose,

For that. In ways a lot
Less fondly matter-of-fact

Might Eskimo enact
His bond with Hottentot . . .

So be it. Dried and clad,
We took our homeward way,
Stopping for a parfait
Aux fraises at the Old Grad.

ALABASTER

I

The original word
Eddied and forked, to mean (a) the soft stone
In use today—flamboyant, vaguely lewd
Honey-pink volumes flounced with lard
Like Parma ham, like the blown-up
Varnished nipple of a Titian nude.

Then (b) the ancient one—
A kind of Pharaonate of Lime,
Cosmetic white, or unbleached-linen white
Through which waves cresting purer white
Make a river seem to stand upright
When the jar fills with sun.

You could say that vagabond gypsum and sacerdotal
Calcite embody the two
Mainstreams of Western thought—Aristotle
And Plato, gristle and dream;
Also that on those mornings they're shone through
Both are supreme.

2

Thanks to it, for centuries a glow
Not quite of this world lit
Sanctum, princeling, folio.
Always too late
We saw the stricken cow, the rabble below
With catapult and crossbow.

Now came the age of glass.
Each room boasted a device whereby
Misbehavior, even miles away,
Could be perceived. (Uh-oh.
From then on it was curtains, both for us
And for the window.)

Visible meanwhile, we had to clean
Our act up. Probity, good sense?
Zero to 1 on the Mohs scale—yet, we'd learn,
Indistinguishable on a wide screen
From marble, rosy with concern:
The stuff of Presidents.

3

And if a tissue-thin
Section of self lay on a lighted slide,
And a voice breathed in your ear,
"Yes, ah yes. That red oxide
Stain is where your iron, Lady Hera,
Entered him.

And in this corner, boldly intricate
As agate, zigzagging
Bays and salients —plans of a fortress?—date
From his twentieth spring,
When we had set the dials at *First Love*.
Up here's the opalescent fossil of—"

Dream on. Dodo and roc
Did without your pious autopsies.
Nor will the self resist,
Broken on terror like a rack,
When waves of nightmare heat decrystallize
Her lucid molecules to chalk.

4

Landscapes about to disappear
Absorb what life
They can. Tamped rainbows tallied
The eons of one banded cliff.
Time pressing hawk and asp and onager
Each to its hieroglyph,

Gods fled to high ground. The dam totally
Quashed—like a warlord—
The future of that past. Henceforward
As text and text alone would the sacred valley
Invite construction. Shall we
Go to the blackboard?

October Flood Sun Set
[The] *Water Table Rising Presences*
[Balance the] *Mirror* [upon] *Granite Knees*
[A] *Scorpion* [made of] *Gems* [in it]
—The so-called "zodiac" cartouche of Sut
Found (1904) by Cômte de Guise.

5

In Spring but also now in Fall
Earth's tilt allows
Early sun to flow straight through the house,
So catching a catch-all
Thrift-shop table in the upstairs hall
That its translucent inset glows,

Mild, otherworldly, from the underside.
As once in love or infancy
Yesterday's cargo—pine cone, junk mail, key—
Floats on a milky tide,
Grime-swirled, with blood-pink glimmerings. For me
The time I dread

Is coming, thinks the table. Yet despite
All that, these fine, late days,
Long minutes after dawn, whatever weighs
Upon me light
Bears up, as to recall it does
Through the dry channel of a starless night.

SNOW JOBS

X had the funds, the friends, the plan.
Y's frank grin was—our common fate?
Or just a flash in just a pan?
Z, from the tender age of eight,
Had thirsted to officiate.
We hardly felt them disappear,
The crooked and the somewhat straight.
Now where's the slush of yesteryear?

Where's Teapot Dome? Where's the Iran
Contra Affair? Where's Watergate—
Liddy—Magruder—Ehrlichman?
Their shoes squeaked down the Halls of State,
Whole networks groaned beneath their weight,
Till spinster Clotho darted near
To shroud in white a running mate.
Ah, where's the slush of yesteryear?

Like blizzards on a screen the scan-
dals thickened at a fearful rate,
Followed by laughter from a can
And hot air from the candidate.
With so much open to debate,
Language that went into one ear
Came out the—hush! be delicate:
Where is the slush of yesteryear?

Omniscient Host, throughout your great
Late shows the crystal wits cohere,
The flaky banks accumulate—
But where's the slush of yesteryear?

HOME FIRES

for John Hollander

I peered into the crater's heaving red
And quailed. I called upon the Muse. I said,
   "The day I cease to serve you, let me die!"
And woke alone to birdsong, in our bed.

The flame was sinewed like those angels Blake
Drew faithfully. One old log, flake by flake,
   Gasped out its being. Had it hoped to rise
Intact from such a wrestler's give-and-take?

My house is made of wood so old, so dry
From years beneath this pilot-light blue sky,
   A stranger's idle glance could be the match
That sends us all to blazes.—Where was I?

Ah yes. The man from Aetna showed concern.
No alarm system—when would people learn?
   No outside stair. The work begins next week.
Must I now marry that I may not burn?

Never again, oracular, wild-eyed,
To breathe on a live ember deep inside?
   The contract signed in blood forbids that, too,
Damping my spirit as it saves my hide.

Take risks! the crowd chants in a kind of rage
To where his roaring garret frames the sage
   Held back by logic, by the very thought
Of leaping to conclusions, at his age.

Besides, the cramped flue of each stanza draws
Feeling *away*. To spare us? Or because
   Heaven is cold and needs the mortal stuff
Flung nightly around its barenesses, like gauze.

Last weekend in a bar in Pawcatuck
A boy's face raw and lean as lightning struck.
    Before I knew what hit me, there you were,
Sweetheart, with your wet blanket. Just my luck.

I touched the grate with my small hand, and got
Corrected. Sister ran to kiss the spot.
    Today a blister full of speechless woe
Wells up for the burnt children I am not.

Magda was molten at sixteen. The old
Foundryman took his time, prepared the mold,
    Then poured. Lost wax, the last of many tears,
Slid down her face. Adieu, rosebuds and gold!

That slim bronze figure of Free Speech among
Repressive glooms woke ardor in the young,
    Only to ring with mirth—a trope in Czech
Twisting implacably the fire's tongue.

One grace: this dull asbestos halo meant
For the bulb's burning brow. Two drops of scent
    Upon it, and our booklined rooms, come dusk,
Of a far-shining lamp grew redolent.

The riot had been "foretold" to Mrs. Platt,
The landlady, by a glass ruby at
    The medium's throat. "Next she'll be throwing fits,"
Gerald said coldly. "I shall move. That's that."

Torchlit, the student demonstrators came.
Faint blues and violets within the flame
    Appeared to plead that fire at heart was shy
And only incidentally to blame.

Consuming fear, that winter, swept the mind.
Then silence, country sounds—and look! Behind
    Me stands the blackened chimney of our school,
Crowned with a stork's nest, rambler-rose-entwined.

A sunset to end all. Life's brave disguise—
Rages and fevers, worn to tantalize—
   Flickers to ash. What's left may warm itself
At the hearth glowing in its lover's eyes.

≈

Dear Fulmia, I thought of you for these
Obsidian trinkets purchased, if you please,
   In a boutique at the volcano's core.
(Extinct? I wonder.) Love, Empedocles.

THE *RING* CYCLE

1

They're doing a *Ring* cycle at the Met,
Four operas in one week, for the first time
Since 1939. I went to that one.
Then war broke out, Flagstad flew home, tastes veered
To tuneful deaths and dudgeons. Next to Verdi,
Whose riddles I could whistle but not solve,
Wagner had been significance itself,
Great golden lengths of it, stitched with motifs,
A music in whose folds the mind, at twelve,
Came to its senses: Twin, Sword, Forest Bird,
Envy, Redemption through Love . . . But left unheard
These fifty years? A fire of answered prayers
Burned round that little pitcher with big ears
Who now wakes. Night. E-flat denotes the Rhine,
Where everything began. The world's life. Mine.

2

Young love, moon-flooded hut, and the act ends.
House lights. The matron on my left exclaims.
We gasp and kiss. Our mothers were best friends.
Now, old as mothers, here we sit. Too weird.
That man across the aisle, with lambswool beard,
Was once my classmate, or a year behind me.
Alone, in black, in front of him, Maxine . . .
It's like the *Our Town* cemetery scene!
We have long evenings to absorb together
Before the world ends: once familiar faces
Transfigured by hi-tech rainbow and mist,
Fireball and thunderhead. Make-believe weather
Calling no less for prudence. At our stage
When recognition strikes, who can afford
The strain it places on the old switchboard?

3

Fricka looks pleased with her new hairdresser.
Brünnhilde (Behrens) has abandoned hers.
Russet-maned, eager for battle, she butts her father
Like a playful pony. They've all grown, these powers,
So young, so human. So exploitable.
The very industries whose "major funding"
Underwrote the production continue to plunder
The planet's wealth. Erda, her cobwebs beaded
With years of seeping waste, subsides unheeded
—Right, Mr. President? Right, Texaco?—
Into a gas-blue cleft. Singers retire,
Yes, but take pupils. Not these powers, no, no.
What corporation Wotan, trained by them,
Returns gold to the disaffected river,
Or preatomic sanctity to fire?

4

Brünnhilde confronts Siegfried. That is to say,
Two singers have been patiently rehearsed
So that their tones and attitudes convey
Outrage and injured innocence. But first
Two youngsters became singers, strove to master
Every nuance of innocence and outrage
Even in the bosom of their stolid
Middleclass families who made it possible
To study voice, and languages, take lessons
In how the woman loves, the hero dies . . .
Tonight again, each note a blade reforged,
The dire oath ready in their blood is sworn.
Two world-class egos, painted, overweight,
Who'll joke at supper side by side, now hate
So plausibly that one old stagehand cries.

5

I've worn my rings—all three of them
At once for the first time—to the *Ring*.

Like pearls in seawater they gleam,
A facet sparkles through waves of sound.

Of their three givers one is underground,
One far off, one here listening.

One ring is gold; one silver, set
With two small diamonds; the third, bone
—Conch shell, rather. Ocean cradled it

As earth did the gems and metals. All unknown,
Then, were the sweatshops of Nibelheim

That worry Nature into jewelry,
Orbits of power, Love's over me,

Or music's, as his own chromatic scales
Beset the dragon, over Time.

6

Back when the old house was being leveled
And this one built, I made a contribution.
Accordingly, a seat that bears my name
Year after year between its thin, squared shoulders
(Where Hagen is about to aim his spear)
Bides its time in instrumental gloom.
These evenings we're safe. Our seats belong
To Walter J. and Ortrud Fogelsong
—Whoever they are, or were. But late one night
(How is it possible? I'm sound asleep!)
I stumble on "my" darkened place. The plaque
Gives off that phosphorescent sheen of Earth's
Address book. Stranger yet, as I sink back,
The youth behind me, daybreak in his eyes—
A son till now undreamed of—makes to rise.

THE PONCHIELLI COMPLEX

"Suicidio!"

Husbands, by my time, dozed beneath the gilt.
The Golden Age was ending, that began
With ominous panache. It was the man
Back then who, lighthouse-monocle aflash
From the deep, twilit loge, willed Malibran
To go insane and ripplingly expire.

He or the likes of him had tamed the wild
Horses of steam, made fiction of the trees.
Soon cables would floor Ocean, factories
Sweat dusk at noon, dehydrating the child
Lighter and bleaker than a lump of coal.
Already Nature, footlit in the guise
Of a wronged maiden (did he realize?),
Expressed what this was doing to the soul.

A woman who had spent her youth at scales
Until hers glinted undertook the role.
Given her life—alone and badly paid—
She needed a protector. That old score
Had ups and downs aplenty, which she played
Also to the hilt. His noisy shirt.
His wife. His friends who treated her like dirt.

Each latest outburst caused increasingly
Fine sunsets round the world. Just so, the sweet
Unsullied heroines of her first decade
Were changing. Now consumptive milliners,
Demi-mondaines and fat Venetian street
Singers driven to verismo's brink
Got their deserts. I poured a triple drink

And wrote: *The end. No more roulades.* But then
Our high seas quieted and the sun shone.
What would acting on that mood have meant?

614

Strangling the lamia whose decibels
Were slowly turning the proscenium
Muses to plaster? Or bankrupting him,
Yearly stouter and more somnolent,
Who backed whatever war-horse she starred in?

Neither. It would have meant once and for all
Extinguishing the footlights across which
Their glances met: desire, intelligence,
Asperity, ennui . . . —per carità!
Not with her clutch-and-stagger scene beginning,
That brings the house down and him backstage grinning.

TO THE READER

Each day, hot off the press from Moon & Son,
"Knowing of your continued interest,"
Here's a new book—well, actually the updated
Edition of their one all-time best seller—
To find last night's place in, and forge ahead.
If certain scenes and situations ("work,"
As the jacket has it, "of a blazingly
Original voice") make you look up from your page
—But this is life, is truth, is me!—too many
Smack of self-plagiarism. Terror and tryst,
Vow and verbena, done before, to death,
In earlier chapters, under different names . . .
And what about *those* characters? No true
Creator would just let them fade from view
Or be snuffed out, like people. Yet is there room
(In the pinch of pages under your right thumb)
To bring them back so late into their own?—
Granted their own can tell itself from yours.
You'd like to think a structure will emerge,
If only a kind of Joycean squirrel run
Returning us all neatly to page 1,
But the inconsistencies of plot and style
Lead you to fear that, for this author, fiction
Aims at the cheap effect, "stranger than fiction,"
As people once thought life—no, *truth* was. Strange . . .
Anyhow, your final thought tonight,
Before you kiss my picture and turn the light out,
Is of a more exemplary life begun
Tomorrow, truer, harder to get right.

VOLCANIC HOLIDAY

for Peter Hooten

I

Our helicopter shaking like a fist
Hovers above the churning
Cauldron of red lead in what a passion!
None but the junior cherubim ask why.
We bank and bolt. Shores draped in gloom
Upglint to future shocks of wheat.
Your lips, unheard, move through the din of blades.

2

A Mormon merman, God's least lobbyist,
Prowls the hotel. All morning
Sun tries to reason with the mad old ocean
We deep down feel the pull of. And in high
Valleys remote from salt and spume
Waterfalls jubilantly fleet
Spirit that thunder into glancing braids.

3

Thunder or bamboos drumming in the mist?
Tumbril or tribal warning?
Pacific Warfare reads the explanation
For a display we'd normally pass by:
Molars of men who snarled at doom
Studding a lava bowl. What meat
Mollifies the howl of famished shades?

4

Crested like palms, like waves, they too subsist
On one idea—returning.

Generation after generation
The spirit grapples, tattered butterfly,
A flower in sexual costume,
Hard-on or sheath dew-fired. Our feet
At noon seek paths the evening rain degrades.

5

Adolescence, glowering unkissed:
The obstacle course yearning
Grew strong in. Cheek to cliff face, sheer devotion. . . .
To be loved back, then, would have been to die.
Then, not now. Show me the tomb
Whose motto and stone lyre compete
With this life-giving fever. As it fades

6

From the Zen chapel comes that song by Liszt.
Is love a dream? A burning,
Then a tempering? Beyond slopes gone ashen,
Rifts that breathe gas, rivers that vitrify,
Look! a bough falters into bloom.
Twin rainbows come and go, discreet,
As when together we haunt virgin glades.

7

Moments or years hence, having reminisced,
May somebody discerning
Arrive at tranquil words for . . . mere emotion?
Meanwhile let green-to-midnight shifts of sky
Fill sliding mirrors in our room
—No more eruptions, they entreat—
With Earth's repose and Heaven's masquerades.

RESCUE

Dusk. Rain over   but asphalt hissing
flooded clear   with sea light.
Sharply, sweet heart,   you swerved, pulled off,
ran back and snatching   the three-inch turtle
we almost hadn't   missed as it started
its perilous crossing   deposited it
there! at the far   pasture's edge—
mission so nimbly,   raptly accomplished
where dizzying beams   rushed both ways
and tears broke   from the tall trees
that I who saw   the marvel simply
filed it away   for future use.
We'd seen so many   marvels those days:

Water welling   from a mountain top.
The Fire goddess   faithfully bleeding
into the Sea,   our helicopter's
crawling shadow   a fly on folds of
charcoal lamé.   From higher yet,
eye to eye   with the ever grander
rising Sun,   the full Moon setting.
Our own two bodies   burnished by foam
—ah, and Rainbows   appearing in pairs
(the showy male,   his mate shyer,
like a Japanese   bride and groom)
peaceably browsing   on the jacaranda
grove in palest   purple bloom.

Back to the turtle,   here's a tale
it can tell   till the end of time:
"Night was falling.   Too frightened to shrink
into my shell,   as the shattering lights
hurtled past   I took despairingly
slow steps   to appease them.
Upon chelonian   powers that shouldered

Terra herself   from a waste of waters
childlike I called   for help. Was heard!—
only then turning   to instinctive stone.
Shame upon me: I had shut myself to
life even   as it uplifted
and heaved me into   a green haven."

II

THE INSTILLING

All day from high within the skull—
Dome of a Pantheon, trepanned—light shines
Into the body. Down that stair

Sometimes there's fog: opaque red droplets check
The beam. Sometimes tall redwood-tendoned glades
Come and go, whose dwellers came and went.
Now darting feverishly anywhere,
Manic duncecap its danseuse eludes,

Now slowed by grief, white-lipped,
Grasping the newel bone of its descent,

This light can even be invisible

Till a deep sparkle, regular as script,
As wavelets of an EKG, defines
The dreamless gulf between two shoulder blades.

NOVELETTES

1

We have settled into this resort hotel.
Our blue suite, linked to others, overlooks a lake's
Cloudless reflections. People we more or less know
Make up the clientele. Next door, for instance,
Two little girls of six, one fair, one dark
(Summer and Winter you called them) are at play—
Hear their shrieks of laughter . . . of pain? *Of pleasure!*
The children, obscenely compliant, are being tortured
By white men dressed in black. You race for the sauna
To fetch their mother from the blinding steam.
She comes forth dripping, red as fire. What next
Happens happens in a flash. Our entire wing
(In conformance to some prevailing "binary plan")
Is now a museum: walls, tables, floor to ceiling
Dense with memorabilia—wrenches, fingernails,
Theater stubs, half-done needlework. Or rather
Not these but laser projections of the lost originals.
I move, on my cane, through crowds; it's the last day.
Concerning one exhibit, a young Eurasian
With a press card stops me: "Sir, can you tell our viewers
How much, in those old plays of yours, were the actors paid?"
Rough figures come to mind. "So little? That's
What you called a living?" Still bent on finding you,
I hobble past. Here's a window onto a world of moonlit
Cubes and arches in ruins, populated by cats.

2

A mesa at cloud level. Over the side, tucked far,
Far down in emerald crevices, appear
Signs of civilization. The descent is sheer,
Yet sturdy dappled ponies have been bred
For just this purpose. We dismount—we three—

624

To an enchantment of cobbled streets and foggy
Lantern-lit shops: an English town. From the speech,
The bonnets and coins, the cakes and tortoiseshell,
Lamia & Other Poems (three mint copies)
We deduce that nothing has changed since 1820.
We take rooms. Time stands still—and flies. Each day
New charms emerge. People are reticent
But ready, we feel, to accept us. So much so
That the blow stuns, when it falls. Two officers
Materialize interrogating J
Who counters, with reason, that we've shown good faith,
Asked from the start no better than to stay.
"Ah," says the tall one in a more civil tone,
Ushering us past gawking groom and barmaid
Out of the inn, " 'tis so, you three well-nigh . . .
But here are your horses." The ascent is harrowing
Into the faceless glare and windhowl. In its course
A fan of stiffened gauze—our only proof,
M will keep laughing later, fighting back tears—
Falls from her sash, through cloud-shreds, past retrieval.

3

The house has filled and darkened. *The Magic Flute*
Begins in silence. A gang of urchins
Racked like pool balls as the curtain parts
Break through the audience, spraying the faces
Of a startled few with luminous paint. A chill
Quick-drying coat transfigures mine. Thus chosen,
We're herded—old subscribers left behind
Blinking about in confusion—onto the stage.
It brightens. We must not look back. The theater
Has no back. In twos (our guides older by now,
More reticent—yet some first true chord is struck)
We have an endless pier of planks to walk, a white
Ramshackle xylophone set low above the flats.
All is tranquillity. To soaring strings
The gradual wavelets glitter, their bluegreen deepens

—But my friend? He's fallen (did the staves give way?)
Head downward, sinking like a stone. I jump in after,
If only to—but there he goes, borne past me
Limp in the jaws of a great fire-gilled sunfish!
A line I've made him grasp will haul him back
To air, the dominant. Except that now *I'm* lost
Beneath the surface, among these milkily glinting
Minors, these time-colored motes, precipitate
Of music, from which I must be saved. I hear him
Piping, trying to reach me. And wake unafraid. He will.

MY FATHER'S IRISH SETTERS

Always throughout his life
(The parts of it I knew)
Two or three would be racing
Up stairs and down hallways,
Whining to take us walking,
Or caked with dirt, resigning
Keen ears to bouts of talk—
Until his third, last wife
Put down her little foot.
That splendid, thoroughbred
Lineage was penned
Safely out of earshot:
Fed, of course, and watered,
But never let out to run.
"Dear God," the new wife simpered,
Tossing her little head,
"Suppose they got run over—
Wouldn't *that* be the end?"

Each time I visited
(Once or twice a year)
I'd slip out, giving my word
Not to get carried away.
At the dogs' first sight of me
Far off—of anyone—
Began a joyous barking,
A russet-and-rapid-as-flame
Leaping, then whimpering lickings
Of face and hands through wire.
Like fire, like fountains leaping
With love and loyalty,
Put, were they, in safekeeping
By love, or for love's sake?
Dear heart, to love's own shame.
But loyalty transferred
Leaves famously slim pickings,
And no one's left to blame.

Divorced again, my father
(Hair white, face deeply scored)
Looked round and heaved a sigh.
The setters were nowhere.
Fleet muzzle, soulful eye
Dead lo! these forty winters?
Not so. Tonight in perfect
Lamplit stillness begin
With updraft from the worksheet,
Leaping and tongues, far-shining
Hearths of our hinterland:
Dour chieftain, maiden pining
Away for that lost music,
Her harpist's wild red hair . . .
Dear clan of Ginger and Finn,
As I go through your motions
(As they go through me, rather)
Love follows, pen in hand.

THE GREAT EMIGRATION

On the low road to Skye
Many a scenic detour,
Oddly few people—
Who's to say why?

THE GLEN.   They were my brave lads and I failed them. Failed to believe their oaths, sworn in my very bosom. To grasp how that matter of a royal line kept leading not to the stanza where weapons glanced peaceably from walls of Spanish leather, but to the battlefield. Small wonder my flowers of manhood sprang up blood-red in clearings of a far, uncharted land. Yonder would follow them no agent of the Crown.

More braes, more lochs . . .
Ever fewer bipeds. Ghosts of rain,
A West grown tame and woolly,
Flocked by flocks

—Sheep or stones? Scrambling to their feet
As we whiz by
A local rock group
Begins to bleat.

Yet where cloud-rents
Brighten up ahead
The scene gives back its promptest gleam so far
Of intelligence.

THE LOCH.   Don't be fooled. Man-shaped at first, distended now by spasms old as the hills to this stretch-mark of twilight upon barren green, my mind is failing something wonderful. No more ideas, no more fair faces quizzing me. It's gust and peak from now on, it's brute beak of swan. I seem abstracted? Don't be fooled. When no one's looking the Thing surfaces.

Wrinkled and barnacled—each a whale
Shaped by unplumbable pressures—
Stone after standing stone
Breaches into the gale.

And the sunlit moon, strange as the moor we cross
Toward a meal featuring
"Medallions of peat
Smothered in rich cream sauce" . . .

THE HAG.   I go on. And on. Brick by brick, the same old story. In the palsied hovels it comes to light—comes rather to eye-watering reek. Dogged as Auld MacAdam cutting into my squelchy terrine, the new crust forms. Brick by brick—but there I go, repeating myself. And no one listens any more.

Those crags, at noon so threatening to approach,
Midnight wears on her bosom
Backed by expiring day,
An onyx brooch.

BEN NEVIS.   With the sailing of the first ships such a grief shook us. Folk left behind fell onto the shore weeping like children. Another year and the grievers, too, set sail—hear their skirling in the skua's throat? Naught remains but to rise in lonely mist above my old, contrary fault. For I too had defected; had by slow unwitting eastward millimeters broken faith with titans whose bones today, ground fine as sugar, seal up the Fountain of Youth.

Sunrise. "The Sands of Uig"—
Quaverings by Schumann
Of a transparence
Marked *sanft und ruhig.*

THE MONSTER.   They have diagnosed my presence, never found me. A shape-shifter, I mutate, I metastasize. Hairshirt tweeds from the gaunt weavers of Bigotree. The broken vow, the cell's implosion. A dread my hostess dissembles with cloudlets, rippling puns, the carnival mask of the swan. But [*a whisper*] beneath that silver evening gown she's wasting away.

Should the rainbow fret,
Each color in its parched enamel cot,
Deftly, inspiredly
Like a healer, your wet

Brush makes the rounds. And presently, mixing *their*
Mothers-of-pearl and pale
Kelp-scribbled creams,
The little coves bid fair

To last. Heaven's eye
Sparkles from the crater of one huge
Lava-purple cowflop, marking a path
Wisps of white prettify:

"Lamb's wool in ears
Before our dip, love!"—Nanny's voice.
Thirty degrees of latitude away
And twice that many years

Welcome palm, plumbago, joy
Of the live deep sapphire
Key-studded Stream
I swam in as a boy—

THE NORTH ATLANTIC.   You caught my Drift! Aye, aye, I love you
still. Who else contrived this rendezvous with mildness, here at journey's
end? Subtly reversing the trend from youth to age, from Key to Loch,
from New World to Old Country, I am the quittance you sought. Pray do
not thank me. The trouble is lost in the pleasure.

Pleasure? Or just Geography cloud-swirled
With Time, a moonwalk's black-and-blue
Postage stamp of Earth . . . Well,
News from a far corner of the world,

Our only envelope. But what to say
Inside, and who to mail it to?
"Great Hermes, Psychopomp,
We're all packed. Lead the way . . ."

THE SWAN.   Would ye hear my song? Tune in another morning.

The postmistress in her fluorescent hole
Weighs (before cancelling) this latest
History of slow-motion joys and grievances
Under remote control.

631

MORE OR LESS

Nature copies Art, said Oscar Wilde.
Out therefore with the old inheritance,
Rooms so overfurnished the heart sinks,
Moulding and fringe, high ozone-whitened panes,
Precious woods and mirror cataract,
The million doodad species catching dust.
In with lack of clutter, starkly styled,
Only the fittest vertebrates and plants,
Cactus habitat and goldfish bowl,
Little to smarten up our costly prefab
Unless a holograph of (say) Einstein—
Bespectacled, white-maned, a breathing sphinx—
Prints ever-thinning air with the myopic
Simplicity of those who live here still,
Their sad know-how, their fingertip control.

ON THE BLOCK

1 / LAMP, TERRACOTTA BASE, U.S., CA. 1925

If when you're old and musing
Upon my whats and whys
Another one should flicker
Its last before your eyes

Don't worry, they give out, too,
Those burning filaments,
Imagination's debris
Englobed still in a sense

Briefly too hot to handle,
Too dim a souvenir,
Then, for the deft unscrewing
Unless you first, my dear,

Feel for what it shone from,
Ribbed clay each night anew
Hardened to its mission:
Light for the likes of you.

2 / MANTEL CLOCK, IMITATION SÈVRES

Time, passing, glances at the clock
Perhaps with pity—who's to say?
Still rose and ormolu, its hands
Clasped in dismay . . .

"Stay then, thou art so fair," he smiles,
To put the pretty thing at ease.
"I will, *I have*," the latter sighs.
"Now what, please?

Teach me to tick without the touch
I took my life from—ah, those years!"

It's dusk; the dial brims with faint
Firefly tears.

The arbiter reviews a face
Flawless in its partial knowing:
"Child, think well of me, or try.
I must be going."

SCRAPPING THE COMPUTER

Like countless others in the digital age, I seem
To have written a memoir on my new computer.
It had no memories—anyone's would have done,
And mine, I hoped, were as good as anyone's.
This playmate was programmed for my "personal" needs
(A bit too intricately, it would transpire),
But all was advancing at the smooth pace of dream

Until that morning when a faint mechanical shriek
Took me aback. As I watched, the paragraph
Then under way deconstructed itself into
Mathematical symbols, musical notation—
Ophelia's mad scene in a Czech production
Fifty years hence. The patient left on a gurney,
Returned with a new chip, the following week.

Another year or two, the memoir done
And in the publishers' hands, the pressure's off.
But when I next switch it on, whatever Descartes meant
By the ghost in the machine—oh damn!—gives itself up:
Experts declare BRAIN DEATH. (The contriver of my program
Having lately developed a multiple personality,
My calls for help kept reaching the wrong one.)

Had it caught some "computer virus"? For months now a post-
Partum depression holds me prisoner:
Days spent prone, staring at the ceiling,
Or with an arm flung over my eyes. Then sleepless nights
In which surely not *my* fingertips upon the mattress
Count out Bach, Offenbach, Sousa, trying to fit
Into groups of five or ten their metronomanic host.

Or was the poor thing taking upon itself a doom
Headed my way? Having by now a self of sorts,
Was it capable of a selfless act
As I might just still be, for someone I loved?
Not that a machine is capable of anything *but*

A selfless act . . . We faced each other wordlessly,
Two blank minds, two screens aglow with gloom.

Or perhaps this alter ego'd been under "contract"—*Yep,*
You know too much, wise guy . . . Feet in cement,
A sendoff choreographed by the Mob.
But who the Mob is, will I ever know?
—Short of the trillionfold synaptic flow
Surrounding, making every circumstance
Sparkle like mica with my every step

Into—can that be sunlight? Ah, it shines
On women in furs, or dreadlock heads on knees
(Hand-lettered placards: BROKE. ILL. HELP ME PLEASE),
This prisoner expelled to the Free World,
His dossier shredded. Now for new memories,
New needs. And while we're at it a novice laptop
On which already he's composed these lines.

A LOOK ASKANCE

Skyward mazes
Rise at right angles to a downstream
Current (left), eluding the pedestrian

Only at the steep cost of fixed scope
And enforced togetherness. Head tilted
In appraisal, see how their concrete poem

Keeps towering higher and higher. See also at dusk
Meaning's quick lineman climb from floor to floor
Inlaying gloom with beads of hot red ore

That hiss in the ferry's backwash, already
Turning to steam where strobe-lit X trains quake
For the commuters of our day

To night. And tomorrow when muggy noon
Films the slow float of peacenik or militant deviate
Down who'll be left to say which of the straight

White avenues between these tercets, when the confetti
Punctuation, the tickertape neologisms begin to pour
From the mad speed-writer plugged into the topmost outlet,

Will it be heat of his—our—bright idea
Makes that whole citywide brainstorm incandesce,
Sets loop, dot, dash, node, filament

Inside the vast gray-frosted bulb ablaze?—
The fire-fonts, the ash script descending
Through final drafts of a sentence

Passed upon us even as we pass into this
Fossil state thought up, then idly
Jotted down on stone.

PRESS RELEASE

Now comes word that a new synthetic substance
Crystallized in Sacramento for the first time.
After much coaxing. These virgin substances
Don't know how. Or it "hurts" like the first time
You were kissed by a man. From then on, each time
Gets easier and perhaps—with crystals, who knows?—
More pleasurable. So now this enlightened substance,
Its code (so to speak) cracked, its maidenhead taken,
Unblinkingly reenacts, time after time,

And in remote labs, a rite of passage unknown
Two weeks ago. Will someone please undertake
To say how the leak occurred? As far as we know,
It didn't. Yet there were no double takes,
No wrong turns such as *our* intelligence takes.
Seems as though Chemistry, allegorical figure
In robes the color of thought, had looked up, knowing
That the sampler she is here depicted as working
Called for a new molecular stitch. Where it takes

Root in her field—for the sampler, too, is a figure—
Buff canvas foothills, happy to be worked,
Turn green and gold, each morning's taller figures
Put forth leaves. Magic—and how it works
I begin to see. There've been hours, alone at work,
Or with you last spring, watching the clabber of rapids
Under the bridge reanimate, refigure
The inert shadows we cast, when I felt my side
Pierced by her needle, and knew that in the works

Were disciplines to be mastered proudly, rapidly,
And without fuss. Whether you are at my side
Or off shooting a film, or tigers, or rapids,
Gemlike projects keep forming deep inside
Our mine. Under what pressures? Today's nine-sided
Figure, prismatic epitome, may at a turn
Of the kaleidoscope—nightfall is rapid

In these parts—yield to a fly's faceted vision
Hatching a micromorgue of suicides

From one poor sleeper. Buzzed awake, he turns
The light on—ah, how old! Who could have envisioned
Twenty years' loneliness, ill health, wrong turnings?
He opens a book, squinting to clear his vision:
"Against such dark views, Nature's best provision
Remains the tendency of certain organisms
Long on the verge of extinction to return
At depths or altitudes they had once been unfitted
To endure . . ." Eyes shut in all but visionary

Consent, he lets the words reorganize
Everything he lives for, until it all fits
Or until he forgets them. What's the inorganic
Teardrop in Bulgari's window to *these* fits
And flashes of blankness? But after just three fittings
Our black suits were ready. Quietly becoming,
Worn forth at midnight into the Piazza's organ-
Grinding hilarity, they offset the scene
Without exposing it as counterfeit.

Not that it was—confetti thick as the coming
Snow, lanterns, mock dirges—merely that this scene's
Flats and floats trundled out over the years had come
To seem less touching. Where we stood a throng obscenely
Masked went dancing through us. Us the unseen
Ghostly headsmen of their Hallowtide?
Now only was it dawning. Harsher lives would come,
Not of necessity human. Meanwhile our natures
Slept in Earth, awaiting the unforeseen.

Solutions whereby molecules are untied
Ribbonwise, or (to quote the technician) "denatured,"
Enervate the long lank threads of polypeptide.
Their one hope then's the prompt recall to nature,
To postures even of some preternatural
Kinkiness, as in yoga. Or like our lovers' knot.
Looming through psychic azure—woe betide

Its severer!—it also, if we concentrate,
One dawn will glitter from a further peak. In nature,

To reach the pass, you must follow, like it or not,
Trails of loam and caustic. By concentrating
On flamework overhead, ice to sun slipknotted,
Each climber sweats his own salt concentrate
Of courage. Innumerable, faster-stabbing traits
Reorient themselves within the substance
He has contracted to become. So let us not
Act like children. These are the Alps. High time
For the next deep breath. My hand. Hold. Concentrate.

Room set at infrared,
Mind at ultraviolet,
Organisms ever stranger,
Hallucinated on the slide, fluoresce:

Chains of gold tinsel, baubles of green fire
For the arterial branches—
Here at *Microcosmics Illustrated,* why,
Christmas goes on all year!

Defenseless, the patrician cells await
Invasion by barbaric viruses,
Another sack of Rome.
A new age. Everything we dread.

Dread? It crows for joy in the manger.
Joy? The tree sparkles on which it will die.

TONY: ENDING THE LIFE

Let's die like Romans,
Since we have lived like Grecians.
—VOLPONE

Across the sea at Alexandria,
Shallow and glittering, a single shroud-
Shaped cloud had stolen, leaving as it paused
The underworld dilated, a wide pupil's
Downward shaft. The not-yet-to-be mined
Villa, a fortune of stone cards each summer
Less readable, more crushing, lay in wait
Beneath the blue-green sand of the sea floor.
Plump in schoolboy shorts, you peered and peered.
For wasn't youth like that—its deep charades
Revealed to us alone by passing shades?
But then years, too, would pass. And in the glow
Of what came next, the Alexandria
You brought to life would up and go:
Bars, beaches, British troops (so slim—yum yum!),
The parties above all. Contagious laughter,
Sparkle and hum and flow,
Saved you from weighty insights just below;
Till from another shore
(Folégandros, the western end of Crete)
Age, astonished, saw those heavy things
Lifted by tricky prisms into light,
Lifted like holy offerings,
Gemlike, disinterested,
Within the fleet
Reliquary of wave upon wave as it crested.

≈

One year in Athens I let my beard grow.
The locals took it for a badge of grief.
Had someone died? Not yet, I tried to joke.
Of course beards came in every conceivable format—

Dapper, avuncular, deadbeat . . .
Mine warned of something creepier—uh-oh!
For over throat and lips had spread a doormat
On which to wipe filth brought in from the street.

Unfair! The boys were talkative and fun;
Far cleaner than my mind, after a bath.
Such episodes, when all was said and done,
Sweetened their reflective aftermath:
The denizens discovered in a dive
Relieved us (if not long or overmuch).
"Just see," the mirror breathed, "see who's alive,
Who hasn't forfeited the common touch,

The longing to lead everybody's life"
—Lifelong daydream of precisely those
Whom privilege or talent set apart:
How to atone for the achieved uniqueness?
By dying everybody's death, dear heart—
Saint, terrorist, fishwife. Stench that appalls.
Famines, machine guns, the Great Plague (your sickness),
Rending of garments, cries, mass burials.

I'd watched my beard sprout in the mirror's grave.
Mirrors *are* graves, as all can see:
Knew this emerging mask would outlast me,
Just as the life outlasts us, that we led . . .
And then one evening, off it came. No more
Visions of the deep. These lines behave
As if we were already gone—not so!
Although of course each time's a closer shave.

One New Year's Eve, on midnight's razor stroke,
Kisses, a round of whiskies. You then drew
Forth from your pocket a brightness, that season's new
Two drachma piece, I fancied, taking the joke
—But no. Proud of your gift, you warned: "Don't leave
The barman this. Look twice." My double take
Lit on a grave young fourteen-carat queen
In profile. Heavens preserve us! and long live

Orbits of Majesty whereby her solar
Metal sets the standard. (A certain five-dollar
Piece, redeemed for paper—astute maneuver—
Taught me from then on: don't trust Presidents.)
Here it buys real estate. From the packed bus's
Racket and reek a newly-struck face glints
No increment of doubt or fear debases.
Speaking of heavens, Maria, a prime mover

In ours, one winter twilight telephoned:
Not for you to see her so far gone,
But to pick up, inside the unlatched door,
A satchel for safekeeping. *Done and done,*
You called from home to say. But such a weight,
Who lifted it? No one. She'd had to kick,
Inch by inch, your legacy down the hall,
The heavy bag of gold, her setting sun.

≈

The sea is dark here at day's end
And the moon gaunt, half-dead
Like an old woman—like Madame Curie
Above her vats of pitchblende
Stirred dawn to dusk religiously
Out in the freezing garden shed.

It is a boot camp large and stark
To which you will be going.
Wave upon wave of you. The halls are crowded,
Unlit, the ceiling fixtures shrouded.
Advancing through the crush, the matriarch
Holds something up, mysteriously glowing.

Fruit of her dream and labor, see, it's here
(See too how scarred her fingertips):
The elemental sliver
Of matter heading for its own eclipse
And ours—this "lumière de l'avenir"
Passed hand to hand with a faint shiver:

Light that confutes the noonday blaze.
A cool uncanny blue streams from her vial,
Bathing the disappearers
Who asked no better than to gaze and gaze . . .
Too soon your own turn came. Denial
No longer fogged the mirrors.

You stumbled forth into the glare—
Blood-red ribbon where you'd struck your face.
Pills washed down with ouzo hadn't worked.
Now while the whole street buzzed and lurked
The paramedics left you there,
Returning costumed for a walk in Space.

The nurse thrust forms at you to sign,
Then flung away her tainted pen
 . . . Lie back now in that heat
Older than Time, whose golden regimen
Still makes the palm grow tall and the date sweet . . .
Come, a last sip of wine.

Lie back. Over the sea
Sweeps, faint at first, the harpist's chord.
Purple with mourning, the royal barge gasps nearer.
Is it a test? a triumph? No more terror:
How did your namesake, lovesick Antony,
Meet the end? By falling on his sword

—A story in Plutarch
The plump boy knew from History class.
Slowly the room grows dark.
Stavro who's been reading you the news
Turns on a nightlight. No more views.
Just your head, nodding off in windowglass.

b o d y

Look closely at the letters. Can you see,
entering (stage right), then floating full,
then heading off—so soon—
how like a little kohl-rimmed moon
o plots her course from *b* to *d*

—as *y*, unanswered, knocks at the stage door?
Looked at too long, words fail,
phase out. Ask, now that *body* shines
no longer, by what light you learn these lines
and what the *b* and *d* stood for.

III

PLEDGE

House on alert.
Sun setting in a blaze
Of insight kisses book and budvase
Where they hurt.

Did the page-turner yawn and slacken,
Or an omen flip by unread?
Prime cuts that once bled
Now blacken.

Her brimming eyes say
More than they see.
He is all worried probity
About to get its way.

Dance steps the world knows curiously well
Ease them asunder—
Friends "rallying round her,"
His "move to a hotel."

Which one will get
The finger-wagging metronome,
Which one make a home
For the agèd cricket

Who sang togetherness ahead
From a hearth glowing bright?
It's dark now. I write
Propped up in bed:

"You who have drained dry
Your golden goblet are about to learn—
As in my turn
Have I—

How life, unsweetened, fizzing up again
Fills the heart.
I drink to you apart
In that champagne."

COSMO

I

Because you are a terrier
—"earth-dog," a digger—
it's only natural, once on the bed,
you'll burrow fast and far as you can
between the strata of percale
dark geometric green/black/red
and in the heat of *our* four feet
frantically storm the badger's "hole"—
one of the many in your head.
What's going on here—instinct? art?
The cave, by all your faith undeepened,
is worried wide awake, a lover's heart.

2

You have some funny genes. Your grandfather
is known as One-Take Toby. There he stands
in the latest *Life*: on his hind legs, tongue-happy,
spangled tutu, Hedda Hopper hat.
Noticing your interest in our closets,
we exchange the eyes-to-heaven look of parents.
We want you to grow up to be All Dog,
the way they wanted me All Boy. My mother at least
seems reconciled. Last week when your "other Daddy"
manhandled you, planted kisses on your belly,
she laughed, "If there's a life after this one,
I wouldn't mind coming back as Peter's next dog."

3

Alpha males? That's what your other
Daddy and I must practice being—

to which end we wrestle your Feistiness
onto its back (lucky you're still a puppy).
The hand of the cradling arm clasps your hind feet,
my right hand lightly steadying your jaw.
Now a mesmeric "gaze of dominance"
initiates convulsions. Whimperings.
Two or three mortifying yawns.
Eyes rolling like an oracle's, Ego fades
into the submissive trance . . .
There! You learn quickly. It took me decades.

4

Housebroken (almost) and street-wise
—if wise is the word for those ecstatic
genital explorations, that intent
snuffling-up of germs four gleaming hypodermic
angels guard you from—you are rehearsing
in microcosm years I hardly remember,
being three hundred times your twelve weeks old.
You're gaining on me steadily, but still:
each time a new dog thrills you, the excitement—
(What *is* that in your mouth—a frozen turd? . . .
And what's that flutter in your nerves—a bird!)
Yes, yes, it comes back. With a difference.

5

Daddies also have their differences,
smelt out by you in the first hour; by us
only this tenth year faced as terminal.
So parting lies ahead—oh, not this month
with snow whipping and howling round the block,
but "in the season of flowers" (*La Bohème*).
And you? You'll go with him. He'll go
to his recuperation, I to mine;
not that a simple "Heal!" is all it takes.

When (if) I go to visit, there you'll be,
our Inner Dog, in perfect loyalty
    . . . to whom? Is this how it was meant to be?

6

(Next summer, when the visit comes to pass,
Surprise: the neighbor's big fat iron-gray mammy
at tether's end. Like one of my formative loves,
she yearns to take that white child on her lap
and teach him the songs of slavery . . . Then, the cat:
both of you at it—bark, hiss, chase—all day
like Hepburn and Tracy in a 40s movie
or scenes from the love going on above your head
ever since you can remember. Well. Time to plant
what but a bed of cosmos by the fence,
then lick your master's hands goodbye—just kidding—
and leave you in them. Meanwhile—) Winter still:

7

three gelid souls in the city. P at a runthrough,
me tired by errands. Heading back to bed,
I pass you open-eyed deep in your bed
on the toy-littered pantry floor,
jaw propped upon a ledge of faux sheepskin . . .
I lay myself down deep and open-eyed
lonely upon the ramparts of goosedown—
doing what? Experiencing Repose.
Each in the same position, the same mood.
Cold, shutter-filtered sun. A lassitude
learned from you by me? by me from you?
Nothing to think of or look forward to.

Timelessness passing. Man and his best friend.

RADIO

Behind grillwork (buff plastic
In would-be deco style)
The war goes on. With each further
Hair's-breadth turn of the dial:
"Kids love it—" "Sex probe in Congress
Triggers rage and denial,"

The weatherman predicting
Continued cold and rain,
Then high-frequency wails of
All too human pain.
Announcer: "That was a test. Now
'Nights in the Gardens of Spain'."

A black man's mild, exhausted
"Honey, I could be wrong . . ."
Gives rise to snickers of static
—But wait. Listen. This long
Ghastly morning, one station
Has never stopped playing our song.

FAMILY WEEK AT ORACLE RANCH

I / THE BROCHURE

The world outstrips us. In my day,
Had such a place existed,
It would have been advertised with photographs
Of doctors—silver hair, pince-nez—

Above detailed credentials,
Not this wide-angle moonscape, lawns and pool,
Patients sharing pain like fudge from home—
As if these were the essentials,

As if a month at what it invites us to think
Is little more than a fat farm for Anorexics,
Substance Abusers, Love & Relationship Addicts
Could help *you*, light of my life, when even your shrink . . .

The message, then? That costly folderol,
Underwear made to order in Vienna,
Who needs it! Let the soul hang out
At Benetton—stone-washed, one size fits all.

2 / INSTEAD OF COMPLEXES

Simplicities. Just seven words—AFRAID,
HURT, LONELY, etc.—to say it with.
Shades of the first watercolor box
(I "felt blue," I "saw red").

Also some tips on brushwork. Not to say
"Your silence hurt me,"
Rather, "When you said nothing I felt hurt."
No blame, that way.

Dysfunctionals like us fail to distinguish
Between the two modes at first.

While the connoisseur of feeling throws up his hands:
Used to depicting personal anguish

With a full palette—hues, oils, glazes, thinner—
He stares into these withered wells and feels,
Well . . . SAD and ANGRY? Future lavender!
An infant Monet blinks beneath his skin.

3 / THE COUNSELLORS

They're in recovery, too, and tell us from what,
And that's as far as it goes.
Like the sun-priests' in *The Magic Flute*
Their ritualized responses serve the plot.

Ken, for example, blond brows knitted: "When
James told the group he worried about dying
Without his lover beside him, I felt SAD."
Thank you for sharing, Ken,

I keep from saying; it would come out snide.
Better to view them as deadpan panels
Storing up sunlight for the woebegone,
Prompting from us lines electrified

By buried switches flipped (after how long!) . . .
But speak in private meanwhile? We may not
Until a voice within the temple lifts
Bans yet unfathomed into song.

4 / GESTALT

Little Aileen is a gray plush bear
With button eyes and nose.
Perky in flowered smock and clean white collar,
She occupies the chair

Across from middleaged Big Aileen, face hid
In hands and hands on knees.

Her sobs break. In great waves it's coming back.
The uncle. What he did.

Little Aileen is her Inner Child
Who didn't . . . who didn't deserve. . . .
The horror kissed asleep, round Big Aileen
Fairytale thorns grow wild.

SADNESS and GUILT entitle us to watch
The survivor compose herself,
Smoothing the flowered stuff, which has ridden up,
Over an innocent gray crotch.

5 / EFFECTS OF EARLY "RELIGIOUS ABUSE"

The great recurrent "sinner" found
In Dostoevsky—twisted mouth,
Stormlit eyes—before whose irresistible
Unworthiness the pure in heart bow down . . .

Cockcrow. Back across the frozen Neva
To samovar and warm, untubercular bed,
Far from the dens of vodka, mucus and semen,
They dream. I woke, the fever

Dripping insight, a spring thaw.
You and the others, wrestling with your demons,
Christs of self-hatred, Livingstones of pain,
Had drawn the lightning. In a flash I saw

My future: medic at some Armageddon
Neither side wins. I burned with SHAME for the years
You'd spent among sufferings uncharted—
Not even my barren love to rest your head on.

6 / THE PANIC

Except that Oracle has maps
Of all those badlands. Just now, when you lashed out,

656

"There's a lot of disease in this room!"
And we felt our faith in one another lapse,

Ken had us break the circle and repair
To "a safe place in the room." Faster than fish
We scattered —Randy ducking as from a sniper,
Aileen, wedged in a corner, cradling her bear.

You and I stood flanking the blackboard,
Words as usual between us,
But backs to the same wall, for solidarity.
This magical sureness of movement no doubt scored

Points for all concerned, yet the only
Child each had become trembled for you
Thundering forth into the corridors,
Decibels measuring how HURT, how LONELY—

7 / TUNNEL VISION

New Age music. "Close your eyes now. You
Are standing," says the lecturer on Grief,
"At a tunnel's mouth. There's light at the end.
The walls, as you walk through

Are hung with images: who you loved that year,
An island holiday, a highschool friend.
Younger and younger, step by step—
And suddenly you're here,

At home. Go in. It's your whole life ago."
A pink eye-level sun flows through the hall.
"Smell the smells. It's supper time.
Go to the table." Years have begun to flow

Unhindered down my face. Why?
Because nobody's there. The grown-ups? Shadows.
The meal? A mirror. Reflect upon it. Before
Reentering the tunnel say goodbye,

8 / TIME RECAPTURED

Goodbye to childhood, that unhappy haven.
It's over, weep your fill. Let go
Of the dead dog, the lost toy. Practice grieving
At funerals—anybody's. Let go even

Of those first ninety seconds missed,
Fifty-three years ago, of a third-rate opera
Never revived since then. The GUILT you felt,
Adding it all the same to your master list!

Which is why, this last morning, when I switch
The FM on, halfway to Oracle,
And hear the announcer say
(Invisibly reweaving the dropped stitch),

"We bring you now the Overture
To Ambroise Thomas's seldom-heard *Mignon*,"
Joy (word rusty with disuse)
Flashes up, deserved and pure.

9 / LEADING THE BLIND

Is this you—smiling helplessly? Pinned to your chest,
A sign: *Confront Me if I Take Control*.
Plus you must wear (till sundown) a black eyeshade.
All day you've been the littlest, the clumsiest.

We're seated face to face. Take off your mask,
Ken says. Now look into each other deeply. Speak,
As far as you can trust, the words of healing.
Your pardon for my own blindness I ask;

You mine, for all you hid from me. Two old
Crackpot hearts once more aswim with color,
Our Higher Power has but to dip his brush—
Lo and behold!

The group approves. The ban lifts. Let me guide you,
Helpless but voluble, into a dripping music.
The rainbow brightens with each step. Go on,
Take a peek. This once, no one will chide you.

10 / THE DESERT MUSEUM

—Or, as the fat, nearsighted kid ahead
Construes his ticket, "Wow, Dessert Museum!"
I leave tomorrow, so you get a pass.
Safer, both feel, instead

Of checking into the No-Tell Motel,
To check it out—our brave new dried-out world.
Exhibits: crystals that for eons glinted
Before the wits did; fossil shells

From when this overlook lay safely drowned;
Whole spiny families repelled by sex,
Whom dying men have drunk from (Randy, frightened,
Hugging Little Randy, a red hound) . . .

At length behind a wall of glass, in shade,
The mountain lioness too indolent
To train them upon us unlids her gems
Set in the saddest face Love ever made.

11 / THE TWOFOLD MESSAGE

(a) You are a brave and special person. (b)
There are far too many people in the world
For this to still matter for very long.
But (Ken goes on) since you obviously

Made the effort to attend Family Week,
We hope that we have shown you just how much
You have in common with everybody else.
Not to be "terminally unique"

Will be the consolation you take home.
Remember, Oracle is only the first step
In your recovery. The rest is up to you
And the twelve-step program you become

Involved in. An amazing forty per cent
Of our graduates are still clean after two years.
The rest? Well . . . Given our society,
Sobriety is hard to implement.

12 / AND IF

And if it were all like the moon?
Full this evening, bewitchingly
Glowing in a dark not yet complete
Above the world, explicit rune

Of change. Change is the "feeling" that dilutes
Those seven others to uncertain washes
Of soot and silver, inks unknown in my kit.
Change sends out shoots

Of FEAR and LONELINESS; of GUILT, as well,
Towards the old, abandoned patterns;
Of joy eventually, and self-forgiveness—
Colors few of us brought to Oracle . . .

And if the old patterns recur?
Ask how the co-dependent moon, another night,
Feels when the light drains wholly from her face.
Ask what that cold comfort means to her.

These city apartment windows—my grandmother's once—
Must be replaced come Fall at great expense.
Pre-war sun shone through them on many a Saturday
Lunch unconsumed while frantic adolescence
Wheedled an old lady into hat and lipstick,
Into her mink, the taxi, the packed lobby,
Into our seats. Whereupon gold curtains parted
On Lakmé's silvery, not yet broken-hearted

Version of things as they were. But what remains
Exactly as it was except those panes?
Today's memo from the Tenants' Committee deplores
Even the ongoing deterioration
Of the *widows* in our building. Well. On the bright side,
Heating costs and street noise will be cut.
Sirens at present like intergalactic gay
Bars in full swing whoop past us night and day.

Sometimes, shocked wide awake, I've tried to reckon
How many lives—fifty, a hundred thousand?—
Are being shortened by that din of crosstown
Ruby flares, wherever blinds don't quite . . .
And shortened by how much? Ten minutes each?
Reaching the Emergency Room alive, the victim
Would still have to live *years,* just to repair
The sonic fallout of a single scare.

"Do you ever wonder where you'll—" Oh my dear,
Asleep somewhere, or at the wheel. Not here.
Within months of the bathroom ceiling's cave-in,
Which missed my grandmother by a white hair,
She moved back South. The point's to live in style,
Not to drop dead in it. On a carpet of flowers
Nine levels above ground, like Purgatory,
Our life is turning into a whole new story:

Juices, blue cornbread, afternoons at the gym—
Imagine who remembers how to swim!
Evenings of study, or intensive care
For one another. Early to bed. And later,
If the mirror's drowsy eye perceives a slight
But brilliant altercation between curtains
Healed by the leaden hand of—one of us?
A white-haired ghost? or the homunculus

A gentle alchemist behind them trains
To put in order these nocturnal scenes—
Two heads already featureless in gloom
Have fallen back to sleep. Tomorrow finds me
Contentedly playing peekaboo with a sylphlike
Quirk in the old glass, making the brickwork
On the street's far (bright) side ripple. Childhood's view.
My grandmother—an easy-to-see-through

Widow by the time she died—made it my own.
Bless her good sense. Far from those parts of town
Given to high finance, or the smash hit and steak house,
Macy's or crack, Saks or quick sex, this neighborhood
Saunters blandly forth, adjusting its clothing.
Things done in purple light before we met,
Uncultured things that twitched as on a slide
If thought about, fade like dreams. Two Upper East Side

Boys again! Rereading Sir Walter Scott
Or *Through the Looking Glass*, it's impossible not
To feel how adult life, with its storms and follies,
Is letting up, leaving me ten years old,
Trustful, inventive, once more good as gold
—And counting on this to help, should a new spasm
Wake the gray sleeper, or to improve his chances
When ceilings flush with unheard ambulances.

QUATRAINS FOR PEGASUS

Breakfast over, to Memorial Park we'd go
On sunny Saturdays, I and Nanny McGrath.
We took care to approach the monument each time
By a new swamp oak- or palmetto-shaded path.

The paths converged at the heart of a parched fairway
Where Earth, not looking her best, rose out of the blue
Reflecting pool: Earth starved to a global ribcage,
Meridians of bronze the empty sky glared through.

Yet round it four horses of stone still fairly white
(Or just the one horse times four—with reflections, eight)
Held up the globe in a caracole that thrilled me,
Eager like them for the further, the ultimate

Thrill due on the stroke of nine. A black man in rags—
Making no secret of it as we looked his way—
Grasped something below ground level and gave it a turn.
The circulatory system brought into play

Filled the air with a magical diamond surf
Hoofs came plunging through, jets like fireworks rocketed
In four directions, as though from the horses' brows.
I wondered if passing through a white horse's head

Was curing the municipal water for good
Of its butts and tinfoil? Making trees toss with joy,
Flagstones glitter and steam? Would the process also
Help Nanny's bad hip, make me a good boy,

And keep—for each morning paper brought fresh horrors—
Our whole world from starving like the Armenians,
Its bones from coming to light like the Lindbergh baby's . . . ?
Nanny McGrath's young brother lay buried in France,

And these were questions—what if she knew the answers?—
I was too little and tactful to ask my nurse.
The more she said, the wickeder the world got.
Don't let it, I begged the horses, get any worse.

THE PYROXENES

Well, life has touched me, too.
No longer infant jade,
What is the soul not made
To drink in, to go through

As it becomes a self!
Admire this forest scene,
Dendritic, evergreen,
On Leto's back-lit shelf—

"Forest" that long predates
The kingdom of the trees.
Move on a step to these
Translucent spinach plates

Morbidly thin, which flake
On flake corundum-red
As weeping eyes embed.
You'd think poorhouse and wake,

Fury, bereavement, grief
Dwelt at Creation's core,
Maternal protoplast,
Millions of years before

Coming to high relief
Among us city folk.
Out of her woods at last,
On the Third Day we woke

From cradles deep in mire
At white heat: elements-
To-be of hard, scarred sense,
Strangers to fire.

PEARL

       Well, I admit
A small boy's eyes grew rounder and lips moister
To find it invisibly chained, at home in the hollow
Of his mother's throat: the real, deepwater thing.
    Far from the mind at six to plumb
X-raywise those glimmering lamplit
Asymmetries to self-immolating mite
        Or angry grain of sand
Not yet proverbial. Yet his would be the hand
      Mottled with survival—
   She having slipped (how? when?) past reach—
   That one day grasped it. Sign of what
But wisdom's trophy. Time to mediate,
Skin upon skin, so cunningly they accrete,
   The input. For its early mote
        Of grit
   Reborn as orient moon to gloat
In verdict over the shucked, outsmarted meat . . .
One layer, so to speak, of calcium carbonate
   That formed in me is the last shot
   —I took the seminar I teach
    In Loss to a revival—
Of Sacha Guitry's classic *Perles de la Couronne.*
     The hero has tracked down
His prize. He's holding forth, that summer night,
At the ship's rail, all suavity and wit,
   Gem swaying like a pendulum
From his fing—oops! To soft bubble-blurred harpstring
Arpeggios regaining depths (man the camera, follow)
Where an unconscious world, my yawning oyster,
     Shuts on it.

OVERDUE PILGRIMAGE
TO NOVA SCOTIA

Elizabeth Bishop (1911–1979)

Your village touched us by not knowing how.
Even as we outdrove its clear stormlight
A shower of self-belittling brilliants fell.
Miles later, hours away, here are rooms full
Of things you would have known: pump organ, hymnal,
Small-as-life desks, old farm tools, charter, deed,
Schoolbooks (Greek Grammar, *A Canadian Reader*),
Queen Mary in oleograph, a whole wall hung
With women's black straw hats, some rather smart
—All circa 1915, like the manners
Of the fair, soft-spoken girl who shows us through.
Although till now she hasn't heard of you
She knows these things you would have known by heart
And we, by knowing you by heart, foreknew.

The child whose mother had been put away
Might wake, climb to a window, feel the bay
Steel itself, bosom bared to the full moon,
Against the woebegone, cerebral Man;
Or by judicious squinting make noon's red
Monarch grappling foreground goldenrod
Seem to extract a further essence from
Houses it dwarfed. Grown-up, the visitor
Could find her North by the green velvet map
Appliquéd upon this wharfside shack,
Its shingles (in the time her back was turned)
Silver-stitched to visionary grain
As by a tireless, deeply troubled inmate,
Were Nature not by definition sane.

In living as in poetry, your art
Refused to tip the scale of being human
By adding unearned weight. "New, tender, quick"—
Nice watchwords; yet how often they invited
The anguish coming only now to light

In letters like photographs from Space, revealing
Your planet tremulously bright through veils
As swept, in fact, by inconceivable
Heat and turbulence—but there, I've done it,
Added the weight. What tribute could you bear
Without dismay? Well, facing where you lived
Somebody's been inspired (*can* he have read
"Filling Station"?) to put pumps, a sign:
ESSO—what else! We filled up at the shrine.

Look, those were elms! Long vanished from *our* world.
Elms, by whose goblet stems distance itself
Taken between two fingers could be twirled,
Its bouquet breathed. The trees looked cumbersome,
Sickly through mist, like old things on a shelf—
Astrolabes, pterodactyls. They must know.
The forest knows. Out from such melting backdrops
It's the rare conifer stands whole, one sharp
Uniquely tufted spoke of a dark snow crystal
Not breathed upon, as yet, by our exhaust.
Part of a scene that with its views and warblers,
And at its own grave pace, but in your footsteps
—Never more imminent the brink, more sheer—
Is making up its mind to disappear

. . . With many a dirty look. That waterfall
For instance, beating itself to grit-veined cream
"Like Roquefort through a grater"? Or the car—!
So here we sit in the car wash, snug and dry
As the pent-up fury of the storm hits: streaming,
Foaming "emotions"—impersonal, cathartic,
Closer to both art and what we are
Than the gush of nothings one outpours to people
On the correspondence side of bay and steeple
Whose dazzling whites we'll never see again,
Or failed to see in the first place. Still, as the last
Suds glide, slow protozoa, down the pane,
We're off—Excuse our dust! With warm regards,—
Gathering phrases for tomorrow's cards.

ALESSIO AND THE ZINNIAS

One summer—was he eight?—
They gave him a seed packet
Along with a 2′ by 4′
Slice of the estate.

To grow, to grow, grim law
Without appeal!
He, after all, kept growing every day . . .
Now this redundant chore.

Up sprouted green enough
For the whole canton, had one known to thin it.
Michaelmas found him eye to eye
With a gang of ruffians

Not askable indoors,
Whose gaudy, rigid attitudes
("Like pine cones in drag")
There was scant question of endorsing

—Much as our droll friend, their legatee,
Would reap from them over the years. For instance:
Think twice before causing
Just anything to be.

Then: *Hold your head high in the stinking*
Throngs of kind.
Joyously assimilate the Sun.
Never wear orange or pink.

SELF-PORTRAIT IN TYVEK (TM) WINDBREAKER

The windbreaker is white with a world map.
DuPont contributed the seeming-frail,
Unrippable stuff first used for Priority Mail.
Weightless as shores reflected in deep water,
The countries are violet, orange, yellow, green;
Names of the principal towns and rivers, black.
A zipper's hiss, and the Atlantic Ocean closes
Over my blood-red T-shirt from the Gap.

I found it in one of those vaguely imbecile
Emporia catering to the collective unconscious
Of our time and place. This one featured crystals,
Cassettes of whalesong and rain-forest whistles,
Barometers, herbal cosmetics, pillows like puffins,
Recycled notebooks, mechanized lucite coffins
For sapphire waves that crest, break, and recede,
As they presumably do in nature still.

Sweat-panted and Reeboked, I wear it to the gym.
My terry-cloth headband is green as laurel.
A yellow plastic Walkman at my hip
Sends shiny yellow tendrils to either ear.
All us street people got our types on tape,
Turn ourselves on with a sly fingertip.
Today I felt like Songs of Yesteryear
Sung by Roberto Murolo. Heard of him?

Well, back before animal species began to become
Extinct, a dictator named Mussolini banned
The street-singers of Naples. One smart kid
Learned their repertoire by heart, and hid.
Emerging after the war with his guitar,
He alone bearing the old songs of the land
Into the nuclear age sang with a charm,
A perfect naturalness that thawed the numb

Survivors and reinspired the Underground.
From love to grief to gaiety his art
Modulates effortlessly, like a young man's heart,
Tonic to dominant—the frets so few
And change so strummed into the life of things
That Nature's lamps burn brighter when he sings
Nannetta's fickleness, or chocolate,
Snow on a flower, the moon, the seasons' round.

I picked his tape in lieu of something grosser
Or loftier, say the Dead or Arvo Pärt,
On the hazy premise that what fills the mind
Shows on the face. My face, as a small part
Of nature, hopes this musical sunscreen
Will keep the wilderness within it green,
Yet looks uneasy, drawn. I detect behind
My neighbor's grin the oncoming bulldozer

And cannot stop it. Ecosaints—their karma
To be Earth's latest, maybe terminal, fruits—
Are slow to ripen. Even this dumb jacket
Probably still believes in Human Rights,
Thinks in terms of "nations," urban centers,
Cares less (can Tyvek breathe?) for oxygen
Than for the innocents evicted when
Ford bites the dust and Big Mac buys the farm.

Hah. As if greed and savagery weren't the tongues
We've spoken since the beginning. My point is, those
Prior people, fresh from scarifying
Their young and feasting in triumph on their foes,
Honored the gods of Air and Land and Sea.
We, though . . . Cut to dead forests, filthy beaches,
The can of hairspray, oil-benighted creatures,
A star-scarred x-ray of the North Wind's lungs.

Still, not to paint a picture wholly black,
Some social highlights: Dead white males in malls.
Prayer breakfasts. Pay-phone sex. "Ring up as meat."

Oprah. The GNP. The contour sheet.
The painless death of History. The stick
Figures on Capitol Hill. Their rhetoric,
Gladly—no, rapturously (on Prozac) suffered!
Gay studies. Right to Lifers. The laugh track.

And clothes. Americans, blithe as the last straw,
Shrug off accountability by dressing
Younger than their kids—jeans, ski-pants, sneakers,
A baseball cap, a happy-face T-shirt . . .
Like first-graders we "love" our mother Earth,
Know she's been sick, and mean to care for her
When we grow up. Seeing my windbreaker,
People hail me with nostalgic awe.

"Great jacket!" strangers on streetcorners impart.
The Albanian doorman pats it: "Where you buy?"
Over his ear-splitting drill a hunky guy
Yells, "Hey, you'll always know where you are, right?"
"Ever the fashionable cosmopolite,"
Beams Ray. And "Voilà mon pays"—the carrot-haired
Girl in the bakery, touching with her finger
The little orange France above my heart.

Everyman, c'est moi, the whole world's pal!
The pity is how soon such feelings sour.
As I leave the gym a smiling-as-if-I-should-know-her
Teenager—oh but I *mean*, she's wearing "our"
Windbreaker, and assumes . . . Yet I return her wave
Like an accomplice. For while all humans aren't
Countable as equals, we must behave
As if they were, or the spirit dies (Pascal).

"We"? A few hundred decades of relative
Lucidity glinted-through by minnow schools
Between us and the red genetic muck—
Everyman's underpainting. We look up, shy
Creatures, from our trembling pool of sky.
Caught wet-lipped in light's brushwork, fleet but sure,

Flash on shudder, folk of the first fuck,
Likeness breeds likeness, fights for breath—*I live*—

Where the crush thickens. And by season's end,
The swells of fashion cresting to collapse
In breaker upon breaker on the beach,
Who wants to be caught dead in this cliché
Of mere "involvement"? Time to put under wraps
Its corporate synthetic global pitch;
Not throwing out motley once reveled in,
Just learning to live down the wrinkled friend.

Face it, reproduction of any kind leaves us colder
Though airtight-warmer (greenhouse effect) each year.
Remember the figleaf's lesson. Styles betray
Some guilty knowledge. What to dress ours in—
A seer's blind gaze, an infant's tender skin?
All that's been seen through. The eloquence to come
Will be precisely what we cannot say
Until it parts the lips. But as one grows older

—I should confess before that last coat dries—
The wry recall of thunder does for rage.
Erotic torrents flash on screens instead
Of drenching us. Exclusively in dream,
These nights, does a grandsire rear his saurian head,
And childhood's inexhaustible brain-forest teem
With jewel-bright lives. No way now to restage
Their sacred pageant under our new skies'

Irradiated lucite. What then to wear
When—hush, it's no dream! It's my windbreaker
In black, with starry longitudes, Archer, Goat,
Clothing an earphoned archangel of Space,
Who hasn't read Pascal, and doesn't wave . . .
What far-out twitterings he learns by rote,
What looks they'd wake upon a human face,
Don't ask, Roberto. Sing our final air:

Love, grief etc. ★ ★ ★ ★ for good reason.
Now only ★ ★ ★ ★ ★ ★ STOP signs.
Meanwhile ★ ★ ★ ★ ★ if you or I've ex-
ceeded our [?] ★ ★ ★ ~~more than time~~ was needed
To fit a text airless and ★ ★ as Tyvek
With breathing spaces and between the lines
Days brilliantly recurring, as once *we* did,
To keep the blue wave dancing in its prison.

AN UPWARD LOOK

O heart green acre   sown with salt
by the departing   occupier

lay down your gallant   spears of wheat
Salt of the earth   each stellar pinch

flung in blind   defiance backwards
now takes its toll   Up from his quieted

quarry the lover   colder and wiser
hauling himself   finds the world turning

toys triumphs   toxins into
this vast facility   the living come
dearest to die in   How did it happen

In bright alternation   minutely mirrored
within the thinking   of each and every

mortal creature   halves of a clue
approach the earthlights   Morning star

evening star   salt of the sky
First the grave   dissolving into dawn

then the crucial   recrystallizing
from inmost depths   of clear dark blue

The Black Swan

(1946)

To Kimon Friar

Keats on board ship for what we shall call Rome
In waterlight watching his shadow fall,
Mingle with written water, observed that time
Obliterates nothing but those public pulses
Nibbling his wrist; so at the difficult prow,

Feeling that all things fail but love that is
Rainbowed by the last raveling of his hand,
Illumined beyond hope, he and his world
As blood and seawater, meeting only in death,
Retain like lovers their chemical sympathies.

Foxglove, larkspur have morning by the throat
   And all the gardens cry
   Poetics of neveraday
And have forgotten all they had learned of passing,
By blue refractions each fixed moment caught;
   Mica-winged dragonfly,
And the pale sky, mild as though milk were laughing,
   Enter the dreamer's eye;
Morning is on us, morning, one might have thought,
Always was on us with no blue bloom missing.

The larkspur, blue, takes morning by surprise;
   The blue, the hours shimmer
   In the mirage of summer,
But this was never the morning of innocence
Caught in a smile of grass by children's cries,
   The sky a child-eyed charmer,
But the cold morning we have sought since gardens
   Burst, and we like swimmers,
Hands plunged for the blue core of morning, rose
Long minutes later, empty, with cold veins.

Nettle and thorn have mourning by the heart,
   The heart, the helmeted,
   Lured by sharp leaves to wed
Mourning like statues in a summer house
Of mirrors, quicksilver eyes in its glass caught;
   So mourning is the bride,
And sunny hours, chilled and thickened, close
   All but the eye inside;
For the young heart, crowned in its mourning, laughed
In abstract noon, turned stone, discovered loss.

Now larkspur, thorn seize morning by the heart:
   Seize it the morning after
   The child's world we were offered,

The morning past the stone noon of our death,
Unmirrored and by no child clamoring caught.
    Morning is ours forever;
After the search it lies whole in our mesh
    Waiting to be delivered,
Its colors trebled, its summer fixed without
One blue bloom missing. It has become our flesh.

THE COSMOLOGICAL EYE

Vivid to the myopic is the blue
Bewilderment prismed in his looking-glass.
He muses on glassed vistas imprecise
And asks his vision why blurred things should be
Still blurred, why on the clear ideal surface
An inch away a parallel vagueness lies.

An inch removed is spread out the appearance
Of sea and sunlight. The sharp elegance
That is birds flying, however, he never knew.
His cloven gaze withdraws, and all at once
Upon the pure expanse of dream begins,
Fluent in the idiom of blue.

The sky is realest: the sky cannot
Be touched and in the mirror it cannot
Be touched. He is enchanted. The rare *azur*
Is flawless; happily blurred blue is no whit
Less exquisite than blue unblurred. And what
He misses he would never know was there.

The mirror and the rare *azur* alas
Are not the same. The keen-eyed have seen this
And tell of birds, foam, subtleties of blue,
Smoke, bone, a sail, blue shells that are of less
Being to him than ideal blues. It is
His proud despair that he will never, now,

Turn to the broad, unbleached experience: Sea,
That as an egg belies complexity;
Blue of horizons made of yes and no
Clasps him from his fulfillment, from seeking wet
Shells and a blue wet feather. Nor is it
The mirror that numbs him. It is his ultimate eye.

PERSPECTIVES OF A LONESOME EYE

In a green twilight the avenues of our love
Are shadowed by an unseen running child;
Pennanted, the tower pointing informed perspectives
Discloses how the emotions are least artless
When most experienced. And the grand lonesome
Artifice is needed to mask the primitive

Sensation. If wholly within or without, artless
Is what the eye sees. Disbelieving in perspectives,
The earliest artist is the child, the child
Holding the handsome beetle to the lonesome
Glass, unafraid to mingle primitive
Sensation with science, profane with sacred love.

The canvases like landscapes in a lonesome
Eye flicker upon the iris, the primitive
Sensation altered, enhanced by love, but love
Of a peculiar kind, not passion but perspectives
Seen through the glass of personal feeling, not artless:
Binding the duplicate verities of the child.

Or take the pointillists—how their perspectives
Illustrate through complexity the artless
Plein-air delight, expound the primitive
Sensation with lucidity that a child
Could understand; yet, not unlike love,
Always about to fail, expose the lonesome,

The more than lonesome terror beyond the child,
The void without nuance, abyss with love
Curiously insignificant, as the artless
Shows, through the careful device of dots, perspectives,
In all its fearful rawness, the primitive
Sensation. Catastrophe. We wander, lonesome,

Each of us, in the gallery, lonesome.
And there is no arrangement of perspectives,

We feel occasionally, will cause these primitive
Longings to meet harmoniously. O child
Within us, do not be artful or artless,
Speak to us clearly, in any language: love.

Perhaps the primitive is the least lonesome.
Perhaps the child has never once been artless.
Bound by perspectives, we are loosed by love.

PHENOMENAL LOVE SONG

Look sharp, love, for here
Lovers, chameleon-wise, are quick to alter
   The unmistakable shore
   To something else again,
Mirror love's windings in bright insects, water,
   Palm parrot-greens, and stain
   All spare and positive things,
Like worlds of some incredible primitive painter,
   With multiple meanings.

Here not the atmosphere
Conditions the mirage: striped butterflies
   Cling upon dung, and where
   Sun sings through the leaves
Wasps riddle the rotting tangerines like eyes
   Burning past ruin; waves
   Of purest blue sieve shells
On the beach, and from the most abundant trees,
   Bruised before falling, fruit falls.

Here the involving shell
Is fretted by salt waves so it appears,
   Inside and out as well,
   Glass-lined and barnacled;
In brilliant hours this skillfullest lecturer
   Tells, has forever told,
   The joys of pure form:
Fear this no less than your ill-nourished cheer,
   And in your tropic warmth,

Love—for in each of these
Mix all extremes of failure and applause,
   Your wreath and booby-prize,
   And no surrender seen—
Watch like a sailor where the rip-tide goes:
   Deep in aquamarine
   The flounder, Picasso-faced,

Hides in the grass, and far-off quicksand draws
    The gazer with his glass.

    O love, where the prismed rocks
Arrow the treacherous statement of the reef,
    And fish that your net takes
    Themselves are the slick lure,
Winding net-fashion in and out of your life
    As their wet flashings scour
    Wherever your heart has failed:
O where the muscular tide whelms your last laugh,
    Love, keep your eye peeled.

THE FORMAL LOVERS

The windowframe behind the blind
Defines oblongs in the late light
That change dimensions till the bland
Walls, blond floor, flowers, quiet
Faces in barred patterns blend.

Like a Mondrian the windowframe
Restricts the room and tells the lovers
They must be still, let light be firm
In gold geometry, subject their favors
To a fevered dominance of form.

All petaled lassitudes or passions
Or the chaste delicacies of fern
Are shown suspect by the exclusions
Of such a pattern; only are stern
Unmoving silences conditions

By which the lovers will survive,
Who measure brilliance by the somber
Scripture of need, who now achieve
Years of green loving through the love
That these strict minutes have remembered.

2

I mean, of course, that form and fever
Have never once been separate;
The bowl of shade we cannot sever
From the hydrangeas drinking light
In heavy air, cannot deliver

Pattern from passion, love from loss.
Here must our feeling like a mould

Harden to this harmonious
Order, and all the lovers melt
Their cries into the silences,

Their gestures into the shadowed wall
—So music has been heard to phrase
Our words as echoed from a well—
And form evolves because they place
Themselves within it. Their own will

Is at once fever and form, is like
Sun in the littered studio,
Seurat's destruction of a lake,
Or my desire to utter you
In words, in movement, in a stroke

Of bronze: a fever that assumes
Clarity through increase of ardor;
As when in legendary rooms
Lovers damned for old extremes
Built out of these a braver order.

3

In evening's deepening you swerve your eyeball
Not into mine nor the dark blue beyond
But to the mirror which you feel is able,
Being at once pursuit and what is found,
To reconcile the eye to its quick double:

As though a shuttle wove a universe
Between these two initial points of vision;
As though in glass simplicity a voice,
Articulate through infinite repetition,
Sang chords portending labyrinths of ice.

For in this difficult hour one supposes
Objects are objects only as we see them,
That there are silver unsuspected prizes

And unbelievable words if we will say them—
But such are altered as the night's chill voices

Change into doubtful whisperings by day;
Shift as our eyes must shift, my love, to live,
From the terraced hearts of mirrors wherein die
All urgent imperfections; cease to move
Like frozen swans in a poet's tragedy;

Shift out to unglazed landscapes and relinquish
For actual vision the elusive dream,
Or even the vision burning in the ambush
Of utterance, hopelessly burning, and distinguish
Flame from an inner barricade of flame.

4

The postulate of dark is light:
As diagrams of shade ascend,
Loom on the ceiling, candlelit,
The hourglass beside your hand
Reflects, convex, our silhouette.

Hurtling, the near necessity
Of praising you, of making words
Conform to your distinct beauty,
Rises as fireworks shower upwards
In dark, then startle all the sky.

Whereby illumined you are real
With the extreme reality
Of hands that do not touch, a still
Life that grows more alive for merely
Being still. My love, how shall

I speak of these illuminations?—
Such lighted mercies as the night
Spills on the structure of our patience

To show it real, extreme, innate
Beyond what calculated sessions

An hourglass measures. We have found
That emptied in its curving clings
A single singular grain of sand
As though nowhere exists a thing
Enclosing, even at its end,

A crystaled purity. Meanwhile
We hunt love in each other's eye,
Learn loss as artists always will,
Probe for such crystal, fevered by
The creed of the impossible.

But sand's progression from first to last
Is less immense than this: from love
To lover. Since, now the light has passed,
Nothing is ever for the lover lost,
Dark is the perfect thing we have.

SUSPENSE OF LOVE

No greater turbulence than light restores
The postures of our loving as within
A ceremonial noon
We pause and of all noons make reckoning:
At last our reckless songs
Subside, and in these galleries appears
The one skylight that clears
All questioning; at last
A quietness happens like dark light through glass
Distinctly seen. The lovers have fared well
Who know remembrance is a ritual.

Between the candle and the mirrored flame
The air preserves a staunch relationship
That while it burns bears up
The hour of wine and gestures. For the will
Is unpredictable,
And love, a pearl that grows in rhythms, some
More personal than dreams,
Shines like a keepsake passed
Between us, back and forth, a pearl whose cost
We doubt till it is bitten; then we know
The fine extravagance of being two.

Two circus poles sustain the merry ring
Of acrobats and lion-tamers: come,
Prop up this tent of time
That stands as long as we both may stand, that holds
Revolving worlds and worlds
Evolving. The laugh in tights, daredevil song
Waver, for they are young,
But clarities of speech
Like spotlights on the bareback riders touch

Moments of calm, skillful and dangerous,
That we prolong, bearing our worlds with us.

Between, between our facing faces, not
Upon them, the secret of our loving lies,
For intricate disguise
Weighs on the private eyelid; only between
Lip, look and its twin
Our landscapes hang like flowers in a net,
Or stars in a lucky night
Whose wishbone winds foretell
Miraculous constancy. Love's windowsill
Gestures securely: silent, face to face,
We span whatever countryside we choose.

No matter what landscape, it hangs like a net
Between your face and mine. Clowns, animals,
Flowers, whatever else
Blooms in this season are suspended there
As sunlight on a tear
That never falls. Our quietness draws it taut
Until the net is not
Wielded in eagerness
But holds rich action with our memories;
Or as a trellis, may have moved through time
Until with morning glories it stands overcome.

EMBARKATION SONNETS

I

Across the limelit balconies of sleep
Where on occasion I have surprised your eyes
Or felt your hand throb or watched panic slip
Like tallow from your quiet smile, I move
Remembering every moment of our days,
Questioning each least glance that balances
On its tightrope, as tightrope dancers thrive
In dangerous air between our love and us.

Acrobat hearts, we watch their tricks and swear
It must be done with mirrors. The acid light
Threatens each failure but they persevere,
Knowing that only as such dancers poise
In constant peril, love, shall we relate
Love to the disparate gestures love may make.

2

All parting is conceit. The images
Of hands, brash water in the wake of steamers,
The piecemeal kiss beneath the clock express
Only the mischief of abandon. Love
Is never at a loss for its lost summers'
Memories: they loom between our smiles,
Read fate into the last half hour we have,
Concerned as godmothers in fairy tales.

Our love is not our memories of love
No matter how we love them. Nevertheless,
Now you are leaving, these are what you leave.
Ah, to suspend as Lamartine his lake
These urgencies, and parting face to face
Know our farewell, know what farewell is like.

THE YELLOW PAGES

(1974)

THE DIARY OF THE DUC DE L***

I

On such a day even the sun stops, even
The leaves hang white as powdered eyelids, even
The queen snores at her pale embroidery.
I watch my hand as it writes. From England, news:
My childhood love, Mme. de V., is dead.

Man of all parasites most excellent
Clings to the world as on a flower's leaf
An insect that devours the tenderest fringes
Is flicked with a grimace off and trodden quite
By the red heel of an aging botanist.

So she is dead, lips yellowed, hair in lockets,
Hands folded like the dusty wings of a moth.
I am unmoved; and shall in a moment rise
To greet the young ambassador from the East
Who with what daring flits to our dry court . . .

An hour in D's abundant greenhouses
Where a new orchid blooms amid moist glass;
After eight years of stress in a mild air
Is now to his ravenous shears accessible
The plant of paradise—his name for it.

2

The king stroked velvet as though it had been his youth
And called at random for lutes, forks, and Chartreuse.
His Majesty, the court historian wrote,
This tenth of August holds no audience
Save with indispositions of the heart.

Morning intruded; one had an obligation
To be like the sun which signed its name on streets,
On men, as on important documents.
But the king scowled at so discreet a counsel
As to how all things most reasonably might be seen.

And how the prince cavorted at his knees!
And how the child musicians' fingers smarted!
But the king's desire sat at an upper window
Turning the pages of *Les Très Riches Heures,*
Thinking of time and smiling at her thoughts.

How senseless, then, that she would take no ring
And that the king, while a whole kingdom languished,
Shuttered the windows? No, the court poet said,
Reason's a dynasty at whose emblazoned pall
The young pretender love cries interval.

3

This night after the opera we walked
Where marigolds, obedient populace,
By day lend flame to the fountains but at night
Are caught up wholly in a quenching dark.
There were stars and, elsewhere, fireworks; and we went

Until we heard inside the summerhouse
The ancient princess at her spinet playing
And talking to herself when the music stopped.
What music fleshless as a theorem
And what mad voice—voice wise yet stammering,

The voice almost of youth, yet never pure,
As though the river of the tongue were clogged
By an upheaval of the intellect:

Of one disaster the most ruined diction—
A voice, I must confess, a horrible voice.

It seemed, for an instant, we had ceased to be
Except as basins brimming with that speech.
But she who was with me touched my sleeve and brought
Me back to the boxwood and the marigolds,
Stars and wet fountains, back to her laugh and the world.

1947

A VALENTINE IN CRAYONS

As the masque went on Sehnsucht was seen to change
His Nordic cowl for Milanese lozenges,
Playing the clown Fiasco. And I mean
He was funny. Butterfingers, stumblebum,
False feet in gum, bloom of the incomplete.
Given a moment more, one thought of a vase
Fallen to smithereens before having held
Queen Anne's lace or even the water for Queen Anne's lace.
And this would have made for pity; nay, it welled
In many a heart before the pink past-master
Could in a single sublime huff disperse
Those wan nosegays, white pollen on the floors
Of dressing-rooms, or turned to paste in water,
The moon face patted rigid as it dries.

1949

EUROPA

The air is sweetest that a thistle guards.
But the lean scholar, reading Buffon and Horace,
Shuts his brown book, marking the place with a flower
Picked from the fragrant riot below his terrace,
And the sea rings with doubloons, and the blossoming words
Of no poet are cleanly about him in a loud shower.

Those feasts, the jubilant quince and bursting pear,
The Judas tree and page in the wind rinsed.
He watches the young laundress of the shore
With blueing and suds rear linen virginals
In sprays of gold, her cloths, white birds, careless;
She stands like any maiden loved by Zeus.

His murkiest deeds, night-thoughts that hammer him
Upon his bed, are charmed into the light,
As when on one day of each year at noon
All creatures of the midnight wake and fly
In a fine sport under the lavish sun
To greet once what they are least succored by:

His dark thoughts whirl until they fall unconscious,
And the warm noon stoops over them then, anxious,
Passionate—ah, the ceremony of rape!
Rape, though of no flesh, nor of mind indeed,
But of the eye, in gauzes negligent,
That, scorched by the flowering nostrils, overstreams.

Then sudden ease: beyond the straits, the climb
Ecstatic of cloud-whites on porcelain, while
Supinely through high morning like a girl
Innocence glides, dipping a wrist in time,
On a white bull of cloud, a full white belle
Smiling, a bridal in the wastes of pearl.

1947

701

LECTURE: THE SKELETON

Nude but for sun
We see the skeleton
Stripped beyond handshake, heartburn, eyesore,
Much mere undimpled bone with string
At every hamstrung joint, aswing
Dire from its gibbet over the sunstrewn floor.

We know each bone
From foot, freed of heelbane,
To crown, the milkweed brain off prickly stem
Now blown; and yet inside the skull
Finger its grooves, conceive a skill
Would outwrest words recorded in their prime.

Always will sorrow
Some for the spire of marrow
And mincemeat torn for worms to undertake,
Cajole an elegy where most
Muscle is mourned or eyeball missed,
By dint of lack divine what life was like.

Ah but will be
Some whose mortality
We'll never stomach, though a pill so gilded
(By peaceable words they spoke) it might
Possibly be the cure-all we must eat
For stamina till we also are piecemealed:

Till against lack
The whole skeleton sunstruck
Quickens, and we see lift in the sunspill
A populace of dust who spin
Gilded about the Gothic spine,
Dust of that ilk, and unappeasable.

1948

THE BED

Where do we go, my love, who have been led
Afire and naked to our firelit bed?
For look! someone is sleeping there, his head

Pinned to the pillows by his own left arm,
Who sinks, who in swift currents of alarm
Sinks glistening (as though the night were warm)

Down through the rocking fathoms of the skin
To where the dreamers, brows on arms, begin
Bearing the dream each has been trammeled in.

Love at the sea's edge turns the turbulent waves
To sculpture, silken body that behaves
As if no paths were but the path love paves.

So with the stranger tangled in our sheet:
Seeing his mouth move, hearing his heart beat,
No lover hears the word his lips repeat,

And none dares question if the dream is good
That plunges him in nothing understood
Down down until, like bait beneath a flood

Suspended where the unseen mouthings feel
For food in darkness, it is him they steal;
And none knows—when to grasp the spinning reel

The mind wakes, winds it back in joy and fright—
If what has torn him in our own bed might
Not first have sought us there! Ah for tonight

Let us seek out a bed that's less our own.
There is a kind of sleep which we have known
Pleasurable and calm. Leave him alone,

Come leave him to his dream. Too long we've kept
Watch by this bed familiar except
For one strange sleeper. It is time we slept.

1950

CUPID

You are one wild boy
For Time to tame, or me to,
Hand in glove with him.

1965

ZENO REMINDED OF A FAMILY QUARREL

As for continuance of the race
I can foresee, far down the blinding course,
A sluggishness, a stubbornness, a force
Bears heaven and earth upon its carapace.

It stops me in my tracks, I go all limp
As once in childhood. Somebody not invited
Was lunching with us, the gentle and inbred—
A swarthy lout humped over jellied shrimp.

Promptly the word *thick-skinned* took on new meaning.
Sublime in crisis, Mother found strength to utter
The dry remonstrance, little dreaming
She'd be snapped back at with a reptilian glitter:

"Madam, your fair-haired champion still
Has not caught up with me, and never will!"

1953

BATH POEM

The wrinkled hand, like one already soaked
Too long in water, reaches round her neck.
Nurse picks him up, inert old man who reeks
Of tears, forgetfulness and wrath,
And lowers him into a nice warm bath.

It does help. He can move one leg, move both.
A knot of vein brightens, a wetted pebble
She soaps. A crooning treble seeps through lather.
Warm, glittering drops, displaced, splash onto tile.
No Archimedes need instruct the bather

Why the gold crown that, young, he bargained for
Has grown so heavy, so impure.
What is there for him but the woman's jokes
As back to life she bears him, whimpering, flushed
With consciousness of the whole dirty hoax?

1958

BIRTHDAY

Beloved dog, in from the wet
Reeking of earth, licking my face like a flame,
Your red-brown coat and glowing eyes
Clearer than anything in human nature
Tell me I will live another year.

1967

EARLY SETTLERS

Finally two of them go high up to live
In a prodigious crystal without flaw.
The slow red setter westward of each day
Lopes nearer, stretches at their feet, and sleeps.

They see one mountain miles and miles away
Blush and grow small. Why, the whole land is shy!
They draw rein over stunted evergreens
Clinging to canyons carved in pots of rouge.

What the scene lacks is any human trail
To give it scale. Crossing the mountain face
A shadow once more leaves the prospect huge.
Well, they arrive and try to make a life

And fail—being after all the first to try.
The cabin built, he mutters over pans;
She lapses from a helpmate to a wife;
The game hangs upside down with glassing eye.

Evenings, the air thins. One of them must kneel
Fumbling the skein of fumes till a dead branch
Puts brilliant leafage forth, whose buffets draw
From their drawn skins the same loud, senseless pulse.

A life is something not invented yet,
A square of linen worked in colored wools
To stand between its maker and that drumming,
Twitching, gibbering source of light and pain

They turn to, hand in hand, themselves becoming
Gnarled, then ashen, upon some hearth not seen
But tended in impassive silence by
A leathery god or two, crouched there for warmth.

1958

INDIA: THE DANCE OF GIVING

Stranger, you go from tomb
To shrine. If a dust forms,
Ours, shod in dust, if thirst
Untunes our prayers about you,
These hands trembling like fumes
From oily cloths in sun,
You give no sign at first

But float within the fierce
Spotlights of your skin
Above pale drip-dry weeds.
We close in—corps of shadows
Cast by you? A thin
Ash our needs burn down to
Flutters on your shut lids

Until at length you shudder
As from an age-long swoon,
Recoil and, whirling once,
Hurl your constellation
Into our dark. And then?
Darkly a gratitude
As much for the twinkle of coins

As to see thus renewed,
In mime, that covenant
Whereby, now you have shown
Yourself neither entirely
God nor truly man,
You go, with our consent,
Your last blind way alone.

1957

PACT WITH THE ASTROLOGER

Suppose I put aside
My past unwound,
Expose the band of paler skin,
Still pulsing, to your fire;

And you your dozen charms leave strewn
The length of their scorched track;
And we, unfettered arm
In arm, take flight . . .

World aimless, lit, minute
Flushed agate underfoot, begun the free
Fall's updraft of afterwit,
The life written in blood.

1966

ROUGH SCHEME FOR AN EON IN THE ALPS

One day in autumn an old god sees red,
Screams, drops like something mowed.
Coming to himself in a brown pool of blood,

He blinks round the wrecked room.
There is so much that he will never fathom
Still pounding in his system.

His emotions are those of the shepherd gaping
At huge, half human tracks, a trail smoking
Upward, most of his flock missing.

He has no choice now, he must think
Winter. In a trice the mercury has sunk
Like a numb slug into its bubblebank,

And at the lake's heart the immense
Valves clash shut. Silence.
He nods through white crocheted curtains—

Obedient, the Jungfrau knits her brows.
The shape that stalked him, in her vise,
Cannot so much as push up edelweiss.

Queer valley mists, though, have begun to weave
Up past him, forming a ceiling. If
Messages reach him, who is he to give

An answer, a coherent one? His head
Fills with the creaking of a bed
Where someone lies unsleeping, exhausted.

The room just seems to be illumined.
Knowledge of life ebbs from the god's mind.
Creation mourns a friend.

Above the clouds, meanwhile, the mountain's
Whole being confronts the heavens.
She strains, in air that burns and thins,

To keep cool, hide the hard core of her shame,
That body huge and haired, and for all time.
Sweating a steep, clear stream,

She musters atmospheres against the fact—
Pleat-shaded-pink now, amorous, abject,
Now gemmed and ruthless. It is quite an act,

And it concludes with avalanches! . . .
Much later, when things could focus, they hung on the eyelashes
Of the unearthed. A strangeness equal to the fantasies

Employed to flee it. These it effortlessly
Called back into its corpse. The sun drew near. The valley
Turned green out of pure susceptibility.

The lake shook on the brink of grave disclosure.
When grunts and tinklings filled the ether
Then it was the old god's eyes ran over.

He sniffed. *Who willed this warmth?*
No answer. *I am not a god of wrath—*
I shall be able to endure the truth!

In its own time came a stench of corruption
In some high place, potent as saffron.
Hallooings from the deranged mountain

Heralded discovery of the beast.
The next day young and old could taste
Their ancestor. It was already harvest.

The god, extinguished at his window,
Gazed into bonfires far below
And manikins black against the glow.

His face worked. He wanted to know why
They did not come after him with cutlery
Instead of feasting on his effigy.

1957

LOVER BY FULL MOON

Before he undergoes
What he must, let all be stripped
And stifled in white gauze.
Let, high above, a silent
Luminous maw have crept
Into position, open.
Does he at last consent
To anything that may happen
During the operation?
Searching a woman's face
For courage, let him then
Inhale this gas
Made by the cricket's voice
Acting on indigo oxygen.

1959

ASCENDANCY OF CHILDREN

For weeks, for years perhaps, they have been playing
Upon the ten-mile boardwalk xylophone
Outside, that joins a given stilted dwelling
To the next and the next and the next one. To and fro
They romp, shrieking. A cluster drops for fun
Into shallows the milky yellow of Pernod.

They are everywhere. Now some have taken to milling
Round a certain doorway, thrusting in their heads
(The door having long since vanished) until pressure
From the foot of the stairs forces an unwilling
Littlest one, all belly, beads,
And panicked, painted eyes, across the threshold.

When it appears no violence will befall
The visitor, five or six larger ones permit
Themselves to be pushed in. What do they see?
A squat white Mover ticking menacingly,
A square leaf with blue marks—look, some are wet!
A woman under glass, white-haired and small,

Fearfully small, and smiling, though not a child.
A devil surely. More, many more, have come.
They babble and touch things. They appear unskilled
In telling metal from cloth, or wood from flesh.
As the confusion mounts it is guessed in a flash
That one of them will discover the occupant of the room.

He has been sitting rigid, pen in hand,
Before his mother's picture. But now he flinches.
As from one throat, ravenous cries rebound.
The waters seethe and smoke with images
Whose parent glares unblinking from on high
And will not long be borne by the naked eye.

1959

MEN'S SONG AT WEDDING

Tjokele's woman—ayiii!
They have dressed her in rattan raiment,
Dyed red her shaven scalp.
See how she stamps her foot!

You who cost our friend four fields,
Listen no longer to your blood-uncles' drumming.
Divide with Tjokele the marital yam, wench
As the dugong timorous, as the peewee cute.

1967

THE CANDID DECORATOR

I thought I would do over
All of it. I was tired
Of scars and stains, of bleared
Panes, tinge of the liver.
The fuchsia in the center
Looked positively weird.
I felt it—dry as paper.
I called a decorator.
In next to no time such
A nice young man appeared.
What had I in mind?
Oh, lots and lots of things—
Fresh colors, pinks and whites
That one would want to touch;
The windows redesigned;
The plant thrown out in favor,
Say, of a small tree,
An orange or a pear . . .
He listened dreamily.
Combing his golden hair
He measured with one glance
The distance I had come
To reach this point. And then
He put away his comb.
He said: "Extravagance!
Suppose it could be done.
You'd have to give me carte
Blanche and an untold sum.
But to be frank, my dear,
Living here quite alone
(Oh, I have seen it, true,
But me you needn't fear)
You've one thing to the good:
While not exactly smart,
Your wee place, on the whole
It couldn't be more 'you.'

Still, if you like—" I could
Not speak. He had seen my soul,
Had said what I dreaded to hear.
Ending the interview
I rose, blindly. I swept
To show him to the door,
And knelt, when he had left,
By my Grand Rapids chair,
And wept until I laughed
And laughed until I wept.

1959

WORDS FOR THE FAMILIAR SPIRIT

1

The tongues leap on the summit of your will.
The dead shine back like planets. They don't know
Whose livingness they shiver round, until
A glancing shape leans up and out from it.
This is yourself. Your body sits below,
Clenched upon vertigo, mouth slack, brows knit.

2

The speech condensing on your breath is mine,
Is me. Thick, fast, gemmed round you, it exceeds
Meaning. Tomorrow, blinking in sunshine,
You won't recall it. But down the sheer face
Behind your features it will have run in beads,
Seeking a level miles beyond this place.

3

Your body crouches on red earth beside
The broad and inmost serpent of my drift
Whose dream is only more and more to glide,
As yours is to awaken from the dream
Transfigured. Rippling, neither slow nor swift,
The condor's shadow widens on the stream.

4

Poor savage, never once do you suppose
My river something more than eddies made
In blood by devils twirling on their toes.
You've yet to see, upon the gleaming lip
Of an immense and immanent cascade,
Sun, sky, volcano totter, shatter, slip;

5

To hear from far below the god's own roar
Raveling utterance like an end of rope
Till all is iridescent breath once more
(The speaker having drained his foaming cup);
Then to endure, green fire in a soap-
Bubble, the quetzal floating up and up.

1959

LANDSCAPE WITH TORRENT

Thus far he has not seen her, a spoke
Of fire transfixes him, a boulder's
Heart pounds beneath the plunging, black
Rainbow of his course.

She, she is all abristle, rearing
Into scarlet air at the scent of danger.
Will it not end, end soon, this thing
They equally fear and share?

Will it not end, this trance of violent
Yet predictable movement, as when all heaven
Dances? Ah, but from another viewpoint
It has ended already, he has fallen

At her feet, too near her now,
Warm stones, bells, flocks, to comprehend
Her heights, there in the serene afterglow
As though nothing had happened.

1958

MUSIC FROM ABOVE

Lying, looking up
At the perfectly white ceiling,
Or later, writing this down
On a smaller, erasable white rectangle,
Feeling the piano's
Crystals descend,
Slow fourths and fifths or a pair of flakes together
Struck more numbingly than the rest,
Discords perhaps intended, perhaps not,
The piece being only a trifle less familiar
To me than to its performer,
I wonder who is playing
(The child? the old uncle? the cat?)
And why. Not expecting, surely,
Ever to play well. Isn't it more a matter
Of just getting through the afternoon
Without releasing, so to speak,
That pedal held,
Blackbrimming pool, at body temperature
Until the final phrase
Of all has lighted and dissolved, of all.

1960

FOUNTAIN IN DISUSE: ATHENS

Thunder? A distant footfall? Has somebody
Grasped what governs me, there below
The level of the dirt? For all about me
Alters to drizzle, fine,
Refreshing—or would be if one enjoyed
A cool and usual manna.
Dances of praise, let the snail perform them:
The peacock lift his worn, soiled tail
Above the frost-nipped oranges.
Undeceived, I hug the scallops
Of my proper shell. I bless
No days but those of the tallest beakers,
Whole suns the oleander drained, rocking and fraying
Until I could no longer contain myself!
Above their organs and their objects
Forth through small leaden pipes and ducts
To startle each in light, drunk artisan
And bauble alike of the rich setting,
Wanting no climax, shameless, infantine,
My senses leapt and played,
Not before sundown to be called back
By a ghostly overall'd figure
Into the wetted body whose one joy
Was ever more to dream them free again.
Does that answer your question, Eleni and Kosta,
With your books and your complexions,
Already learning, already forgetting?
It is why at all seasons,
Here in the park at the convergence
From no less than six directions
Of little-pebbled myrtle-bordered paths,
I wait for what I think
Will not have been withheld much longer, or in vain.

1960

LANDSCAPE WITH VW

This votive spansule driven at top speed
Away from hell—shivering Primavera,

Ingest the bitterness, spark and exhaust,
Of pangs all day deferred. Have me be one

With cub and violet, your whole wildlife
Sanctuary hurt into blossom, healed by it.

1969

ORACLE

Suddenly as of today
The weeping beech in the next garden
Is making large doomed signals.
After an August spent on the lawn's edge,
Wrapped, like myself, in a thousand light inflections,
Look at it now! The tree is in a trance!
And high time. Just this once
It may have something really important to say.
Or is that fair?
One or two simple characteristics,
Such as a weakness for somber ornament
Combined with that congenital slight deformity
That crooks us earthward into the gloom we shed—
Mightn't those, if heeded,
Have uttered truths the flailing
Limbs never will, an all but weightless
Claw of bamboo haunts, an early
Figment of blue smoke crazes?
I should like to put a hand out saying *Hush!*
Be still. It doesn't matter.
Too late. The sky is hoarse with birds.
The leaves have started up their stylized wailing.
The shutters beat themselves against the wall.
Already leaves of three colors are racing ahead of me
(Why am I always the last to know?)
As I step from the house into my element,
The old progress resumed
Complete with mourners and outriders
Through a kingdom vast and cold;
Freely resumed, for in this middle season
What is not driven where it means to go?

1960

ENVOI

As I crossed the lot next door, one page I wrote
And had copied to send you struggled and broke away,
Collapsing sunwards, an unribbed kite, a mote.
Here on earth trees were swaying,

Nodding and neighing like horses. The thrilled, sweet-smelling
Grasses, the molten sea—what *was* it? My hair, my coat,
My mouth forced open, made to smile,
The song half sung thrust back into my throat—

1963

It is time. The fire crackles. Drugged by heat
And habit, the book lies open on my knees.
It breathes the light in lazily, debauched
By this or that impressed on it,

By deeds done, loves I can no longer feel,
Leaving me almost jealous—why go on?
Today snow fell. Women went wrapped in scarves
Through the near whiteness. I saw their tracks fill.

(How many like them, entering Juan's life,
Had trusted he would not detain them there,
Foxing their passage with jet character,
A fire-flushed virgin overleaf.)

Clearing at sunset, I took from its shelf
The diary, knowing what remained to do.
It opened, "All is over. She has left . . ."
The page began to quiver of itself,

Though that one did not leave, or not that year,
And never wholly; we are good friends still.
Indeed our Persian, bronchial now and cross
And too much the voyeur to interfere,

Stares me to the brink of the ordeal.
I want to say—there is no other word
But one half blasphemous, half absurd—
To say *This is my body* and so kneel

To place it among flames. Burn, little book!
You gasp and writhe, you kindle. My cheeks burn.
What have I done! What can I do but turn
Dumbly back to my view, and look.

(Landscape would be what speaks to him these days.
The vacant, untrod road arrives at dark
Exactly where, thrust outward by a pane
And in transparent effigy, the years blaze.)

1960

ECONOMIC MAN

Perhaps it is being off the gold standard
Makes times particularly hard.
Dark brings the jingle and glint of waning coin.
The Huntress pokes through a vast pantheon
Of paper, each leaf sacred to someone
Like Richelieu or Hamilton.

How many genial flames
Gutter and flee the nation's household shrines!
These days the people I know, like raccoons,
Squat over streams to wash their hands
In the clear thinking of John Maynard Keynes.
And nothing clings to the pans.

Meanwhile the heavens fill with counterfeit
Bodies and lights, which seem to circulate.
The woman of the world puts on
These trinkets with a frown.
They poison her compliance and the love
We had no other way to prove.

The diehards cry: "Restore
The monarchy! Our buried King
Lent significance to everything,
Made the desert bloom and the heart soar.
Uranium the jet-black President is insane.
Ah to be loyal subjects once again!"

Personally I would leave him at Fort Knox
And look for something better—yes but what?
Each time you butter bread
Paid for with money that your money made
The debt grows more prohibitive
To those luxurious lives you didn't live.

Infants (the Master said) in the erotic filth
Of their own bodies first imagine wealth,

729

Then sweat to purge it from the very bone.
With shaven head and climbing eyes
A priesthood grew. Soon Cities filled the skies,
Of gold and precious stone.

The next step was to build one here below.
Less rich, conceivably, but no
Less real, these concrete blocks
Up from whose monumental bowels jokes
Pharaoh's ghost: "Such interest we accrue,
We may some day relent and cover you."

Forty floors down is Wall Street; forty years
Ago, the merger of Heart & Hurt
That made me. Sunset. The gilt cages halt,
Fill up with financiers
And sink. Not one of us but will revert
To his original value in the vault.

1960

TABLE TALK

"Food!" exclaims Charles. "Each new dish I have tried
Moves me more strangely than the last.
Often my hostess, as an aproned bride,
Will enter to a blast
Of burning biscuits, and her screams
Shake the red, gas-lit theater of my dreams.

Those nights, the marquee spells out plenitude:
SARAH BERNHARDT IN *HEARTBURN HOUSE.*
The opening speech ('If physic be the mood
Of love,' said by the Doctor to his spouse)
Quite glues me to my seat.
'More please!' I clamor. We are what we eat.

Deep in original dirt and secrecy
Which none but boiling waters wash away,
The lowliest tuber speaks to me.
I have been scalded in my day,
A raw youth carapaced
By shyness. Now I'm plump, with almost perfect taste.

Come autumn, I am one who broods
On the hot-dog man. His hawking of full-fleshed
And sizzling nudes
To frozen, fur-clad adepts in
Vicarious contact with pigskin
Is unsurpassed by anything in Brecht.

Or chestnuts . . . Through the blue dusk their opaque
Cabuchons pop and glow—too late!
The girl has set before me a ham steak
Glazed thick and pale as its own plate.
Red neon lights through diner windows splash
The stupid succotash

Till tears of rapture burn my throat.
Even the slovenly unthinking sloth

Cauldrons hem in, who adds by rote
The salt and gristle to her nameless broth,
Obeys, through clouds of steam,
The oracle: Transfigure and Redeem.

At higher levels you are apt to get
A Vinaigrette or Aïoli
So strong it makes you sweat,
And in your fever it will seem that she
Who serves it has advanced gyrating with
Armpits shaved blue, a white rose in her teeth.

Or just to think of bittersweet
Oranges veiled in flickering blue rum,
Or—but you must be starving! Shall we eat?"
He goes. And from an inner room
Brings out the bird acrackle in its nest
Of spices, asks who will have leg, who breast.

Charles is a marvelous cook. Still, there are meals
He serves that make me wonder, as tonight,
What it all means, and what my neighbor feels.
Somehow I cannot touch a bite.
I wish a doctor or at least
A jolly Roman priest
Were here to tell me: *Go ahead, my son, enjoy the feast!*

1961

A BAG OF PEANUTS FOR
JOHN HOLLANDER

As the double feature began, so did you to un-
do one by one the fiber-waisted corsets of some
thirty miniature, soiled torsos (like a month of
     the same headline: EX-ACTRESS SLAIN)
and to remove from each those two or three posthumous
red-skinned ivory-fleshed diptychs of guilt, to divide
the adulterers, neither's face, now, able to save
     the other's. Nor does it matter,
that kiss once broken, if a random beam on any
one pair sheds the wooden, vertically indented
amour propre of people by Modigliani, "her"
     liplessness, "his" fringed pout alike
dumb, who ideally (for the goobers if not for
you, slumped there popping them into your mouth regardless)
might have been spared to sow with new and edible stars
     the future's dirt spectaculars.

1961

THE KITCHEN KNIGHT

O my white armor, my copper or stainless steel
Or aluminum brainstorms, each with its steam panache!
The woman comes, goes, turns me off,
Wipes me dry, and sits down to her meal.

A fussy, elderly muse, who needs a man,
She looks at raw experience with distaste.
Who doesn't? . . . though when she passes it on to me
My code constrains me to do what I can.

1967

AUTUMN ELEGY

Sumac, your running wild
In bad seasonal verse
Depresses me no longer. Spelt anew
In the mind's mirror, child,
Your dark dry blood reverts
To that of the young demi-god Camus.

1960

THE BEQUEST

My sorrow was a little child,
    Exacting, innocent.
It looked upon the world and smiled,
Whereupon all grew vivid in its gaze
    Including me. It went
From this into a second phase.

With others its own age and size
    It struggled to compete.
Coming home flushed from exercise
It sprawled at table in a wordless rage.
    Love was its milk and meat.
Enough. So passed the awkward age.

Fullgrown, my sorrow settled down
    Into the dull routine
Of one who daily rides downtown
To calculate his worth in red and black,
    And all night scans a screen
For glimmerings of his heart attack.

Stricken at last, it lay in bed.
    I brought it a new book
And a new friend. It shook its head
And plucked the crazy quilt as if to say
    With malice in its look,
You will be sorry one fine day.

I doubted that—but now behold
    My sorrow's word come true!
It died in second childhood, old
And blind with laughter for no cause, unless
    For having left me you,
My happiness, my happiness.

1961

ON THE BRIDGE

Leaves burn green
Over the stupid little wooden bridge.
Almost the same swan
Feeds at the pond's edge.

The sun is high. The shadow of my head
Floating blank in its flame-dusty halo
Lets me so see down through it to a bed
Of mire inert and pale

That all at once this outlook, cross-plank, rung
And worn handrail,
Is wrong, is wrong
To seem unchanged—have *I* been faithful

To what I came here with
Less than one love ago?
Hush. At my feet a diabolic wraith
Remains obscurely so.

Not quite out of the blue A asks B, for when it must end between them, to
help him behave nicely. Her whole face beams—as if he could ever not be
nice! Weeks pass. He tries a new tack: "Don't burn our bridge. Whole
families, feelings, habits, etc., still use it every day." But C has all along
been using B, so there is only the usual way out. At the park gates A
pauses. Inside are thickets, mazes, mirrors charred & croaking, which he
will never again visit after dark, alone.

The sun is low. A golden fleece
Drowns the toy water.
Boys call their boats in. It is more and less
Than they had set out after.

And at the zenith of the bridge somebody
Else is enduring
With shut eyes, like a god,
That bounced-from-below uppouring

Of rapid pulses, ripple, flash,
Whose drunken script
Scrawls on the scene, on the seer's very flesh,
A message undecipherable except

For its tone of buoyant impatience
With anything downcast—
Long sad truths let fall misshapen
By one and all, to skitter in the dust.

All but that one. *His* shadow melting, flowing
Upwards into the green and azure flue, fire-pale.
At the stake, but smiling unharmed, he is not going
To die, no, no. He has put wind into a sail

Designed never to bear his weight and mass;
And now, having seen this last of many float
To a white standstill on the burning-glass,
Will not recoil, feeling the deck grow hot.

1962–1966

FROM "THE BROKEN HOME"

Small beyond great swaying glooms
Over driveway gravel strewn
With golden acorns and shed plumes
From the pigeon-lariat
Twirled of a long afternoon
Stands the house of fifty rooms.
In front the white Isotta gleams
Like a solar chariot.
Everything is as it seems:
Servants loyal, mistress kind,
Master wise, and cupid mossy-blind
At the fountain's heart; and all
Imperceptibly grown small.
It is the house of dreams.

1963

HOURGLASS

Dear at death's door when you stand
I will run to let you in.
You may know me by my grin
And the joints of this right hand.

You will follow unafraid
As one seldom does in life.
I will say to Pluto's wife,
"Please your Majesty, this shade

Is my friend's who kept your Spring,
Showed me how to wear your green.
Twenty winters intervene
Yet I glow, remembering."

She will then unlock a chest,
Shake our senses out like robes
Fine and warm to naked ribs,
Make a sign when we are dressed

For one hour in which we fill
With ten thousand joys and pains.
Then, reversed, the burning grains
Back through her transparent will

Drain, and the robes are blown apart,
Two more bat shapes in the cave,
Little dreaming now they have
Blessed each other heart to heart.

1968

DELFT

What's left? No place.
After Vermeer
The storm roves elsewhere;
The fates make lace.

Houses left to steep
In teabrown water
Stretch and totter
On the brink of sleep,

Or by arrangement steal
Meekly from sight
As once more his great
Late light strikes tile

And in the cauldron
Of their own high glaze
Even nowadays
Small figures drown.

1961

741

CROCHETED CURTAIN

The zany interplay
Of thread and motive, oh,
Twenty-five years ago,
Left me drawn, left me gray,

While a duenna not
So dense yet as to screen
The worlds I come between.
Both take note somewhat.

That young man of the streets
May if he please infer
A demure glancing fire
Behind my marguerites,

And she who nods alone
Within, good soul, confuse
His noble looks with views
Hooked into them by bone.

1968

THE CASEWORKER

Door by door, story by story,
You can devote a lifetime to the side streets.
They run from North to South. Each house
Has a family, or five, or twenty-five;
Each family, a name. When you arrive
They put away the telephone directory
In whose yellow pages, dense with doctors and gadgets,
They had been looking for help,
And give themselves to you without reserve.
Rapturously the cat kneads your thighs.
The youngest child brings you a bruise to kiss.
More iced tea? Hours have passed. You rise. So soon?
You can't go yet! Look at this photograph
Of a mammoth Junior High School senior class.
The father and mother were schoolmate sweethearts.
In five seconds you have picked them out.
He clasps your hand. Tears fill her eyes.
Come back and see us! Come back anytime!

Mid-afternoon. From the sixtieth floor
Where you present your findings, the side streets
Have receded through waves of heat, exhaust, and sound
To ten thousand rippling backdrops
On microfilm, stacked
In a deep file of umber haze—
Baby elevations soured by sun
As days and years have soured their architects.
And at this height, moreover, a plan emerges.
The city is built on the Chinese gridiron.
Now you can see what you had not been allowed
To see before: clogged glitter of avenues
Down which the mind alone speeds. These
Run from East to West. At the end of each

Ought to be a palace or a temple,
Guards, gods, trumpeters, lacquer carriages,
Where in fact there is only a brown-gray cloud
And rumor of a river.

1965

A SILENCE

No coffin without nails.
This one you drive into mine
At least is golden.

1968

MOSQUITO

The sheet strains and pulls loose,
The needle dances, the eye rolls,
The soul falls to its knees

Desperate for that mild land
Where, once the Horn is rounded,
No tiny star of sound

Malign, unshining, flickers
Over the frail vessel
To lure it from its course

Through tall glooms, heaving, slapping,
Drenched with refusal
Of the faint siren song.

1959

642719

I will not dial that number, never fear.
When the phone rings it won't be me for you.
It will be another voice you hear,

Younger no doubt, more eager, more sincere
And simpler, you can simply answer to.
I will not dial that number, never fear.

You will turn back to backgammon and beer.
Breathed into bones as hollow as bamboo
It will be another voice you hear.

What will I do? Play *Rosenkavalier*
Three times a week. Whatever else I do,
I will not dial that number, never fear.

The 2 kneels down, the 1, erect, severe . . .
No. In the hush of tonight's rendezvous
It will be another voice you hear

Whispering, "Experience comes dear.
Don't learn. Pay nothing. To yourself be true."
I will not dial that number, never fear.
It will be another voice you hear.

1966

AT A TEXAS WISHING-WELL

Stranger, look down (the jingle said) *& you*
Will see the face of one who loves you true.
Will do. My face looks back at me
Sheer above a ground of hard cold cash—

Pennies aglint from either eye,
Silver in hair, teeth, value everywhere!
Drop my coin and make my wish:
Let me love myself until I die.

1967

THE SEVENTH ROUND

Give it to him!
To you, they mean.
As always (mezzanine
Gone dazzling dim,

A crown at stake)
Before you stands
The giver with clenched hands.
Drop your own. Take.

1971

CASTAWAY

The letters you no longer write
Go forth in bottles I have drained,
Bobbing above your profile drowned
But debonair, night after dream-racked night.

Mulling them over, ocean learns
That it is hateful, salt and wide.
Self-knowledge—ha, who needs it! fumes the tide.
By dawn each courier returns.

Roll up the blind on palm trees, sham
Blue stutterings from trunk to wrinkled trunk.
A pink eye-level sun falls drunk
Into my arms. The clockface burns with shame.

What shall I do today? What can I do
But sit down in this shadow toothed with gold
And trust the light to shift, time to be told,
Someone else to save me if not you.

1965

THE ROMANCE LANGUAGE

When first in love I breakfasted by water.
The chestnut trees were in full bloom, I fear.
A voice at my elbow breathed, "Monsieur désire?"
I understood perhaps, but could not utter.

Some stay years, and still are easy to lie to.
Frog and prince have been witty at my expense.
My answers when they come make less than sense
Although I tell the god's own truth, or try to.

1965

TSIKOUDHIÁ

Given us through a misunderstanding,
Its name and what it does
We keep forgetting. Paroxysms. Tears.
Enter the cautioner: Last spring
(Ten, fifty springs ago)
An "English lord" drank one glass and dropped dead.
Now that we've heard the tale
Told by a blood, a grandfather, a child,
Each time in a new village,
Its incidental whitewash, flies, the spit
Still turning above unseen flames,
Even—ah stop!—those baked
Blue eyeballs in the walrus mask
Have grown discardable as straw round shimmering
Curves fullblown, glass-green, the hueless
Lightning fills. Nobody hereabouts
But comes to swallow with it
Some apprehension of the dead man.
He too grows daily nearer.
Smooth-faced by now, slim in unwrinkled white—
See him lift his little tumbler gaily.
And, though we gag at its taste,
Are in no hurry to die,
Would not anyhow choose one quick
Exit over another, we lift ours
To a survival less in earth's black libraries
Than in these cubic miles
Of midday, tavern above wine-blue pines,
Then gurgle winking from the flagon
Down next year's beardless throat
That drinks as yet no dying of its own.

1965

NO WORD

The river flowing from you
By day is warm and slow.
It plays back each chord
Of augmented willow
Flawlessly, each cloud,
Each cormorant, unheard
On the dummy keyboard.

Never coming nearer,
That rower and his lady
Are a postcard written
Backwards, to be read
Held just above the mirror
(Which has by heart already
The sweet nothing said).

And after dark there's only
The small arms factory
Big as a matchbox—
Blisters of phosphorus
Bursting along blackness
Gasping now and racing
In its narrow bed.

1968

FULL MOON: LETTER TO T

Under your bald spell who could prevent
This upsurge of—oh call it poetry
Effacing, overwhelming the real me:
Sandcastle, peachpit, Friday's footprint.

Inland, too, I daresay whole
Meadows gleam with bubblings-up.
Homage? Defense? Over the drowned crop
Of clover hoofless cattle drool.

Held by your unbreathing glow
Nothing live but waters like a mouth.
Too bad that you will never know

My dry, reasonable stretches. Thank you though
For this brilliant, dancing path
By which I arrive at saying so.

1965

TRELLIS

Again, ramshackle skeleton,
You spare the house what is about to happen.

Out of nowhere, up from the bleak ground,
My greedy twinings overcome your frame,

Climb, put blue suns forth, suicidally thicken,
And, spoiled at summer's end no doubt

By so much wooden acquiescence, brag
Of having woken a response in you.

Who can say? A night is coming, I remember,
When I share your body with frost. A second,

And I withdraw into myself for winter.
Never mind. I'll bloom next year.

You only, love's uncomprehending object,
Will be replaced after a season or two.

1966

COUNTRY MUSIC

Catbirds have inherited the valley
With its nine graves and its burned-down distillery

Deep in Wedgewood black-on-yellow
Crazed by now, of bearded oak and willow.

Walls were rotogravure, roof was tin
Ridged like the frets of a mandolin.

Sheriff overlooked that brown glass demijohn.
Some nights it'll fill with genuine

No-proof moonshine from before you were born.
This here was Sally Jay's toy horn.

A sound of galloping—yes? No.
Just peaches wind shook from the bough

In the next valley. Care to taste one, friend?
A doorway yawns. A willow weeps. The end.

1967

OPAQUE MORNING

W.C.W. 1883–1963

Cold mottles gray and lichen mustard
The porous balustrade's
Outermost shapeliness plotted
Against these windless white

Plungings. Upon it also,
Two drained wineglasses standing guard
Next to a fog-spangled book
Left out, face down, all night.

Night. As if her black luxuriance
Hairpinned with roving points of light
Might never again be shaken loose,

We strain to see beyond the stone
That has soaked upward into words
That have soaked downward into it.

1963

SEASIDE DOORWAY, SUMMER DAWN

Hot low notes undulate the stave,
Color the riser in his element
As in a tumbler flushed above
Pajamas windstreaked blue and wine.

Risen, dear carouser more than rose,
The step from bed to watery grave
Could take forever, fissionable moment,
So many bubbles pinking any spine.

West then this least interior's
Greasebeaded skillet, stove, splintery beam
Grain of a fingertip restores

Flame with the whole East. In unison
Both ripple meaning to become
The other upon passage through its frame.

1968

TOMORROWS

The question was an academic one.
Andrey Sergeyvitch, rising sharp at two,
Would finally write that letter to his three
Sisters still in the country. Stop at four,
Drink tea, dress elegantly and, by five,
Be losing money at the Club des Six.

In Pakistan a band of outraged Sikhs
Would storm an embassy (the wrong one)
And spend the next week cooling off in five
Adjacent cells. These clearly were but two
Vital details—though nobody cared much for
The future by that time, except us three.

You, Andrée Meraviglia, not quite three,
Left Heidelberg. Year, 1936.
That same decade you, Lo Ping, came to the fore
In the Spiritual Olympics, which you won.
My old black self I crave indulgence to
Withhold from limelight, acting on a belief I've

Lived by no less, no more, than by my five
Senses. Enough that circus music (BOOM-two-three)
Coursed through my veins. I saw how Timbuctoo
Would suffer an undue rainfall, 2.6
Inches. How in all of Fairbanks, won-
der of wonders, no polkas would be danced, or for

That matter no waltzes or rumbas, although four
Librarians, each on her first French 75,
Would do a maxixe (and a snappy one).
How, when on Lucca's greenest ramparts, three-
fold emotion prompting Renzo to choose from six
Older girls the blondest, call her *tu*,

It would be these blind eyes hers looked into
Widening in brief astonishment before
Love drugged her nerves with blossoms drawn from classics
Of Arab draftsmanship—small, ink-red, five-
Petaled blossoms blooming in clusters of three.
How she would want to show them to someone!

But one by one they're fading. I am too.
These three times thirteen lines I'll write down for
Fun, some May morning between five and six.

1967

THE PARDONER'S TALE

Writing to kill, whose wiles
No longer captivate,
I glean from what I am
A fine self-centered glue.
The wingèd words comply.
By dusk their hum of hate
And stinging innuendo
Deck my page to you

But leave the web in tatters—
Away! This must not be!
Concoct for the next hedgerow
A foolproof stratagem.
Yesterday's words moreover
Begin to disagree
With me, as if I had
Already eaten them.

Down ever cooler, bluer
Vistas of argument
You would be little apt
To enter or pursue
Daily I weave another
Missive left unsent.
Of late my lines are studied
Only by heavy dew.

Soon rains will wash the mirror
You praise my silence in,
A printlessness I ponder
Whiten my very hair.
No less kind than cruel
(Wipe off that stupid grin)
Yours will be the brightest
Nature I can bear.

Summer's wasp by now
Is a mere wisp of spite.
The gemskull fly
Dusts the deep clover.
Unconstructive magic
Streams from me tonight.
Sleep. No one all winter
Will have a better lover.

1967

WE WALK IN WOODS

Of our own words.
Our fathers planted the strangler vine,
Perspectives, glooms of meaning.

The taproot enfolds
Earth's heart and ours.
A topmost verbiage whispers
Not only silence is golden.

Nevertheless one dreams
Of the ringing ax,
Shudder and crash,
Light streaming in.

Whose speech am I
And what is being said
When, tightlipped and barehanded,
I make a silence, briefly?

1963

DESERT MOTEL WITH FROG AMULET

Fairweather thunder smote. Who then
(The old man I had become wondered)

From every height and hollow of the scene
Glowed like a flame cupped by seductive features?

Rarely so rosy an incognito,
A stirring, dream-flushed child—I mean,

Were there many loves or only one?
The eyeslits burned and guttered, light from lips

Broke, a voice in answer: "You
Who happen on me here, return

To the chamois pouch around my neck
This stone charm. Small but powerful,

So often shattered and made whole,
It kept me young in either element."

Deep in the waste one room was green as water
And tall erosions rippled what it faced.

1969

LUNCH WITH A SCHOLAR

Waters lowering, lion and red vole
Will see one lofty crater (Vulcan? Jove?)
Overlaid in the hot lull with vibrant
Silver leaf, quicker than I can write

Doctor of dead letters, lift the veil,
Lick clean your luster platter's oval
Of its tough liver, throw these louvers open,
Volumes unspoken, for the dove to light.

1971

CHILD OF THE EARTH,

They call you here. The scorpion's
Harmless country cousin, taking time

Across the terrace toward small purple
Windfall plums that deep in shade

Would hatch the thunderstorm . . . An illegitimate child,
Said her pajama'd friend, deadpan, the day

We found you drowned in Lesbia's pool.
Fished out, you lay in a great crystal reliquary

Between the desert and those nodding
Trees of heaven, as they call them here.

Already clouds were massing. The poodle and I
Sniffed at your sheepskull visor, your shiny brown armor,

Stilt-joints gartered each with tiny claws.
You'd taken upon yourself the sins of the insect world

In errantry no doubt very quixotic and selfless
But ill-timed, sure to fail—our vertebrate empire

Being, if only in the short run, stronger,
More . . . plausible. (Lesbia plausible? God help us.) Child,

Away with you. Sped by no prayer of mine,
Storm within storm you must weather,

These margins infiltrate of hardened clay
And beaten marigold to reach

Me reading by some future
Light the book where both our names are written.

1969

MASTER AND MAN

for Christos Alevras

Services that can be bought
Make mock of the essential thing,
Whatever that is. Two whole years, come spring,
You're with me—who'd have thought?

Is it affliction or godsend,
This odd dependency of each,
Unlike in background, character, and speech;
And where will it all end?

Each morning at my study door
You knock, impetuous to earn
That bread I know no better than to turn
Into a metaphor.

So presently a nice white grime
Of plaster lies on chair and page.
Cracks in my ceiling, sanctified by age,
Will seep no more. High time.

Or from the hardware store you phone
To ask me what you've gone to buy.
What's "bearing" in your language? As if I
Could tell you in my own.

Shades of the Don and Sancho Panza,
Unless I mean Batman & Co.,
Flit at dusk (plink! your guitar below)
Through a distempered stanza.

(Or shriek! your changeling making scenes
In the loud and local tongue,
Which leave her mother proud, yourself unstrung.
That child is full of beans.)

When to the mirror strides my fellow
Libertine, all sword and ruff,
You like the style but can't count high enough
To serve as Leporello.

What then to tell your good square face
Toothed like a saw with pearl and gold.
The tale *it* tells me has been told, told, told.
Just open the bookcase,

Read how from here to Trebizond
Burly reliance, a real burr,
Clings to its deluded arbiter
According to their bond.

"Nos valets feront ça pour nous,"
Said Villiers de l'Isle Adam
Of living. Or is it I by now who am
Upstairs to live for you?

Lurching through worlds we hardly see,
So rich and awful, fast and loose,
You wave Good night, sweet dreams! from the caboose
Of my train de vie.

1970

THE CATCH-ALL

Here you came, poor armoire
Jolting down the street,
Mirror in your door
Seasick, flashing speechless
O's of shock the driver
Of the open van
Did nothing to compose—
All this in August heat.

Once in place, you knew
No worse or better than
To stuff yourself with clothes.
A nasty rash of red
Plastic hooks broke out
Along your sides. Old *Times*
Got piled up on your head
(Kept, now, through thick and thin).

One cold day, when the bedside
Lamp seemed far too dim
To dress by, a light gold
Oval swung ajar—
Dear eyesore, placidly
Reflecting on your roommate
Once more left unmade
By forms that sprang from him.

1972

TRANSLATIONS

LES COLLINES

Above Paris one day
Two big airplanes were fighting
One was black and the other red
While in the zenith flamed
The eternal solar airplane

One was the whole of my youth
And the other was the future
They fought furiously
So against Lucifer fought
The Archangel with radiant wings

So the estimate to the problem
So night against day
So my love destroys
What I love so the hurricane
Uproots the crying tree

But look what sweetness all over
Paris like a young girl
Wakens languorously
Shakes her long hair
And sings her lovely song

O where did my youth fall
You see the flaming future
Know that I speak today
To tell the whole world at last
The art of prediction is born

Certain men are hills
That rise from among men
And see far off all future
Better than the present
More clearly than the past

Ornament of times and of roads
Passes and lasts with no pause
Let us hiss the snakes
In vain against the south wind
Snake charmers died with the sea

Order of times if machines
At last began to think
Upon the jeweled beaches
Gold waves would shatter
Foam would be mother still

Less high than man the eagles fly
It is he who delights the seas
As he scatters to the winds
Shadow and the dizzy humors
Where spirit and dream meet

Youth goodbye jasmine of time
I have breathed your fresh perfume
At Rome on the flowery carts
Laden with masks with garlands
And the tinkle of carnivals

Goodbye youth white Christmas
When life was only a star
Whose reflection I observed
In the Mediterranean sea
More pearly than meteors

Downy as a nest of archangels
Or the garland of the clouds
And more lustrous than halos
Emanations and splendors
Singular sweetness harmonies

I stop to watch upon
The incandescent lawn
A serpent twine it is myself
Who am the flute I play
And the whip that punishes others

A time comes for suffering
A time comes for goodness
Youth goodbye this is the time
When we will know the future
Without dying from our knowledge

It is the time of ardent grace
Man's will alone will act
Seven years of incredible proof
Man will divine himself
More pure more alive more wise

He will discover new worlds
The soul declines like flowers
From which come delicious fruits
That we watch ripening
Upon the sunlit hill

I tell what is really life
I alone could sing this way
My songs fall like seed
Be silent all you singers
Do not mix the tares with the wheat

A ship came into the harbor
A liner decked with flags
But we found no one on it
But a handsome crimson lady
She lay there assassinated

I have examined what none
Can in any way imagine
And many times I have weighed
Even imponderable life
I may die with a smile

I have often soared so high
So high that goodbye to everything
The strangenesses the ghosts
And I no longer wish to admire
This boy who mimics fear

This is the time of magic
It is returning be ready
For millions of prodigies
That have midwived no fables
None having imagined them

Depths of consciousness
We will explore you tomorrow
And who knows what live things
Will rise from these abysses
With whole universes

These are prophets ascending
Like blue hills in the distance
They will know precisions
As thinkers think they know
And will carry us everywhere

The great force is desire
And come let me kiss your forehead
O weightless as a flame
All whose suffering you bear
All whose ardor all whose blaze

The time is coming we shall study
All that it means to suffer
It will not be courage
Nor even renunciation
Nor all we have power to do

We shall search in man himself
More than has ever been sought there
We shall scrutinize his will
And what power may spring from it
With no machines no instruments

Even the helpful waver
Mingling themselves with us
Since the days that overtake us
Nothing begins nothing ends
Look at the ring on your finger

Time of deserts of crossroads
Time of places and of hills
I come to take strolls here
Where a talisman plays its part
Dead and more subtle than life

I have at last detached myself
From all natural things
I may die but I may not sin
And what has never been touched
I have touched it I have felt it

Another time I was begging
They gave me only a flame
That even burned my lips
And I couldn't say thank-you
Inextinguishable torch

Where are you O my friend
Who entered yourself so well
That only a well remained
Into which I threw myself
Down to the colorless depths

And I hear my steps return
Along the paths that no one
Has traveled I hear my steps
All day they go by there
Slow or swift they come or go

Winter you grower of beards
It snows and I am unhappy
I have crossed the splendid sky
Where life is a music
The earth is too white for my eyes

Accustom yourself as I have
To these marvels I announce
To goodness that will rule
To the suffering I endure
And you shall know the future

It is of suffering and goodness
That beauty will be made
More perfect than the beauty
That came from proportions
It snows and I burn and I tremble

Now I am at my table
I write what I have felt
And what I have sung up there
A slender tree balancing
The wind where the hair blows away

A top hat is upon
A table weighted with fruit
The gloves lie near an apple
A lady cranes her neck
By a gentleman who swallows himself

The ball revolves in the depths of time
I have killed the handsome orchestra leader
And I peel for my friends
The orange whose flavor is
A marvelous fireworks

All are dead the head waiter
Pours them unreal champagne
That foams like a snail
Or like a poet's brain
While a rose was singing

The slave holds a bare sword
Similar to springs and rivers
And each time that it falls
A world is disembowelled
From which new worlds are born

The chauffeur steps on the gas
And each time on the road
He blows his horn at a corner
There appears on the horizon
A still virgin universe

And the third is the lady
She goes up in the elevator
She goes up goes up always
And the light unfurls
And these clarities transform her

But these are little secrets
There are others more profound
That will soon unveil themselves
And divide you into a hundred
Pieces each an original thought

But weep weep and weep again
And whether the moon is full
Or whether it's only a crescent
Ah weep weep and weep again
We have laughed so much in the sun

Golden arms sustain life
Enter the gilded secret
It is all but a rapid flame
That bears the adorable rose
From which rises an exquisite perfume

from the French of Guillaume Apollinaire

1946

THE MALLEABILITY OF SORROW

how lovely the russian lady is
and listen to what she says:

I'm just an ordinary lady
no lady of the russian court

I've long been troubled by insomnia
but luckily all that's past

my favorite food is snails
my favorite man a sailor

nights I love to look up at the stars
and luckily we still die at last

when the whole world was one big bed
I took to it and stayed

how lovely the russian lady is
and listen to what she says.

from the Dutch of Hans Lodeizen

1970

FOR MY FATHER

o father we've been together
in the slow train without flowers
which pulls the night off and on like a
glove, we've been together
father when the darkness slammed us shut.

where are you now out for a ride
in the gay breeze of a green coupé
or didn't the day leave her glove
on a table to which twilight and
sweet recovery are bound to come.

my lips my tender lips composed

16 July 1950

from the Dutch of Hans Lodeizen

1970

THE WATER

in the pale pink sky
and in the immense quiet
he heard a voice
a gentle voice of
yellow reed that called to him
in the pale pink sky
called to him
and in the immense quiet

there stood a man
on the far side of the water
who waved to him
in the pale pink sky
a man among the yellow reeds

he waited a long time
and did not answer
the gentle voice
of yellow reed that called to him
in the pale pink sky
and in the immense quiet

he did not answer
and waited

from the Dutch of Hans Lodeizen

1970

SECOND ROSE MOTIF

to Mário de Andrade

However much I praise, you do not listen,
although in form and mother-of-pearl you could be
the uttering shell, the ear whose music lesson
engraves the inmost spirals of the sea.

I place you in crystal, in the mirror's prison
past all undertone of well or grotto . . .
Pure absence, blind incomprehension
offered to the wasp and to the bee

as to your acolyte, O deaf and mute
and blind and beautiful and interminable rose
who into time, attar and verse transmute

yourself now beyond earth or star arisen
to glisten from my dream, of your own beauty
insensible because you do not listen . . .

from the Portuguese of Cecília Meireles

1972

VIGIL

As the companion is dead,
so we must all together die
somewhat.

Shed for him who lost his life,
our tears are worth
nothing.

Love for him, within this grief,
is a faint sigh lost in a vast
forest.

Faith in him, the lost
companion—what but that
is left?

To die ourselves somewhat
through him we see today
quite dead.

from the Portuguese of Cecília Meireles

1972

BALLAD OF THE TEN CASINO DANCERS

Ten dancers glide
across a mirror floor.
They have thin gilt plaques on Egyptian bodies,
fingertips reddened, blue lids painted,
lift white veils naively scented,
bend yellow knees.

The ten dancers go
voiceless among customers,
hands above knives, teeth above roses,
little lamps befuddled by cigars.
Between the music and the movement flows
depravity, a flight of silken stairs.

The dancers now advance
like ten lost grasshoppers,
advance, recoil, avoiding glances
in the close room, and plucking at the din.
They are so naked, you imagine
them clothed in the stuff of tears.

The ten dancers screen
their pupils under great green lashes.
Death passes tranquil as a belt around
their phosphorescent waists.
As who should bear a child to the ground
each bears her flesh that moves and scintillates.

Fat men watch in massive tedium
those cold, cold dancers,
pitiful serpents without appetite
who are children by daylight.
Ten anemic angels made of hollows,
melancholy embalms them.

Ten mummies in a band,
back and forth go the tired dancers.
Branch whose fragrant blossoms bend
blue, green, gold, white.
Ten mothers would weep at the sight
of those dancers hand in hand.

from the Portuguese of Cecília Meireles

1972

THE DEAD HORSE

I saw the early morning mist
make silver passes, shift
densities of opal
within sleep's portico.

On the frontier, a dead horse.

Crystal grains were rolling down
his lustrous flank, and the breeze
twisted his mane in a littlest,
lightest arabesque, sorry adornment

—and his tail stirred, the dead horse.

Still the stars were shining,
and that day's flowers, sad to say,
had not yet come to light
—but his body was a plot,

garden of lilies, the dead horse.

Many a traveler took note
of fluid music, the dewfall
of big emerald flies
arriving in a noisy gush.

He was listing sorely, the dead horse.

And some live horses could be seen
slender and tall as ships,
galloping through the keen air
in profile, joyously dreaming.

White and green the dead horse

in the enormous field without recourse
—and slowly the world between

his eyelashes revolved, all blurred
as in red mirror moons.

Sun shone on the teeth of the dead horse.

But everybody was in a frantic rush
and could not feel how earth
kept searching league upon league
for the nimble, the immense, the ethereal breath
which had escaped that skeleton.

O heavy breast of the dead horse!

from the Portuguese of Cecília Meireles

1972

PYRARGYRITE METAL, 9

The piano tuner spoke to me, that tenderest
attender to each note
who looking over sharp and flat
hears and glimpses something more remote.
And his ears make no mistake,
nor do his hands that in each chord awake
those sounds delighted to keep house together.

"Disinterested is my interest:
I don't confuse music and instrument, mere
piano tuner that I am,
calligrapher of that superhuman speech
which lifts me as a guest to its high sphere.
Oh! what new Physics waits up there to teach
other matters to another ear . . ."

from the Portuguese of Cecília Meireles

1972

THE HOUSE OF THE CUSTOMS MEN

You do not remember the house of the customs men
above the cliff-face on a lurching rise:
desolate, it awaits you since the evening when
your thoughts swarmed in,
there restlessly to pause.

For years the libeccio has lashed the old walls
and the sound of your laughter is no longer gay:
the compass spins haphazard, the dice-score
adds up no longer. You do not remember;
another time distracts your memory;
a strand is drawn back into the skein.

I still have hold of an end; but the house recedes
and high upon the roof the weathercock
smokeblacked keeps revolving mercilessly.
I have hold of an end; but you remain alone
nor here do you breathe in the dark.

O fleeing horizon, where but rarely shine
lights of the tanker! Is the passage here?
(Breakers still spring against the plunging cliff . . .)
You do not remember the house of this evening of mine.
And I do not know who goes and who remains.

with Ben Johnson, from the Italian of Eugenio Montale

1952

THE EEL

The eel, siren
of cold seas who leaves the Baltic
to come to our waters,
our estuaries, rivers
whose depths she swims, under the adverse flood,
from branch to branch, then
from vein to tapering vein,
ever more inward, ever more into the heart
of rock, filtering
through runnels of mud until one day
a light, darted from the chestnut trees,
kindles a flashing in pits of stagnant water,
in ditches binding
cliffs of the Apennines to Romagna;
the eel, torch, whip,
arrow of Love on earth
whom only our gullies or the parched
Pyrenean brooks lead back
to the paradise of her spawning;
the green soul seeking
life where only
drought gnaws, and desolation,
the spark saying
all begins when all seems
to burn and blacken, an interred bole,
the tiny iris, twin
of the one you mount in the midst of your eyelashes
and make glisten untouched among the human
children, sunk in your slime, can you not
think her a sister?

with Ben Johnson, from the Italian of Eugenio Montale

1953

NEW STANZAS

Now that the last shreds of tobacco
die at your gesture in the crystal bowl,
to the ceiling slowly
rises a spiral of smoke
which the chess knights and chess bishops
regard bemused; which new rings follow,
more mobile than those
upon your fingers.

The mirage, that in the sky released
towers and bridges, disappeared
at the first puff; the unseen window
opens and the smoke tosses. Down below
another swarming: a horde
of men who do not know this incense of yours,
on the chessboard whose meaning you
alone compose.

My doubt was once that you perhaps ignored
yourself the game that on the board
evolves and now is storm cloud at your doors.
Death's frenzy (for you inciting
the god of chance, when he helps) subsides at no
small cost, if small be the flame in your gaze,
but, past the close-meshed curtains, asks
a further blaze.

Today I know what you want; la Martinella
tolls faintly and frightens
the ivory figures in a spectral
snowfield light. But he resists and is

rewarded for the lonely vigil
who can with you, to this burning glass
that blinds the pawns, oppose
your eyes of steel.

with Ben Johnson, from the Italian of Eugenio Montale

1956

CAFÉ AT RAPALLO

from "Poems for Camillo Sbarbaro"

Christmas in the tepidarium,
gleaming, masked by fumes
rising from cups, veiled trembling
of lights beyond the closed
panes, profiles of women
in the dusk rayed through by gems
and whispering silks . . .
                    They are come
to these your native beaches,
the new Sirens! And you are wanted here,
Camillo, friend, chronicler
of shudderings and desires.

We hear great fanfare in the street.

Out there has gone by
the unutterable music
of tin horns and of children's cymbals.
This innocent music has gone by.

A gnomish world went with it:
clatter of mules and carts,
a bleating of papier-mâché
rams, and a glinting
of sabers sheeted in tinfoil.
By went the Generals
in their cardboard hats,
brandishing spears of nougat;
and then the simple soldiers
with tapers and lanterns
and the little rattles shaken
to produce the tritest of sounds,
tenuous stream that enchants
the doubting mind
(marveling to my ears).
The crowd went by with the din

794

of a stampeding herd
that nearby thunder routs.
And pastures welcome them
such as for us no more are green.

with Irma Brandeis, from the Italian of Eugenio Montale

1962

IN THE GREENHOUSE

A pattering of moles
filled up the lemon trees,
in a rosary of cautious drops
the scythe was glittering.

Upon quinces ignited
a point, a ladybug; the pony
was heard to rear under the curry-comb
—then dreaming overcame.

Ravished, all air, I was permeated
by you, your form became my own
hidden breathing, your
face melted into mine, and the obscure

idea of God descended
upon the few living, among
celestial soundings and infant drummings
and hanging spheres of lightnings,

upon me, and you, and the lemon trees . . .

from the Italian of Eugenio Montale

1962

IN THE PARK

In the magnolia's ever
stricter shade, at one
puff from a blowgun
the dart grazes me and is gone.

It was like a leaf let fall
by the poplar a gust of wind
uncolors—perhaps a hand
roving through green from afar.

A laughter not my own
pierces through hoary branches
into my breast, a thrill
shakes me, stabs my veins,

and I laugh with you on the warped
wheel of shade, I stretch out
discharged of myself on the sharp
protruding roots, and needle

your face with bits of straw . . .

from the Italian of Eugenio Montale

1962

THE SHADOW OF THE MAGNOLIA

The shadow of the Japanese magnolia
thins out now that its purple buds
have fallen. At the top intermittently
a cigale vibrates. It is no longer
the time of the choir in unison, Sunflower,
the time of the unlimited godhead
whose faithful it devours that it may feed them.
It was easier to use oneself up, to die
at the first beating of wings, at the first encounter
with the enemy; that was child's play. Henceforth
begins the harder path: but not you, eaten
by sun, and rooted, and withal delicate
thrush soaring high above the cold
wharves of your river—not you, fragile
fugitive to whom zenith nadir cancer
capricorn remains indistinct
because the war was within you and within
whoso adores upon you the wounds of your Spouse,
flinch in the shivering frost . . . The others
retreat and shrivel. The file that subtly
engraves will be silenced, the empty husk
of the singer will soon be powdered
glass underfoot, the shade is livid—
it is autumn, it is winter, it is the beyond
that draws you and into which I throw myself, a mullet's
leap into dryness under the new moon.
                                        Goodbye.

from the Italian of Eugenio Montale

1962

THE BLACKCOCK

Where you beat downward after the brief gunshot
(your voice boils up again, redblack
slowburning stew of heaven and earth)
I too repair, I too burn in the pit.

The sob cries help. Sweeter it was
to live than to founder in the muck,
easier to scatter oneself in the wind
than here in slime, encrusted over flame.

I feel in my breast your wound, beneath
a clot of wing; my heavy flight
attempts a wall and what is left of us?
Only some feathers upon the frosted ilex.

Tussle of nests, O loves, nests of eggs, all
marbled, divine! And now the gem
of the perennials sparkles like the grub
in darkness; Jove is underground.

from the Italian of Eugenio Montale

1962

THE AUTHOR IN EXILE TO HIS PUBLISHER IN PRISON

Dear Theodore,
    Going through some old papers
which have just reached me from our native land,
I found a contract we both signed back then
when you were still a publisher, and I a writer.
Well, "the said agreement stipulates"
I owe you one per cent "in the event
of foreign sales." The book sold, Theodore.
Foreigners, ever since the dictatorship,
have taken enormous interest in whatever
we tell them about the good old days before it.
But now, that money, where can I send it?
Letters are sent back stamped UNKNOWN from there.
They wouldn't let you receive so much as a box
of food and clothing. And I have been upset
because you hadn't, not until this debt,
been on my mind at all. So tell me, what
shall I do about it? Put it in a bank
in your name for you to collect as soon as
they let you out? Or try to have some third
person take it to your family?
I know so well, I can see that shrug of your shoulder
where once you caught a chill—as if to say,
"Stop worrying, just drink it up to my health."
How are you, Theodore? How are you feeling?
I remember noons at the bookstore—now, I hear,
A "House of Italian Imports." Well. Ah well.
All must start afresh from the beginning.
Obviously. And will start. Yes. As for
that one per cent, I write you about it only
because, as the saying goes, careful accounts
make good friends.

from the Greek of Vassilis Vassilikos

1970

THE AFTERNOON SUN

This room, how well I know it. Now
they're renting it, it and the one next door,
as offices. The whole house has been taken
over by agents, businessmen, concerns.

Ah but this one room, how familiar.

Here by the door was the couch. In front of that,
a Turkish carpet on the floor.
The shelf then, with two yellow vases. On the right—
no, opposite—a wardrobe with a mirror.
At the center the table where he wrote,
and the three big wicker chairs.
There by the window stood the bed
where we made love so many times.

Poor things, they must be somewhere to this day.

There by the window stood the bed: across it
the afternoon sun used to reach halfway.

. . . We'd said goodbye one afternoon at four,
for a week only. But alas,
that week was to go on forevermore.

from the Greek of C. P. Cavafy

1987

ON AN ITALIAN SHORE

The son of Menedoros,   Kimos, a Greek-Italian,
fritters his life away   in the pursuit of pleasure,
according to the common   practice in Magna Graecia
among the rich, unruly   young men of today.

Today, however, wholly   counter to his nature,
he's lost in thought, dejected.   There on the shores he sees
with bitter melancholy   ship upon ship that slowly
disgorges crates of booty   from the Peloponnese.

Greek booty. Spoils of Corinth.

Today don't be surprised   if it's unsuitable,
indeed impossible,   for the Italicized
young man to dream of giving   himself to pleasure fully.

from the Greek of C. P. Cavafy

1987

DAYS OF 1908

That year he found himself without a job.
Accordingly he lived by playing cards
and backgammon, and the occasional loan.

A position had been offered in a small
stationer's, at three pounds a month. But he
turned it down unhesitatingly.
It wouldn't do. That was no wage at all
for a sufficiently literate young man of twenty-five.

Two or three shillings a day, won hit or miss—
what could cards and backgammon earn the boy
at *his* kind of working class café,
however quick his play, however slow his picked
opponents? Worst of all, though, were the loans—
rarely a whole crown, usually half;
sometimes he had to settle for a shilling.

But sometimes for a week or more, set free
from the ghastliness of staying up all night,
he'd cool off with a swim, by morning light.

His clothes by then were in a dreadful state.
He had the one same suit to wear, the one
of much discolored cinnamon.

Ah days of summer, days of nineteen-eight,
excluded from your vision, tastefully,
was that cinnamon-discolored suit.

Your vision preserved him in the very act of
casting it off, throwing it all behind him,

the unfit clothes, the mended underclothing.
Naked he stood, impeccably fair, a marvel—
his hair uncombed, uplifted, his limbs tanned lightly
from those mornings naked at the baths, and at the seaside.

from the Greek of C. P. Cavafy

1987

PREVIOUSLY UNCOLLECTED POEMS

BEGINNER'S GREEK

To one
  Who smells the sun,
    Eyes shut, and tastes that rain is sweet;
Who hears
  Music, but fears
    Its presence in empty gardens; or, discreet,
Only observes
  The nerves
    And fibers of a painting—shade, technique;
What is
  Beyond analysis
    Is perilous: we must not wish to seek
And cry
  "This is what I
    Love, what I cherish!" Instead, be wary of such
Intensity
  That we
    May never be hurt or happy or anything too much.

1946

How rich in opportunity! Part of a wall
Gave back a hollow sound. Forthwith, intrigued,
The Contessina knew her mind, consulted
No one. A door! Annunziata darkly
Swept up after the workmen and withdrew.
Lost in thought, her mistress was already
Rehearsing what to say in thirty years:
"Only after our marriage did I begin
To fear your father"—but she broke off
And went with a candle down the dank stair
Leading she knew not where. What sweet alarms
Had gone unfelt for lack of this provocative
Circumstance! There gathered about her brow
Tenuous webs of not quite human weaving.
What though the passage led but to the chapel?
Might not her adventure, rightly told, set him
To brooding on a crime? might she not still
Reproachfully die in childbirth, or be undone
By the majordomo who had held his tongue?
Infant alternatives to the workaday,
These musings led her on, which ever after
(The door by that time sealed afresh in fright)
Will seek her out, handsome, unscrupulous,
Quick to extort costly precautions, turn
Her forelock white, a matron suddenly—
Become, in short, a life, a trodden path.
Dazzle of choice, anon there shall be none:
The candle gutters at a breath, her own.
Put down the book unread. The tale is done.

1957

AT MAMALLAPURAM

The site relives its tender monotone
In the begging children's bodies, thin and dark.
They even sleep here, watched over by a far dog's bark
Setting its faint pockmark onto the stone

Up out of which, every morning, small temples have grown
Like organs, those that nourish or beget,
At the onset of a pubescence yet
More longed-for and more alien than our own.

1958

Yoo-hoo! This way, dear reader, I so hoped
You'd find us. We have neither *Sward* nor *Bowers*
Nor imaginary *Gardons,* yet a peasant *Plath*
*Wilbur*ing you through *Ciardi* perennials of many
Hughes to our—hardly a *Villa,* more a *Warren.*
For fine old *Holmes* you'll have to look elsewhere.
The unfrocked *Bishop* next door used to call
Our *Bogan*villea'd turrets "frozen music's
Swensong"—which was *Garrigue* to me, *Kumin.*
Tsk! Watch your head. Here in the simple *Hall*
Is an engraving of the *Bly*nded *Simpson,*
Next to a holograph page of "*Shapiro* Lunaire."
Reflected in the mirror's a door marked
T. ELIOT—that's where we got our training.
You've not *Eaton?* Can you *Sitwell* in this *Booth?*
We've nothing out of the *Auden*ary—no *Wiener*s, no *Koch.*
One *Combs* the shops for a *Pound* of *Hamburger*
In a paper *Bagg.* Have some, it's on the *Howes.*
Now for our tête-à-*Tate.* Yes, we're all here.
Tomlinson? Ginsberg? Meredith? Great *Scott,*
How names like that *Kinsella* line beats me.
Why, any *Lehmann* will tell you—Beg your pardon?
Miles is as good as *Amis?* Ha, that's *Rich!*
Oops! Butterfingers! Should have tucked in a *Dickey*
Or two. Come upstairs while I change. This view
Is of the *Moore* where only *Heath-Stubbs* grow.
It's full of *Graves.* Here, *Raine* or shine, the *Sexton*
Succumbs to *Skully Fitts.* Here, *Larkin*spired,
Hard by an upturned *Baro*—no, a *Wain*
(Where are you, *Wagoner? Abs*ent? There's no *Justice!*)—
Dwell the *Moss*-gatherer and the *Berryman,*
That shallow, *Merrill*y chattering stream, where bends
The unthinking *Reid* and bobs the *Corke,* flows seaward.
Yon far out speck will be the *Hollander* sailing

Under a curse . . . What, leaving? Not so soon!
Do stay. Don't jump the *Gunn*. We'll *Lowell* about
And—You smell something *Brinnin*? Well, bye-bye.
Please *Wright*—I'll just lie down with a wet *Pack*.

1963

TWO DOUBLE DACTYLS

1 / ABOVE ALL THAT?

Higgledy-piggledy
Mary of Magdala
Said to the dolorous
Mother of God:

"Parthenogenesis
I for one left to the
Simple amoeba or
Gasteropod."

2 / NEO-CLASSIC

Higgledy-piggledy
Jacqueline Kennedy
Went back to Hydra and
Found it a mess—

Neon lights, discotheques . . .
"Landlord, what's *hap*pening?"
"'Ανθρωπιστήκαμε*
Go home, U.S."

---

*Or, roughly, "We have become human beings!"

MOUTHPIECE

in memoriam Marius Bewley

Might and must now cast upon the hearth,
Great mouldy figurehead, slow to ignite,

Also the mummy of a membrane-red bouquet
Cut "to straw thy way" in ages past,

Offsprings of dew and dust, of will and wilt,
Catching their deaths where the flue rages.

Set among coals to roast the atoms' apple.
Relatives, at its fat hiss of pain,

Wince on the live branch: who next?
Listen. From far within, our princess phone,

She of blue curves ajangle in darkness,
Of disembodied pangs and sparks of pitch

Bone-tingling jars the nerveless sperm
Whale's tooth etched with pennants and dead sails

At her side awake. Seaward in perfect time
Her wreaths float zeroed on moonset.

Between them silence and beneath them threat?
Tidings? Don't ask. Don't answer. Lines grow taut,

Up looms the spectral kinship after blood,
Harpoon glissando, absolute

On which in a livelier vein once bud from sleet
She plucked, and fruit from fire. Statements to burn

Rake us, heart's ash. The oracle forever
About to be struck dumb, or repossessed,

A not till then surrendered-to
Friend or fiend keeps shawling with phenomenal

Red-blue infringements his own fiat calling
Halt to wave, to flame, that foam-lipped series,

This flickering tongue, grain of the wooden Ceres
Translated by it, blind with salt.

1973

ACROSTIC

Take first some pleasure in the maker's

own. Let who he was bring back the original gifts
of light &

measure inexhaustible. Only then let the fellow-
ship of all shapes, from toy to omen, be deduced
and (by one who knew better) alerted.

Is this a truth? Was that? No longer brook, pueblo,
handclasp, percussion riff, or even the trail, on
snow on dirt, of a now bleached, impromptu rainbow
torn-up & scattered so as to return unharmed from
the enchantment, these are constructions resolved
that

no other be put upon them. Bearing his plus sign,
they have come far enough past gusto & misgivings
alike to share in that austere

gaudiness of objects used by the gods. A

language one grew radiant

erasing.

1974

FIVE INSCRIPTIONS

1 / WITH A GREEK COIN (HEADS, ATHENA IN PROFILE;
   TAILS, HER OWL) FOR A SILVER ANNIVERSARY

The face of love is very old
And one with wisdom's wingèd shape.
Mary and Charles, this coin keep
Until it turns to gold.

2 / COPIED ONTO THE THING ITSELF

Although the gingko's older far
   Than most trees here below
      This leaf is Art
         Nouveau.

3 / IN A NOTEBOOK FROM DELPHI

Apollo's whim
Consulted as to Stephen
Bespoke a volume even
Slimmer than him.

4 / ON A PHOTOGRAPH OF THE AUTHOR PRESENTED TO
   HIS FORMER STUDENT AFTER A STAY IN GREECE

New wrinkles I daresay
From many a summer day
One more Hellenophile
Made the Old Master smile.

5 / WITH A FOUNTAIN PEN

Together half in love and half in pain
Missing the point, we dipped
Our pens—but who can read such flowing script?
Where hearts are humbled, words are vain.

1974

FORT LAUDERDALE

Listless old women,
Fiber faces the thin milk
Long ago drained from—

Sparkle of their engagement
Rings in April sun.

≈

On the horizon
One toy tanker pitches south
Playing hide and seek.

Broad as a fan, each rust-pocked
Leaf of the sea-grape.

≈

Japonaiserie!
—Yet these dwarf forms have made for
A fair, calm crossing:

Self-effacement on both sides
Of the looking-glass.

1976

EN ROUTE

The needle on the gauge
I noticed suddenly
Had been pointing all this time at E.
Traffic-light foliage
Was turning yellow, red—
The whole world grinding to a stop? Instead

It all kept whizzing past
At 60, uphill, down,
Church spire, bleak reservoir, town after town,
If anything too fast
To clock in miles per hour.
Tank dry, this eerie, by now selfless power

Was bearing me beyond
The windblown kids with signs
Upheld in hope: New Haven, Providence . . .
Their mouths worked. But a wand
Had grazed me. On I drove
Under the curse or blessing of no love.

1977

HER CRAFT

Elizabeth Bishop—swan boat or
Amazon steamer? Neither: a Dream Boat.
Among topheavy wrecks, she stays afloat.
Mine's this white hanky waving from the shore
—In lieu of the requested "essay." (Faute
De pire, if I may say so. Less is more.)

29.vii.77

THE SUPPLIANT

Tiny, half-blind life
Crouched by the marble stoop,
A hand huge and impulsive
Gathers you up

Past fear into a space
Peopled with dark woods,
Hushed airs, and high transparent
Rectitudes:

Odor of human law,
Its kissing sounds, its crumb
Of cheddar on a chair . . .
Study. Become.

(A phone call to Welfare
To distance you and us,
All, from the crushed paw
And eye-slit pus,

Then day will flame and swerve
About a moving car
This one time. You'll be far
Too gone to care.)

Ensconced upstreet, the sphinx
Of slacker household gods,
Great-great-grandmother blinks—
Against all odds

Still going strong, while you just
Blur into print, who for
That least of mercies came
To the right door.

1981

GARONCE

Think small. My scene no sooner lit
Than animation flows
Simply from candy-apple cheek
And bodkin nose.

The operator's hand, you see,
That wears me like a glove
Makes me lurch upright, arms outspread,
Inviting love

—*But feeling it?* A headshake. *Ah,*
Too much to ask? A nod.
Both of us moved in one breath by
The hidden god.

1981

EPITHALAMIUM

Look! in full view, the woman's hands at his throat—
Embracing? strangling him?—the young man rocks
Forward, back, too glazed to struggle, wax
In those quick hands, a smile on his lips, remote,

For of course he's only a dummy. She's knotting the tie.
Manhattan this morning is full of other such lovers
Behind glass overlaid with clouds and gliding towers,
Trucks of the garment district, passers-by.

1981

SNAPSHOT OF ADAM

By flash in sunshine "to reduce contrast"
He grins back from the green deck chair,
Stripped, easy at last, bush tangle rhyming
With beard and windblown hair;
Coke sweating, forearm tanned to oak,
Scar's lightning hid by flat milk-blaze of belly
—But all grown, in the sliding glass
Beyond him, unsubstantial. Here I dwell,

Finger on shutter, amid my clay
Or marble ghosts; treetops in silhouette;
And day, his day, its vivid shining stuff
Negated to matte slate
A riddle's chalked on: Name the threat
Posed never long or nakedly enough.

1982

SIESTAS OF AN ARCHITECT

Those afternoons you'd wake
No longer in your "working girl's
Room-and-a-half economy flat"
But in a storied tower of stone, with views.

Here shone a mirror, there a lake;
There burned autumn, here the ingle-nook.
Which was inside, which out?—
Not that you had to choose.

Above would be the starswept parapet
A headless Presence roamed by rote;
Below, steam-rancid, smoke-
Dimmed groinings, cauldron clang and mastiff glare;

And below that, a sort
Of unfloored cellar, or vast oubliette
—Drop a pebble? No report . . .
It is still falling through black air.

1982

HUBBELL PIERCE (1925-1980)

Well and good to take the fortune, Life,
And spend it all. Such prodigality
Meant backing, though, by deep reserves. Too often
Ego-inflation heralded collapse
Of Type; one's tyrant features hadn't found
Proper metal on which to stamp themselves.
You, by contrast, did no better—did,
Better yet, no worse—than simply *be*
The Tailored Man too spruce to toil or spin,
Or Minstrel, or the Jester whose calling allows him
Acerb, outrageous flashes; at the end
(His standard brightening as day drew in)
To be the upright, stricken Chevalier.
Tokens of idiom and decoration,
Those little pillows worked for friends, my dear,
Your paper labels, Social Register,
H of diamond, smoky blues of Cole
—Your faith transformed these things. So that a whole
World one might otherwise have written off,
Its cults and creeds, as a poor counterfeit
Through you took on resonance, magic, wit
And while you sang, rang true. It's what
The fortunately not quite mortal do.
Those features we shall see again (we're told,
"But who knows where or when?") had come to rest
In your odd moments upon gold, pure gold.

1982

ANOTHER POSTSCRIPT

Like someone blind from infancy
Whose eyesight is restored
—Quickly, the mirror! (Long pause.) Lord,
That old man, who is he?

Now to uncrumple and spell out a face
Barely foreknown
In lines you'll shrink to call your own,
They are so worn by time and lit by grace.

1982

Here in SoHo
The tabletop sticks.
We spread Vallejo
On pumpernickel,
Suck the ferocious
Char from chopsticks.
Tonight I've stewed a
Fat, skinned Trakl,
Mike's made some Ritsos—
Tuck in! We'll guzzle
Red Neruda
And stub our roaches
Of home-grown ghazal
Out in the meat sauce.

1982

TO A POCKET CALCULATOR

Quiz kid,
Behavior's midget
Mime or mirror,
Push-button cogitation sets
You racing, brow clear, up to the ninth digit,
A dawn-tipped pyramid—
At which point enter E for ERROR:
The tabula "forgets"
(But we know, don't we, what *that* means?)
In cool gray fog its orgiastic genes
And all the naughty things they did.

Joking
(Your patron's abysses
Bore you? Embarrass?)
Aside, aren't you that periodic peon
Translated from his peaks by Mrs.
X or Count Y to the choking
Lianas of a Paris—
Cocteau, cocaine, the Natansons, the neon—
Mad, till he foundered in the West,
For "l'impassivité sauvage, funeste"
With which he wore his smoking?

Proud in-
nocent, beware.
I, too, possess
A magic memory. Can in a decade's
Flash extract the square
Root of whatever rapture or chagrin.
Atop a pyramid no less
Dense than yours with figures light pervades,
Can by this downward thumb
Undo our frail continuum
And lift its heart out, live but paper-thin.

1983

THE ILLUSTRATIONS

Slide upon slide,
Transparencies of Nile and Sphinx,
Dragoman, hieroglyph,
Dark sunset golds, hot pinks
Over old Dr. Bean's white shirtfront glide
Each then, as if

Through gorges worn
Smooth by his voice and theme,
Is swept, borne backwards, up tonight's
Eerily narrowed, smoky-crystal stream.
Back, sigh the date palms, mourn
The circling kites,

Back!—as the hole
Drilled in darkness, radiant nil
Of the projector's brow,
Calls each in turn, from banks that overspill,
Back to the Source. The soul
Will keep her vow.

1984

PIPE DREAM

Perfectly still. Yet smoke,
Ionic-columnar,
Rises from meerschaum just so far
Before imploding to baroque

Cumuli. Such behavior
Of the idyllic—state or weather—
Is a kind of dubious feather
In all our caps that, waverier

When tyrants reminisce and scribes orate,
Tickles a Chaos brought
Simply to heel in the garden, not
Shown the gate.

1985

GADFLY TRIOLETS

Three packs a day
Simply won't do.
I mean to say,
Three-packs-a-day
Is both outré
And bad for you
Three packs a day
Simply won't *do*.

That airless room
Reeking of smoke:
It's like a tomb,
That airless room.
Come on, exhume
Yourself, old soak!
That airless room
Reeking of smoke . . .

You are life's clear-
Eyed, smiling rhyme.
Why rage? why fear?
You *are*. Life's clear.
I need you here
To last my time.
You are life's clear-
Eyed, smiling rhyme.

1985

834

PHILIP LARKIN (1922-1985)

He's gone somewhere
But left his writing,
Plain and inviting
As a Windsor chair.

The sitters? Every sort.
Each struck that artless pose
We face our maker in. God knows
The likeness hurt.

His signature's
Worm-drill and gleam of cherry
—Vacant now? Unwary
Reader, all yours.

1986

HERE TODAY

Looking up from my craft,
I recognized nothing.
Sun was about to set, it shone through my clothing.
From the bank a bird laughed,

The death-watch beetle chirred.
Wherever root
And vine strung their vast zither underfoot
Could now be heard

The myriad priesthood
Of the tree toad,
Minutely ceremonial in woad,
Chanting. I understood

Voice after voice to utter
My welcome to a place
Entirely strange, strange as the staring face
In the wrinkling water.

It had to be very far
From where I started,
Paddling out, that earliest, faint-hearted
Morning, all mist and star,

Afraid, if I was afraid,
Of having nowhere to go—
Had there been talk of a landing, a bungalow
Set in a glade?—

And hardly daring to feel
How fine the going was,
Brown-skinned current throbbing lover-wise
Under my keel.

And sleeping through noontime
When the head's shadow

Might have seen through its calm, flame-dusty halo
To beds of slime

—Wake up! The condor,
Wings wide,
Scything a golden rush on either side
—Listen! Thunder

Of the god drawn near,
On whose obsidian lip
Jungle and sky, tottering, shattering, slip
Off into sheer

Veils of breath—green fire
Caught in your prism,
Quetzal spiraling up out of the chasm,
Higher and higher—

    The End
           (of a life I may
Have lived once, or be going
To live, or be living still without my knowing,
Here, today.)

1986

DOMESTIC ARCHITECTURE

Honestly now! Another White House scandal—
Denied at every level. Can't they at least
Skip the sincerity? Nope (says the analyst),
That fair flag of the land'll

Flap long and loud from its pole. It's our democratic
Need to Come Clean, unfurling above the latest
Infrastructure framed by a mad elitist
To keep his realm secure and his facts hermetic

—As I well know. Glass-eyed or beheaded, dressed
In dust, forms exiled to the poem's attic
Wake at my passing candle.
Stick to the parlor, Reader, where it's brightest,

Though even here—! Foul drafts and dragging feet
Haunt this house once white as a blank sheet.

1987

IDEA

If when you're old and musing
Upon the whats and whys
Another one should flicker
Its last before your eyes,

No matter, they wear out too,
Those burning filaments,
Illumination's debris
Englobed still in a sense

Briefly too hot to handle,
Too dark a souvenir,
Then, for the deft unscrewing
Unless you now, my dear,

Feel for what it shone from,
This ribbed clay form each night
Hardens to iteration
Of nothing if not light.

1987

SONG

Gretchen wishes she weren't blonde.
Cleopatra long in tooth
Heaves a sigh for vanished youth.
Wally hates his choirboy ass.
Few of us *au fond* are fond
Of the likeness in the glass.

Odd how each adores to sit
Peering into the half-blind
Shallows of his/her own mind.
Vast reflections upside down
Leave us queasy? Not a bit:
Awed, and dreaming of renown.

1987

Before our day, what had the sawfish seen—
His own snout's toothy, prehistoric blade?
His own tank's sun and shade? . . .
Flat white lips of a ghost or libertine

Open and shut, as do the strenuous gills
Which even admit light. Bored in mid-swim,
He sees you—and a sunbeam fills
That frightful mouth. Now if I speak for him,

A fellow captive, lips that kissed and told
Declare me—well, almost—
Not of this world, transparently a ghost

Into whom still the bright shaft glides. One old
Disproven saw sinks out of mind:
Love's but a dream and only death is kind.

1987

PEELED WANDS

Peeled wands lead on the pedophile. Give me
Experience—and your limbs the prize.
Too scarred and seasoned for mere jeopardy
Ever now to fell them, trunk and thighs
Rampant among sheet lightning and the gruff
Thunderclap be our shelter. Having both
Outstripped the ax-women, enough
Uneasy glances backward! Nothing loath!
Roving past initial bliss and pain
Visited upon you, I have gone bare
Into the thicket of your kiss, and there
Licked from that sly old hermit tongue—
Life's bacon not yet cured when we were young—
Eternal oaths it swore with a salt-grain.

1988

NOVEMBER ODE

The blow has fallen, our dear dim local grocery
 been shut down by the State—not yet for good, though
  how, in whose wildest dreams, will it get
   its act together?

The son picked to succeed him never lived up to the
 seigneurial old man. Yet his clientele
  kept brightly toeing the line of least
   resistance, taking

with a grain of salt (Aisle 3) all talk of heavy drugs
 and light women, closing Republican eyes
  to dead mouse and decimated shelves,
   the padded statement;

nodding with vague good will to the taciturn widow
 upon her rare, black-shawled manifestations
  by the meat locker, or pausing the
   length of a joke with

the handsome, cock-eyed daughter (-in-law?) and her teenage
 sidekick—Zig-Zag cigarette-paper pirate
  freshly tattooed, indigo on bisque,
   upon his shoulder;

but failing to check a wave of perfect unconcern
 each time we stepped into sunlight. Alas for
  their compulsive *Havaniceday!* We
   had made other plans.

Small wonder the plate-glass windows one night were whited
 out as by frost (butcher's paper), and pumpkin
  faces promised REDECORATION!
   GRAND REOPENING!

or that during those weeks of grace no light from inside
    shone, no rumor escaped. Like an old servant,
        face to the wall, refusing comfort,
            the place rebuffed us.

The big day came and went. So did the customers in
    disbelief. I could have warned them. Why, only
        mornings before, a rip in wintry
            blankness let me peer,

peer like Thoreau, cheek to the skylight of his glaucous
    parlor, down at wall-eyed denizens by cold
        and apathy hypnotized. There my
            three were suspended:

the aproned boy, head raised as if checking an order,
    the young woman at her counter, the old one,
        shawl held tight, mute in the gloaming still—
            their living simply

switched off at the source by the electric company?
    Plainer than day was how, next summer, this prime
        square footage would be developed in
            the usual way.

Oh well, what don't we learn to live without? Our drugstore—
    gone forever. Likewise the rival grocer,
        the Syrian tailor, and the Greek
            who resoled our shoes.

Now, having watched their premises without exception
    change to antique shop or real estate office,
        and our neighbors into strangers charmed
            by what these offer,

we must ourselves go forth in hollow-eyed addiction
    to malls where all is maya, goblin produce,
        false-marble meats, tinned tunes, the powder
            promises of *Cheer*.

Victims of a force that in guises far more ghastly
elsewhere upon our planet squanders its fruits,
let us give thanks for what we've been spared,
and let what is lost

(says the adage) be for God. Varying eerily
from truth to truth, his voice—and never more than
when speaking American—sounds like
that of the people.

1988

NAVARINO

No sleepy harbor is a dream come true
More than when you pull away by sea.
If the cubistic chorus in whiteface,
Led by that lighthouse, blind seer of the rocks,
Predicts disaster, certain bygone ones,
However dire or petty, a Pasha's fleet
Sunk in the name of Freedom, or today's
Balcony-flung breakfast meat,
Pink floppy disk recoiled from by the schools,
Only make you row faster. Stroke by stroke,
Veiled in atmospheric Alzheimer's
Above the waterfront's retreat,
Rise forest, woodsman's hovel, hilltop castle—
Fairytale touches—till the scene, complete
At last without you, brightens. There
From under a blue neon O. T. E.
Appears a lone, white-shirted manikin
Programmed to clamber over rocks, to climb
The iron lighthouse ladder, reach the top,
Lift the clear visor of the lamp, ignite it
—How, you're not near enough to tell—
Then climb down, clamber off and disappear.
Dazzling, and he does it every day?
The very first beam seeks you, looks away
Too fast, back and away, away and back,
Despite yourselves attracted. The space between,
Moments ago a slack accordion,
Starts pumping tangos, sea-caves full of blood
The sun is slipping into: Quick! before
World transubstantiates into wordplay
(Ondine's Treacherous Empire? Oh, too easy!)
You've come about in the unsocial web
Oars chop to pitch and pearl, making for shore,
And gained in a dead heat with evening's height
The navel of this world: one satellite-
Transmitted, thrill-packed, 17″ ballgame

Deep in a yawning tavern. Round it the teenage
Blowtorch motorcade outside would be
Careening even now, had Matron not—
Frugally shining, ego on the wane—
Risen to cool it in your can of wine.

1988

STORM

ROCK: Control yourself! I've been shattered
       Blind and dumb—
       Three mortal days bespattered
       With odium!

WAVE: You're talking to *me*, who was shattered
       Each time anew!
       When have deep feelings mattered
       To the likes of you?

MOON: Nights I recall would come
       In which these sorry two
       Lay in a dream
       Of silver, stirring but to kiss and gleam.
       Ah, how that flattered
       My self-esteem . . .

1988

CHINESE POEM

In the course of many lives before this one,
I may have been born to influential parents
And been given a proper education. For all I know,
I too have languished as an army clerk,
Loved and been loved, wept on my friend's tomb,
Traveled, meditated, written verse . . .
Now, drunk by noon, I watch the dandelion
Turning to seed the weightless moon shines through.

1989

"... Or take TV, where relatively crude
Gradations of black and white come to express
The moral, or subjective, realm no less
Than that of appearances. If some days a mood
Of buzzing blankness overcomes the screen,
A 'snow' through which Zhivago plods unseen,
The viewer, thus alerted, seeks the flaw
In his own consciousness, and hardly blames
Dealer or Manufacturer—their claims
Look small as print in courts of Higher Law.
Delinquencies of image, to conclude,
Invite self-reexamination. Jude?"

"You hung up in old times, man. You forgets
All us kids got they fail-safe color sets."

1989

MORE BITS

1 / THE POEM AS CRUTCH

Be that as it may, there are some few I've hung
Within Your old clay temple, Mother Tongue,
Then strode forth whole and free
Until (the pain
Striking again)
I reached for a gnarled rhyme to steady me.

2 / WOMAN LEAVING SHOP

That was Clarissa Dalloway!
She's how old? Yet the high
Comedy of her face is a fresh lie
Made up three times a day.

3 / IN CARAVAGGIO'S STUDIO

The boy's lips parting, a ripe fruit,
Sleep took him. Morpheus with his loot.

4 / PEOPLE WILL TALK

Awesome. The nitty-gritty. Wannabes.
Pustules of idiom we itch to squeeze.
What can the Muse do for the common weal?
Make an appointment for a facial peel.

5 / APRIL IN ATHENS

The young Cycladic goddesses
Hug themselves, shivering
Against the cruel Aegean spring—
If only they had bodices.

6 / REST HOME

They've given up everything—affection, strife—
To feed their habit. Here they sit,
Scarred, infirm, consumed by it:
Addicts of life.

7 / LIFE IN THE MEZZOGIORNO

Silenzio? Solitudine? cried the family's
Neapolitan cook
On hearing the Signora needed these
In order to complete her book.
Nothing in life's more offensive to You Know Whom!
—Rolling her eyes at the plaster skies
And clattering out of the room.

8 / WORD MADE FLESH

Dronning. It's the Danish word for Queen.
A stroller near the Palace will have seen
Her driven past, in picture hat and poils,
Making that gesture only known to Royals,
A kind of . . . wave? "Young man,"—her smile is stunning—
"I'm farther out than you think, and not waving but dronning."

9 / HOW LONG?

The lawyer pursed his lips: "Well now, let's see . . ."
We shared a vision of Attornity.

1992

AFTER CAVAFY

Why is the Rising Sun aflutter from ten thousand flagpoles?
    Because the Japanese are coming today.
And why do our senators, those industrious termites,
Gaze off into space instead of forming a new subcommittee?
    Because the Japanese are coming today.
    Congress will soon be an item on their Diet.
What's gotten into the President, trading quips with reporters
As he bails out his Whitewater bubble bath? How will posterity
        judge him?
    Well, the Japanese who are coming today
    Have their own scandals. His we can forget.
Why does the waterfront swarm with clumsily bandaged apprentices,
And the garment district ring with the mirth of transvestites in
        whiteface?
    Because the Japanese are coming today,
    Bringing their sushi-bar legerdemain
    And female impersonators second to none.
But our artists and writers? Funny—somehow one had pictured
        them flocking
To greet the compatriots of Utamaro and Lady Murasaki.
    They won't be missed. The Japanese of today
    Want spicy space-pirate comics and Van Gogh.
Midnight already? Times Square is a semiologist's heaven:
Mitsubishi, Sony, Suntory, Toshiba, Kirin, Benihana . . .
But horrors! Great wings hide the moon. Are the Japanese passing
        us over,
As an in-depth update asserts, for the shores of Gimme Gucci?
    The sun has risen in Rome. By dark not a pair
    Of lizard loafers will be left unbought.
Leaving us where? With egg on our faces, or tofu. Those people
Were some sort of golden opportunity, but we blew it.

1994

MINOTAUR

A young one who'd have thought
dreaming in late light
before a portico
pinker than nougat
His father's terrible head
laid aside uncovers
an ink sketch by Cocteau
The earlobe's cunning nugget
Colors of Crete   Sun washing
black locks blood-red

Pale ankle firm as cactus
escaping from his cloak
dense with soft black spines
To see not quite a threat
to touch not quite a joke
A vital rivulet
pulsing along his throat
he looks up   Shafts of blue
fatally attract us
Drawn two by two

after him through the maze
we've come as tribute   Ten
old women ten old men
This youngster is expected
to feed on what we are
or were   Mind's meat heart's blood
all that we've seen and known
treasured up rejected
will now become his body
Devour my life each prays

Amazement   Golden beeline
for greenest dark   Strong fusion
of grape and cardamom

As for the "sacrifice"
one lightning-fleet contusion
sparklers of ice
farewell's euphoric hail
It must have been benign
if we lived through it   *Did* we
Depends who tells the tale

1994

ORANGES

His mother wore, as in a fairy tale,
A fragrant crown upon her snow-white veil.
   The photograph obsessed him. Didn't she know
What grievous crops such blossomings entail?

≈

There was that sweetness just beneath the skin,
A single night of frost undid: blood kin
   To acrimony; the boy's crush rebuffed;
Sour notes drawn from a solar violin.

≈

Abroad, at the Orangerie, he came
Upon Monet's great mirrorings aflame
   With water blues, sky purples, greens and pinks . . .
The past lending no color but a name.

≈

Followed those winters when the mercury dove
Past all endurance. What could simple Love
   Hope to accomplish? Yet each night he lit
His sorry smudge-pot in the shivering grove.

≈

Segment by segment, nonetheless a mind
Made up of taste and sunlight. May the blind
   Gods who drink its juice be satisfied,
Disposing gently of the empty rind.

≈

After Jim's funeral the marmalade
Deathmask tomcat Agent Orange stayed
   Far from the house. Time passed and, mourning done,
One bright dusk up he sauntered, undismayed.

1994

IN THE PINK

From under a duvet the pink of dunes
In first light tantalizing fragments peek,
Rosy alabaster flecked with buff:
Here a foot, there a forearm, a bent knee . . .
Their disposition so mysteriously
Right, we have no plans to trouble them
Just now. Aren't they the thermostats
That regulate the desert's warms and cools?

Armed, unamusable at the dune's crest
Our nightly Bedouin, his glance
A slit of glitter between cloak and cloud,
Stood guard, or seemed to. As the last star fades,
He mounts his camel; slowly both dissolve.
Tonight again? We have no words in common,
No way to question him, or thank—
Yet it was he who led us to the trove.

The finest, most absorbing piece thus far
Will be this lower half of a royal head
Sliced in two by a catastrophe
Lost in the mists of time. The upper half—
Eyes, forehead, serpent crown—may sooner or later
Come to light. Meanwhile notice the lips:
Work of such quality belongs
To the last great period of portraiture.

The chin rests on an incurved hand we took
At first for a second figure's—a suppliant?—
Clasping the narrow sisal "beard" required
For ritual. (Did he obtain his boon?)
This morning's theory, though, deems it the ruler's
Own knee bent, his own hand making bold
To approach its godhead, even that part
Deepest nearby in pink oblivion . . .

Wake up! It's May, it's daybreak in the City.
Already I've pulled some random selves together
Sufficiently for "us" to draft these lines
Which thus far, like the duvet, show
Stray pieces of only the Sandman's trick.
So, presto, off with that magician's cloth!
The complete sleeper stretches, blushes, yawns
A tear from either spring's lighthearted blue.

1994

RHAPSODY ON CZECH THEMES

for Allan Gurganus

I

A mauve madness has overrun Moravia—
"Mauve" used loosely to include lavender,
Fuchsia and puce and pansy-violet,
But even the oxymoron of *strict mauve*
Is everywhere. Those posted notices,
Purple on mauve—five or six crudely-printed
Words in Czech, like losing draws in Scrabble—
What do they spell? and whom to ask? Meanwhile,
Mauve workpants, mauve shopfronts, mauve sunglasses:
Accents vividly standing out against
The obvious ochers of the Hapsburg heritage.
Or is it an early symptom of one of those
Artistic movements (mauvement in this case)
Whose hyperactive brushwork swept the Flore?
Part of the Paris Mucha's manikins
Hoped sleepy Prague would wake as—statues on bridges,
Art Nouveau . . . as if appearances
Were everything. But aren't they? and doesn't thought
—Lend me your clippers, ghastly these long nails—
Make provisions when the real thing fails?
Why else booth upon booth of marionettes?—
Our childhood intimates, known then as now
Chiefly by how they dress and do their hair.
Why else Princess and Troubadour, Hermit and Crone
(Whose joints are stiff, like mine)? Why else entangle
Ourselves for life in the Seven Deadly Strings
Or the Seven Adorable ones?—same difference.
Why else yet one more spruce façade upon
The same old miseries? The baby's vomit.
Grandfather's gunshot cough, his uniform
Faded, mildew-bemedalled. Ludmila's fits
The neighbors set their clocks by. Joys no doubt
As well. We know, we *know*. (Why bring it up?
Because, as page after notebook page blackens

With these and other musings, a small voice warns:
"James, don't leave out the humanity!")

2

A waking dream: I'm ten, I'm Dorothy
In one of the *Oz* books. Called on to set free
From their translation into bibelots
The members of a royal family.
Which of the chill cave-full will they be?
Three wrong guesses and the child that was
Becomes a nut dish of Depression glass.
(Of course the dream was telling me to set
Myself free—but from what half-humorous
Manipulative bondage I forget.)
On Dorothy's third try a purple budvase
Wakes back into a gurgling year-old princess.
So! purple was the clue, and those doomed selves
Childsplay from then on to disenchant.
As with the bloodless "Velvet Revolution,"
Its dawn till then unknown except in dream,
People now jubilantly woke—free, free!
How can you doubt the color of that velvet?

3

Far from the capital proliferates
A (what to call it?) terminal prettiness.
Houses of cards. A whole square, poker-faced,
Each frontal in broad sunset strung with gems,
Like MGM's generic frontier town.
In the antique shop, uncollectibles
Collecting dust. Gnawed cushions, carpet ends,
Postcards in savage, ego-driven script,
Dead woodcuts, loose beads, ossified crochet—
One's weakness for that terrible old stuff . . .
But look who through a pendant of chipped crystal

Exuberantly sidles in—by turns
Furnace-red, fire-emerald, glory-blue:
It's Light! snapping his fingers to a beat
Our own eyes pick up, ardently repeat.
And here's a two-foot-high medicine chest,
Oak unpainted and unhinged. Try picturing it
Painted mauve, or a purple mercy-mild,
That would at the right touch grow tall and glow,
Its baby mirror door (the mottled face
Of an old man seems to peer from) opening
In expectation—ah but you're not at home,
Just your pure concentrated know-how
Bottled in amethyst. Compounds, elixirs
Bringing us wisdom, youth, fertility . . .
In a word, change. Unstoppered as we gawk,
Those vials release through evening sun a swarm
Of whirring mothlike sprites, to do your bidding
Within the small gilt theater each of us
Reserves for rapture. Gravely they hold our gaze,
Then by imperceptible degrees
Into the afterglow of the scene played
Sink back.

4

                    Woodsmoke. Night falling. Black
As one of President Havel's comedies.
Not so much as a streetlight after ten
Shining in Telĉ. The town's young people
Head for homework, freed from the spell of a late
Mauv—clippers again, please [*cuts the string*]—
There, no more jokes—of a late movie.
Too dark to see the kids in their true colors—
Colors, those "deeds and sufferings of light"
That flood your book's great honeycomb—But whoa!
What's this live whiteness pulsing from below?
We've all but pitched into an underground
Cube of fluorescence eerie-dense as snow
Where one lone figure in white coveralls—
Grave robber? master mechanic? have we names

861

For what he so candidly is and does and knows?—
Works night-shift magic. It's the school basement.
Upstairs all day the priests (in black) rehearse
A past, by termite zeal beneath our feet,
Made ever quainter and more obsolete.
What lies in store for that Old World depends
Soberingly on this dew-bright whiz and friends.
Tomorrow we'll be shown scenes from a play
They're working on ("It still needs work") performed
By eight reactors huge on the horizon,
Titans letting off steam. Some latterday
. . . Not yet Chernobyl, not yet Auschwitz. We
Trust in the dreamwork, although who's to say
What the exact works are that make us free.

5

Remember (the inner wireless crackles on)
These people have known centuries of oppression—
Magyar, Hapsburg, Nazi, Soviet
(And now the Swiss are investing—blue skies ahead)
And come through with their liveliness intact.
Would Americans be capable of that?

You're asking *me*? Oh well, America . . .
[*Deep sigh*] Who hasn't OD'd on those Carl Sandburg
WPA frescoes-in-words. Wheat sheaves,
Civic street scenes, torsos brawny-bare . . .
State art of just the sort then reaching us
From the Soviet Union. One small difference:
We had the freedom to make fun of it
And They did not. Freedom to trust all's well
Once we have made the other person smile
(As you've been doing, Reader, this whole while?).
Freedom when confronted to disarm
With openness. (Talking of other things
While stitching up my finger numb as wood,
The old blood swabbed away, "*Of course,*" said Susan,
"I'm telling you the truth, I'm from Nebraska!")
Freedom to ignore our own spellbinders

While millions behind the Iron Curtain knew
By anguished heart voices the State had schooled
In irony, shades of meaning, stratagems
Worthless now that everybody's free
To trade threadbare Camus for *Dynasty*,
Freedom to justify bad deeds by pleading
Good intentions. To shoot down those who don't
Believe what you and I do. To oust from office
The gladhander we put there in the first place.
Freedom not to wave flags on May Day
And lose our visas as a consequence
—That last detail by way of nice Jan Rippl
Who runs the pension we've settled in.
His English is piquant, he doesn't—won't?—
Speak German. His teenage children want to shame him
Into a job "worthy of his education."
Such jobs don't pay; he made more as a fireman . . .
Now, "free" to run the pension, he leads
A life that answers, sort of, to his needs.
Without TV as yet, his personal dial
Ranges from uphill Castle to The Trial
(A grim pub we avoid) downstreet. Then there's
His packed, glass-fronted bookcase below stairs
—Germaine Greer, Robert Ludlum, Wittgenstein—
To which I add a paperback of mine.
(Thank you. This dry, opinionated stretch
Has left us thirsty for the purpler patch.)

6

Eureka! Mr. Rippl, stripping beds,
"Englishes" what those crude mauve posters say:
EQUAL RIGHTS FOR SECONDARY COLORS
—A taunt "not printable" while the Red Army
Ran the show.
                    (Merciful god, those "reds"
One went to school with? Their brave attitudes
Over long nights of argument and smoke

Mixed with subliminal piano blues . . .
Result? This new, seductive shade.)
                                        But hey,
It's our show now, as that blond kid asserts
In hoarse convulsions over his guitar.
All Prague agrees. The citywide street fair
Gathers momentum—bangles, jugglers, beer,
And yes, at every stop along our way,
Another puppet government for all
Whom ideologies of Type enthrall:
Devil and Priest, Tycoon and Commissar,
Death himself, white bones on a black robe—
Pull the right strings, and look, you've made him dance!
Our crucial selves, they're all here for the having,
All but [*ominous chords*]—all but the Golem.
Rabbi Löw's masterwork, the Golem, lurching
Unstrung, red-eyed through nightmare wails of grief,
Bent on the bonbon Child, wrapped in gold leaf.
("Will you believe," wrote Natalie reading this,
"We met the Golems at *The House of the Dead*?
She is enchanting, knows the whole world, spoke
Affectionately of you. *He's* something else,
Not—one hates to say it—a nice person.
No soul, I mean.") Just that foul Being made
Of the resurrectionist's odd limbs and organs,
Abstracted from the graves of infidels.

7

Does the Rabbi rest in this Ghetto graveyard?
Among the markers handy to our path,
Unskewed enough for the next step,
Pause. Perform what the wisest, most
Compelling life at length comes down to:
The pious placement of a pebble
Upon the good man's golden, weather-
Gimleted stone. The whispering of a wish
Some wraith of wry complaisance underground

Will try to grant.
                  Dear Heart, come, time to go.

Have we sufficiently seen? have we had our humanity?
Were our travels true, our words worthy
(As if one could say) of the unassuming
Reb Sholem of Belz, who in a minor mode
Enjoined his juniors:

                               Keep your nail-parings
for burning and never   *talmidim fail to*
add when the toy fire   *fondly whistles*
its color-carol   *two willing chips of*
seasoned wood   *as witnesses*

                                           1994

CHRISTMAS TREE

          To be
      Brought down at last
From the cold sighing mountain
Where I and the others
Had been fed, looked after, kept still,
Meant, I knew—of course I knew—
That it would be only a matter of weeks,
That there was nothing more to do.
Warmly they took me in, made much of me,
The point from the start was to keep my spirits up.
I could assent to that. For honestly,
It did help to be wound in jewels, to send
Their colors flashing forth from vents in the deep
Fragrant sables that cloaked me head to foot.
Over me then they wove a spell of shining—
Purple and silver chains, eavesdripping tinsel,
Amulets, milagros: software of silver,
A heart, a little girl, a Model T,
Two staring eyes. The angels, trumpets, BUD and BEA
(The children's names) in clownlike capitals,
Somewhere a music box whose tiny song
Played and replayed I ended before long
By loving. And in shadow behind me, a primitive IV
To keep the show going. Yes, yes, what lay ahead
Was clear: the stripping, the cold street, my chemicals
Plowed back into the Earth for lives to come—
No doubt a blessing, a harvest, but one that doesn't bear,
Now or ever, dwelling upon. To have grown so thin.
Needles and bone. The little boy's hands meeting
About my spine. The mother's voice: *Holding up wonderfully!*
No dread. No bitterness. The end beginning. Today's
      Dusk room aglow
      For the last time
      With candlelight.
      Faces love lit,
      Gifts underfoot.
Still to be so poised, so
Receptive. Still to recall, to praise.

1995

866

KOI

Snow today, the first in seven years,
As major a blizzard as the mildness here can muster.
Big slow skydiving flakes, their floating filigrees
Aspiring to come back as a field of Queen Anne's lace.

Then it is over, and the terrain resumes its menace.
Coyotes patrol it, watchful for a small
Privileged dog to steal. Premonitions! Whole nights
Preliving the yelp of pain and disbelief

As we helplessly watch our Cosmo borne struggling off.
We keep him on a stout red leash, but still . . .
Behind these garden walls it's safe. Birds, olive trees,
A rectangular pool of koi. Twin to the urban

Gempool south of us. Last night again: a moon,
Big stars, white clouds—no, wait, clouds colorized
To the exact tint of the white patches on the koi. A white
Ever so faintly suffused by blood and gold.

And from the clouds, or far beyond them, at intervals
Our upturned faces receive a mild pinprick of dew.
Feel the world drop away it whispers. *Seven years more*
Breathes the melting snow. To which the koi can only

Reply *Carpe diem*. Next morning to their skylight comes a human
Silhouette edged by radiance, and they cluster to be fed.
Hold a fistful of pellets underwater, your hand will be kissed
By the tenderest mouths. It's too much: our "Lindbergh puppy"

Is barking—he's losing his footing—he's fallen in!

1995

DAYS OF 1994

These days in my friend's house
Light seeks me underground. To wake
Below the level of the lawn
—Half-basement cool through the worst heat—
Is strange and sweet.
High up, three window-slots, new slants on dawn:
Through misty greens and gilts
An infant sun totters on stilts of shade
Up toward the high
Mass of interwoven boughs,
While close against the triptych panes
Rock bears witness, Dragonfly
Shivers in place
Above tall Queen Anne's lace—
More figures from *The Book of Thel* by Blake
(Lilly & Worm, Cloudlet & Clod of Clay)
And none but drinks the dewy Manna in.

I shiver next, Light walking on my grave . . .
And sleep, and wake. This time, peer out
From just beneath the mirror of the lake
A gentle mile uphill.
Florets—the mountain laurel—float
Openmouthed, devout,
Set swaying by the wake of the flatboat:

Barcarole whose chords of gloom
Draw forth the youngest, purest, faithfullest,
Cool-crystal-casketed
Hands crossed on breast,
Pre-Raphaelite face radiant—and look,
Not dead, O never dead!
To wake, to wake
Among the flaming dowels of a tomb

Below the world, the thousand things
Here risen to if not above
Before day ends:
The spectacles, the book,
Forgetful lover and forgotten love,
Cobweb hung with trophy wings,
The fading trumpet of a car,
The knowing glance from star to star,
The laughter of old friends.

1995

TEXTUAL NOTES

1   In his first selection of poems, *From the First Nine: Poems 1946–1976* (1982), Merrill chose to reprint five poems from *The Black Swan* and ten from *First Poems*. In a note, he explained: "Poems from the first two books have been touched up, in a few cases drastically. The practice is frowned upon, I know. Yet they should otherwise have been dropped altogether, and with them the earliest inklings of certain lifelong motifs I hope I may be forgiven for keeping faith with, even while seamlessly breaking it with the hollow phrase and plain ineptitude of the beginner." His revised versions can be found in *From the First Nine;* their originals are printed here.

53   "Saint," "The Day of the Eclipse," and "The Power Station" were added to the "new and enlarged" edition of *The Country of a Thousand Years of Peace* in 1970. "At Mamallapuram," which originally appeared between "Voices from the Other World" and "Dream (Escape from the Sculpture Museum) and Waking," was dropped. It can be found here on p. 811.

314   When he reprinted "18 West 11th Street" in *From the First Nine*, Merrill added an explanatory epigraph: "a house in Manhattan, our home until I was five, carelessly exploded by the 'Weathermen'—young, bomb-making activists—in 1970."

359   *Divine Comedies* was originally divided into two sections. The first section of nine poems is reprinted here. The second section consisted entirely of "The Book of Ephraim," which subsequently became the first part of *The Changing Light at Sandover* and can be found there.

677   Five poems in *The Black Swan* were reprinted, with minor changes, in *First Poems*, where they appear in this edition. The original order of the poems in *The Black Swan* was:

     The Black Swan
     The Broken Bowl
     From Morning into Morning
     Accumulations of the Sea
     The Green Eye
     The Cosmological Eye
     Perspectives of a Lonesome Eye
     Phenomenal Love Song
     The Formal Lovers
     Medusa
     Suspense of Love
     Embarkation Sonnets

695 In 1974, Merrill gathered into *The Yellow Pages* certain poems he had published over the years but never collected. That book was issued by Temple Bar Bookshop, not the poet's regular publisher. He added this prefatory note to the volume:

> Verses that gave blood to others and were thrust aside for their pains; others no less that went a flighty route their maker chose not to call his own—neither kind was apt to "go" in the collection then being put together. Where *did* they go? Yellowed, brittle with reproach, these of mine are felt, this rainy weekend, to have deserved more than the pauper's ditch of a bottom drawer or dispersal in the pages of twenty magazines. Their chronology is approximate; no matter; they date themselves. Without further ado I offer them to friends.

739 Merrill excluded this sonnet stanza from "The Broken Home" (p. 197) when that poem was first published.

771 Two other translations appeared in collections: "Pola Diva" (p. 271) and "Paul Valéry: *Palme*" (p. 472).

812 "Poets at Home," which first appeared in the September 26, 1963, issue of *The New York Review of Books* under the pseudonym "Raoul Marx," was printed as a review of the anthology *Modern Poets,* edited by John Malcolm Brinnin and Bill Read.

BIOGRAPHICAL NOTE

James Merrill was born in New York City on March 3, 1926, the son of the financier and philanthropist Charles E. Merrill, one of the founders of the brokerage firm Merrill Lynch & Co., and his second wife, Hellen Ingram. Merrill, who attended St. Bernard's School, was raised in Manhattan and Southampton, Long Island, where his family had a country house that was designed by Stanford White, and in Palm Beach, Florida. His parents divorced in 1939, and the reverberations of the "broken home" can be heard throughout his poetry. After attending the Lawrenceville School, Merrill enrolled at Amherst College, his father's alma mater, took a year off to serve in the army, and graduated *summa cum laude* with the class of 1947. He taught at Bard College in 1948–1949, and although he fought shy of academe in the following years he did accept short appointments at Amherst, the University of Wisconsin, Washington University, and Yale University. In 1954 he moved with his companion, David Jackson, a writer and painter, to a house in Stonington, Connecticut, which is still maintained by Stonington Village and houses an artist-in-residence every year.

In 1957 Merrill and Jackson undertook a trip around the world, and for two decades beginning in 1964 they spent a part of each year in Greece. They owned a house in Athens at the foot of Mt. Lycabettus and were famous among the local *literati* for the terrace parties they threw. Beginning in 1979 Merrill spent winters in Key West, Florida, where he and Jackson acquired another house. It was a place he had an affinity for partly because it had previously attracted two of his favorite poets, Wallace Stevens and Elizabeth Bishop, the latter his close friend for decades. Merrill, a gifted linguist and a lover of different cultures, always traveled widely, and the displacements and discoveries of his travels, along with the routines of his life in his different homes, are the stuff of many of his poems. He died away from home, in Tucson, Arizona, on February 6, 1995.

A selection of Merrill's earliest writings, taken from his contributions to the *Lawrenceville Literary Magazine,* was privately printed by his father as a sixteenth-birthday gift in 1942, under the title *Jim's Book.* The young writer proudly distributed most of the one hundred copies as soon as possible—and before long began to retrieve as many of those copies as he could. A group of his poems appeared in *Poetry* in March 1946, the same year that saw the publication in Athens, Greece, of a limited edition of poems entitled *The Black Swan.* He published his first full-fledged book, *First Poems,* when he was twenty-five, in 1951. He next tried his hand at playwriting: *The Bait* was produced at the Comedy Club in 1953 (and published in 1960), and *The Immortal Husband* was performed at the Theater DeLys in 1955 (and published in 1956). Meanwhile, his first novel, *The Seraglio,* a Jamesian roman à clef, appeared in 1957 (it was reissued in 1987), and his second commercial volume of poems, *The Country of a Thousand Years of Peace,* in 1959 (revised edition, 1970). His third volume of poems, *Water Street*—its title refers to the street Merrill lived on in Stonington—came out in 1962, and his second, experimental novel, *The (Diblos) Notebook,* based in part on his first experiences in Greece, in 1965 (reissued in 1994).

In 1966 his collection *Nights and Days* received the National Book Award. The judges for that year, W. H. Auden, James Dickey, and Howard Nemerov, cited the book for its author's "scrupulous and uncompromising cultivation of the poetic art, evidenced in his refusal to settle for an easy and profitable stance; for his insistence on taking the kind of tough, poetic chances which make the difference between esthetic success or failure." *The Fire Screen* appeared in 1969, followed in 1972 by *Braving the Elements,* which was awarded the Bollingen Prize for Poetry, and in 1974 by a selection of previously uncollected poems, *The Yellow Pages.* When *Divine Comedies* came out in 1976, it won the Pulitzer Prize.

The narrative poem "The Book of Ephraim," which was originally included in *Divine Comedies,* later served as the first installment of an epic visionary poem based in large part on Merrill and Jackson's communications with the Other World by way of the Ouija board. The subsequent two parts were *Mirabell: Books of Number,* which received the National Book Award for Poetry in 1978, and *Scripts for the Pageant,* published in 1980. In 1982 Merrill brought together these three long poems and "Coda: The Higher Keys" in a comprehensive edition of the work he now called *The Changing Light at Sandover.* That landmark volume won the National Book Critics Circle Award in 1982, the same year in which Merrill published his first selected poems, *From the First Nine: Poems 1946–1976.* His book of poems *Late Settings* was published in 1985, and a collection of essays, interviews, and reviews entitled *Recitative* appeared in 1986. In 1988 *The Inner Room* was honored with the first Bobbitt National Prize for Poetry, awarded by the Library of Congress. Merrill's memoir, *A Different Person,* came out in 1993. *A Scattering of Salts,* the last book of poems that he saw through production, was published posthumously in 1995.

INDEX OF FIRST LINES

INDEX OF TITLES

A NOTE ON THE TYPE

Pierre Simon Fournier *le jeune,* who designed the type used in this book, was both an originator and a collector of types. His services to the art of printing were his design of letters, his creation of ornaments and initials, and his standardization of type sizes. His types are old style in character and sharply cut. In 1764 and 1766 he published his *Manuel typographique,* a treatise on the history of French types and printing, on typefounding in all its details, and on what many consider his most important contribution to typography—the measurement of type by the point system.

Composed by NK Graphics, Keene, New Hampshire
Printed and bound by R. R. Donnelley, Harrisonburg, Virginia
Designed by Chip Kidd